AN ECOLOGY OF KNOWLEDGES

EXPERIMENTAL FUTURES: TECHNOLOGICAL LIVES,
SCIENTIFIC ARTS, ANTHROPOLOGICAL VOICES
A series edited by Michael M. J. Fischer and Joseph Dumit

MICHA RAHDER

An Ecology of Knowledges

Fear, Love, and Technoscience
in Guatemalan Forest
Conservation

DUKE UNIVERSITY PRESS

DURHAM AND LONDON / 2020

Designed by Matthew Tauch
Typeset in Minion Pro and Chapparal Pro
by Westchester Publishing Services

Library of Congress Cataloging-in-Publication Data
Names: Rahder, Micha, [date] author.
Title: An ecology of knowledges : fear, love, and
technoscience in Guatemalan forest conservation /
Micha Rahder.
Description: Durham : Duke University Press, 2020. |
Series: Experimental futures: Technological lives,
scientific arts, anthropological voices | Includes
bibliographical references and index.
Identifiers: LCCN 2019034466 (print)
LCCN 2019034467 (ebook)
ISBN 9781478006107 (Hardcover) ISBN 9781478006916
(Paperback)
ISBN 9781478007524 (eBook)
Subjects: LCSH: Forest conservation—Guatemala—
Reserva de la Biosfera Maya. | Sustainable forestry—
Guatemala—Reserva de la Biosfera Maya. | Reserva de
la Biosfera Maya (Guatemala)
Classification: LCC SD414.G9 R34 2020 (print) |
LCC SD414.G9 (ebook) | DDC 333.75/16097281—dc23
LC record available at https://lccn.loc.gov/2019034466
LC ebook record available at https://lccn.loc.gov
/2019034467

Cover art: Girl in two jaguar masks, taken in a Q'eqchi'
migrant community inside the Maya Biosphere Reserve
(photograph by author).

Duke University Press gratefully acknowledges the Department of Geography and Anthropology at Louisiana
State University, which provided funds toward the
publi-cation of this book.

In loving memory of my father, HARRO RAHDER

When somebody threatens you, in my experience, that's when you're safest. That's the thing. You have to be worried about when people greet you and shake your hand, then when you turn around they kill you. That's the real threat.

Wildlife Conservation Society worker, 2011

Certainty itself appears partial, information intermittent. An answer is another question, a connection a gap, a similarity a difference, and vice versa.

Marilyn Strathern, *Partial Connections*

CONTENTS

LIST OF ABBREVIATIONS

ACOFOP	Asociación de Comunidades Forestales de Petén [Association of Forest Communities of the Petén]
AFISAP	Asociación Forestal Integral de San Andrés, Petén [Integrated Forestry Association of San Andrés, Petén]
ARCAS	Asociación de Rescate y Conservación de Animales Silvestres [Wildlife Rescue and Conservation Association]
CALAS	Centro de Acción Legal Ambiental y Social [Center for Legal Action in Environment and Social Issues]
CARE	Cooperative for Assistance and Relief Everywhere
CEH	Comisión para el Esclarecimiento Histórico [Commission for Historical Clarification]
CEMEC	Centro de Monitreo y Evaluación de CONAP [Center for Monitoring and Evaluation of CONAP]
CI	Conservation International
CICIG	Comisión Internacional contra la Impunidad en Guatemala [International Commission against Impunity in Guatemala]
COCODE	Consejo Comunitario de Desarollo [Community Development Council]
CONAP	Consejo Nacional de Areas Protegidas [National Protected Area Council]
CONRED	Coordinadora Nacional para la Reducción de Desastres [National Coordinator for Disaster Reduction]

DFID	United Kingdom Department for International Development
DIPRONA	División de Protección de la Naturaleza [Nature Protection Division of the Guatemalan National Civil Police]
DOI	U.S. Department of the Interior
FARES	Foundation for Anthropological Research and Environmental Studies
FYDEP	Empresa Nacional de Fomento y Desarollo Económico de Petén [National Enterprise for the Promotion and Economic Development of Petén]
GIS	geographic information systems/science
GPS	global positioning system
IDAEH	Instituto de Antropología y Historia de Guatemala [Guatemalan Institute of Anthropology and History]
INAB	Instituto Nacional de Bosques [National Forest Institute]
INACIF	Insituto Nacional de Ciencias Forenses [National Institute for Forensic Sciences]
INGUAT	Instituto Guatemalteco de Turismo [Guatemalan Tourism Institute]
INSIVUMEH	Instituto Nacional de Sismología, Vulcanología, Meteorología e Hidrología [National Institute of Seismology, Vulcanology, Meteorology, and Hydrology]
IUCN	International Union for Conservation of Nature
MARN	Ministerio de Ambiente y Recursos Naturales [Ministry of the Environment and Natural Resources]
MBR	Maya Biosphere Reserve
MINUGUA	United Nations Verification Mission in Guatemala
MODIS	moderate-resolution imaging spectroradiometer
NASA	National Aeronautics and Space Administration
NGO	nongovernmental organization
NOAA	National Oceanic and Atmospheric Administration
NTFP	nontimber forest product
OMYC	Organización de Manejo y Conservación de Uaxactún [Management and Conservation Organization of Uaxactún]
PACUNAM	Fundación Patrimonio Cultural y Natural Maya [Foundation for Maya Natural and Cultural Patrimony]

RA	Rainforest Alliance
REDD+	UN Collaborative Programme for Reduced Emissions from Deforestation and Forest Degradation in Developing Countries
SIPECIF	Sistema Nacional de Prevención y Control de Incendios Forestales [National System for Prevention and Control of Forest Fires]
SNEM	Servicio Nacional de Erradicación de Malaria [National Service for the Eradication of Malaria]
SRTM	Shuttle Radar Topography Mission
STS	science and technology studies
TNC	The Nature Conservancy
UCSC	University of California, Santa Cruz
UN	United Nations
UNESCO	United Nations Educational, Scientific, and Cultural Organization
USAID	United States Agency for International Development
WCS	Wildlife Conservation Society

ACKNOWLEDGMENTS

First, I must thank the forests of Central America for inspiring me with enduring curiosity, beginning with my first trip to Costa Rica at age sixteen. I heard a howler monkey for the first time and never looked back. I thank the forests for hanging on despite the powerful destructive forces working toward their end and for providing endless nourishment to my mind, senses, and politics. These are not things that forests can do alone, however, so I must also thank some of the people who have helped along the way.

The people living and working in Guatemala who welcomed me, with my quiet curiosity and strangely obvious questions, are many. Victor Hugo Ramos at CEMEC-CONAP and Roan Balas McNab at the Wildlife Conservation Society made this project fundamentally possible, opening the doors of their institutions to my presence and facilitating my entrance into so many other places and spaces of the conservation worlds of the Maya Biosphere Reserve. Several other people played an enormous role in my life and work in the Petén, particularly Melvin Mérida, Julio Morales, Miriam Quinonez, Daniel Trujillo, Julián Zetina, and Julio Zetina. Juan Pablo Noriega, with his goofy jokes and daily provision of rides, and América Rodríguez, with her propensity for picking me up when I was at my lowest, deserve special mention. Paola Morrill, Elena Baum, and Oseas Obed Hoil Bertruy provided the best possible company for strolling around the Flores Malecón and thinking aloud in the evenings. Miguel Xol and the family of Don Nicolás Mo, in Paso Caballos, have given me a small but essential sense of welcome in the village since I first showed up in 2007, while Doña Mirna's place in Uaxactún provided an essential source of local gossip. To all of the above, and the many more in

Guatemala who are not named individually, I am overwhelmingly grateful. In particular, their warmth and care made it possible not just to conduct ethnographic research, but to do so as a chronically ill and sometimes disabled researcher, a challenge that far surpassed my well-laid plans.

Back in the United States, many more people have enriched this work over the years. The seeds of this research were first planted in 2007 at the Yale School of Forestry & Environmental Studies, and Carol Carpenter deserves credit for my initial forays out of ecological science into anthropology, with Michael Dove providing additional support. At the University of California, Santa Cruz, Andrew Mathews was the kindest and most engaged supervisor I could hope for, helping grow the project from seeds into the rich ecologies it now represents. Anna Tsing always reminded me to look at the bigger picture and inspired me to bravery in experimenting with writing and ideas. Mark Anderson kept me grounded and accountable to those academic conversations I might try to sneak out of sideways, and Karen Barad demonstrated incredible generosity while systematically undermining everything I thought I knew. Together, these advisors provided me with many giants' shoulders to stand upon.

Others at Yale, UC Santa Cruz, and Louisiana State University contributed not just to this work but to the vibrant academic communities in which it could flourish: Patricia Alvarez Astacio, Meg Arenberg, Don Brenneis, Mary Jill Brody, Jeff Bury, Zac Caple, Natalie Ceperley, Kerry Chance, Chris Cochran, Craig Colten, Brent Crosson, Rachel Cypher, Laura Alex Frye-Levine, Melinda González, Donna Haraway, Susan Harding, Jed Holtzman, Joyce Jackson, Cat Jacquet, Peter Kamau, Liam Lair, Jake Metcalf, Katy Overstreet, Triloki Pandey, Licia Peck, Pierre Du Plessis, Joseph Powell, Helen Regis, Danilyn Rutherford, Lisa Rofel, Teresa Sarroca, Yuliya Shmidt, Craig Schuetze, Peyton Smith, and Matthew Wolf-Meyer have all proven "good to think with" over the years. Kyle Bikowski at LSU helped with last-minute preparation and tinkering with images and text, with good humor and patience throughout. Celina Callahan-Kapoor provided both intellectual and emotional support throughout research and writing, without which this book would never have been possible.

I also owe thanks to the many reviewers and commenters who have provided feedback on this work over the years. Key arguments were honed with the help of audiences who listened to presentation of works in progress, particularly at the Aarhus University Research on the Anthropocene (AURA) group in Denmark, the Cornell University Science Studies Reading Group, and the

LSU Philosophy Salon, in addition to innumerable conferences. Earlier versions of portions of chapters 1, 4, and 7 appeared, in different form, in *Ecología Política*, *Science as Culture*, and the *Journal of Political Ecology*, respectively. Each of these benefited from the comments of both editors and anonymous reviewers. My two anonymous reviewers through Duke University Press offered extraordinary detail and generosity in their reports on this manuscript and helped push my arguments much further than I had initially envisioned. At Duke, Courtney Berger, Sandra Korn, Liz Smith, and Jenny Tan offered editorial guidance ranging from the mundane to the sublime, and I am deeply appreciative for their patience and help at all levels. In particular, Courtney's enthusiastic support for the project kept me moving when other simultaneous work stalled under the weight of daily to-do lists.

This research was financially supported by grants and awards from the Wenner-Gren Foundation, the National Science Foundation, the Northern California chapter of Phi Beta Kappa, the UCSC Anthropology Department, the UCSC Science and Justice Graduate Training Program, and the LSU Department of Geography and Anthropology and College of Humanities and Social Sciences.

Thanks beyond words are also owed to my mother, Barbara Rahder. Her financial support made the absurdity of medical care during field research possible (thereby saving this research from the compost heap). More importantly, she taught me, along with my father, to think broadly, creatively, and critically, to fight for social justice, to care for all kinds of environments, and to work passion, compassion, and intellect together in the pursuit of a better shared world.

Finally, I thank those who have helped me keep balance and joy in my life while working hard to bring this book to fruition. Summer Renault-Steele, Ana Shepherd, and Teoma Naccarato somehow all grew up to be brilliant, strong, extraordinary women; the shared love between our lives and families keeps mine humming even at a distance. Friends and family who could ask how the book was coming without calling forth monstrous anxiety are rare, and deserve mention: Skyler and Mary Koski-Vogt, Katie Stem, Jed Holtzman, Jerson Liam Livingston Lopez, Sergio Pastor, Desmond Ramirez, Megan Harrington, Taya Koschnick, Tara Anderson, Nat and Robin Magder, and Tracy Beard all contributed emotional labor to this creation. I have also been thrilled by the support of the extended Mitchell family, especially Roland, Roman, Chaunda, and Faith, who kept me company and kept me well fed in Baton Rouge. Above all, I thank my partner in life, love, and intellectual exploration—Reagan

Mitchell. Without his undying belief in this work, ridiculous jokes, and the recliner he bought for me to write in, this book may never have made it.

Any names that I have forgotten here should be read back into these acknowledgments, much as any errors in the following text are purely my own and should not be attributed to those named here.

What on Earth Is a Nooscape?

Hiking through Laguna del Tigre National Park, my friend Luis—a Guate-malan veterinarian employed by the Wildlife Conservation Society (wcs)—stopped to point out tracks in the mud. First, a tapir track in dried earth, fading with time. Then, a large feline print in fresh mud, recent. Luis crouched to point out the differences between jaguar and mountain lion tracks—round toes indicated jaguar: endangered, rare, and exciting. Then, a human boot print; its analysis yielded less certainty than the jaguar's. Luis wondered aloud: was this trail walked by a park patrol recently, or did the print signal some intrusion of illegal presence or activity? I was left with an ominous sense of unknowing, unsure how to reconcile the feral excitement of the predator with the shadowy possibility of the poacher, the land usurper, or the drug trafficker.

Laguna del Tigre National Park is part of Guatemala's Maya Biosphere Re-serve (MBR), the largest protected area in Central America. The MBR stretches over 21,600 square kilometers of thick, tangled tropical lowland forests, boggy wetlands, and—increasingly—cleared agricultural or ranching landscapes. The reserve overlays the top half of the Petén department, which represents a third of Guatemala's land and shares extensive borders with Mexico and Belize. A patchwork of national parks like Laguna del Tigre, a buffer zone, and a large multiple-use zone divided into concessions, the reserve was in-tended to balance biodiversity conservation with local livelihoods (see plate 1). While some parts of the reserve have successfully maintained forest cover, other areas are overrun by agricultural expansion and by the cattle ranching, oil extraction, and criminal interests that are muddled with the small-scale action of peasant migrants.

Many MBR conservation institutions avoid Laguna del Tigre, preferring to work in other, better-conserved parks, or with the community-run forest concessions that offer integrated conservation and development opportunities.

Yet abandoning the park poses risks to the future of the entire reserve. With continued frontier migration, oil exploitation, and illegal movement of drugs and humans across the border into Mexico, Laguna del Tigre is one of the MBR's most threatened—and now threatening—areas. In 2017 alone, more than 54,750 acres of forest (larger than the area of Seattle, WA) were burned inside the park. A few of these fires were permitted agricultural burns within semilegalized settlements; some were the unregulated fires of agricultural migrants without settlement agreements; and most were attributed to wealthy ranchers and drug traffickers, for whom clearing wide swaths of forest is a land-grabbing technique. These impacts on the park were invisible during our hike, except through the haunting possibility, offered by the boot print, that this part of the forest might soon be swept up in the violent dynamics of landscape change.

Like a boot print in the forest, flames index human presence, but differences between humans can make these signs as illegible as their interpretation is urgent. Distinguishing between the traces left by agricultural migrants, park protectors, or drug traffickers is a vital but impossible task. The tapir and jaguar tracks tell another, partially connected, story. Here, the tools of tracking that distinguish between species are a good enough way of knowing (at least until it becomes necessary to tell individuals apart, as when a wild cat develops a taste for domestic cattle). Where a boot print can equally index the failure or success of park management, a jaguar print along the same path points to the necessity of continued intervention—which requires knowing the difference between humans. Understanding what is happening on the landscape becomes an urgent act, creating the sites, scales, and possibilities for the never-ending project of forest conservation.

To know that a human, a tapir, and a jaguar walked this path required Luis and me to walk along it as well, leaving new traces as we traced the paths of others. If reported to WCS, our steps might count on future maps of institutional presence, translated into an authoritative measure of state control of the landscape. Reporting the jaguar and tapir prints might translate into evidence of the value of conservation efforts in spaces that carry risk of kidnapping or death. The traces of our walk might therefore attract or deter others from walking the same path, depending on whether those traces are marked by boot prints, scent, sound, patrol reporting form, word of mouth, or GPS points on a map. Each of these traces might shape the future of interventions in this place and across the wider MBR. Throughout the reserve, conservationists labor through the promises and perils of a landscape home to jaguars and drug traffickers, rare birds and returned refugees. Entangled with irreconcilable difference, violence, rich forest ecologies, inequality, struggle, and hope, conservationists are left with a powerful desire: for clarity, certainty, knowledge of the landscape that might provide a way to change it.

To know a place in order to change it.

This desire drives much conservationist action across the MBR, a landscape beset by many forms of violence, uncertainty, and precarity. In this book, I trace an ecology of knowledges in the reserve. The *knowledge ecology* framework reflects this core conservationist desire, drawing attention to the mutually transformative effects of knowledge-making practices and material more-than-human landscapes. Like the twisted loops of knowing, unknowing, and material change created by Luis's and my reading and leaving of traces along a forest path, the book traces how environmentalist knowing is always about intervening, in multiple ways. I offer two introductory chapters to develop this idea in depth, oriented to somewhat different audiences—the remainder of this brief introduction outlines the theoretical framework of a knowledge ecology and the related concept of a *nooscape*, while the next chapter provides a richer historical and descriptive introduction to the many worlds of the MBR.

Knowledge Ecology and Nooscape

My approach to knowledge ecology builds on long histories of exchange between anthropology and the ecological sciences, as well as on recent work in science and technology studies (STS), political ecology, and the environmental humanities. This approach focuses on two key properties of knowledges: materiality and relation. First, knowledge remains rooted in the material world: I examine how knowledges emerge from situated encounters and relations, and how they fold back into real material impacts on more-than-human landscapes like the MBR. Second, this approach emphasizes relations between a multiplicity of knowledges, examining the coentanglements of distinct and incommensurable epistemologies and worlds.[1]

Knowledge ecology is a form of analysis, the epistemic framework I use to describe and incorporate a multiplicity of epistemic frameworks, like a snake eating its own tail. But ecology is a type of inquiry; it is not an object, place, or space. Like all methods, knowledge ecology enacts its object of study. As global ecology enacts and describes the biosphere, or ecosystem ecology enacts and describes ecosystems, knowledge ecology enacts and describes what I call a nooscape—patterns of collective thought and action that emerge from and fold back into the material-ecological worlds of northern Guatemala.

The word "nooscape" draws together two very different streams of thought. The first is the idea of the *noosphere*, first proposed by Jesuit priest, geologist, and philosopher Pierre Teilhard de Chardin (1956) and developed further by Vladimir Vernadsky (1945), the Soviet geochemist best known for popularizing the idea of the biosphere. While their two versions of noosphere differed somewhat, the general idea was the same: an emergent global mind.[2] Just as the biosphere is rooted in and emergent from the geosphere, so too is the noosphere rooted in and emergent from the biosphere. Emergence does not mean escape—the biosphere is intimately intertwined with the geosphere through biogeochemical processes, not an independent layer like icing over top of a cake. Similarly, there is no noosphere without interconnection and relation to the whole of the biosphere, and therefore also to the geosphere within that. The noosphere is very literally the mind of the earth. Early versions of this concept described the noosphere as a directed global form of human exceptionalism, but recent reworkings push against both the imagined coherence and anthropocentrism of these framings (Turner 2005; Margulis and Sagan 1995). Margulis and Sagan describe the noosphere as "the aggregate net of throbbing life, from flashing fireflies to human e-mail. . . . Polymorphous, paranoiac, confused, yet intensely imaginative, [it is] the thinking layer of Earth that is largely the unexpected product of animal consciousness" (1995, 138).

I build on these latter conceptions of noosphere, which root more-than-human collective thought in the materiality of earthly life. But this is a book about northern Guatemala, not the whole earth, and the noosphere is locked into the global. Beyond that, the concept remains too holistic for my purposes, too rigidly tied to systems theories of closed loops, nested hierarchies, and discrete levels.[3] Bridging the noosphere with an analysis of partial connections (Strathern 2004), I introduce the alternative of the nooscape. Nooscapes are situated flashes of ecological-knowledge-worlds-in-the-making, emergent phenomena based on relative and situated scalar processes of partial connection rather than nested part-whole relationships.[4] I join the *noos*- prefix, the ecologically emergent mind, with the suffix *-scape*, particularly following Arjun Appadurai's use of the latter in his work on globalization to indicate "fluid, irregular shapes" (1990, 297). Appadurai writes, "I use . . . [the] suffix scape to indicate first of all that these are not objectively given relations which look the same from every angle of vision, but rather that they are deeply perspectival constructs, inflected very much by the historical, linguistic and political situatedness of different sorts of actors" (1990, 296). Unlike the holistic noosphere, nooscapes do not assume the existence of hierarchically organized spatial or temporal scales (though scalar relations can emerge within them). They are defined in situated practice and lively intra-action, and approach knowledge as an emergent property of contingent but not fully indeterminate more-than-human encounters and relations.

My focus on the embedded materiality of knowledges also builds on recent conversations that link questions of knowing (epistemology) with questions of what is real (ontology). I draw heavily on Karen Barad's (2007) agential realism, particularly her theory of intra-action, which entangles knowing and being together through mutually constitutive encounters and relations (she uses the conjoined term *ontoepistemology* to describe these entanglements). She writes, "the point is not merely that knowledge practices have material consequences but that *practices of knowing are specific material engagements that participate in (re)configuring the world*. . . . Making knowledge is not simply about making facts but about making worlds" (Barad 2007, 91, emphasis in original). Following this insight, I describe how different practices, especially knowledge-making practices, enact multiple ontological realities of the MBR (Mol 2002; Law and Mol 2008), and I use the words "enactment" or "world" to signal these multiples in order to remain focused on their situated creation through particular epistemic practices and embedded ecological relations.[5] My ethnographic ecology of knowledges traces how multiple enactments of the MBR emerge from intra-actions between individual human minds and bodies, institutions, documents, technologies, nonhuman critters, and others. The emergent knowledges and worlds then fold back into other relations across the nooscape, shifting and changing processes like land cover change, drug war violence, neoliberal transparency measures, sustainable timber harvesting practices, and so on.

Multiple enactments of the MBR come together in conservation practice in situated moments of partial connection, producing a nooscape that is more than one but less than many (Strathern 2004; Haraway 1991).[6] The approach to relations and multiplicity that I build within the knowledge ecology framework differs from many ethnographic studies of knowledge, particularly scientific knowledge, which describe the creation of singularity or cohesion out of fields of difference and contradiction. There are many versions of this many-into-one analysis, from classic actor-network theory, in which heterogeneous networks stabilize into something recognizable as fact or truth

(Latour and Woolgar 1986), to Annemarie Mol's (2002) work on multiplicity in medical practice, in which worlds are coordinated to appear ontologically singular despite fundamentally incommensurable enactments of body or disease. This kind of stabilization or singularity is simply not the lived reality for people working or living in the MBR. Enacted MBR worlds do not stay neatly bounded and separate from each other, nor do their exclusions remain manageably in the realm of the unreal. One cannot so easily dismiss the real possibility (or possible reality) of a drug trafficker in the forest, the way one might an aberrant lab result in a hospital. If enactments of multiple natures occur through what Barad (2007) refers to as "agential cuts," my work attends to the ways that these cuts continue to bleed.

Haunted Conservation

The multiplicity of worlds in the MBR does not remain invisible and cannot be coordinated away to the weakened position of perspective. The contradictions between incommensurable enactments are too filled with the potential for violence, the shifting between frames too saturated with embodied affect, such that a singular reality rarely coheres. There is little, if any, agreement about what the landscape is or should be, even within conservationist institutions, projects, individuals, or sites. Rather than presume any enacted reality's ability to deny or exclude its alternatives, then, each enactment in fact relies on its alternatives, on the always incompleteness of their denial and suppression, for the production of certainty, power, profit, or violence—and sometimes too, for love, hope, and the possibility of ongoing life. This produces a sense of haunted conservation practice, where "haunting" refers to the presence of worlds otherwise, multiple MBRs enacted through multiple epistemic encounters.[7]

Following an introduction to the MBR's many worlds, this book is divided into three sections emphasizing different aspects of the nooscape. The first, "Double Visions," explores the symbiotic relations between technoscience and paranoia as two dominant epistemic frames in conservationist knowledge production (chapter 2), understandings of the state (chapter 3), and in the formation of controversies (chapter 4). The second section, "Patchiness and Fragmentation," examines the spatial and temporal heterogeneity of the nooscape, using the examples of population (chapter 5) and fire (chapter 6) to explore the uneven distribution of knowledges and their effects. Finally, the third section, "Composing and Composting Knowledges," explores how multiple knowledges and worlds are turned back into material interventions and impacts on the MBR landscape, including unexpected and unintended effects. This section includes conservation-influenced identity and livelihood shifts in one reserve village (chapter 7), experimental interventions in wild animal populations (chapter 8), and how imagined futures of the reserve reshape its present (chapter 9). Winding around this structure are short narrative vines, tendrils of connection that grow between and through chapters (indicated by insertions that will direct you elsewhere, like the one beside these lines). In wrapping around the chapters, these vines form spirals of meaning as they appear repeatedly at different points in the text, emphasizing the nonlinear relations between different sites and scales of the nooscape.

Learning How to See 10

Finally, the afterword revisits the idea of the nooscape, particularly the effects of my own embeddedness in MBR knowledge worlds. Throughout this book, I describe the creation of partial, often problematic knowledges in one moment, and in another cite their measures and products as evidence in my own argument. Similarly, my substantial presence throughout the text reflects the shift from a reflexive ethnography to a diffractive one: "[diffractive methodology] is a commitment to understanding which differences matter, how they matter, and for whom" (Barad 2007, 90). Diffractive analysis attends to the patterns that result from relations of difference, including between myself and conservationists, between knowledge-in-the-making and knowledge-as-fact, and between the many other humans and nonhumans intra-acting in the reserve. Diffractive analysis is embedded in agential realism, acknowledging that "we don't obtain knowledge by standing outside the world; we know because we are *of* the world. We are part of the world in its differential becoming" (Barad 2007, 185). As this work has grown from my encounters with multiple worlds of the MBR between 2007 and 2017, it also folds back into material impacts— even though these are buffered by relatively large geographic, linguistic, and sociopolitical distances. In other words, my knowledge claims are not immune from my own analysis of knowledge- and world-making in the reserve. To remove my presence from the text would be ethically and politically at odds with my argument about the impacts of knowledge projects on the landscape.

Above all, this argument works to open space for reflection on the contradictory harms and benefits wrought by environmental projects on contested landscapes like the MBR, in order to push these projects in more just and equitable directions. As a result of the contingent, partial, and contested nature of the MBR's many enacted worlds, conservationist actions end up reactive, contradictory, and deeply incoherent. Ultimately, however, the apparent incoherency and ad hoc nature of conservation in the MBR is in fact coherent when acknowledging the haunting presence of multiple worlds, particularly those that threaten violence. Conservation actions are oriented not toward an abstract evaluation of best practice on a singular knowable landscape, but toward a carefully calibrated tightrope act balanced between efficacy and danger. This is not exceptional—most conservation projects around the world take place on landscapes crowded with too many possible worlds to ever settle on a best practice or ultimate solution. The stories that follow throughout this book do not represent an isolated case, but rather one instructive for thinking through the complex dynamics of environmental knowledge and action in contexts of instability, inequality, and violence around the world.

Protected areas and conservationist projects in such troubled places are often critiqued as "greenwashed" extensions of (neo)colonialism, state territorial control, ethnic exclusion, or militarized security discourses (Chapin 2004; Bray and Anderson 2005; Berger 1992; Sundberg 1998, 2003; Bryant 2002; Ybarra 2012; Lunstrum 2014; Duffy 2014). Ethnographies of conservation often reveal deep inequalities between transnational environmental organizations and local people (West 2006; Lowe 2006; Doane 2012). These problems and inequalities appear here too, as differential access to networks of power, knowledge, and capital. But they appear differently, based on the difference of my ethnographic location—instead of situating myself primarily among MBR residents, I spent my time in conservationist institutions, with state and nongovernmental organization (NGO) employees. What emerges from this vantage is different from traditional environmental anthropology: with a few exceptions, reserve residents appear mostly in moments of encounter with conservation institutions and their personnel—filtered, in some way, through institutional lenses. I describe a conservationist nooscape, not a local one, the situated knowledges of conservationists taking precedence over MBR residents' relations to the landscape. The latter appear in patches and always in partial connection to institutional worlds.

This may make some readers uncomfortable. My goal is not to disregard local perspectives or needs, but rather to push back against common critiques of conservation by addressing the ways that people working in conservation institutions (many of whom are themselves local) attempt to understand and reconcile multiple human needs with multiple environmental priorities. As repeatedly becomes clear in the chapters that follow, many conservationists struggle deeply with exactly the same questions and issues that academics mobilize in their critiques. To acknowledge this struggle is not to absolve conservationists of harms done by their programs, practices, or institutions. But recognizing the struggle opens up possibilities for reflection on the part of academic researchers—What are we contributing, if launching criticisms that conservationists themselves are already well aware of? What kinds of worlds do our own knowledges compose and compost into? I do not let conservationists off the hook for policies or practices that further perpetuate violence and inequality. At the same time, I resist the temptation to write off nature conservation as a totalizing project, attending instead to the ways that people working in the reserve enact a contingent and shifting set of discourses and practices, attempting, against incredible odds, to shape a landscape that might be hospitable to both humans and the many nonhumans that make up its tropical lowland forests.

LEARNING HOW TO SEE

Late one night in Uaxactún, I wander the small yard between WCS buildings with Juan Castellanos, WCS's field technician in the village. Juan teaches me to hunt for tiny jumping spiders—*saltarinas*—by shining my headlamp across the yard and watching for flashes of electric blue as the light reflects off their eyes. We find spiders less than half a centimeter wide, from over ten meters away. We crouch to watch one dance haltingly from side to side, silvery gray with a dark geometric pattern etched on its back. Transfixed by its staccato skipping, a slower movement in the corner of my vision makes me jump back—a tarantula crawled beside our tiny dancer, unnoticed with her secretive eyes, though hundreds of times larger.

The spiders remind me of a lesson I learn again and again: sometimes bigger, scarier, more powerful things are harder to see. It all depends on how you go looking. My mind turns to CEMEC's map of environmental crimes, scattered with dots color-coded by category: illegal logging, fraudulent sale of state-owned protected land, land usurpation, kidnapping. The map shows isolated events sprinkled across the reserve like flashes of saltarina eyes. These crimes were identified by reports made to the Ministerio Público (attorney general's office). Looming just out of view: activities unseen by patrollers; crimes encountered but not reported; lack of follow-up or prosecution of reported cases; connections of money and power that link isolated dots to each other, to drug traffickers, to criminal organizations, to wealthy politicians. I would later sit with a group of conservationists as they looked over the map and considered these possibilities, trying their best to reconcile visible and invisible.

Later that night in Uaxactún, a few of Juan's friends from the village join us in the yard, and we play in the dark with a vivid curiosity. We examine new growth on a young coconut palm, and find a smooth sac of spider eggs tucked up beneath the lightest green leaf. We guess at the animal that left tooth marks in a fallen avocado. We watch streams of ants swarm across a concrete patch, and one man comments on the patterns they make: "I've seen bats hunting together, and they fly in exactly the same way." I remember images of similar patterns in the fungal-informed ecological theory of Alan Rayner's (1997) *Degrees of Freedom*, which traces energetic patterns common to streams of water, ants, fungi, and others. I say, "Yes, the patterns stay the same across many species. Herding buffalo, too, run that way." The men laugh as I struggle to describe buffalo in Spanish, then we let the conversation lapse, watching the ants, standing together in the thick of night.

The patterns of ants are like bats, like streams, like buffalo. The same patterns inspire human imitation in the name of forest protection: Plan Hormiga (Ant Plan) was devised by WCS to spread patrols through the forest as crawling sets of eyes, rather than leaving them predictably clustered in control posts, camps, or around archaeological sites. Plan Hormiga now crawls along the eastern border of Laguna del Tigre—the pristine/damaged forest edge known as "the shield." Plan Hormiga was the result of an exploratory trip into deep jungle, with expectations of untouched wilderness betrayed by evidence of illicit occupation and a threatening encounter with armed *huecheros* (archaeological looters). In this story, the WCS explorers got away by smooth-talking the huecheros and promising not to report them, insisting they were only interested in looking for fire damage. Later, they heard that these huecheros were themselves shot dead by competitors.

Some ants are harmless to humans (like my favorites, the fungus-farming leaf cutters) and others' bites will hurt like a bullet wound. I learn to tell the difference, to spot the most dangerous ones. Some people encountered in the forest are harmless, and others ready to shoot. It is not always so easy to tell the difference by just looking.

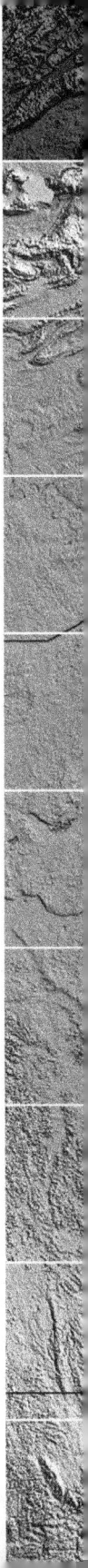

ONE

The Many Worlds of the Maya Biosphere Reserve

> The attempt to banish the specter creates the possibility and the likelihood of a haunting. In the very moment of exorcism, the specter is named and invoked, the ghost is called to inhabit the space of its desired absence. The more one attempts to render it invisible, the more spectacular its invisibility becomes.
>
> J.-K. Gibson-Graham, *The End of Capitalism*

"I was there when they drew the line on the map," Sheri told me, "when they were drawing up the boundaries of the reserve. It was in this room with a bunch of biologists. I had this friend, this biologist, and he said, 'Let's draw the line right here, across the seventeenth parallel. That'll look so good on maps. The politicians will all like that. It'll fly well. It looks so good.' And they didn't know, or didn't care, that there were already these people inside—Uaxactún, Carmelita, Paso Caballos—all these loggers and hunters and looters, you know. Living off the forest." We were sitting at the top of Tikal National Park's Temple V, watching early morning mist clear from the tops of the forest crown and gazing out toward the peaks of other ancient temples stretched out in front of us. Sheri was acting as a tour guide, but between her professional explanations of Classic Maya architecture and recitation of forest facts, she talked about the upcoming 2011 presidential election, Guatemala's problems with machismo and anti-indigenous sentiment, the money-grabbing motives of NGOs, and the environmental destructiveness of local people. When she talked about the history of the MBR, she spoke with bitterness, sadness, and anger. This was a landscape she loved and wanted to see protected, but in her eyes, conservation in the reserve was a failure.

I disagreed with much of what Sheri said. She was resolutely against any human inhabitation of the forest, even as she romanticized ancient Maya traces. She placed responsibility for ecological destruction and violence on locals, ignoring both structural pressures and powerful wealthy actors. She did not differentiate between NGOs that swept in for one-off projects and those that built long-term local collaborations and commitments. Yet at the heart of her perspective was the same problem I had identified: the 1990 MBR map drew a line to declare the existence of a new northern Guatemalan landscape, one composed of pristine nature and sustainable development opportunities for local residents. But the map failed to erase the landscapes that had come before.

Guatemala's national imagination of the Petén has shifted wildly over the past fifty years, from a backwoods jungle, to a colonization frontier, to an epicenter of horrific civil war atrocities, and then to the site of a global environmental crisis that necessitated the intervention of multiple international agencies (Schwartz 1990; Meyerson 1998; Primack et al. 1998; Nations 2006). Home to fewer than 30,000 people until 1970, the Petén's population is now estimated at around 750,000 and growing. As a result of this spectacular population growth, more than half of the Petén's forests were cut down by the mid-1980s, leading to the declaration of the MBR in 1990.

By 2001, the population inside the MBR was over 80,000, already triple that of the entire Petén department only four decades before (Ramos, Solís, and Zetina 2001). A 2011 estimate raised this number to 118,000 (WCS 2011), which includes both legal settlements—like Uaxactún and Carmelita, Petenero communities predating mass migration that now manage forest concessions—and illegal settlements holding out in tense relation with conservationists and park patrols. Militarized evictions of illegal settlements have increased in recent years, but other communities like Paso Caballos bely this oversimplified legal/illegal dichotomy: the Q'eqchi' migrant village has a signed agreement with the National Protected Area Council (CONAP) allowing them to stay within a national park. MBR communities are primarily Ladino (the Spanish-speaking ethnic majority in Guatemala), but about 20 percent of the population are Q'eqchi' Maya who migrated to the Petén following centuries of land dispossession (Grandia 2012), followed by a small minority of Itza' Maya, indigenous to the region (Ramos, Solís, and Zetina 2001).

The region's tremendous population growth was caused by a confluence of factors that continue to shape the landscape today. The first was a state-led program to colonize the region, known as the National Enterprise for the Promotion and Economic Development of the Petén (FYDEP). In the late 1960s, in order to relieve political pressure caused by vast land inequality without addressing the roots of that inequality, the U.S.-backed military government began a program of road building and colonization into the Petén's lowland forests. While political rhetoric focused on opening the Petén as an outlet for poor, landless peasants, the financial rewards of this campaign flowed to the oligarchy and military generals via lumber, cattle, oil, and mining development (Berger 1992; Colchester 1993). By the late 1970s, FYDEP colonization operated on a massive scale, with over U.S. $5.6 million donated by the U.S. Agency for International Development (USAID) to support rural resettlement programs (Wittman and Tanaka 2006). Despite U.S. support, these colonization projects were underplanned, underfunded, and beset with infrastructural problems: not enough and substandard housing, no health facilities, poor soils and tough-to-clear jungles, and isolation from national markets. The Petén was used as a release valve for social and land pressure in other departments, but its continued isolation and agricultural undesirability quickly marked it as a place for the most desperate of the landless poor. As migrants flooded the region in excess of the state's ability to manage them, the government soon reversed its rhetoric and declared them land invaders (Berger 1992, 131).

La Violencia

Carlos suggested I take a hard look at the Wildlife Conservation Society's work on evicting illegal cattle ranchers, in alliance with CONAP and the military. "It's hard. It's really hard. I mean, if you're going to kick out some huge cattle finca [large landholding], inevitably there's some poor campesino there tending the cattle, and what can you do?" He continued with a dark joke referring to recent narco violence: "You're out there, breaking fences, burning houses . . . at least we don't chop off their heads."

Layered over this rural development program was the violence of the civil war (1960–96). During the height of state violence in the 1970s and early 1980s, the jungles of the Petén provided a relatively safe path of flight for hundreds of thousands of internally displaced people whose highland villages were razed in scorched-earth campaigns. But the safety of the forest did not last for long, and the Petén became an epicenter of military massacres in the early 1980s (Egan 1999).[1] The lines between agricultural migrant and people fleeing the war were rarely clear, and the push of military violence and the pull of available land intersected in complex ways with ethnic divisions in Guatemala. From their beginnings, political debates surrounding state colonization programs focused heavily on racial and ethnic identities among migrants. In 1967, the head of FYDEP, Oliverio Casasola, stated that what the Petén needed was Ladino businessmen, not indigenous peasants: "No matter how much sympathy we have for the Indian problem, it is not this human contingent which the Petén process needs" (quoted in Berger 1992, 148). State brutality during the war heavily targeted indigenous Maya, amplifying racialized divisions between migrants. These war-hardened divisions haunt conservation discourses and practices: Q'eqchi' migrants are sometimes assumed to be more harmful to Petén landscapes than Ladinos due to their misplaced indigeneity, the idea that their farming systems are "naturally" adapted to different environments (Nations 2001, 2006).

People fleeing violence competed for land with those pulled by the promises of colonization programs, both groups displacing the forests that predated their arrival. Competition between migrants and refugees has continued into the present over the attention and resources of conservation and development NGOs (Egan 1999; Bailliet 2000; Carr 2006). Many people that moved to the region through FYDEP programs later fled across the border into Mexico, returning in the 1990s to a landscape newly overlaid with conservation concerns (Egan 1999). Their former settlements were now inside protected areas, or resettled by later migrants, who were encouraged to suspect the returning refugees as guerrilla sympathizers who might bring renewed military attention (Egan 1999). The experiences of refugees in Mexico with NGOs, UN agencies, and Mexican government support programs gave them access to health, education, and other key services, arming them with new knowledge and skills. They learned to organize within their communities and access institutional resources, all while buffered by distance from some of the brutal psychosocial effects of the conflict. When they returned, then, refugees who settled in the Petén were often able to garner greater attention and support from NGOs than other migrants (Carr 2006) and were more resistant to the last vestiges of the war: "One can look at return communities as small islands of resistance in the sea of militarization which was rural Guatemala. Within the Ixcán and west Petén, the return communities were relatively large, well organized, and based on relatively democratic principles. Return communities refused to participate in Civil Patrols, something most other rural communities did not dare to do" (Egan 1999, 9). Those who never left Guatemala were almost certainly witness to, victims of, or forced participants in state violence (via Civil Patrols), and the channeling of development funding to those who fled led to resentment and conflict between communities in the late 1990s and early 2000s.

Layered histories of violence and death, as well as of thickly flourishing forest life, erupt into the present. The Petén's landscapes have been the milieu for violence, but so too have they been subjected to it, through catastrophic loss of lively ecologies. Forests and wetlands have become resource frontiers, converted to fields, ranches, and plantations. This is a frontier in the sense described by Anna Tsing (2003): neither place nor process, but a brutal imaginative project built on paradox and contradiction. Cycles of violence here extend beyond the human: thin soils pounded to bare rock beneath the hooves of cattle, cattle lost to the attacks of jaguars, jaguars' habitat converted to ranchlands. For many, agriculturalists still deserve the blame for forest loss in the reserve, as they often do around the world (Tsing 2003; Forsyth 2002; Sundberg 1998; Kull 2000; Lambin et al. 2001). But agricultural migrants and refugees are only the first wave of the deforestation frontier. Those who follow behind are those who drive it: cattle ranchers, oil companies, and ecocidal palm oil plantations snatch up small subsistence farms, pressing the poorest further into the forest.

Increasingly, these land grabs are the work of corrupt politicians and organized crime syndicates, especially drug traffickers. Known as narco-ranchers (*narcoganaderos*), the latter clear huge swaths of forest, then use cattle as thin cover for their territorial claims. Drug trafficker presence has grown throughout the reserve over the past decade, contributing to widespread fear and paranoia as hidden connections periodically erupt into spectacular violence—like the 2016 murder of community conservation leader Walter Manfredo Méndez Barrios, or the 2011 beheading of twenty-seven farm workers just outside MBR borders. Most of the time, it is impossible to know for sure who is a narco, and who a campesino (peasant/agriculturalist). Even when rumors make these differences known, it is difficult to pursue action against criminal land grabs when the police, public prosecutor's office, and judges are frequently bribed or threatened into compliance. In the face of a feeble justice system, drug trafficker presence solidifies troubling new alliances between conservationists and the military, who still have not been held meaningfully accountable for the genocide of indigenous peoples committed during the war (Nelson 2009, 2015).

The army has been instrumental in evicting individuals, cattle, and even whole communities from the reserve. Then-president Álvaro Colom declared a new "green battalion" dedicated to the MBR's western national parks in 2010, and by 2014 military presence in the reserve had more than doubled from 2008 (CONAP and WCS 2015). Military personnel account for 42 percent of patrols walked in the reserve, more than any other institution, including CONAP. They are present in control posts that check movement through parks, especially clustered around oil extraction sites. The border with Mexico, across which drugs and humans are now trafficked by the same violent networks, is increasingly militarized on both sides. Militarized evictions have led recently to forest regrowth in a few small patches of the reserve, celebrated under the neutral-technical term "recuperating areas." While over two decades have passed since the 1996 peace accords declared an end to the war, continued impunity for state-orchestrated genocide haunts this new military presence on the landscape. As a result, even successful evictions can become a larger failure: backlash against military action has bolstered international support for settlements in the MBR's parks, undermining their status as conservationist spaces (e.g., Grandin 2017; Escalón 2017).

Institutional Confusions

> *Joking around with a group of NGO field technicians, Chepe demonstrates how his CONAP uniform is designed so that he can choose whether to show or hide the CONAP insignia. The logo is printed along the top of the breast pocket; the flap to close the pocket can either be tucked inside, showing the image, or buttoned over top to hide it. "Ustedes son engañosos!" (You all are deceitful!), somebody comments, laughing. "Was it a mistake, or done on purpose?" asks another. "On purpose, I think," responds Chepe. He laughs and folds the cover flap carefully over the logo, leaving it anonymous, the way he likes it.*

Overlaying the reserve's lived worlds are a mind-boggling number of state agencies and NGOs, with overlapping and contradictory projects, jurisdictions, and constantly shifting alliances between them. Individual career paths move through these institutions along with the ebb and flow of funding and politics, from state agencies to NGOs and back again. These movements create new institutional ties and sever old ones, as gossip and skill travel with laboring bodies. Rumors, expertise, and experience travel easier through some connections than others, and the possibility of unknown motives or connections haunts many interactions. Fearful of hidden agendas, conservationists working in the MBR talk constantly about what they perceive as conservation's failures. Mistrust and disorganization have bred confusion on the ground: managerial boundaries are drawn and redrawn, with new projects, governing bodies, and physical zoning limits layered on top of old ones rather than replacing them outright.

The confusions of institutional responsibility have existed since 1989, when the Guatemalan congress passed the law cocreating the MBR and CONAP, the government agency responsible for its management. Immediately, the fledgling agency's jurisdiction over the northern Petén landscape was outsourced to three international NGOs, underwritten by USAID. These three were the Cooperative for Assistance and Relief Everywhere (CARE), Conservation International (CI) and the Nature Conservancy (TNC).[2] Notably, none of these original three appear much in this book, despite the wide range of NGO actors I encountered; NGO presence and power on the landscape has shifted repeatedly over time, as national politics and donor and institutional priorities change. Similarly, some of the institutional formations described in the ethnographic present in this book (2011–12) have since disappeared. But even when institutions disappear, traces—of projects, priorities, relationships, and material landscape changes—are left behind.[3]

The irony lurking in these proliferating institutional interests in the early MBR landscape was a lack of institutional presence. The MBR's borders were drawn on maps in the faraway capital in 1990, and its management was funded and outsourced via international aid, but the material presence of those lines on the landscape did not appear in many places until years later. This delay allowed further intrusion of migrants and others onto a landscape apparently empty and without clear control. When CONAP and others did show up, especially in the western national parks of Laguna del Tigre and Sierra del Lacandón, they encountered many more people living on and working the land than had been present when the parks were established by law. Paso Caballos, for instance, was not yet settled in 1990, but was fully established before the arrival of CONAP in 1997. Accounting for this human presence inside human-exclusive parks has now become one of the key issues in the reserve, especially as these two parks are prime territory for narcotrafficking.

Multiple States, Multiple Conservations

Swimming in Lake Petén Itzá off the docks of Flores, my friend Cheny and I talk about how she came to study conservation biology after growing up in Guatemala City. Despite her commitment to the field, she tells me that she sees conservation across Guatemala as a "cover." "I'm not really sure; I just have this sense . . . this question . . . What are protected areas really protecting?" She explains that many protected areas were set up around resource extraction sites: oil or mines. Resigned, Cheny sighs, "At least we're trying to do something."

Many conservationist strategies and practices described in this book—from the good-governance priorities of international agencies to payment for environmental services programs—are typically ascribed to neoliberalism.[4] In Guatemala, the transition to neoliberalism is most often located with the 1996 peace accords ending the civil war. The accords provided not just an end to conflicts but also structural adjustment to taxation structures, economic development programs, indigenous and human rights agendas, agrarian reform, protection of natural resources, and streamlined government (Blum 2001; Robinson 2003; Wittman and Tanaka 2006; Hale 2006). These reforms overwhelmingly prioritized market-based, decentralized governance, and opened Guatemala to new levels of influence by major multilateral organizations.

The structure of the peace accords led to an influx of international NGOs, as well as encouraging the proliferation of new, smaller Guatemalan NGOs (Blum 2001). Dependency on international donors quickly became standard for these Guatemalan organizations, which then had to adjust to meet these donors' demands—a trend that continues with current emphases on governance and transparency in the reserve. This process reshaped a wide variety of local political agendas into a single liberal democratic model, leaving many

Guatemalan organizations feeling that their accounting and reporting practices were of greater importance than the quality or nature of their work (Pearce and Howell 2002). As NGOs take on many former state roles, they are often less transparent and institutionally accountable than governments, and therefore are criticized as less democratic (Bebbington and Thiele 1993; Ribot and Larson 2005).

These critiques, while valid in many cases, do not capture the complexity of the Petén's institutional landscape. Despite recent efforts to curb widespread corruption and impunity, the Guatemalan state is not particularly transparent or accountable, either, making critiques of NGOs on these accounts somewhat moot. More importantly, critiques of neoliberal governance tend to represent the state as a coherent, unified object, while states are in fact highly multiple and constructed in practice.[5] Tracing an ecology of knowledges reveals how the state—what it is, what it does, its legitimacy, roles, and responsibilities—is not simply reshaped under regimes of global neoliberalism, but multiply so. The Guatemalan state is not a singular, newly weakened set of institutions, arranged in the service of global capital. Rather, it is a variable, shifting, deeply contradictory set of practices, techniques, knowledges, and material politics.

Viewed through this lens, corruption, organized crime, and military dominance within ostensibly democratic institutions are not signs of polluted purity of an ideal state, but multiple enactments of what the state is. The Guatemalan state is simultaneously the site of democratic reform, anticorruption measures, and postwar liberal restructuring, and their opposites, the continuation of centuries of military-elite domination and deeply unequal and nontransparent power structures. Nature protection and antidevelopment conservationism exist within the state, as do their opposing pro-extraction policies. Much like the lived landscapes of the MBR, the Guatemalan state is multiple, fractured, and contradictory.

Tracing an Ecology of Knowledges

Flying low in a six-seater plane with a camera strapped to its open side, I got a much more impressive—in terms of the impression left on me— picture of the difference between well-conserved and poorly conserved areas in the MBR. I felt the landscape in ways that I hadn't before.

On the ground, it is easy to get a sense of the size of open, deforested areas—like the expanses of cattle ranches and burned fields stretching to the horizon from the road to Carmelita. But it is harder to understand the size of the forest, which crowds close around you when you are inside it. Even from lookout towers or the tops of temples, the forest seems local, if large. Coasting for forty-five minutes over endless green is a different thing.

The nooscape of the Maya Biosphere Reserve grows from the encounters of many worlds, competing and crashing together amid complex fields of power. Patterns emerge and move in unexpected ways, cutting across scales, reworking temporal orders, and undermining the possibility of certainty at every turn. My own encounters with these patterns and worlds grew over eighteen months in and around the MBR between 2007 and 2017, including a fourteen-month stretch from 2011 through early 2012. I learned from people, plants, smells, sounds, maps, animals, technologies, documents, and others, relying mostly on the intensive sensory attunements of daily ethnographic fieldwork recorded in hundreds of pages of field notes. Most of my time was spent with two institutions: (1) the remote monitoring computer lab CEMEC (Center for Monitoring and Evaluation of CONAP), which creates and distributes geographic information system (GIS) analyses, maps, and reports; and (2) the Guatemalan branch of the U.S.-based NGO the Wildlife Conservation Society (WCS), which also coadministers CEMEC. Both are located in the central urban area of Flores–San Benito–Santa Elena (three towns grown together); I spent my days in their offices and followed their staff as they went out to meetings, press conferences, community or field sites, or other workplaces. As a participant as well as observer, I offered labor on minor tasks, like translating English-language cartographic guides for CEMEC or analyzing community survey data for WCS. As time went on, I also joined staff in the spaces of friendship: homes, bars, or evening strolls around the *malecón* (the concrete antierosion wall around the island of Flores).

These sites offered vantage points into the production, movement, interpretation, and application of conservationist knowledges. I watched CEMEC's mundane office routines like data processing or map making, and followed their products out toward conservation practice through the work of WCS. With WCS (and sometimes with the Guatemalan NGO Asociación Balam, with whom they work closely), I visited the reserve communities of Paso Caballos, Uaxactún, and Carmelita, attuned to their different conservation engagements and alliances. Returning to these villages without NGO staff, I sought further input from residents on monitoring practices and conservation programs. I conducted over fifty in-depth interviews, the majority with CEMEC and WCS employees and residents from the three above communities. I also interviewed staff and directors of other NGOs working in the MBR, archaeologists, various departmental directors of CONAP-Petén, a USAID representative, and people in the tourism industry.

My research was shaped by the particular set of accesses and limits available to me as a white Canadian American woman, living with chronic illness and disability, trained in biology, ecology, anthropology, and STS. Whiteness and a North American passport (or two) go a long way toward opening institutional doors in Guatemala, and I follow local uses of the word *gringa* to describe this positionality. Guatemalans use *gringo/a* to point to uneven structural relations with North Americans who come to their country, so I retain the word to foreground my own embeddedness in the power-laden relations of knowledge making in the reserve.[6] My gender brought both advantages (men curious to talk to me, a nonthreatening appearance) and disadvantages (harassment, condescension, bodily threat). My fieldwork was deeply defined by the rhythms of intensive medical care for my chronic illness (chronic inflammatory demyelinating polyneuropathy)—rhythms that were thrown off by arrival in the field, resulting in a bedbound week in which conservation staff I had not yet met showed up in shifts to bring food and care. Following this episode and extensive insurance battles, I ended up flying back and forth to the United States once a month to receive medical treatment. This rhythm disrupted some opportunities in the field, and provided others, like the depth of conversations in shared ten-hour rides to the capital, Guatemala City.

The majority of my trips to the *campo* ("field," used to refer to rural or wild spaces in the reserve) were limited to villages, but much conservation labor takes place in the wilder parts of the campo—patrols, exploratory expeditions, biological research, veterinary wildlife interventions, firefighting, and other deep forest work. I did spend some time in the forest, but never for more than a few days at a time. My bias toward villages was an artifact of choices made amid the limitations of multisited fieldwork and a variably disabled body—I could not always manage a hike, and village trips tended to be shorter and more easily arranged than forest work, allowing more flexibility to move back and forth between office and campo spaces.

I also draw heavily on analysis of documents and technical artifacts—including maps, images, reports, Skype chats, PowerPoint slides, and others—considering these artifacts and the technologies involved in their creation as lively actors in the construction of the MBR nooscape, not just passive objects. I observed the creation of these artifacts, collected copies whenever possible, and tracked their movements through and across institutions and contexts. I attended to how particular technologies shape (though do not determine) representations of the reserve contained in these artifacts, performed my own close reading of texts and images, and noted others' interpretations of them in different contexts. I used several of these maps, images, and texts in one-on-one interviews, for example using the aerial photographs taken by CEMEC to estimate population in interviews with the villagers whose houses are being counted from above.[7]

I draw together these traces of my time in Guatemala—field notes, recorded interviews, and documents and artifacts—and analyze diffractively across them to identify emergent patterns that cut across the many sites and sources. By using the term "diffraction," I draw on methodological insights developed by feminist STS scholars Donna Haraway (1997) and Karen Barad, the latter of whom defines diffraction as "a tool of analysis for attending to and responding to the effects of difference" (2007, 72). The importance here is in attending not just to difference itself, but to its effects, and always with an eye to response (and, therefore, to responsibility). As an example, I track how CEMEC's maps, data, and reports move across the nooscape. The movements illuminate their power—as they move, these artifacts gather new attachments and alignments. But they can also change completely as they encounter different contexts—even from evidence of environmental success to evidence of environmental harm.

The effects of these extreme differences in meaning are not neatly dismissed between contexts, but haunt these artifacts, pointing to excluded worlds that undermine claims of technoscientific objectivity. Thus the effects of difference can destabilize conservationist claims or practices, leading to further mistrust or even violence. The knowledges and enactments that grow from situated intra-actions across the MBR twist together in strange relation, jumping scales and reversing the presumed linearity of causality. Embodied experience, technical documents, rumors, transnational discourses, profits, jokes, and fears offer different ways to know and to change the reserve landscape. The mutual transformations of these knowledges can turn wildlife encounter into policy, policy into violence, violence into coalition.

Three epistemic frames—which I gloss as technoscience, paranoia, and love—dominate the conservationist MBR nooscape. Technoscience and paranoia drive most conservation decisions, while love motivates continued work in the face of fear and loss. (These are not the only epistemologies present in conservation, nor in this book, but they are dominant in conservationist institutions in the MBR.) Technoscience offers clarity: as a multitude of institutions and actors attempt to slow the ongoing rush of deforestation in the reserve, they rely increasingly on knowledge produced by CEMEC. But these official, objective knowledges are haunted by the presence of hidden networks of power and violence. So paranoia fills in the gaps, fueled by competing networks of rumor and silence. Finally, embodied encounters with wild life inspire love and motivate conservationist action in the face of difficult and dangerous problems. These three ways of knowing—and the many others that shape conservation practice, including local or indigenous environmental knowledges, nonhuman worldings, historical memory, and others—enact fundamentally incommensurable worlds. As conservationists shift between them, the contradictions within their own knowledges and practices further amplify experiences of radical uncertainty, nonlinearity, and precarity.

Technoscience

> This report contains twenty-one indicators distributed into four categories. . . .
> The indicators have different baselines and unequal temporal resolution, largely
> due to the limitations of available information, but it is estimated that they
> adequately . . . allow understanding of the MBR and support those responsible
> for its management in making informed decisions.
> CONAP and WCS, "Monitoreo de la Gobernabilidad en la Reserva de la Biosfera Maya"

The MBR is a hotspot for international researchers—between 120 and 150 academic articles mentioning the reserve are published in English each year. These academic sources are occasionally drawn into conservation practice, but most MBR institutions turn to the hybrid state-NGO institution CEMEC when they need authoritative knowledge about the reserve. As a central clearinghouse for remote monitoring, GIS mapping, and reporting of key information about the MBR, CEMEC has garnered an exceptional reputation for two key characteristics: neutrality and usefulness. Responding directly to conservationist desires for clarity, certainty, and actionable knowledge, CEMEC carefully balances between producing knowledge that is specific and detailed enough to inform decision making while avoiding knowledge that might be politically or materially dangerous.

One of the most powerful effects of CEMEC's work is to continuously enact the reality of the MBR itself. Through its many maps and reports, CEMEC helps make real a coherent, bounded reserve object, beset by knowable, measurable problems. Mapping this reserve coproduces state control, management, and definition of a landscape that is otherwise a highly varied patchwork of projects, institutions, ecosystems, and human dynamics (Jasanoff 2004). Asking people to describe the reserve as a whole inevitably leads to answers broken down into smaller geographic pieces, or hedging and uncertain generalities. Imagining the reserve as a singular object is difficult, but maps and monitoring reports from CEMEC, with their solid reenactments of the familiar outline shape of the reserve, work to make this imagining possible.

What can this singular biosphere reserve do that an unruly patchwork of parks, settlements, and timber concessions cannot? For one thing, the reserve enables connection to globally circulating models of conservation and development that attract major funders, including the UN Man and the Biosphere program within which the MBR was designed and developed. It facilitates state claims to territory that are otherwise difficult to manage or control—and the Petén has historically been exemplary of these difficulties (Sundberg 1998; Gould 2006; Ybarra 2012). Most powerfully, the reserve object enacted by CEMEC's reports enables conservation action to occur, on the part of the state, NGOs, and other actors. Problems are teased apart from each other—deforestation rates, crime, fire, population growth—and defined numerically and spatially, enabling strategic, directed response in defense of forests. Feeding conservationists' hunger for clarity and action, technoscientific knowledge thrives in the nooscape of northern Guatemala, facilitating collaboration across social and political difference while also reinforcing those differences and their embedded power dynamics.

Paranoia

A man was shot and killed in Paso Caballos in early 2012, leading to a rush of rumor and speculation on the part of conservationists as to whether it was related to recent illegal land sales. Rosa, WCS's technician in the

village, explained to me that the murder was unrelated to land: some-
body had recognized someone else from back in the war—an old grudge,
not a new one. She also explained that the proliferation of rumors to the
contrary was routine, elaborating with another example: There was a
man in the village who saw a strange car parked outside his house. Not
knowing who it was, he went to hide elsewhere, not returning home
until the car was gone from the village. The car turned out to be from
WCS; when the visiting staff looked for the man and couldn't find him,
they called Roan (director of WCS-Guatemala) to report the "missing"
man as kidnapped. Roan then called Rosa in a fury: "What the hell is
going on out there!? People are being kidnapped now?" Rosa, feeling
that Roan and others were holding her responsible, tried to calm them
by saying nobody knew what had happened—maybe he was bitten by
a snake; maybe something else happened. But others just responded,
"He's been kidnapped. He's definitely been kidnapped." She went to his
home to investigate, and found him there, ready to explain what had
happened. It took a while, still, to assure others in her institution that
no kidnapping had occurred.

On a landscape overrun with historical and current violence, people reach far beyond objectivity to make sense of real and unreal, known and unknown. As the old saying goes, knowledge is power, and power in Guatemala is violent, hidden, fractured, and deeply threatening. This leads to a paranoid epistemology, a kind of double vision in which knowledge is always haunted by terror of the unknown. George Marcus argues that paranoid thinking can, in certain contexts, be "within reason, a 'reasonable' component of rational and commonsensical thought and experience" (1999a, 2). Following Marcus and others, I use "paranoia" to refer not to individual psychological pathology, but rather to a mode of thought borne of social contexts in which suspicion of hidden dealings is a perfectly reasonable response. Paranoia grows from the relation between violence and the ordinary that Veena Das describes: "The affect produced on the registers of the virtual and the potential, of fear that is real but not necessarily actualized in events, comes to constitute the ecology of fear in everyday life. Potentiality here does not have the sense of something that is waiting at the door of reality to make an appearance as it were, but rather as that which is already present" (2007, 9).

Paranoia describes a distributed affect of fear and mistrust, in which the distinction between things known and unknown is the source of dangerous power. It is fed by the precarity of human and nonhuman life in and around the MBR, by horrific news reports, and by mundane daily experiences of violence or corruption that never appear in those reports—rampant domestic violence, muggings, extortion, and other incidents heavily underreported due to widespread distrust in the police and justice system. It is fed by the regularity of death threats made against those working in conservation institutions, in which those speaking politically dangerous opinions, or just patrolling the wrong park at the wrong time, might have to sweep their families into hiding at a moment's notice.[8] While paranoid thought—seeking the hidden beneath the apparent, assuming the existence of malicious secretive powers—is a common mode of political thought around the world, it is especially prevalent in Guatemala, where networks of brutal criminality mix easily with entrenched military-backed oligarchies.

Paranoid epistemologies are exhausting, exhaustive, terrifying, and enlightening: there are always things too dangerous to say, and you must always listen carefully to others' silences. Rumors and secrets come to seem more credible than things declared transparent.[9] Rumors run richly through the nooscape, alongside, against, and sometimes even woven into the artifacts of official technoscientific knowledge. The same is true of this book, as the interplay between formal and informal knowledges and settings affected my field research immensely, with official recorded interviews and informal conversations working with and against each other. While most individual identities have been anonymized throughout the text, several figures—like Roan Balas McNab in the story above—appear under their real names due to their positions as institutional leaders or public figures. When people were acting as official representatives of institutions, or when drawing on quotations from public forums, I use real names and affiliations. At other times these same individuals appear under pseudonyms when I draw on material from more confidential contexts. Similarly, most places and institutions are given their real names, but there are exceptions for exceptional stories.

Part of fieldwork amid paranoia means that the most interesting information comes when recorders are turned off. Some people didn't want to be recorded at all, though they were happy to talk to me while I scribbled notes. Others would ask, mid-interview, for me to turn my recorder off for a few minutes, while they spoke about narcotraffickers or criminal politicians. In the text, I collapse these moments with others from more relaxed settings: conversations on shared rides out to remote villages, or after a few rounds of beer at a Flores bar. I collect these various unrecorded, less (and more) guarded moments under the category *chisme*—rumor or gossip. In reporting chisme I sometimes approximate quotations, especially when people used memorable turns of phrase. More often, chisme haunts my text as insinuation, slippery with passive-tense construction—vague, sourceless information, *some people say . . .*

The ways chisme intertwines with official technoscientific information in the nooscape is central to my analysis, but decisions on when and how to include chisme are ethically fraught. There are things that I, as an ethnographer, will not say or write even now—names, places, events, and dangerous connections between them. I will not name them, nor name those who named them to me, and even acknowledging the fact of my own dangerous knowledge produces a shadow of terror in my own mind. I participate in paranoid anticipation, choosing which stories and quotations to include carefully, wondering and worrying about whether or not those who were brave enough to share things with me will be safe, and, too, whether it will be safe for me to return. I walk a line between the safety of silence and trying to write stories that might make a difference. I see this line in the work of conservationists as well—a careful navigation of unknown threat, the safety of inaction and silence, and trying to make a difference.

Love

> Luis told me of a jaguar he and others saw lying in the middle of the road in eastern Laguna del Tigre. By the time their vehicle stopped, the jaguar had jumped up and run into the forest. The men got out of the car to check the spot where it had been lying. With childlike joy in his voice, Luis told me, "It was still warm and everything! Bien bonito!"

If the twists of many entangled worlds mean success can become failure, if a field visit carries risk of kidnapping or death, why keep working? Conservationists across institutions turn to stories of their encounters with wildlife to answer this question. Most people working in MBR conservation move back and forth between the worlds of urban office and wild campo. These movements bring extreme sensory shifts, producing at first a heightened awareness akin to the culture shock of arriving in an unfamiliar ethnographic field site. I call this "nature shock": a loss of familiar environmental cues and easily discerned meaning.[10] In their daily work, MBR conservationists encounter and deal with incommensurable human-enacted worlds. Here, these incommensurabilities are compounded by even greater gaps of difference, those between human and nonhuman worlds. Encountering this unbridgeable difference is part of nature shock. Like its cultural counterpart, nature shock wears off with time, repeated visits, and familiarity: learn to name a few trees, distinguish dangerous from harmless spiders and snakes, and things are not quite so overwhelming. Yet as the initial disorientation is replaced with the relative comfort of recognition, a deep, affective sense of difference between wild campo and office continues to pervade bodily experience.

For conservationists, this difference is identified by powerful words: love, and the real. Love grows from the fertile ground of nature shock, from encounters with wild animals, from smells and sounds rich with abundant life. It is this richness of life that makes the MBR a special place for those working to preserve it. I mean "make place" literally: while the conservationist space of the MBR is enacted through official maps, policies, and practices, the MBR as place is enacted through multispecies collaborations (Raffles 2002; Moore 2005; Tsing 2005, 2012). This love motivates conservationist action, even in the face of uncertainty, threat, or failure. This love grows into bodies that enter conservation work in the Petén not because of environmentalist principles, but because these are decent jobs: many field staff talk about how their belief in the values of conservation grew slowly from their time in the forest.

The love inspired by wild spaces and species is often contrasted with the difficulties of working with people. As a U.S. biologist visiting WCS stated, "Our species is really messed up. That's why I prefer to work with jaguars." She was not the only one. One of the field technicians who has been with WCS the longest, Mario, echoed this sentiment, saying he preferred working with scarlet macaws to people. Roan had asked if he was interested in community-oriented work, but he declined: "I don't like to work with people. It's too hard. The thing is, you always want to be on good terms with everybody, and you just can't. It's impossible. So I don't like it. I prefer the *montaña* ['mountain,' referring to wild spaces], the forest, discovering new things."

This theme of discovery was frequently associated with the wild. The campo promises access to the real, the immediacy of bodily sensation appealing amid the uncertainties of a multiple nooscape. Never mind the false impressions that may be given by our senses; that which happens right in front of one's eyes feels seductively certain. Personally getting to the campo, or at a minimum getting trustworthy reports from field teams, was seen in WCS as a necessary complement to remote technoscientific knowledges about the reserve.[11] Driven by desires to have these knowledges make a difference, technologies ranging from camera traps to field reports to global positioning system (GPS) wildlife collars are used to epistemically tame the wild "real" of the campo, translating the sensations of wild encounters into generalizable forms such that they might be able to travel across the nooscape and make a difference.

Encounters among Many Worlds

The following chapters trace the interconnections, disconnections, flows, transformations, effects, and affects of knowledge forms, including the dominant frames of technoscience, paranoia, and love. While conservationist strategy in the MBR has recently shifted toward militarization in defense of parks, previous approaches like participatory community engagements continue at the same time. Caught amid fields of uncertain identities and motivations, conservationists work within and around contradictions: instituting programs to reduce human-wildlife conflict at one site, and sending in the army for evictions at another. These contradictions result from the haunting presence of alternate epistemologies and worlds that contradict those being used to act or intervene at any particular scale, site, or moment. Maps of state presence are haunted by a lack of accountability associated with that presence; scientific descriptions of wild species are haunted by the radical unknowability of their lived worlds; declared conservation success is haunted by the incoherency of a multitude of actors and institutions working at odds with each other. The haunting exclusions of conservation emerged with the very first attempt by environmentalists to know and intervene on the northern Petén landscape: the many worlds left out when the line was drawn on the map.

SILENCES OF MEMORY

I remember the first time I encountered Kaibiles, the Guatemalan special forces responsible for the worst massacres and brutality of the civil war. It was 2009, and a couple dozen uniformed men in red berets poured out of the back of a truck in the middle of the Santa Elena market. Rosa, whom I was with, quickly grabbed my arm and hustled me away. She explained who they were once we had some distance, but only barely. Mostly, she just said she did not like to be near them. This was the most common way of referencing war memories I encountered among (mostly Ladino/a) conservationists: short, evasive statements of discomfort; careful avoidance of physical proximity, eye contact, or direct statements. It is no coincidence that the report of the Commission for Historical Clarification (CEH), tasked with making sense of the senseless violence of the war as a step toward peace and reconciliation, was titled *Guatemala: Memory of Silence, Tz'inil Na'tab'al* (Tomuschat, de Cotí, and Tojo 1999).

Many people continue to make extraordinary efforts to account for the people killed and disappeared, for the communities razed and turned violently against themselves, for the depth of terror ground into bodies, minds, and social relations (Nelson 2015). They work to undo long-ingrained practices of silence. These people are mostly Maya, who were most heavily targeted by the military, and they are primarily working in the densely populated highlands of Guatemala. Yet a massacre of mostly Ladino villagers in the Petén town of Dos Erres has been among the very few cases to result in formal consequences. This massacre of over two hundred people, which took place over four days of systematic cruelty, led to a 2012 conviction of five Kaibiles and a public apology from President Álvaro Colom. But even as this case proceeded through trial in 2011, it was largely surrounded by silence in conservation offices. Reconciliation documents are named as a memory of silence, but in many spaces, the silencing of memory continues to work against the possibility of reconciliation.

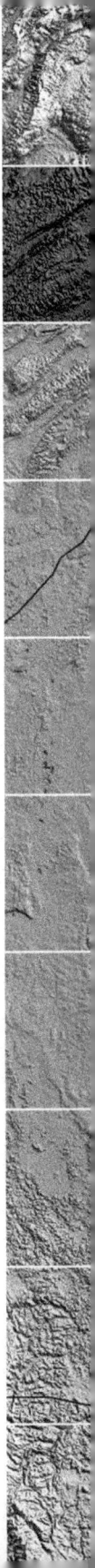

Fantasy . . . is not opposed to reality but
constitutes its "psychic glue."
Begoña Aretxaga, "Maddening States"

I / DOUBLE VISIONS

Technoscience and Paranoia

What happens when widespread paranoia intersects with technoscientific environmental knowledge? Science and paranoia
are often assumed to be contrasting epistemic frames, undermining or competing with each other (Lewandowsky, Oberauer,
and Gignac 2013; Lahsen 1999). But their relations in the MBR
nooscape are more like a complex symbiosis, like a legume and
nitrogen-fixing bacteria: these belong to different kingdoms of
life, live on different temporal and spatial scales, and participate
in uneven exchanges, but neither exists without relation to the
other. So too with science and paranoia in northern Guatemala,
which rely on each other for the ongoing production of radical
difference. In the MBR, calls to urgent action strengthen local
desires for certainty and objective truth as the basis for decision making. Yet these desires are never fulfilled by the partial
nature of technical knowledge, nor can its embedded authority banish conservationists' lived experiences of precarity, violence, or loss. Decisions are declared on the basis of data, but

the data too are haunted by silences and exclusions. Here, paranoia is not a pathological context in and against which scientific environmental reasoning must work, but offers visions of other (terrifying) worlds inaccessible to techniques of rational knowability. The incommensurabilities between these worlds produce and reproduce double visions of paranoia/technoscience, known/unknown, opportunity/threat, and conservation success/failure.

TWO

Eye of the Storm

Mapping in the Morgue

In the back meeting room of the WCS office in Flores, I watch as Julio, a CEMEC technician, displays a draft of the ambitious *State of the Maya Biosphere Reserve* report (WCS 2011) to a group of NGO staff and visiting project funders. He clicks through PowerPoint slides of maps and data, presenting each one in brief, technical terms: deforestation, reported environmental crimes, local livelihood sources. After each slide, the room erupts in discussion about the political implications of the information, how, when, and where it might be used effectively, what kind of responses or shifts in strategy it implies, or how the description of the data should be worded in the final report. Each time, Julio waits patiently, silently, for the others to indicate that he should move on to the next item. Calm, neutral, and quiet. As I watch, I realize that his behavior matches the way the data are supposed to be read—and, too, that his quietness that stands out so distinctly in WCS is how I am always used to seeing him, where it doesn't stand out, back in the computer lab at CEMEC.

The office of CEMEC is a world apart. Where the surrounding streets of San Benito are hot, humid, and alternately dusty or muddy depending on the season, CEMEC is very cold—the air conditioner always blasting on high—and clean. People outside its doors weave a constant stream of conversation, preferring to run the same words over rather than be without *plática* (chat), but CEMEC is silent, an open room full of ten friendly people sitting next to each other with little interaction. When visitors enter beyond the plywood barrier separating the reception area from the rest of the lab, they make rounds through the desks with hard-slapped handshakes and loud friendly greetings to the men, and gentler, more formal salutations to the women. The technicians smile, shake, and greet, then slide their gazes back to their screens, discouraging further intrusions. These visitors usually then pull up a stool next to the desk of whoever is preparing a map or other request for them and lower their voices. Only a very few interrupt again to repeat their rounds on the way back out.

For six months, I rode to and from CEMEC in the car or on the back of the motorcycle of one of the technicians who were my neighbors. We would chat through the ride, into the halls of CONAP, right up to the CEMEC office door. But stepping through the door, our voices would quiet, the conversation dropped until we stepped back out again for lunch or at the end of the day. Maybe one of us would issue a subdued "Good morning" to those already settled at their desks, but not always. When leaving, somebody might murmur "See you tomorrow," answered with a round of quietly echoed "tomorrow" from a few desks, but not always. Outside CEMEC's door, talk is the air Guatemalan sociality breathes; without it, the space inside CEMEC feels hollowed, hallowed.

Early in my field notes, I wrote this description: "There are no windows in the office. It is totally *encerrada* [closed in]. Used to be a hospital. Julio joked one day that CEMEC used to be the morgue." CONAP had indeed occupied a former hospital building for its regional office, and the CEMEC-as-morgue jokes were recurring (though inaccurate). But it wasn't the deathly cold atmosphere that I had gotten wrong. A couple of weeks later, another field note:

> I was wrong—there are windows here in the office! . . . There are four windows lining the wall behind me, shuttered and with turquoise curtains that almost exactly match the turquoise paint of the office walls. Perhaps it was this clever camouflage that kept me from noticing them before, although the room still feels *encerrada*, even when I look straight at the windows. They are covered with both curtains and the translucent plastic blinds so common here, so you can't see out, and the office's artificial lights are brighter than any light coming through—it just doesn't feel like there are windows.

Even staring straight at openings to the wider world, CEMEC felt cut off, closed in, and separate.

A Keystone Knowledge Actor

A small monitoring institution embedded within a regional state agency, CEMEC is the eye of the storm at the center of the Maya Biosphere Reserve's management regimes. This description works in two senses: first, as a figurative eye tracking and organizing vast amounts of social and ecological data about the reserve; and second, as a widely trusted source of apparent political neutrality in a nooscape characterized by intense conflict. The opening image of Julio quietly providing data to an unrestrained interinstitutional audience captures both of these facets. For most actors and institutions in the MBR, the adjectives "neutral," "objective," and "trustworthy" are nearly impossible to come by. Yet CEMEC garners all of these, both in people's professed opinions and through the widespread use and application of their data. This chapter introduces the practices and politics of CEMEC's knowledge production about the reserve, analyzing how the institution cultivates two powerful properties of technoscientific knowledge: neutrality and usefulness.

The director of CEMEC is Victor Hugo Ramos, a focused, brilliant autodidact from the western highlands department of Huehuetenango whose local stature (and full facial hair) lives up to that of his notable namesake. He and Roan Balas McNab, American expat director of WCS-Guatemala, have worked closely together for many years, and are good friends. When I arrived in Flores in 2011, the two met with me together to discuss my research plans and referred to themselves as "elephants" (giants) in the world of MBR conservation. Together, the two hold extraordinary institutional knowledge—not just of their own institutions, but also of the broader landscape of individual conservationists, state agencies, NGOs, private interests, local community factions, and both domestic and foreign funders that might be called upon to support new projects. When Ramos talks about retiring to pursue less stressful work—a recurring, and recurrently deferred, dream—McNab responds with worries about who might possibly step in to fill his shoes. Indeed, Ramos's mix of technical acuity, political savvy, and ability to manage ever-increasing numbers of technicians and projects with humor and authority is essential to the success of the institution.

I would meet strangers in other contexts who, upon learning that I was doing research at CEMEC, would beam and spontaneously heap praise upon the office, telling me that they were "damned good at making maps!" (*son cabrones para los mapas!*), or launching into stories of how much a certain technician had helped them in their work. During fieldwork otherwise filled with rumors, secrets, doubts, and constant undermining of truths, I heard only a single challenge to CEMEC's neutrality, from a tourism developer who suspected that the data in a GIS model of future deforestation might have been "manipulated" due to "bias." (Even then, this challenge was not directed at the lab per se, but at the community-run forest concessions in the reserve, which he did not believe could protect the forest in the way that the model predicted.) Given the power of the lab's work to determine land rights, conservation and/or development plans, and other highly contentious issues, the absence of accusations of bias, corruption, or political manipulation is truly extraordinary.

Faced with incommensurable possibilities and perspectives at every turn, both state and NGO conservation actors pull from a wide variety of knowledge sources: immediate experience; published and unpublished academic research; traditional, local, or indigenous knowledge; trusted personal contacts; rumors and gossip; institutional documents and gray literature; and official reports like those produced in CEMEC. The knowledges from these sources move unevenly through networks of actors in the reserve, along with their attendant ontological and epistemological frameworks. Contradictions, translations, and practical effects are worked out differently in different spaces, resulting in a wildly heterogeneous nooscape. Yet across many of these spaces, CEMEC's maps and reports act as authoritative sources through which other forms of knowledge are filtered and compared. As such, CEMEC emerges as a keystone actor in the MBR nooscape: the institution plays a critical role in developing and maintaining conservationist regimes in the reserve.[1]

This keystone role is explicitly recognized by many outside the institution. One NGO conservationist, Juan Luis, reported that over his many years working in the reserve, he found that different sectors had "completely different understandings of the way things are, of the state of the reserve." He told me that the ambitious *State of the Maya Biosphere Reserve* report, being prepared by CEMEC, was going to be a powerful tool to build consensus, "to create a unified understanding of how things really are." His anticipatory remarks point to how CEMEC's reputation for objectivity ("how things really are") creates the possibility for reconciling disparate positions.

NGO-State Hybridity

The perceived trustworthiness of CEMEC is even more extraordinary considering that it is part of the widely mistrusted Guatemalan state. As a subdepartment of the Petén branch of CONAP, CEMEC is officially a state institution, and is housed within CONAP's regional offices in San Benito, Petén. But its exceptionality is made possible largely by the support of WCS, which legally coadministers the lab via signed agreement with CONAP and provides approximately two-thirds of CEMEC's funding. The NGO justifies support for the lab as part of its local mandate, which includes biological and ecological monitoring of the reserve. At least one CEMEC technician is dedicated exclusively to WCS projects at all times, so the NGO's mapping requests are relatively buffered from the delays and prioritizations other institutions must undergo.

This state-NGO hybridity offers CEMEC advantages and disadvantages. As Ramos points out, one of the key advantages of being part of the state is that their data are recognized as more or less official. This makes it much easier to work with others inside state agencies and provides a certain level of authority for working with those outside of them. The disadvantages are related to the well-known instability, corruption, and inefficacy of Guatemalan state institutions, including problems such as nepotism, political deprioritizing of environmental issues, lack of continuity in institutional personnel or priorities, and consistently scarce resources. WCS's involvement buffers the small lab against many of these issues; it provides funding stability and a strong external ally during sudden shifts in the political winds. As such, Ramos declared that CEMEC's comanagement by the NGO was the best possible position. While relations between CONAP and WCS surrounding management of CEMEC have not always been tension free, the agreement has endured and has been repeatedly renewed over the years, giving long-term stability and support to the lab. This hybridity is key to the production of knowledge that is both official—attached to the state—and objective—dissociated from the weaknesses of the state.

Eye of the Storm I: Monitoring and Reporting

As a keystone knowledge actor, CEMEC has enormous power to shape conservation in the MBR. What the institution tracks, maps, and reports (and what it does not) creates and limits possibilities for intervention on the landscape. As director, Victor Hugo Ramos constantly seeks out new themes and technologies that CEMEC can tap into for monitoring projects, taking on a much more active role than simply acquiring and distributing data at others' request. Many monitoring activities now considered routine and fundamental to reserve management were dreamed up by Ramos and have since become indispensable across institutions. For example, CEMEC conducts low-altitude flights over the reserve to capture aerial photographs. Ramos told me, "Nobody asked us to do that. And we're doing it. Right now we're using it for specific ends, like demographic monitoring, like monitoring cattle. We're also using the photographs for certain proposals, or to validate our remote sensing products. All this, nobody told us we had to do it. We just started to do it because it seemed like a good idea. And now, they wait for us to do it!" This was in 2011, when U.S.-based charitable organization LightHawk paired with CEMEC to provide donated volunteer flights. When LightHawk pulled out of Guatemala a few years later, CEMEC replaced them with local volunteers with private planes and occasional chartered private flights, but had to scale back the scope of this monitoring. By 2017, the majority of flights carried journalists or representatives of the justice system to see key areas of the reserve, but CEMEC continues working toward other ways to accomplish this aerial monitoring.[2] Most of CEMEC's projects are thought up by Ramos, sometimes in conjunction with McNab or others, and are brought to fruition through their personal commitment, drive, and savvy in negotiating both institutional and technical worlds.

CEMEC now gathers information from satellites, sensors, cameras, and human bodies sent to observe and report on the landscape. Massive amounts of data come into CEMEC from an ever-growing number of sources, where it is tamed into maps, reports, and databases and made freely available to (most of) those who request it. Since its beginnings as a modest three-person operation in 1997, CEMEC has grown into a powerful clearinghouse of information about the reserve, with a wide variety of people and organizations relying on their maps and reports. Some of the most widely used of CEMEC's routine annual activities (and their data sources) include:

- maps of deforestation and land cover change (Landsat, SPOT, and Deimos satellite imagery)
- near-real-time fire reporting during the months of February–May (NASA MODIS satellite data)
- maps of annual fire damage (Landsat satellite images and aerial photography)
- estimates of human population in reserve settlements (aerial photography)
- monitoring of cattle presence (aerial photography)

As a supplement to their land use change monitoring via satellite imagery, the lab has begun georeferencing (precisely locating digitized photos via geographic coordinates) huge numbers of aerial photographs as a way to "ground truth" or verify their deforestation estimates.[3] In 2011, the office also began georeferencing an enormous database of historical aerial photographs of the region from the 1980s, to establish a pre-reserve baseline of forest cover. CEMEC also manages information from a network of climate monitoring stations, some under their purview and some belonging to other institutions—INSIVUMEH (National Institute for Seismology, Volcanology, Meteorology and Hydrology), the NGO ProPetén, and others—and distributes daily and weekly climate updates, particularly during the fire season.

CEMEC regularly supports a wide variety of projects for both the state and NGOS, as well as researchers, educators, and others. They provide maps and data for protected area master plans, five-year management plans, funding proposals, and other documents. They conducted an enormously difficult and successful census of reserve residents in 2000–2001, and aerially monitor population growth on an annual basis. They build sophisticated GIS models of future deforestation and land use change, including taking the lead on a Mesoamerica-wide scenario planning project. They have begun collecting and systematizing data on nontimber forest products harvested by community concessions, with the goal of creating a comprehensive database of extraction activities across the reserve. They collect livelihood data, track financial contributions to reserve institutions, model climate change impacts, settle boundary disputes, monitor water quality in local lakes, prepare mapped routes for field expeditions, track reported crimes, build websites, prepare and present PowerPoint slideshows about the reserve, provide training in GPS and technical skills to a wide variety of actors, and more.

One of the most common activities in the office is simultaneously one of the simplest to complete and yet one of the most powerful: CEMEC estimates that it receives at least 250 requests for location mapping per year. These *constancias de ubicación* (evidence, record, or proof of location) involve the creation of small maps indicating the geographic coordinates and legal jurisdiction of particular locations. This may be either a request to locate an existing structure or place (requiring a GPS technician to go into the field to take coordinates, return to the office to map them, and then report on which jurisdictional area they lie in), or to verify planned locations to build new structures or infrastructures. Schools, farms, cell phone towers, fences—any new construction legally requires precise location, since protected area laws restrict and regulate all activities in the reserve. This is an extremely simple, even dull, task for technicians, but one that determines land access and building rights on a hotly contested landscape.

Technical Exceptionalism

CEMEC staff are extremely proud of their work, in terms of both personal accomplishment in technical skills rare in Guatemala, and their knowledge that the data and reports they produce are widely used and trusted across sectors, actors, and institutions. Of course, the lab's technical exceptionalism within Guatemala sits in tension with the rude intrusions of external infrastructure, politics, or even the lively multispecies landscape itself (one day the secretary spent an hour carefully scooping the sugar next to the coffeemaker from one container to another, sorting out tiny black ants). Their technical skills did not equate with being on the cutting edge, according to most CEMEC staff, largely due to insecure funding. Though far ahead of most Guatemalan institutions, and immensely proud of that fact, they didn't have a dedicated server for the office until 2013. The server enables centralized storage and coordination of the lab's many databases and products; until its purchase, overlapping versions of projects were awkwardly distributed across machines, passed back and forth over a variety of free file-sharing programs like Skype, YouSendIt, and Dropbox. This kind of patchwork approach to limited resources shows up across technical projects: cameras are secured to airplanes by zip ties and bicycle inner tubes; thirty-day trials of expensive software are downloaded to one computer at a time, extending their collective availability.

Infrastructure is reliably unreliable. In remembering the occasional nonsilent soundscapes of the lab, it is not voices that first come to mind, but the beeping of emergency battery systems that punctuated frequent power outages. Loss of electricity (as well as internet and cell phone service) occurs regularly, if unpredictably, in Petén's urban areas. CEMEC's computers have backup power sources to prevent data loss, but not enough power to continue working when the lights go out. When this happens, people sit quietly at their desks, taking the moment to tap out a text message or get up to refill their coffee, waiting as the air slowly thickens without the air conditioner's blast. The midtoned beeps of the backup systems punctuate the lab's silence in syncopated rhythms. Only if the power is out for more than a couple of minutes might a conversation start up—a funny story from the bar last night, chances on upcoming soccer games (with the office divided in loyalties between Barcelona and Madrid). If high-pressure deadlines are bearing down, Victor Hugo might take the opportunity to check in one by one with each technician on the progress of their work, or a few people might gather around a laptop with a reliable battery, working through a problem together until the return of power scatters them back to their own desks.

On one particularly bad day, the electricity began flashing on and off every few minutes, with outages continuing for several hours. I had carried my laptop over to the desk of another technician, David, so we could work through new animated mapping software together. I led him step-by-step through English-only instructions (a translation role I frequently played in the lab), each of us creating the same map in parallel on our two screens. Each time the power dropped, the office would release a collective groan, while David and I tried to make our shared project work on my single remaining screen. After ten or so of these mini blackouts, David asked me, "This doesn't happen in the U.S.?" "No!" I answered quickly and emphatically, causing the rest of the office to burst into laughter. "Only in Guatemala . . ." David replied with resignation, a reminder that despite CEMEC's exceptionality, it was still entangled with the realities outside the office door.

Users and Usefulness

Despite the often mind-numbingly dull day-to-day work in the lab—tasks associated with processing satellite or aerial imagery are highly repetitive—technicians consistently reported that awareness of the ultimate products of their labor, and of the perceived usefulness of those products, was deeply satisfying. Despite his disinterested demeanor in the opening story, Julio's account of preparing the *State of the Maya Biosphere Reserve* report emphasized his excitement about the final product. He described the data processing as mostly uninteresting, chipping away at one indicator at a time. But when he saw the first draft of the report come together, Julio emerged with a new impression of his own work, particularly the way he could read across different indicators to tell a new story:

> The scope that you can have with all that information—whew! Because when I was working on it, I just focused: I'm working on this theme, checking that this detail comes out right, that this comes out right, and then I'd finish with that theme. But then when you look at it all together, you can see how this thing is happening in the same place as that thing, and you start to see something interesting. This plus this. Let's say, for example, control posts with deforestation. So there is deforestation where there are no control posts. Or if there is deforestation where there's a post, what's

happening with that post? Things like that, no? Just as an example. There are a ton of possibilities with this much information.

Possibilities for usefulness are an emergent property of the combination of many individual maps, monitoring projects, and data points. This emergent story told by CEMEC's overlapping maps and reports weaves through conservation practice and policy at all scales in the MBR; its travels, impacts, and encounters with other knowledges and worlds shape possibilities not only for understanding the landscape, but also for intervening on it.

Usefulness does not emerge from data naturally; it must be built by moving CEMEC's knowledge products outward to other actors and institutions. This movement is facilitated by extraordinary care in representational choices. Ramos told me:

> If we're presenting, for example, to *diputados* [members of congress], we make it as simple as possible. Not because the diputados are people who don't know how to think or don't understand things, but sometimes they don't have a lot of time. They're always on the run, and this is one of the arguments that is brought up for making information accessible to people. And with the public as well, we try to make things like that, the most understandable possible. Some things can't be brought down from high levels of complexity; you can't reduce their complexity because they're complex things unto themselves, right? So you just can't. But we try.

Ramos's comments show his keen awareness of the power of communication, simple graphics, and clear messaging. This savvy is one key to the lab's success, as well as a glimpse into the fact that reduction of complexity on the landscape—commonly critiqued by political ecologists—is not a naive technocratic move but a deliberate attempt to increase the political efficacy of CEMEC's data.

In addition to their regularly distributed annual reports and support for ongoing projects, CEMEC estimates that they receive an average of two thousand individual requests for information per year. The lab keeps two logbooks to track requests for maps—one for location maps, and one for everything else. I reviewed the "everything else" logbooks for the period December 2004–May 2011, which concealed as much as they revealed: fields were often left blank, handwritten entries were undecipherable, names referred to multiple possible scales or spaces (e.g., "San Andres" is both a town and municipality), and the books only tracked requests from office walk-ins. This last condition meant that many requests from other CONAP departments and WCS were excluded, as they often came over phone, email, or Skype, skipping the secretary's desk altogether. Increasing internet access and use in recent years also explain why the logbooks showed a consistent decline in requests since 2005, despite CEMEC's increasing influence and number of full-time technicians. I attempted to categorize requesters—state agencies, NGOs, community organizations, and so on—but the confusions of institutional presence and responsibility made determining stable categories difficult. A request might have come from Sierra del Lacandón National Park, which is coadministered by CONAP and an NGO, Defensores de la Naturaleza; should this be counted in the CONAP or NGO category?

Even considering the blank spaces, unidentified actors, and institutional overlaps, the logbooks told a compelling story of short- and long-term trends in the MBR. Data requests follow a clear annual rhythm matching that described by CEMEC technicians: peaking in the fire season (February–May), slumping in June in a postfire rest period, and then declining slowly toward the end of the calendar year. The highest number of recorded map requests in one month (sixty-one) was in March 2007, at the height of one of the MBR's most devastating fire seasons during an El Niño year. (But compare this to the 160 calculated in June 2011 by asking each technician how many maps they had made in the previous month, a figure that includes location maps.) The rise and fall of institutions over time are also visible in the logs, with NGOs appearing and disappearing along project time scales of two or three years. Other events leave traces: the 2010 relocation of CEMEC from a space in Flores next door to WCS to CONAP's San Benito offices shows up as a near-doubling of requests from CONAP. The 2007 fires show up not just in number of maps but also as a record high proportion of requests for maps of Laguna del Tigre National Park, where fires are often the worst. Requests for maps of Mirador-Río Azul National Park ebb and flow with cycles of controversy over the park's future, reaching a peak in 2010 when a new public use plan for the park was drafted. The logbooks point to how CEMEC's history exists in dynamic relation to the larger history of the reserve: they trace shifts in institutional power and attention, and simultaneously reflect CEMEC's own power in shaping that attention.

Figuring out where and how CEMEC's maps and reports move is key to the knowledge ecology approach, illuminating CEMEC's relations to other institutions and actors within the MBR nooscape. Even before entry in the register, requests for information can take different paths through the institution, depending on who is asking. Many CONAP and WCS staff can go straight to a technician, as can Defensores de la Naturaleza, which pays the salary of a technician dedicated to their coadministered park. Students, researchers, or representatives of other state or NGO agencies can usually enter the office and request data directly, while landowners, ranchers, private companies, or unknown Guatemalans (foreigners seem to be given a protective sheen of positive assumptions) must first make a formal request through the Technical Administration department of CONAP, getting clearance from other levels of bureaucracy before being granted access to information. These multiple paths are often determined on the spot by Ramos or others in the office, on the balance of trust and (potential) suspicion—the knowability of a requestor's motivation and potential use of the information. Determination of the acceptability of a potentially suspect user is always outsourced to another CONAP office, buffering CEMEC from accusations of bias or improper politics. These structures of bureaucratic procedure help maintain CEMEC's reputation for objectivity and neutrality, even as they are navigated along lines of paranoid politics, chisme, and established social connection.

Eye of the Storm II: Cultivating Neutrality

Skyping in Silence

For months after I arrived, I was overwhelmed by the obtrusiveness of my fieldwork in the silence of CEMEC. To find out what technicians were working on, I had to leave my assigned desk space and intrude upon somebody else's. I had to make them remove their headphones, break their concentrated silence, and talk to me about what they were doing. And it did not take an outsider like me to notice the strangeness of the office environment. One of my opening interview questions for the technicians—what do you like most/least about working in CEMEC?—came back most often with answers about the silence or the extreme air-conditioned cold. The staff was divided over whether the silence was their most or least favorite aspect of working in the lab, but it was always marked enough to comment on. Some found it satisfying to focus on their individual tasks without interruption; others—especially newer additions to the ranks—were deeply uncomfortable.

Several technicians noted that it must be hard for me to do my research there, jokingly chiding me to keep quiet when I joined them at their desks, or commenting that I must be bored—which I politely denied, but was frequently true. I had a few minor projects to chip away at—writing a brief guide on cartographic design principles, or using English-only software manuals to complete small tasks like the animated map I created with David—but often I found myself dragging through long, cold days without concrete tasks. Starting my fieldwork with six months in CEMEC also had consequences for my local socialization: my language skills and my ability to engage in the idle friendly chat necessary to make myself socially recognizable to most Guatemalans developed late, and only once I had made a friend good enough to tell me bluntly: Micha, you don't talk to anybody; they will think you are rude, a snob, or very strange. I learned first, in the strangest place, to be silent.

I also eventually learned how these silent technicians were not, in fact, being rude to each other. After enough awkward intrusions into others' work spaces, I noticed that the technicians' Skype accounts were always open and popping up with chat messages—including from others in the office. Here was the sociality, sublimated into silent screens. Links to YouTube videos, coordination of shared projects, plans to hang out after work, clarification of data points, cute photos of their kids, all the regular chatter happened over Skype. Once I discovered this, the world of the office opened up to me. I received an invitation to the wedding of one technician over Skype chat—I grinned as I responded, since she was sitting five feet away and facing me, but typed my reply rather than answering her aloud. People started spontaneously sending me maps and images they thought I might find interesting, and I found that it was suddenly easier to ask casual fieldwork questions during the workday: Who was that who just came in? What information were they requesting? All this fit best in the silent Skype box.

It is not just technologies that do this—working at a screen does not determine silence. CEMEC's newest hire told me that the last office he had worked in, a similar GIS lab in Guatemala's National Forest Institute (Instituto Nacional de Bosques, INAB), had been filled with music and conversation. The lab's atmosphere might be partially due to Victor Hugo's preference for uninterrupted quiet, though this is not a total explanation, since the silence remained unchanged during his frequent absences. Eventually, after asking again and again, "Why is it so quiet here?," I decided that the *why* was not only unanswerable, but also not the most interesting question. Instead, I started asking, Might this silence have something to do with the stability, neutrality, and trustworthiness of CEMEC?

I came to recognize the staff's silenced bodies as part of the technical infrastructure of CEMEC. It was more common among conservationists to refer to field staff in infrastructural terms, such as a group of CONAP field technicians who proudly declared: "*We* are the remote sensors!" Similarly, it is easiest to think this way of the two CEMEC technicians devoted to GPS locating—their bodies sent out into the reserve in pickup trucks, on dirt bikes, and on foot for multiday treks, with the simple goal of reaching particular locations and pressing a button on their GPS unit to carry back to the lab and place on a map. But even in the lab, the practices of monitoring and map making shaped and changed bodies, silencing them, removing their eye contact or physical contact with each other, and moving the sociality of daily life through fingertips, keyboards, Skype, and screens rather than lips, tongues, and shared air.

To consider technicians' silent bodies as infrastructure indicates their role in undergirding functions essential to the institution—including that of producing objectivity. Infrastructure has recently surfaced as a generative theme in the humanities and social sciences, with Howe and others (2016) noting that it is the category's paradoxes that make it good to think with. One such paradox is the presumed invisibility or backgrounding of infrastructure, alongside the fact that, "in many instances, the visibility of infrastructure is necessary to assert its political and poetic effects" (Howe et al. 2016, 558). In CEMEC, the technicians' silence makes them visibly invisible—the lab is a semipublic display of quiet, neutral technicality, much like Julio's presentation of data in the opening vignette. Bodies as attached to individual, political humans are backgrounded in order to foreground the data they produce as objective fact. This silence does important (if unintentional) work to build the lab's reputation and smooth the circulation of their maps, reports, and data. It creates a strong impression on all who enter the lab that it is a space apart, somehow different, possibly exempt from the tumult of uncertainty raging throughout the reserve.

The dullness of daily work in CEMEC also explains why the lab space recedes in many of the following chapters, despite its keystone role in the reserve. As a result of this backgrounding of bodies, it was difficult to keep CEMEC from fading out of ethnographic view; the office did not provide many exciting vignettes with which to illustrate their data creation processes (though there are a few). The lab sometimes disappears, even as their work becomes infrastructural to my own account: I critically analyze their data, but also use it to reinforce my arguments and descriptions of reserve dynamics. CEMEC's occasional disappearance in this text is a product of the same dynamics that allow the lab to disappear from people's considerations of its data when they use its maps and reports in their work and decision making. The power of dullness to immobilize the imagination is in fact a sign of a powerful imaginary at work—that of the possibility of apolitical technoscientific clarity.

Technical Stability

That this powerful imaginary of neutral technicality should emerge from a Guatemalan state institution is extraordinary. Where most of the Guatemalan state is broadly understood to be treacherous, corrupt, and highly unstable, CEMEC is characterized by long-term stability and widespread trust and admiration. My fieldwork overlapped with the national elections of 2011 and transition to a new government in early 2012. These events highlighted the widespread instability of state institutions other than CEMEC, including the regional CONAP office within which it is embedded. From the 1996 peace accords through the 2011 election, each presidential contest resulted in the election of the second-place candidate from the previous round, with no party ever succeeding in winning two presidencies in a row (presidents are limited to a single four-year term).[4]

As a result of this political rhythm, the first thing every new president does is distinguish himself (all have been men) from his previous competitor by undoing their signature policies and programs. New presidents also quickly replace the heads of state agencies with their friends, supporters, and donors. These changes ripple down through bureaucratic hierarchies to an unpredictable degree: the national director of CONAP always changes, and this person has historically always appointed a new regional director for CONAP-Petén. The new regional director then may or may not bring in people they trust to head the various subdivisions of the regional office, and so on. In some transition years, everyone down to low-level field technicians are swapped out; in others, the new regional director decides to retain those on hand for the value of their experience.

Over the years, CEMEC has never been strongly affected by these transitions. Victor Hugo Ramos has remained director since the lab's inception in 1997, and while he has had to fight to retain his staff a few times, the computer lab has been protected from the political changes that, sooner or later, have overturned all other departments of CONAP. While CEMEC staff were anxious in 2011 about the transition between governments, these anxieties did not extend to their job security, as they did for every other state employee.

Instead, they worried about having to justify their work—particularly their budget and requests for material support—to an entirely new group of people. Victor Hugo told me, "We're not as affected as other units, but there's always a bit of stress. We have to get to know the new people, and convince them that our work is useful, good for something. . . . You can't tell what's going to happen, because you don't know who the new regional director will be, what their intentions will be, or their politics, their plans for administration." Another technician told me he was worried about the transition because so many people always lose their jobs, but he also knew CEMEC had always been safe from this threat, and that the only person who ever left the institution did so by his own choice.

WCS plays an important role in this stability, offering protection both as a powerful external ally and as a financial buffer from budget changes inside CONAP. But the stability is also attributable to the specialized technical nature of CEMEC's work—there are very few Guatemalans with experience or training in remote sensing or GIS, and even fewer with enough experience to step in as director of a monitoring institution. Ability to produce technical knowledge thus provides some protection against extreme political changes. Crucially, this protection also depends on the production of knowledge that is not too threatening to potential new governments, with their unknown connections, priorities, and motivations. As a result, CEMEC carefully negotiates how much to report, how to represent issues, and what to leave out—always balancing its own institutional stability with producing knowledge that is detailed and specific enough to be useful.

Technopolitical Influence

Even more than specialized technoscientific knowledge production, this balancing of threat and usefulness is where CEMEC truly excels as a Guatemalan institution. The lab's keystone role in the MBR nooscape has grown enormously since the lab's beginnings in 1997, largely as a result of this skillful negotiation. Ramos attributes CEMEC's growth to a combination of technological change and interinstitutional political pressure:

> I believe it has changed because maybe now people are more receptive to technological things, and now it's easier, for example, to make a presentation in PowerPoint, use a projector to show interesting things. It probably has something to do with that. But there's also an insistence from certain

institutions, or certain specific people, in arguing their positions with the data. You have to give credit, for example, to Roan, who has pushed a lot on using the data, using them to advocate [*hacer incidencia*], to make changes, right? And, fortunately, there's been receptivity on the part of people from CONAP, and on the part of other sectors of the government, to start to use data to make decisions, with respect to things that emerge from the field [campo]. It wasn't like this before; it wasn't so easy. For example, now we have a good internet connection. We can send an email to a thousand people without so many problems. Before, not everybody had email addresses. It wasn't so easy to send the information, you know? So it's a mix between the two things, ease of access to information and technology, and also specific work in insisting on using information to make decisions. And to show things that at times aren't particularly agreeable for the government, right? But we have to show them—it's the reality, how it is—and to try to provoke changes with that.

Ramos's explanation is rich and revealing. The growth in technological access, familiarity, and connectivity across sectors and institutions is an important part of CEMEC's increasing influence, in the sense of email and web access, PowerPoint, and wider ability to read and interpret maps, graphs, and tables. At the same time, some aspects of CEMEC's technical abilities, particularly in producing sophisticated GIS maps and remote sensing analyses, are still out of reach of the majority of reserve actors. This bolsters the lab's reputation for objectivity, depoliticizing their technical data through the authority of rare expertise. This expertise is part of what allows Ramos to describe CEMEC's data products as "the reality, how it is." It allows the institution to "provoke changes" in other parts of the state while still maintaining an apolitical reputation. Ramos's explanation reveals that this was not always the case, that this ability to maneuver information into politically powerful arrangements is one that has developed over time, and with the help of external allies—especially WCS. Ramos and McNab use their close relationship to move monitoring data in powerful ways, creating it in the neutral technical zone of CEMEC, then letting WCS (and others) push the data into advocacy as an actor outside the state.

Even as Ramos portrays a positive, progressive change in terms of CEMEC's influence, lurking within his explanation are signs of hesitation, uncertainty, and potential threat. Ramos notes that state institutions' willingness to use data in decision making is both something relatively new—"it wasn't like this before"—and something that has required insistence and pressure from external actors. Beneath these statements lies the reason for resistance: the fact that the alternative to decisions based on data is likely those based on corrupt or criminal motivations. This is also acknowledged in Ramos's delicate statement that some of their data might be politically dangerous, or not "agreeable for the government." Publishing data that makes the state look corrupt, or even just ineffective, can pose a threat to the institution as part of state bureaucracies, even with the protective buffer of WCS. Despite Ramos's claim that there is a moral obligation to speak truth to the state, that "we *have to* show them," there are limits—things that are simply too dangerous to report.

Technoscience and Neutrality on a Violent Landscape

CEMEC is not immune from the paranoid epistemology that infiltrates life and work throughout the MBR. In fact, its reputation for neutrality is evidence of a skillful negotiation of this epistemic frame, not its evasion. In a less politically savvy monitoring institution, knowledge claims would be rejected as biased or plagued by rumor—as are most claims made in the MBR by other institutions and actors. Several of the following chapters trace issues in the reserve along lines drawn by CEMEC: crime and governance (*gobernabilidad*), human population growth, fire, deforestation. In each of these cases, the violence, inequality, and nontransparent forces that permeate MBR worlds shape CEMEC's knowledge production. What to map and who may see the maps are carefully chosen, and thick with threat. Threat might come from a change in government regimes, from unstable budgets, from corruption, or from violent actors outside the state, like narcotraffickers. Often the lines between these threats are imperceptible. Ultimately, the lab is not just avoiding known dangers but also carefully navigating potential and unknown sources of threat.

CEMEC's technoscientific practice in the midst of widespread paranoia poses a challenge to common critiques of technical knowledge in conservation and development work, particularly the role of technoscience in depoliticizing deeply political interventions onto landscapes. These critiques focus on the discursive split between nature and culture or science and politics, arguing that this discursive structure evacuates political claims from anything placed in the realm of nature, science, or the technical.[5] At first glance, CEMEC's production of objective, quantitative reports on a wide variety of ecological, social, and political factors perfectly fits this model of what Tania Li (2007) calls "rendering technical." However, these critiques assume that both producers and users of technical knowledge are so embedded within this hegemonic discourse that they do not or cannot recognize the inherently political nature of their technical problems and solutions.

What becomes apparent in the MBR, however, is that a widespread paranoid epistemology means that people are always listening to the silences where power is assumed to lie. Depoliticization is both desired and necessary in a context in which knowledge can be dangerous, and sharing that knowledge more so. When knowledge moves, threat hangs heavy in the air: Who might be listening? Where is the next threat coming from? The indistinguishability of the silence of protection (let us not say what might get us killed) and the silence of threat (let us not reveal our ties to dangerous networks of power) perpetuate this distributed political affect of paranoia. Reading the silent politics that have been evacuated out of a technical report becomes the natural and obvious way in which to read any technical report. Similarly, reporting some issues (deforestation, fire) but not others (narcotrafficking airstrips, land grabs linked to politicians) is the best way to cultivate a reputation for objectivity and neutrality, while avoiding physical or political threat.

CEMEC's representations deliberately remove politics. This is not an unintended side effect of technocratic schemes but a concerted effort to create possibilities for intervention while sidestepping the most dangerous or threatening problems on the landscape. The resulting depoliticized knowledge then moves smoothly between institutions and up and down political hierarchies. People trust this knowledge, share it, praise its rigor and objectivity, and use it to direct their activities inside the reserve. Here again is the usefulness so deeply prized by CEMEC technicians. It is not enough to simply make a good map. That map must also be able to move through the correct channels, yet not be accessible to those who could use it for illicit or dangerous ends. It must be powerful enough to provoke conservationist action, yet not so threatening that it provokes a dangerous response. The lines delimiting what can and cannot be reported shift with new government regimes, with transformations in institutional alliances, with violent events or swells of public controversy.

CEMEC walks this shifting line carefully, balancing the dangers of knowing with the desire to have that knowledge do some good. Their ability to enact depoliticized technoscientific objectivity greatly facilitates the spread and acceptance of their knowledge, and they know it. The state-NGO hybrid lab sits as the eye of the storm, working always to maintain its stability, neutrality, and trustworthiness, and quietly—silently—turning out maps, reports, indicators,

Certainty Emerges 216

and statistics. They produce representations of the reserve that create a sense of clarity, defining problems and dynamics that everyone may know are not the biggest problem, but which still matter. By pulling single issues and questions out of the morass—fires, deforestation rates, population growth—as if they weren't all tied together into the same unassailable confusion of competing realities, CEMEC enables action.

Above all, the lab's reports are most useful to conservationists as a way of creating a momentary consensus about what the landscape is, if not about priorities or strategies in response. Its reports enact versions of the reserve and its problems that offer clarity instead of contradiction. CEMEC's knowledge products are more successful than any others in creating these moments of consensus or shared reality in the reserve. But ultimately, the realities enacted by their technoscientific monitoring are shifting ground, haunted by their silences and exclusions, and begin to disintegrate almost as quickly as they can be constructed. The following chapters detail many moments in which CEMEC's data create these shared realities through which connection, action, and response can take place, as well as others that reveal the limitations of those enacted realities, their (sometimes violent) conflict with other worlds and knowledges, and outright refusals to engage with the unified understanding that CEMEC offers.

CORRUPTED DATA

After the 2015 Guatemalan spring, a public protest movement against government corruption, state agencies across the country tightened up. New accountability and transparency measures were the norm. In the Petén offices of CONAP, people complained that these new anticorruption measures—in theory a good thing—had a dark side: people were so scared of being accused of corruption that they were afraid to "stick their hands in the pot," even if spending agency money was their job. As a result, one man told me, anticorruption measures had actually increased institutional precarity, making it far more difficult to use the scant resources they did have—leaving park guards stranded in the central urban area, for example, if their supervisors would not pay for gasoline to get them to the campo. Those accustomed to working with corrupt institutional worlds are confounded by practices that stop mundane bureaucratic procedures in their tracks by layering on more bureaucratic procedures. People in CONAP already complained about how much of their work was *tramites*, paperwork and procedure, calling themselves *tramitólogos*. Now, the more that paper moves around, the less people do.

One man, Julián, complained about Jimmy Morales's government (2016–20) in comparison to Otto Pérez Molina's (2012–15): "[Pérez] was corrupt, but at least he was an effective functionary." Pérez needed government programs to run in order to give the contracts and profits to his friends, he explained. But Morales was a puppet and a fool, with no ability to govern.

If corruption is contamination, a state of depravity or decay, it is also the way things work. This state was built by a select few

for their own power and profit, with military and U.S. support to keep everything in line. Even after the peace accords' constitutional reforms, even in the face of the extraordinary advances of the International Commission against Impunity in Guatemala (CICIG), even when the previous two presidents were arrested on corruption charges, even with the current president under investigation, even now these entrenched structures remain resilient. There is no purity at the heart of the state, no ideal core to which Guatemala might return if every cent were counted and accounted for. Instead, people like Julián long for a return to a familiar, functional corruption.

Data too can be corrupted. Files become unreadable, their data loss a frustration shadowed by the idea of what might have been contained in their scrambled ones and zeros. Try passing them through another program; try to find another copy of the files; try to sort through the metadata—but problems remain.

Are data produced by a corrupted state another kind of corrupted data? Legibility is key to statecraft (Scott 1998), while corrupted data imply illegibility. But it is the corruption itself that remains illegible in official state documents, a contamination visible only when run through another (paranoid) program. I and several others attempted in 2011–12 to come up with estimates of funding flowing into the MBR, past and present, with minimal success. Requests for ostensibly public information, like USAID grants or Guatemalan state budgets, resulted in contradictory and incomplete figures. Granting and grantee institutions reported different numbers. Detailed information revealing how money was spent in particular projects or locations was left purely in the realm of wishful thinking. By and large, CEMEC escapes accusations of this kind of corruption. But if corruption is how things work, how resources and bodies are made to move through bureaucracies, perhaps the lab's data *are* corrupted by its origins in the state—produced with just enough illegibility to move and get things done.

THREE

Mapping Gobernabilidad

On May 16, 2011, on Los Cocos ranch in central Petén, twenty-seven poor farm workers were brutally bound, tortured, and beheaded. Straight out of a horror movie, a gruesome message was left written in their blood in two-foot-tall letters on the side of a farmhouse, warning the owner of the farm that Z 200, part of the Mexican drug cartel the Zetas, was after him. Within twenty-four hours, President Álvaro Colom declared a state of siege (*estado del sitio*) in the Petén, and the department was flooded with armored military vehicles heaped with uniformed men carrying machine guns. Tourists visiting nearby Maya ruins who were staying in Flores—about sixty miles northeast of the massacre—were terrified by the news, and by the army trucks trundling over narrow cobbled streets day and night. Almost immediately, the tourism industry's steady stream of visitors dropped to a bare trickle.

The state of siege continued for three months, after which it was downgraded to a state of alarm and then extended, thirty days by thirty days, well into 2012. Over the same period, national news outlets were following the trial of four former Kaibiles, members of the Guatemalan Special Forces. These four (and a fifth, later) were eventually convicted of crimes against humanity for their participation in the 1982 massacre of over two hundred people in the village of Dos Erres, part of the military's scorched-earth campaign during the civil war. What made this doubling particularly haunting in 2011, as both stories cycled through daily news reports, was that Dos Erres and Los Cocos were located very close together in La Libertad municipality, not far outside the borders of the Maya Biosphere Reserve. The echoing of mass murder tactics in these two cases, separated by thirty years, is no coincidence—ex-Kaibiles are heavily recruited by the Zetas, who originated from a similarly trained elite forces branch of the Mexican military.

On the day of the Los Cocos massacre, all government offices in the Petén were closed due to bomb threats, including CEMEC. When the technicians and I returned to the office two days later, the staff broke the tension by cracking jokes about the bomb threats and referring to the surrounding streets as "pure Baghdad." "Watch out!" one technician, David, teased another. "If you make a map of the landing strips, they'll come cut off your head!" Laughing, another responded that one day the Zetas were just going to stroll into the office, politely asking for a base map of the reserve (*mapa base*, a broad-scale general reference map). It wouldn't be a base map, David corrected authoritatively: "They'll want *una hoja cartográfica*" (detailed area maps including fine-scale topographic data). Turning to me, his tone more serious, he clarified that this was only a joke: "But they have good maps, the Zetas. They already have really good maps."

The following week, a Kaibil came striding into CEMEC. A fit, handsome middle-aged man with a machine gun strapped to his hip, he requested large printed maps of the western regions of the reserve, Laguna del Tigre and Sierra del Lacandón National Parks, rolled them up under his arm, and strode out again. As he left, a Skype chat from CEMEC's director popped up on my screen:

VICTOR HUGO RAMOS: Scared?

MR: Yes and no . . . I don't like guns.

VHR: Yeah, me neither

MR: What did they want? General maps of the area? I'm a little surprised that the military doesn't have excellent maps of the whole state

VHR: That's how it is. They always ask us for maps. Always. The maps they have are from the 1960s

Despite the strong statement about state power and territorial control made by rolling tanks through the streets of Flores, actual military knowledge of the territory of western Petén was apparently fifty years out of date. The contrast with David's confidence about the Zetas' maps is striking, and closely tied to the general sentiment that the Petén, like other pieces of Guatemala before it, was becoming Zeta territory.

The Doubled Nature of Gobernabilidad

Bodies, tanks, maps—each of these appear here as technologies of territory, marking presence and power in ways both shocking and mundane. I open with these interwoven stories of violence, the state, and mapping work in CEMEC to begin to explore the question of *gobernabilidad* in the MBR. I leave the Spanish term "gobernabilidad" untranslated in order to allow its double meaning made up of two coconstituted opposites: governability and governance. First, govern*ability* describes a characteristic of the landscape itself: the reserve's thick tangle of jungle, swampy wetlands, and densely layered histories of violence, inequality, and marginality. Here Guatemala's problems with organized crime, human and drug traffic across the border into Mexico, and both extraordinary and mundane violence compete with international imaginings of a pristine nature.[1] Second, govern*ance* describes state (and state-like) efforts at control over the landscape, as well as transparency and accountability for the actions involved in those efforts.[2] The single term "gobernabilidad" was used for both of these entangled opposites in the Petén, such that when somebody was speaking it was often unclear whether they were describing a problem (governability), the response to a problem (governance), or the relationship between the two.

The term "gobernabilidad" thus works well to describe a paranoid double vision of the state, as rampant corruption within the government haunts claims to legitimate authority. A UN commission designated to fight Guatemala's corruption and impunity, known by the acronym CICIG, made extraordinary strides after its arrival in 2007, particularly in pursuit of high-profile cases. Still, President Jimmy Morales expelled the commission's leader, Iván Velásquez Gómez, from the country in 2018 and ultimately ended CICIG by not renewing its mandate when it expired in September 2019. Velásquez, who continued to lead the commission from outside the country until its termination, stated that he was pessimistic in the face of elite backlash and reconsolidation of structural problems (Silva Ávalos and Puerta 2018). Half of all political party funding is obtained through illegal means, with 25 percent coming from organized crime (CICIG 2015). Prosecutors and judges who successfully pursue high-profile cases face death threats or lose their jobs. The National Civil Police are widely mistrusted, known as "rolling sacks of corruption."

As within state structures, violence and organized crime are part of daily life and work on the MBR landscape, though largely invisible except in moments of spectacular eruption, as in Los Cocos. The proliferation of organized crime, particularly drug cartels, competes in western areas of the reserve with land-grabbing cattle ranchers, illegal loggers, archaeological looters, and poor agricultural migrants. The differences between these groups are never immediately apparent: following the Los Cocos slaughter, many people speculated whether those killed were really innocent farm workers or if they were cleverly disguised members of the drug trade. This probing for hidden threat, identity, or connection reflects the widespread fear of duplicity that permeates postwar Guatemala (Nelson 2009). Deforestation rates are also highest in the West, and conservationists muddle threats on the landscape with threats to the landscape.

The 2011–12 state of siege provided a spectacle of state power that had little impact on narco activities or other serious crime, though smaller offenses like motorcycle theft dropped precipitously. The visible displays of military power, which enacted a strong, lawful state in control of its territory, were haunted by both this inefficacy and by memories of the civil war. The war was an era of horrific double visions: violence by, for, and against the state became largely indistinguishable, as civilians were alternately slaughtered and forced into collaboration with military violence against their own communities and families (Tomuschat, de Cotí, and Tojo 1999; Manz 2004; Nelson 2009). Former president Otto Pérez Molina, elected shortly after the Los Cocos massacre on a tough-on-crime platform, is a former general with close ties to this historic violence. He denied that genocide was ever committed even as his former colleagues were put on trial for crimes against humanity. He has since been stripped of his presidential immunity and, along with his vice president, Roxana Baldetti, arrested for participation in a multimillion-dollar graft case. These haunting double visions undermine the narrative that the military straightforwardly acts on the side of good in the Petén.

Despite these problems, the slaughter at Los Cocos strengthened conservationist support for military presence in the MBR. Like Aretxaga's description of "maddening states," relations between the state and criminal actors are characterized by a "mirroring paranoid dynamic" that produces and reproduces the violent "fictional realities" of both (Aretxaga 2003, 402). The militarization of the reserve grows directly from Guatemala's histories of counterinsurgency warfare, from entangled political and petroleum interests, and from the outsourcing of U.S. border security to Mexico's southern border with Guatemala (Ybarra 2012, 2016; Devine 2014, 2017). But this doesn't explain why conservationists are increasingly in favor of this strategy, especially given widespread awareness of historical and present human rights abuses by the military. Conservationists told me that they did not like or trust the military, but needed them. As one man told me, "You can't send a kitten in to fight a rabid pit bull." This need is driven by the sheer terrors of narco violence and its unpredictability.

After years of intensification, this strategy is beginning to double back on itself in unexpected ways. Military evictions in Laguna del Tigre National Park have been technically successful but have met with widespread public backlash and support of evicted communities that ultimately undermine the park as conservationist space. The haunting presences of rights abuses, war memories, and corrupt state actors twist the results of military interventions in strange directions. While a full discussion of violence, crime, postwar state formation, and the inefficacy of Guatemala's justice system is far too extensive for me to cover completely, this chapter begins to examine how these issues overlap with conservation in the MBR.[3] In particular, I explore how militarization is produced as one among many possible enactments of a conservationist state, one with increasing presence and power in the MBR.

Knowing and Intervening in the State

Like the reserve itself, the Guatemalan state is not a coherent, bounded set of institutions, but rather multiple partially connected enactments created through different state-making practices. In addition to the military, I explore enactments of the judicial and administrative state, particularly as conservationists attempt to harness each of these to create change across the MBR. All three are beset by the haunting doublings of gobernabilidad, with criminality and violence connected across state/nonstate boundaries. As a result, attempts to use the state to intervene on the landscape always involve attempts to intervene in the state itself, to make it more just, lawful, and effective. Like their desires to know the MBR in order to change it, conservationists similarly seek to know the state in order to change it.

In 2011, CEMEC began developing practices for monitoring and mapping gobernabilidad, funded by large grants to CONAP and NGOs.[4] These activities offered new access to trustworthy technoscientific knowledges about both criminal and state action in the reserve. Shaped by the conservationist priorities of CEMEC, this is an explicitly environmental gobernabilidad: state presence is equated with governance, and deforestation with ungovernability.

CEMEC's 2015 report on these data includes an introductory letter that defines gobernabilidad as: "consolidation of a democratic state governed by rule of law [*estado democrático de derecho*] in which institutional presence is the principal guarantor of collective values" (CONAP and WCS 2015, frontmatter). In this chapter, I tease apart and follow the haunted strands of this definition: "rule of law," pointing to a judicial state undermined by widespread corruption and impunity; the "democratic state" exposed as unstable fiction during turbulent election years; conservationist "collective values" of ecological integrity hiding certain forms of violence from view; and finally, "institutional presence," signaling the turn toward militarized defense of nature.

Knowing the state relies on double visions of technoscientific monitoring and paranoid epistemologies, which keep the tensions of coconstituted contradictory truths at the center of attention. The state is violent and corrupt; the state must be harnessed to fight violence and corruption. Paranoia and rumor are useful for locating corrupt actors within the state and for ferreting out its violent, criminal enactments. Objective data that can move between institutions or be published in the media are essential for pushing back against these forces in attempts to change them. Balancing these visions is key to navigating a state and landscape filled with uncertain threats, while working to intervene in both.

How Does the State See Itself?

Practices that draw boundaries between state and nonstate are central to enacting authority and sovereignty (Mitchell 1991; Aretxaga 2003; Gupta and Sharma 2006; Hetherington 2011). Though ironic given its own hybrid state-NGO status, CEMEC's reports on gobernabilidad are central among these boundary-building practices, responding directly to the confusions of governability/governance, state/nonstate, legal/illegal, and problem/solution. Designed to represent the state to itself, their reports enact clear boundaries between violence, lawlessness, and hidden dealings on the side of cattle ranchers and drug runners, and transparency, accountability, and right action on the part of the state. These boundaries are essential for the indicators' usefulness as conservationists work to intervene not only on the landscape, but also in the state itself.

Many gobernabilidad indicators were first conceived and developed in 2011, as a draft of the United Kingdom Department for International Development (DFID)-funded *State of the Maya Biosphere Reserve* report came together (WCS 2011). A new CEMEC technician, Julio, was hired to work on the report, and he and Victor Hugo frequently negotiated between the director's vision for data presentation and the realities of time, budgetary, and logistical constraints. I followed the construction of the indicators and report in great detail, tagging along on an aerial cattle-counting flight, helping CEMEC staff adjust sampling and statistical methodologies, attending formal presentations of the report to different audiences, and doing the bulk of translation from Spanish to English for the bilingual website set up to showcase the effort.[5] Every stage, from construction to movement to interpretation, was shaped by double visions of gobernabilidad.

More so than any of their other knowledge products, CEMEC's gobernabilidad data are crafted to navigate between efficacy and danger, which means leaving things out. Official state knowledge is always coproduced with official state ignorance (Mathews 2011); for gobernabilidad, these blind spots are constructed with care. The extra care is due to the doubling of gobernabilidad itself: retaliation might come from within or outside the state. Producing maps of illegal activity must be balanced against the potential for horrific narco violence, and as part of a state bureaucracy, the lab must not expose too much state weakness, incoherence, or corruption, lest the institution be dissolved. Yet the official ignorance of CEMEC's reports is always weighed against the usefulness of its knowledges, which present just enough detail that the state and other actors can be called to action.

Not all that is known can be mapped. A foreign researcher working on risk assessment asked CEMEC for maps of drug trafficking routes through the western national parks and was told that no such maps existed—despite the well-known fact that CEMEC had access to this information. Its monitoring flights over the reserve regularly spot signs of illegal activity, such as landing strips cut into the jungle. This was the same (nonexistent) map that David teased about being beheaded for after the massacre at Los Cocos. Dark jokes aside, CEMEC director Ramos reported that they didn't make these maps because it wasn't within their jurisdiction as a "technical institution," that they didn't get involved with the "dirty work." This explanation made little sense in the context of other gobernabilidad indicators, which explicitly track illegal activity across the MBR. Instead, this was a silence grown from paranoid knowledges: a map like this could find its way into the wrong hands and return in the form of violence.

To make this map would be terrifying even if it never circulated outside of CONAP, as criminal connections always lurk within the state. Rumors (and occasionally, public scandals) point to associations between major political figures and drug traffickers in the reserve. People fear that any published or leaked information—even if sent anonymously to the press or authorities—will somehow be traced back to particular individuals or institutions, with deadly consequences. Even judges were suspect, as I learned from discussion of a new indicator that tracked prosecution rates of MBR crimes. An NGO worker told me, "I think the judges, when they find out that somebody's keeping a tally on them, how effective they've been, what sort of resolutions they've given to cases . . . that can spark some kind of animosity, or . . . it remains to be seen." This indicator edges toward dangerous specificity, with the potential to expose corruption or weakness in the justice system. To balance this threat, CEMEC reports only percentages of prosecution for all cases, without too many details on particular examples. The latter emerge only in conversations between trusted people, weaving the power of chisme and informal paranoid knowledges around and through official reports.

Cleaning Up a Messy State

The Guatemalan state is multiple, and messy. In order to create the clarity and security needed to intervene in the state, some of the mess must be swept out of view. Aggregation and summary statistics are essential techniques for this cleanup, and for balancing efficacy and threat in gobernabilidad monitoring. As in CEMEC's tracking of prosecution rates, lumping all cases into a generic category avoids singling out any judge, prosecutor, or other individual that might be "connected." This enacts a singular judicial state that can be improved by, for example, restructuring the district attorney's (fiscalía) office to diversify the number of people pursuing single cases; this was done in the Petén in mid-2012, spurred by interinstitutional organizing among conservationists. By remaining focused on the collective level, both the indicator and restructuring avoided having to identify any individual as either particularly effective or ineffective, marking them as either potential target or source of threat.

As CEMEC began conceiving and developing new gobernabilidad indicators in 2011, aggregation emerged as a dominant strategy for cleaning up a messy state. A new form was distributed to CONAP field technicians in 2011, asking them to self-report details of each patrol they walked. The forms included a small map on which to trace the patrol route, with space below to include GPS coordinates of key points or findings. The forms came back filled out with

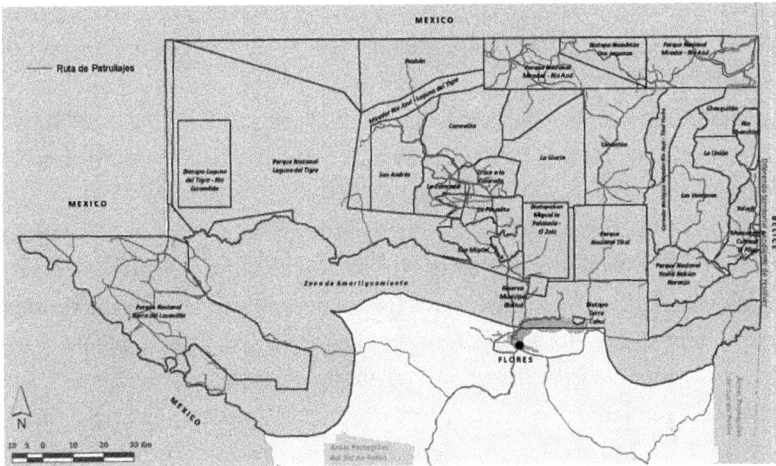

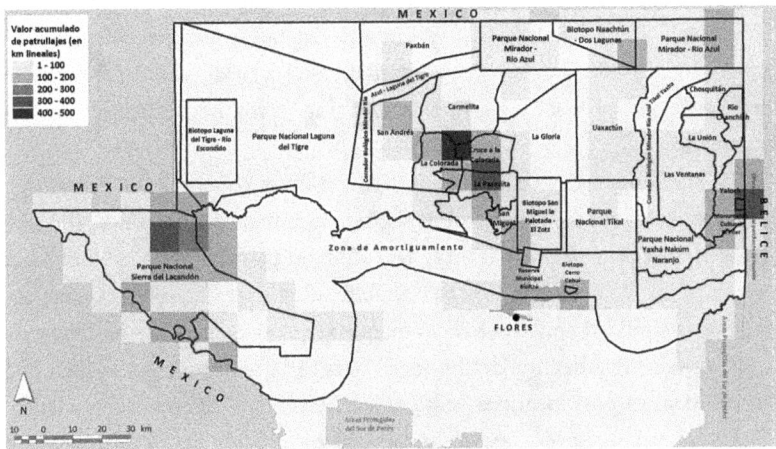

FIGURES 3.1 AND 3.2 Two maps of patrol routes used in the 2011 *State of the Maya Biosphere Reserve* presentation in the National Palace of Culture. The top image traces patrol routes, but attempts to animate the map to indicate number of times each was patrolled failed. Instead, the bottom image was created to demonstrate the density of patrols in different areas (kilometers patrolled/year) (images: CONAP and WCS).

either GPS coordinates or map sketches but not both, or with only narrative description of the patrols. Those that did use the map did so in a myriad of ways: a route traced in a solid line, a series of points or arrows, or one circled location. Some control posts failed to hand in their forms altogether. Still, a CONAP employee told me the system was "a thousand times better" than what had existed before—no formal reporting procedures whatsoever.

When the handwritten forms were brought into CEMEC, technicians traced the patrols onto a digital map by eye, including any wiggles or detours along the way. Later, the lines were cleaned up, straightened out for viewing at the reserve-wide scale. Preparing for the official launch of the *State of the Maya Biosphere Reserve* report, Julio spent two full workdays trying to make a PowerPoint animation of mapped patrol routes come out just right (making the lines change color to indicate the number of times each was walked) before giving up and settling for an imperfect version—one that erased even more detail (figures 3.1 and 3.2). While more detail is not necessarily better (especially given the varied reporting that led to that detail), these multiple forms of cleanup enact a particular meaning, scale, and purpose for this information.

The resulting indicator helped enact a version of gobernabilidad in which "institutional presence is the principal guarantor of collective values" (CONAP and WCS 2015): the important thing was whether patrols happened, not what happened on the patrols. Many gobernabilidad indicators that track state activity were similarly constructed to emphasize physical presence on the landscape, joined together under the term "territorial control." These included patrols, control post locations, staffing statistics from different MBR institutions, and even a map of CEMEC's own monitoring flight paths. Each of these territorial control indicators emphasized aggregated institutional presence on the landscape at a reserve-wide scale, abstracted from questions of accountability or efficacy in finding, reporting, or deterring illegal activity. The measures allow aggregate state presence and absence to appear on maps, which facilitates intervention into these spatial dynamics. More importantly, they do so without ever pointing to individual actors, who might then become either targets or threats.

Quantity over Quality

Besides aggregation, quantification is a key tool for safe communication to other parts of the state. The two are closely related, but numerical measures in particular—kilometers of patrols walked, number of staff in control posts—are most readily targeted for intervention. Numbers are subject to easily measured change, particularly through changing other numbers: those of funding to reserve institutions. This connection was recognized by CEMEC, who designed the visual and narrative presentation of the new gobernabilidad indicators to appeal to both state and nonstate funders. In their 2015 gobernabilidad report, for example, they note a precipitous drop in the number of patrols in 2013, linking this to a loss of project funding that CONAP had used to pay for gas and vehicle repairs. Despite having the staff, skills, and willingness to do their conservationist work, the implication was that without additional funding, CONAP patrollers would remain stuck in the office in San Benito.

The formal launch of the *State of the Maya Biosphere Reserve* report in November 2011 was also designed as a funding pitch. The report was presented at an elaborate press event in the ornate National Palace of Culture in Guatemala City, directed at outgoing president Álvaro Colom, who was on the verge of setting his final budget before leaving office. As an attempt to use monitoring data to intervene in the state, the presentation carefully balanced congratulatory rhetoric with calls for further support. Mariela López Díaz, executive secretary of CONAP, followed a script prepared by CEMEC to accompany their meticulous PowerPoint presentation.[6] Gobernabilidad featured prominently in the presentation, which included six slides outlining key threats to the reserve (or governability, e.g., plate 2 and figure 3.3), and ten slides emphasizing state presence and territorial control (governance, e.g., plate 3 and figure 3.4)

The gobernabilidad section of the presentation ended on a slide showing headlines from the previous year, displaying negative news stories alongside positive ones (figure 3.5). As this slide was shown, López said, "The mitigation of these threats will only be possible by *increasing* gobernabilidad in the MBR. Recently, it was possible to balance the bad news with the good due to *increases* in gobernabilidad. Nevertheless, it is clear that these achievements are fragile, and their sustainability depends on maintaining or increasing levels of human and material effort over the short and medium term" (emphasis added). After a series of maps, graphs, and numerical measures distinguishing criminal problems from state presence, gobernabilidad was evaluated not as good or bad (as in neoliberal "good governance" discourses), but rather as something quantifiable, in which increases (easily supported by more funding from the state) are the measures of success.

This quantification has evolved since 2011–12, as CEMEC has worked to incorporate more qualitative indicators and narrative in their gobernabilidad

FIGURE 3.3 PowerPoint slide titled "Multiple Threats," from the 2011 *State of the Maya Biosphere Reserve* presentation in the National Palace of Culture. The threats are identified as illegal hunting, archaeological looting, land use change, powerful interests, illegal cattle ranching, illegal logging, forest fires, and monocropping. The presence of narcotraffickers and organized crime in the reserve is coded as "powerful interests" and illustrated with a photograph of a downed plane. While other threats on this slide were mapped in detail elsewhere in the presentation, this was the only reference to powerful interests (image: CONAP and WCS).

reporting. Still, the limits around what information can be put in an official state document remain, and aggregation and enumeration act as shields. To point even obliquely to criminal activity within the state is dangerous; risky words including *narcotrafficker, drug, organized crime, corruption,* and *impunity* are all absent from CEMEC's fifty-page gobernabilidad report. The report does nod toward potential corruption or theft in Tikal National Park by reporting major discrepancies in collected entrance fees compared to nearby parks, but this is buffered by repeated mentions that the same discrepancies were already widely reported in the national media. Instead of directly reporting on the effects of state presence on the landscape—using the details of the handwritten patrol forms, for example—CEMEC correlates ecological indicators, like forest cover or fire damage, with that presence. This allows the

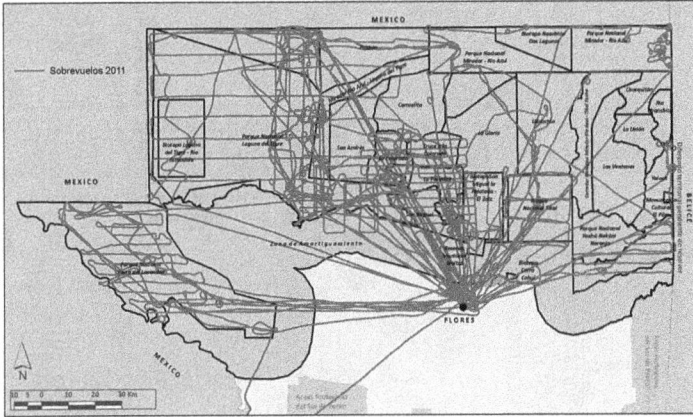

Control del territorio

Sobrevuelos 2011

Entre 2009 y 2011 46,700 km de sobrevuelo, suficiente para dar 1 vuelta entera a la tierra

FIGURE 3.4 PowerPoint slide titled "Territorial Control," from the 2011 *State of the Maya Biosphere Reserve* presentation in the National Palace of Culture. The lines show CEMEC's 2011 aerial monitoring flight paths. The caption reads: "Between 2009 and 2011, 46,700 km of flight paths, enough to fly around the entire world." This slide was animated in the presentation, with each flight path traced individually to create a feeling of watching all the flights taking place at high speed (image: CONAP and WCS).

state to claim responsibility for any conservationist successes indicated by the latter, while avoiding responsibility for any problems or incoherency within the state itself.

Heating Up Cold Data

Aggregate and numerical measures create a narrow understanding of, and clear solution to, gobernabilidad issues. This is easily critiqued as a form of depoliticization, or using quantification to remove questions of responsibility, efficacy, or justice from the presence of institutions on the landscape. But technical depoliticization is always incomplete, haunted by the excluded worlds crowding around carefully plotted maps. CEMEC's visual and technical choices in constructing gobernabilidad indicators mirror the paranoid linguistic work

FIGURE 3.5 Slide from the 2011 *State of the Maya Biosphere Reserve* presentation in the National Palace of Culture. Headlines on the left read (*clockwise from top left*): "Invaders draw closer to Tikal National Park," "Mirador [archaeological site] is in danger," "Land invasions bring danger," "Paradise under threat," "Mayan sites sacked," and "Twenty-seven occupations detected." Headlines on the right read: "Six control posts built in Petén jungle," "Cattle removed from Laguna del Tigre [National Park]," "Protected areas strengthened in the Maya Biosphere," "Government recovers areas of the Maya Biosphere," "Example of forest management," and "Environmentalists applaud recovery of jungle in Petén." The arrangement of news headlines indicates a clear separation between violence, danger, and illegal land invasions on one side and state territorial control and the moral use of force on the other—key to garnering further state support and funding (image: CONAP and WCS).

of avoiding naming that which is dangerous, while those who encounter these data are sensitively attuned to that which does not appear. The 2011 presentation in the National Palace included mentions of "well-funded" land grabs, and identified a key threat to the reserve as "powerful interests," both thinly veiled references to narcotraffickers and other organized crime. These threats were illustrated with a single photograph of a crashed plane, rather than a comprehensive map of associated activities (figure 3.3). Yet the message was clear.

Silences come from many sources. Many of CEMEC's gobernabilidad indicators are incomplete due to the limitations of data collection: patrol forms never handed in, unreported crimes, or financial data that cannot be confirmed. For these indicators, informal knowledge is required to understand the gaps in official reports, intentional or otherwise. Technically, this was sometimes referred to as the difference between cold and hot data, the latter including detailed contextualization, methodological caveats, and practical limitations. Paranoid knowledges also heat up cold data. As an interinstitutional group working on gobernabilidad viewed a CEMEC map of environmental crimes, everyone agreed that Laguna del Tigre National Park should show the highest incidence in the reserve, even though that wasn't how the data appeared (see plate 4). The group did not attribute the discrepancy to CEMEC's monitoring practices, but rather assumed that crimes were taking place but were not reported due to threats or payoffs.

The map was interpreted "properly" by those in the know, while maintaining an official enactment of the MBR as state territory, subject to transparent and rational state knowledge regimes. The spaces between cold data points on the map were heated by shared paranoid knowledges, with rumors of criminal presence in the park overshadowing official measures. CEMEC's ecological indicators for Laguna del Tigre also contributed to this reading, indicating that institutional presence may not be "the principal guarantor of collective values" after all, if those values are conservationist ones. There may be increasing patrols and state activity, but the park's forests keep shrinking—something is missing from the maps, gaps waiting to be filled by paranoia. These interpretations only happened behind closed doors, and in this meeting participants who did not know me well glanced nervously at my presence despite lengthy introductions, assurances, and trusted group members who vouched for me. Later in the same meeting, as an NGO representative presented a plan for the upcoming fire season, he accidentally said the acronym "INACIF" (National Institute for Forensic Sciences) instead of "SIPECIF" (National System for Prevention and Control of Forest Fires), and the room broke out into hysterical laughter. Somebody joked that we were all going to end up dead.

What Is the State?

CEMEC's gobernabilidad indicators enact a singular, coherent state tied to territory, but this enactment must compete against the multiplicity of states arising from varied practices across the MBR. Many administrative responsibilities have been outsourced to NGOs since the declaration of the reserve, creating a patchwork of state-like practices distributed across institutions (Sundberg 1998). While CONAP is officially in charge of administering the MBR, many areas are now or were previously legally coadministered with other institutions: biotopes with the University of San Carlos, Sierra del Lacandón National Park with the NGO Defensores de la Naturaleza, the multiple-use zone divided into concessions operated by community organizations and industrial logging companies, and other arrangements.[7] Less than 50 percent of the MBR is under single administrative control of CONAP, a figure that does not account for informal areas of influence or de facto administration of the army or NGOs.

The responsibility placed on NGOs in the MBR can be attributed in part to the extraordinarily low tax rate maintained by Guatemala's elite oligarchy. In one meeting, an argument over state and NGO roles erupted when a visiting representative of the U.S. Department of the Interior (DOI) asked why CONAP never picked up the bill for interinstitutional meetings. The explanation—that they simply couldn't afford it—led back to Guatemala's tax base: "The lowest in all of Latin America!" one man proclaimed with perverse pride. "The way things stand," he continued, "it's close to a failed state." At this, another Ladino man jumped in to defend his country, arguing that the strength of the executive branch was more important than the fact that there was barely enough money to cover basic functions. Ultimately, this argument concerned what a state is, or should be—a strong hierarchical presidency, or a complex set of bureaucratic regimes and institutions? One state was a success, the other a failure. This double vision of a strong state/failed state mirrored anxieties over conflicting enactments of the conservationist state in the MBR: strong military presence versus chronically underfunded CONAP bureaucracies.

Uncertain boundaries between state and nonstate institutions are reenacted at moments like picking up the bill, or by the ways that NGOs strategically avoid official responsibility for what CEMEC's Ramos referred to as "the dirty work." Of course, as in the closed-door meeting on gobernabilidad, NGOs are extremely active in shaping responses to criminal activity. NGOs rely on state/nonstate boundaries for protection in the same way that CEMEC relies on technical aggregation and enumeration. WCS avoids taking on official coadministration of part of the reserve, as this allows them more flexibility in strategy, timing, and priorities, while leaving the burden of difficult enforcement work to the state. Roan Balas McNab refers to WCS's role as "NGO accompaniment" of the state, emphasizing that as an international institution they should not "substitute" for the state or take over its key functions. (This qualification, that they are not a Guatemalan NGO, makes space for allied Defensores de la Naturaleza's work in Sierra del Lacandón). Of course, as WCS's legal and financial coadministration of CEMEC demonstrates, where this line gets drawn is strategic rather than ideological. Remaining outside the state can be essential to intervening in it.

The Democratic State

National elections and government transitions enact state/nonstate boundaries in particularly illuminating ways. The destabilization of state structures and practices during electoral transitions offers NGOs and other nonstate actors a key opportunity to intervene. MBR conservationists drew heavily on CEMEC's gobernabilidad monitoring during the 2011–12 transition, trying to use these new technoscientific data to push the emerging state in desired directions. NGO intervention during transitions often takes the form of seeking continuity, as conservationists attempt to enact the state as a stable set of institutions from the outside in.

Guatemalan elections also heighten paranoia, as corrupt and violent networks compete for power. Undermining attempts to enact a democratic state, electoral politics are nontransparent, elitist, corrupt, and violent. Physical, psychological, and economic violence against candidates, campaign activists, and their family members are common, as are physical intimidation and violence against voters, vote buying, and ballot burning (Abom 2004; Freedom House 2012; Votes without Violence 2018). Campaign finance laws are flagrantly disregarded by most parties and candidates; voters are trucked to new districts to shift regional party distributions; and social program benefits like food, medicines, and monetary assistance are offered as payoff in exchange for votes. According to CICIG, fewer than 5 percent of criminal violations of election laws result in prosecution—a figure that only accounts for those violations reported to authorities (CICIG 2015).

Building on the momentum of CICIG's investigations, 2015 marked a shift in Guatemalan democratic action, both before and during the elections. The remarkable Guatemalan spring that emerged in April 2015 involved massive public protests leading to the resignation and arrest of Vice President Roxana Baldetti Elías in May, then President Otto Pérez Molina in September, just days before the first round of voting. Both are now awaiting trial for their role in corruption scandals, and Baldetti has also been accused of drug trafficking activities by U.S. prosecutors. Elections followed closely on the heels of these unprecedented peaceful uprisings, which set the stage for the largest voter turnout since the peace accords, as well as a relatively low incidence of violence related to the elections. Widely celebrated as a turning point for Guatemalan popular mobilization and functional democracy, the elections resulted in bringing the television personality Jimmy Morales to power on an outsider, anticorruption platform.

Despite these momentous events, the elections and resulting presidency were still plagued by problems. Repression of rural, female, and indigenous voters was common, and at least twenty people associated with the electoral process were murdered—down from thirty-six in 2011 (National Democratic Institute 2017). Morales has deep military support, including generals directly tied to the genocidal campaigns of the war. His own corruption scandals have since multiplied, including his 2018 exile of the head of CICIG from the country. Although he campaigned on his lack of connections to the elite political establishment, the latter has closed rank around him, entrenched power structures not so easily upended even by the Guatemalan spring.

No hint of these events was yet in the air in 2011, as the election cycle that resulted in Pérez Molina's presidency was taking place. In the Petén, the two leading candidates were widely interpreted as a choice between bad and worse—Pérez Molina, a former general closely tied to the brutality and scorched-earth policies of the civil war, and Manuel Baldizón, a charismatic Petenero business mogul locally called a "thief" and a "narco."[8] As Julián, a Ladino Petenero field technician, told me, "It pains me to vote for a military man, for somebody who committed genocide. But Baldizón . . . I despise him with all my soul. The only thing I hope is that [Pérez's] military patriotism will keep him from completely destroying the country." Pérez won the election with his repressive Mano Dura platform (tough on crime, literally "firm hand"), broadly popular in the face of increasing murder rates, gang activity, and narcotrafficking.[9]

Strategizing for Stability

Guatemalan elections are characterized, even in an extraordinary year like 2015, by violence, corruption, and scandal. But it is the transitions between national governments following elections that are "always catastrophic," as Julián told me. Because of swings between parties each electoral cycle, new presidents always begin their four-year term by wiping the executive slate clean and undoing everything their predecessor started.[10] These rapid shifts in policy are mirrored by top-down waves of personnel changes throughout state institutions, destabilizing the bureaucratic state while enacting a strong executive branch. As a result, the NGO sector in the MBR works to provide a stabilizing force against the unpredictability and drastic changes of transitions. Roan Balas McNab suggested that donors should structure multiyear funding cycles for NGOs to specifically span election periods rather than coinciding with them. The latter, he added, would be a "real recipe for catastrophe and disaster." Roan told me,

> It brings up an interesting issue that's kind of poignant, because, you know, on the one hand our stated mission is to build local capacity, with local NGOs, and especially install capacity in the local government. But then there's this *massive* turnover every four years where you're almost back to zero and you have to start all over again . . . and we have this stated goal of building local capacity, supporting local government, when in fact on many occasions, the civil society programs end up providing some of the stability over time. And continuity. And I think one possible solution, you know, wearing my international NGO hat, is to build capacity in the national civil society institutions. Like Balam, and others . . . ACOFOP, CALAS [Center for Legal Action in Environment and Social Issues], those sorts of organizations [all Guatemalan NGOs]. And that helps somewhat, but you know, it's an ironic situation.

As Roan notes, intervening in the state can ironically take the form of intervening in other nonstate actors, like Guatemalan NGOs. The idea that NGOs provide long-term stability is unexpected given short-term project cycles and the history of shifting NGO presence in the reserve. Still, the upheaval that follows national elections every four years is predictable—in timing, if not in effect—and nonstate actors work to provide a counterbalance.

CEMEC's information about the MBR—both classic ecological measures and new gobernabilidad indicators—took a central role in interinstitutional strategizing for the 2012 government transition. As a full draft of the *State of the Maya Biosphere Reserve* started to take shape in fall 2011, intense discussions arose in WCS and allied institutions about how, when, and where to publicize the collected data. Although much information was already available through the project website, publicly launching the report through formal presentations, press releases, and targeted distribution of the complete document was subject to careful temporal-political calculation. Project staff tried to predict effective political pressure points—should they integrate information into questions for candidate debates, hoping to elicit on-camera campaign promises? Wait until postelection but pretransition, to build alliances with incoming politicians? Wait until the full effects of the transition had shaken down through bureaucracies, so they would know exactly who they'd be dealing with at all levels?

Activities related to interinstitutional gobernabilidad projects were subject to similar calculations. A DOI-funded project involved a capacity-building training (capacitación) with CONAP field staff, and project members debated whether or not to wait until after the transition. Acting quickly could strengthen NGO alliances with the low-level technicians who might make the transition smoother in terms of field practice in the reserve. But this advantage had to be balanced against the possibility that political replacement of CONAP staff would reach too far down the institutional structure, in which case the training would have to be repeated for an entirely new group after only a few months. Each moment offered its own possible risks and rewards.

Overall, people agreed on two central strategies relating to CEMEC's monitoring data. The first was directed at strengthening alliances between NGOs, and with individuals likely to retain their state positions, to help ensure a relatively smooth transition (for example, WCS renewed their legal agreement with CONAP to coadminister CEMEC in late 2011). CEMEC's data could help build these alliances, uniting diverse political perspectives by objectively defining the most important problems in the MBR. Second, publicizing the presence of monitoring itself was seen as a form of creating accountability for incoming politicians. Members of a DFID-funded project decided that drawing attention to ongoing monitoring activity was more important than any specifics of resulting data—sending a message that NGOs (via CEMEC) were watching the transition carefully and ready to report what they saw.

A term often associated with this strategizing was "political will" (voluntad política), lack of which was a common catchall explanation for failure of positive change in Guatemala. Political will was vague but widely desired, and discussions about monitoring data centered on how the proper use of information might create, encourage, or coerce this slippery quality—often through a balance of carrot (reconocimiento, recognition/positive publicity) and stick (palo, negative publicity or legal action) strategies. In both cases, the idea was that objective data, especially CEMEC's new gobernabilidad indicators, should be used to demonstrate political will (or lack thereof) in ways that strategically advanced the political alliances most useful to conservation. These conversations showed a heightened awareness that data could have very different effects and meanings as they move through the nooscape. In a discussion of when to release monitoring data during the government transition, a visiting donor told NGO staff, "*You* will really be responsible for the future state of the Petén"—not, notably, the incoming government. Somehow, responsibility had shifted from those with actual political power to those attempting to use CEMEC's data to influence them.

The Judicial State

A challenge for those maneuvering CEMEC's data in attempts to change the bureaucratic state was how this strategy relied on yet another part of the state—the judicial branch. Here the "rule of law" in CONAP's gobernabilidad definition moves to the foreground. CEMEC has begun tracking MBR environmental crimes as they move from initial reports through final ruling. Defining environmental crime is key to enacting a conservationist judicial state, so CEMEC includes crimes that violate protected area law or that involve threats or harm to conservation actors, but excludes all others. (During one inter-institutional meeting on gobernabilidad, participants discussed two well-known gangs operating in San Benito, but decided it was "not their place" to report these activities because they were not related to conservation.) The Guatemalan justice system is notorious for its ineffectiveness, so in order to intervene effectively, CEMEC and other conservationists narrowed their lens.

According to CEMEC's report, of 620 environmental crimes reported in the MBR between 1999 and 2013, 113 cases were formally concluded, of which 96 resulted in guilty verdicts (CONAP and WCS 2015). This amounts to a total prosecution rate of 15.5 percent, a statistic either disheartening or laudable depending on its contextualization. Fifteen percent is very low, especially given this number's exclusion of unreported and nonenvironmental crimes in the reserve. Yet it becomes impressive when compared to even lower criminal prosecution rates in the country, which hover around 3 percent. While the presence of CICIG in Guatemala made a difference in pursuing high-profile cases, the commission was terminated in 2019 and structural problems continue to plague the justice system. At every stage of a case, from reporting to police capture to sentencing to incarceration, double visions of threat from inside and outside the state can lead to a paranoid paralysis.

The development of a new cross-sector Environmental Justice Forum in the Petén was envisioned as a way to counteract this paralysis, a coordinated attempt to change the dynamics of violence and impunity in the limited sphere of environmental crimes occurring in the MBR.[11] It is designed to improve reporting and prosecution of environmental crimes, and to protect those pursuing cases from retaliation. The forum is a civil association made up of nonstate institutions (WCS, Balam, CALAS, and ACOFOP were founding members, and Defensores de la Naturaleza joined in 2015). This structure was carefully designed to protect individuals, though several participants worried that official NGO membership might further blur their boundaries with the state as the group took on more governance responsibilities. This careful balancing of roles and responsibilities, potency and protection, was succinctly described with an inevitable soccer metaphor: "[The forum] is a ball passed between many, but belonging to nobody" (Es una pelota entre un montón pero de nadie).

Several cases were being considered for the launch of the forum in 2011, including the 2010 public murder of community conservation leader David Salguero, the loss of huge numbers of cadastral records by a government office (linked to illegal land sales), and a case related to looting and trafficking of Maya artifacts into Mexico. Each of these cases carried a shadow set of problems— networks of actors, interests, and alliances, not all of which were known but which nonetheless shaped the possibilities for response. In all three cases, serious discussions were held not just about what kind of evidence needed to be gathered, but the most strategic use of that evidence. This was never a matter of simply turning information over to legal authorities, and in many cases meant collecting additional evidence about lack of follow-up within the justice system. Similar to the use of monitoring data for political pressure during the elections, strategizing over how to use information to intervene in each particular case was intense, heightened by the ever-present possibility of violent retaliation.

The forum began to make headway in late 2011, due largely to the initiative of then–attorney general Claudia Paz y Paz and the national presence of CICIG. Paz had been lauded in the international media for her willingness to prosecute major drug barons and to put former dictator Efraín Ríos Montt on trial for genocide. Still, her eagerness to pursue environmental cases in the Petén surprised conservationists, and this unprecedented action spurred even more fear and self-protection, not least because there was at least one corrupt link within the departmental environmental prosecutor's office. Quite suddenly, as cases started to make headway, the forum was cloaked in silence.

Some who had been involved in its development refused to give official statements; others pretended a total lack of knowledge when they were outside the safety of the attorney general's "fortress-like" office, and all quietly worried about endangering their friends, families, coworkers, and selves. My own inclusion in forum planning meetings abruptly ceased around the end of 2011—I was shut out, most likely for my own protection as well as for those who continued to pursue action.

Through Paz, fears of violence were mediated by a rare shred of hope that the forum would achieve real legal repercussions for crimes that were committed under assumption of total impunity. Of course, Paz's boldness came with a price—not only did she receive numerous death threats, she was forced out of office six months before the end of her constitutional term. Her conviction of Ríos Montt, a globally celebrated accomplishment, was quickly overturned by the Supreme Court on a technicality, and his lawyers successfully prevented a reconviction until his death in 2018. While the Environmental Justice Forum is now well established as a space of interinstitutional coordination and public reporting, members continue to be frustrated by the lack of follow-up and accountability within the justice system. Fifteen percent may be laudable, but it is far from enough.

Institutional Presence and the Military State

NGO conservationists intervene in the administrative state by forming alliances with CONAP, but CONAP staff change with every election. They use CEMEC data to intervene in transitional stability and to create political will, but political will is always undone by criminal connections within the state. They try to intervene in this criminality by reforming the judicial system, but this too is plagued by corruption and threats of violent retaliation. In the face of these frustrations, the confusing double visions of gobernabilidad, and continued threats and violence against conservation actors—like the 2016 murder of another community conservation leader, Walter Manfredo Méndez Barrios—conservationists increasingly throw their support behind military action.

The Kaibil striding into CEMEC at the opening of this chapter is a potent image of this militarization. Army presence is increasing, especially in the reserve's western national parks through the Green Battalion declared in 2010 (see plate 3). CEMEC's institutional presence indicators have tracked this growing influence, with the army now walking more patrols than any other institution in the reserve, including CONAP. In a 2011 public meeting, the director of CONAP-Petén, Mariela López Díaz, defended CONAP's alliances with the Nature Protection Division of the Police (DIPRONA) and the Green Battalion forces as "*importantísimo*" (extremely important). She said, "There are many who say that the Maya Biosphere Reserve is being militarized. And what we have said to this is that those of us who are here, those who know the area well, we know that for any project we want to carry out we first have to have gobernabilidad. . . . There are many sectors that say that CONAP, well, it's a technical institution, and we shouldn't get involved in the matter of gobernabilidad. But it's part of our mandate within protected areas." As Megan Ybarra (2012) argues, this call to gobernabilidad reinforces discursive links between conservation and historical military action in the Petén: both are based on a territorial defense of forests against agricultural and other incursions. Yet López's speech reveals a simultaneous support for militarization and local ambivalence and awareness of critiques. And while it reinforces links to the military, gobernabilidad is also a useful term in official settings like this one to talk about things too dangerous to name directly, including narcotrafficking gangs and corruption within the state itself. López's comment about "those who know the area well" does similar work, calling to mind networks of informal knowledges excluded from official discourse.

Desires to work with the military represent a major shift since the 1996 peace accords. After the declaration of the MBR in 1990, the military served as protection for wealthy ranchers and petroleum companies looking to exploit the previously inaccessible Petén landscape. Now, even those who confronted this military-oil alliance in the 1990s laud the army's commitment to conservation, conveniently ignoring that army presence in Laguna del Tigre National Park surrounds French oil company Perenco's legally ambiguous drilling concession. One NGO staff person, Carlos, told me that he heard a rumor that the military had marked him as a target in the late 1990s, after he helped a reserve village resist the building of an army outpost. But the army of today was a very different thing, he continued, tuned in to the environmental dynamics of the reserve. Carlos added that perhaps the military had just changed their discourse, similar to local community members who "speak conservation" in order to access NGO resources. But especially in contrast to the police, notorious for corruption, the army had gained his respect for its effectiveness, discipline, and ability to follow through on planned actions in the reserve. Spectacular displays of military power, like the 2011 state of siege and more recent evictions, are a powerful way of enacting a territorial state.

The army indeed follows through, but the outcomes of their actions are never quite what conservationists expect. Militarized protected area management is on the rise worldwide, as global conservation discourse is inflected with post-9/11 securitization discourses (Ybarra 2012, 2016; Devine 2014; Meierotto 2014; Bocarejo and Ojeda 2016; Duffy 2014, 2016; Lunstrum 2015). In South Africa, this strategy encourages an arms race between parks and poachers, escalating violent conflict, turning unaligned local actors against the state, and ultimately accelerating wildlife loss (Lunstrum 2014). In the MBR, replacing "poachers" with "land invaders" reveals a similar dynamic. Militarized actions in the reserve and their enactments of territorial control are further undermined by the haunting presence of double visions, which reveal the inefficacy and injustices of the state.

Hints that militarization might not lead where conservationists wanted were beginning to show in 2011. People noted with dismay the gap between the official purpose of the state of siege (to deal with narcotrafficking presence) and the actions being taken (arrests for minor nonviolent crimes, with perpetrators usually released after fifteen days). As conservationists strategized on how they might turn the state of siege to their advantage, they also discussed rumors of rights violations, discussions haunted by continued impunity for civil war brutality. But while several people shared stories of recent intimidation and fear, no one had heard of outright human rights abuses; most agreed that fear induced by military presence was inevitable and therefore acceptable. Behind closed doors, conservationists debated taking military action against land invasions, but the inscrutability of identity was always a sticking point.[12] How could they be sure of the difference between land grabs linked to the Zetas or the Sinaloa drug cartel, or those carried out by poor campesinos?

The effects of these haunting doublings have only intensified over time. Through the double visions of technoscience and paranoia, combining maps of land use change and rumored criminal connections, conservationists have aligned with the military to evict whole communities from the reserve. In May 2017, an NGO worker tipped me off that two evictions were planned in Laguna del Tigre National Park, for the communities of Laguna Larga and La Mestiza. Both had been expanding their illegal settlements in the park, and I had heard rumors of their criminal connections for years. Jose explained that the eviction would act as a hinge for the park's future: "If the army and police are successful in kicking them out, then other communities in the park will see that and settle down [*calmarse*]. But if the community fights them off, it's only going to get worse." Implied in the second possibility was the escalation of a territorial battle between the state and narcotraffickers leading to the end of the park itself.

Within two weeks, thousands of armed police and soldiers stormed into Laguna Larga, but the aftermath followed neither of Jose's anticipated scripts. The villagers did not stay and fight, but fled in advance of the approaching army across the nearby border into Mexico, setting off a flurry of national and international press in defense of community members' human rights. Echoes of the war resonated through the stories, which focused on suddenly homeless women and children, indigenous community members, and the destruction of property carried out by soldiers in the abandoned village. Critics pointed to the injustices of enforcing the law in the case of agriculturalists but bending it to allow oil drilling inside the same national park. Politicians who had been fully aware of the planned eviction suddenly postured in defense of people they had long neglected. Jose's vision of a successful eviction calming other conflicts in the park was crushed beneath this wave of human rights and antimilitarization responses. Under massive public and political pressure, the second eviction of La Mestiza was postponed indefinitely.

Among conservationists, a different debate emerged after the eviction: whether Laguna Larga residents were really poor victims, or whether they (or at least some among them) were funded and protected by other interests. A Facebook post circulated with photos of the empty village's satellite dishes and well-built houses and schools, noting, "Many think that . . . the people who were evicted from Laguna Larga were poor, no my friends, you are very wrong, they had even better conditions than us." Reposted seventeen times, and with dozens of likes and congratulatory comments, the post offered a reassuring counternarrative to the critiques of the mainstream media. But many conservationists saw the eviction in double vision. Another NGO worker, Carlos, reflected on the challenges of ousting "powerful, absentee" land grabbers, with violent impacts falling on the "true campesinos" who work the land for them: "there is no joy, believe me, in seeing any humans impacted negatively by efforts to conserve nature. . . . Complexity exists on every side of this equation, and I do not feel that any single side, including ours, has dominion over a single truth."

Jose's prediction of two possible futures reflects widespread desire for a conservation practice that follows rules of cause and effect, for the clarity of a singular, knowable reserve, managed by a coherent, lawful state. Instead, he and others are faced with a landscape on which current military actions are haunted by memories of the war, community and individual identities are rendered unknowable by hidden and violent networks of power, and the moral positioning of the state as environmental protector is undermined by the opening of the very same park to destructive oil extraction. The total surprise of the eviction's outcome—a backlash against military action that bolstered national and international support for settlements in the park—reflects these contradictory yet copresent worlds, which scramble straightforward relations between action and outcome. The successful eviction of Laguna Larga became a massive failure, threatening the future of the park even when everything unfolded according to plan.

Collective Values and the Law of the Jungle

The Laguna Larga eviction followed on the heels of a catastrophic fire season in Laguna del Tigre, with over 54,750 acres of parkland burned by residents of settlements like those targeted. The urgency posed by the fires helped push conservationists toward military action, as a deep sense of loss, paranoid epistemologies, and the inability of the administrative or judicial states to effect change in the park formed an explosive combination. CEMEC's gobernabilidad indicators are interpreted alongside ecological indicators like forest cover (see plate 5), which come to represent the collective values that institutional presence is supposed to guarantee. Deforestation rates are highest in the west, where drug and human traffic cross to Mexico, where the lag was greatest between national parks declared on paper and institutional presence on the ground, and where Green Battalion army forces now roam. It is these western parks that people imagine when they talk about gobernabilidad. In the MBR, gobernabilidad is innately tied to threats to the forest; in areas where there are few signs of deforestation, concerns over state presence and gobernabilidad disappear, allowing crime and violence to hide among the trees.

Repeated issues with violence and crime in the small village of Uaxactún were protected from major state action by the village's successful conservation programs. The village has a twenty-five-year forest concession in the heart of the reserve's multiple-use zone, and is widely praised for its success in community-led sustainable forestry and development projects, and for its maintenance of forest cover within the bounds of its concession. When people talk about gobernabilidad in the reserve, they are rarely talking about Uaxactún. The concession is a blank spot on several maps of institutional presence (e.g., figure 3.4), but this absence is read as unproblematic because of forest cover. Yet there were many examples of crime and violence in the village while I was there—stolen NGO laptops, slashed concession vehicle tires, and shots fired at a truck carrying cash payments for village laborers, among others.

NGO workers fretted over these events, considering whether or not to include them among environmental crimes—they were not breaking protected area law, but nearly every aspect of life and work in the village is tied to conservation, NGO projects, or concession management. These crimes were reported to the police weeks later or not at all, reflecting reluctance on the part of the isolated community to engage with problematic authorities. As WCS's field technician assigned to the village explained to me, this is both "small town custom" and because there is no protection for those who report—everybody knows who committed the crimes, but everybody also knows who reports what to whom and when. The community prefers to determine responsibility and consequence among themselves, turning to local vigilante justice along with many other communities across postwar Guatemala (Godoy 2002; García 2004; Handy 2004). Even murders have been dealt with internally in the past, with retaliations passing back and forth between families, or somebody run out of town by a coalition of gun-wielding villagers. This is how the village enacts what one NGO worker described to me as *la ley de la selva*, "the law of the jungle."

When conservationists do raise the issue of gobernabilidad in the village, it is in relation to strictly environmental crimes. In late 2011, two men shot a small deer (*cabrito*) that had wandered into the village. The case might have appeared relatively minor compared to gunshots fired at concession staff, but was treated with much greater formality, reflecting its connection to environmental gobernabilidad across the reserve. The case was reported through multiple official channels, by the Wildlife Department of CONAP to Tikal National Park (the accused men worked in Tikal), then by Tikal to the attorney general's office (Ministerio Público). While in the end the men were not prosecuted, the case of the cabrito spurred a flurry of anxious reflection on community-based conservation and gobernabilidad. A CONAP administrator told me that he was disappointed in the lack of follow-up:

This type of thing just increases disorder; it should have been dealt with. Not that much, because it was a cabrito, which is . . . it's a deer, and there are more in the forest. But the fact was, for me the fact was that this was a lack of respect for the law. And in a certain way, it was not just the law, but also the fact of killing an animal that way. It might have been for food, but that wasn't the way to go about it, you know? And I hoped, first, that they would investigate it as a park, directly with the park. Who it was, how it is possible that people who work for the park are doing this, the impacts of this . . . because it was people who work for a government institution. And you'd think that they should be well aware [*consciente*], no? The other thing that interests me is the information in omyc [Conservation and Management Organization of Uaxactún], that they were informed who it was because it's in their administrative area, and I don't think anything is happening with them. It's a problem for me because it was an opportunity to install some order and discipline in the community, and the opportunity was lost. Easier to say, "Ahh, it's a deer, there are thousands in the forest." No. But it was an opportunity to . . . to use this as a strategy, and to try to impose some order.

Confusion over institutional boundaries and responsibilities emerges in this response: Was this the problem of CONAP, as general administrator of the MBR? Tikal National Park, because these men were its employees and should therefore know better? OMYC, within whose administrative area the killing occurred? The attorney general's office, which could follow up with formal prosecution and legal action? In the end, these confusions led to no consequences for the hunters whatsoever.

The administrator also framed the problem in terms of the hunters' awareness and respect for the right way to go about hunting. This was echoed by the response to the incident of an NGO technician who told me that the difficult thing was "*concienciar la gente*"—to educate or raise awareness among the people. Gobernabilidad in Uaxactún is often translated into this frame of awareness, knowledge, or values surrounding conservation and the forest. The implication is that if villagers had the proper knowledge or attitude toward local wildlife, then the question of gobernabilidad would become moot: they would refrain from shooting the deer out of respect for the deer, rather than respect for the law. Uaxactún's well-maintained forest cover, its variety of strong NGO allies, and its international reputation for community conservation mean that responses to problems in the village focus on local environmental education instead of calling up the presence of the army to enforce regulations, as happens in the west.

Hard Questions and Hard Data

Measuring gobernabilidad in the MBR is seen as key to improving it. This shifts responsibility away from the state and onto CEMEC and the NGOs responsible for managing these hard data. The idea of gobernabilidad is tied to CEMEC through dreams of omnipresent vision and technoscientific neutrality, both promised by remote sensing technologies. Their gobernabilidad indicators are designed to untangle double visions, enacting a landscape on which there is a clear difference between state and nonstate, between legality and illegality, or between the moral use of force to protect the environment and illegal violence linked to deforestation. The equating of state presence with governance, and of deforestation with ungovernability, provides the Guatemalan state with an easily improved measure of success that pays little attention to the effects of state and nonstate action on the ground—even when that success, like the 2017 Laguna Larga eviction, twists into failure. Gobernabilidad indicators also harden boundaries between human and nonhuman landscapes, rendering the landscape an inert, passive backdrop to human conflict. Though the nonhuman landscape too is lively, confusing, and sometimes deadly, mapping renders it the victim of environmental crimes and calls forth increasing violence in defense of nature. Woven through with paranoid knowledges, the mapping of gobernabilidad in the MBR reinforces state and international funding for military and police presence while undermining flexible responses to the complex, shifting problems that characterize the reserve.

Their silences reveal that CEMEC's indicators are not simple representations of a coherent, singular landscape and state, but rather concentrated attempts to enact landscapes of possibility and clarity. Attempting to enact alternative landscapes of justice, accountability, or responsibility, even if these are desired, may simply be too dangerous. Those developing strategies for conservation and gobernabilidad in the MBR are trapped between the desire for clarity and its impossibility. Wending their middle path between violence and inefficacy, they end up resigned to their own participation in undemocratic, corrupt, and violent dynamics. One CEMEC technician, Jorge, noted his discomfort with the military, describing support for militarization as a kind of temporary stopgap, until "things improve in Guatemala." He continued that CEMEC couldn't ever put a perspective like his in their reports, because the military was one of CONAP's closest allies. He said, "So even if it's not something we want over the long term, we can't go and put that in a report." When or how this improvement that could bring an end to militarization might come was never clear. In CEMEC's report, they note that recent improvements in gobernabilidad appear to be "working" (with respect to forest cover), but that efforts should be ongoing—including the need both to continue collaborating with security forces and to restrengthen community alliances, as though these strategies were not deeply contradictory to each other.

Militarization can feel like the only option to conservationists faced with overwhelming environmental destruction and unknowable sources of violence and threat. While not absolving conservationists of their responsibility for increasing militarization in the MBR, it is important to remember that they too are caught up in the violent precarity that threatens reserve residents and landscape. They are caught by the technocratic requirements of globalized neoliberal institutions, by the impossibility of knowing who is a threat and who a potential ally, by the failures of efforts, repeated again and again, to make CONAP, the police, or prosecutors and judges effective actors in the battle against ecological change. They are caught in the apocalyptic terror of loss of those places they most love. Instead of blunt critique, these lived contradictions must be acknowledged and contended with.

There is much disagreement among people working in the MBR about how much should be kept under cover, and how to manage the risks involved in exposing or addressing drug and other illegal activity. It can be difficult to get conservationists to discuss kidnappings or threats, even if these are a regular part of their work life and experience. My own quiet exclusion from the Environmental Justice Forum meetings when they got too specific, or drew too close to dangerous information, mirrors this silence. In another moment, a conservationist openly discussed the landing strips he had seen in a recent monitoring flight. Yet when a visitor asked whether he would call to report these locations to the governor or director of CONAP, he replied incredulously, "On their *phones*?! They'll find out. If they don't already know." How knowledge moves through the nooscape matters.

At the same time, people worry about the consequences of participating in these silences. Carlos told me that if conservationists stick their heads in the sand like an ostrich, they're leaving the rest of themselves exposed to "a good screwing" (*una buena cogida*). He continued, arguing for direct and open engagement even as he carefully avoided the word "narco": "There's been a lot of discussion, you know, with people from CONAP, and there's a lot of common knowledge about hot spots. It's a question . . . you know . . . that one of the challenges that faces conservation, that faces local communities, faces the sustainable future of this whole area, are these questions of *really*, you know, thorny gobernabilidad issues. So . . . it's incumbent on us, as people that are promoting conservation, and that live *from* conservation, to find a way to grapple with these things, one way or the other." He continued by acknowledging the limits of direct engagement, praising the director of CONAP-Petén, Mariela López, for her ability to "triage" problems in the reserve along an intertwined continuum of importance and danger:

> There's *this* set of issues over here [at one end of a scale drawn in the air]— these are just too intractable. Anybody that tries to open this Pandora's box is just *gone*. And . . . that means that some yea-sayer is going to come in and just do the bidding of, potentially, some *other* interests. *This* set of issues [at the other extreme of the indicated scale], they're not very complicated; we can address them. *These* [in the middle] are the thorny issues— these are thorny issues that if we set up the right alliances, if we have the resources, if we get certain amounts of backing, we can actually make a real, significant difference here. And that's what [López] did. She focused on that central set. To her credit.

The intractable contents of Pandora's box, the "other" implied in "other interests" and their assumed power to replace key figures in the government— these are the shadowy presences of ungovernability, the hidden powers that make rule of law a strange fantasy in Guatemala.

The multiplicity of the state, and of both sides of a criminal/lawful dichotomy of gobernabilidad, are revealed in these calculations. The terrors of drug trafficker violence, organized criminal connections woven throughout political parties, bureaucracies, and judicial bodies, and the rapid loss of vast swaths of forest to actors with uncertain identities and motives lead to double visions of both landscape and state. To make decisions, conservationists must navigate between contradictory knowledges and worlds—is the army friend or foe of conservation? Is an individual encountered in the forest a poacher, drug runner, or poor agriculturalist? Is it better to provide education and alternative economic opportunities to people in the reserve, or to forcibly evict them? CEMEC's gobernabilidad indicators provide clear answers to these questions, a charismatic clarity that leads to their extensive use. Yet it is a false clarity. Just because a park is patrolled doesn't mean the guards will report what they find. If an innocent farm laborer is killed, perhaps he wasn't so innocent after all. Like Mariela López's triage of problems in the reserve, CEMEC's knowledge creation carefully navigates between too much danger and too little impact, enacting haunted versions of both landscape and state. Translated into conservation action, gobernabilidad indicators lead to a confusion of responses, a striving for control and clarity that only further reproduces violence and contradiction.

GENDER AND VIOLENCE

In early 2012, I ran into Luis in the alley outside WCS and asked about upcoming campo trips, thinking I might tag along. He told me that they were soon heading out to La Corona, in an area of eastern Laguna del Tigre National Park that I hadn't seen. "But," he told me, "I don't know if you can go out there with us. It's a little complicated." I asked why, and he continued, "Well, there's a problem of invaders, or at least it's a possibility. It's a little bit dangerous . . . for women." I shot him a look; we had had conversations about selling women short in the campo before. I also knew he was right—that the risk to me, a gringa, was very different than that posed to his Ladino body. He explained that the government transition had destabilized things; CONAP presence wasn't well established under the new regime yet. Everybody knows what happens when the government changes, Luis explained, so they take advantage and invade new areas. He pointed toward a field tech sitting outside WCS: "He was kidnapped at La Corona one time." To further discourage me, he added, "Also, it takes a long time to get there, maybe eight hours. *If* you get there at all." (I did not go.)

Guatemala has one of the highest rates of femicide in the world, averaging at least two women killed every day. Only 2 percent of these murders are ever successfully prosecuted (Musalo, Pellegrin, and Roberts 2010). Although violence against women is the most commonly reported crime in the country, these reports most likely represent only a tenth of actual cases. Indigenous women face the most barriers to accessing support or justice services in the face of violence (Inter-American Commission on Human Rights 2017). Rape and sexual slavery, particularly of indigenous women, were tactics of army terror during the civil war (Tomuschat, de Cotí, and Tojo 1999). Human trafficking and forced prostitution of women and children are still common today.

When Luis warned me away from La Corona, my memory shot back to an incident months earlier, when I had been mugged in Flores by a young man with a gun. I didn't lose much, but I was badly shaken. The morning after, when I recounted my story in WCS, others flooded in: every woman in the office had been robbed at gunpoint, many more than once. Every man had stories about their wives, sisters, and mothers being robbed. Some women had been mugged up to eight times. Not one man had been robbed.

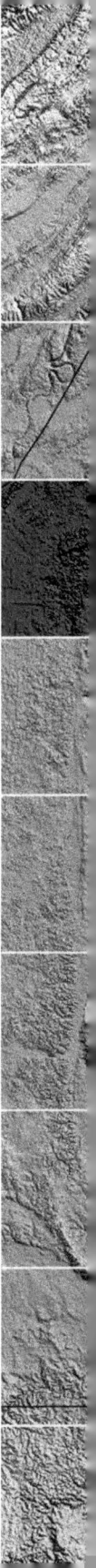

FOUR

But Is It a Basin?

Sitting atop an ancient temple at sunset in the Preclassic Maya city of Mirador, a friend and I swapped stories with our local guide, outdoing each other with increasingly strange tales of the fight over the site's future. Our stories turned to a well-known American archaeologist who has studied Mirador for over thirty years, Richard Hansen. Hansen is locally notorious—not for his archaeological findings, but for his scientific claims about a geological basin (*cuenca*) surrounding the site and his proposals to redraw the boundaries of the northeast corner of the MBR within which Mirador lies. Our guide, a resident of the nearby village of Carmelita, recounted rumors about the motivations hidden behind Hansen's scientific and political positions—stories ranging from planned construction of luxury hotels in the jungle to desires to build an enormous, illegal personal collection of Maya artifacts. I traded back rumors that I had heard in other contexts, while my friend—always up for a good conspiracy story—joined in with wild speculations about worldwide Mormon networks and Hansen's religious drive for domination. Conspiracy theories like these swirl around conflicting scientific claims about the forested landscape that stretched out as far as we could see in every direction.

At Mirador, rumors and paranoia are as deeply entangled with scientific controversy as the vines and roots of the forest are with the abandoned Maya cities that lie beneath them. The ancient city lies within Mirador-Río Azul National Park, tucked away to the north of the MBR's multiple-use zone. It is the most geographically remote part of the reserve, requiring a multiday hike or expensive helicopter ride to access, but the site is far from peripheral in the MBR nooscape. Debates over the site's formation, significance, and legal designation entangle conflicting scientific claims, international media attention, multiscalar political alliances, private interests, and wild speculation about duplicitous manipulation of evidence. In the face of competing scientific-political positions, paranoid double visions cohere into the more structured logics of conspiracy theories, which refer to deliberately hidden coordinated actions with nefarious motivation.

While archaeologists debate interpretations of Mirador's history, the site's primary controversy has formed not around archaeological remains, but around the geological shape of the landscape on which it stands. The site is at the center of an ongoing scientific and political argument over the existence of a geological basin. People ranging from poor local villagers to members of the Guatemalan congress to Mel Gibson, Arab sheiks, and representatives of the UNESCO World Heritage Program line up on one side or the other. While both sides draw on conservation rhetoric, arguments over the presence or absence of a basin delineate struggles over the region's future, with different visions of the landscape competing for legal, social, and economic control over the northeastern corner of the MBR. The existence of a basin is used to argue for a redrawing of boundaries inside the reserve, creating more strict parklike protected areas while removing large tracts of land from forest concessions. Those who deny the existence of a basin support the current mixed-use concession model, particularly community concessions like that managed by Carmelita, which stands to lose the most land if the basin lines get drawn.[1] This comingling of political position and scientific "truth" is a powerful mixture, amplifying rumors of hidden agendas and secret dealings on both sides of the fight.

Chapters 2 and 3 describe how the instability, violence, and nontransparent powers rampant in Guatemala shape a paranoid epistemology that crosses institutional lines. Making certainty impossible yet increasing desires for certainty, paranoia grows with technoscience in the reserve into a haunting symbiotic double vision. Here, that paranoia hardens certainty in the face of contradiction, and lines are drawn in the sand. The knowledge practices I have begun to describe in CEMEC, WCS, and allied institutions are thrown into sharp relief as they encounter controversy and do battle with an opposing political-scientific network. The basin controversy illuminates paranoid epistemologies in a stark way, in particular their power to generate multiple actor networks that compete for truth status in the nooscape.

This chapter centers less on knowledge production and more on assessments of evidence viewed through a paranoid frame. Conspiracy theorizing offers those embroiled in controversy a way to see clearly through the epistemic murk of unstable dynamics, contradictory evidence, and uncertain futures. Usually, when conspiracy theory and science appear together, it's in reference to antiscience "wackos" who deny climate change (Lewandowsky, Oberauer, and Gignac 2013), or to the ways that science can help you prove or disprove conspiracy theories once and for all. But Guatemala's elite and military domination, widespread corruption, and uncertain responsibility for current and historical violence all contribute to a political landscape in which conspiracies do take place, and paranoia is both a reasonable epistemology and a practical political strategy. Here, fears of a hidden reality are inseparable from scientific knowledge claims, not an opposing social field for science to battle. The case of Mirador unsettles the normative assumption that conspiracy theory and science are antipathetic, instead showing how the two are deeply entangled ways of determining truth on a politically fraught landscape.

Mundane Conspiracy

Given new prominence in the posttruth era, the words "conspiracy theory" call to mind pathological extremes, the fearful fantasies of the lunatic fringe. These stories are typically placed in opposition to rationality, but conspiracy thinking is mundane and widespread in political thought (Marcus 1999b; Stewart and Harding 1999). Rather than individual pathology, the term denotes a style of paranoid politics characterized by "heated exaggeration, suspiciousness, and conspiratorial fantasy" (Hofstadter 2008, 3). Epistemologically, conspiracy theories are powerful, flexible explanatory tools that lack clear limits around what is too extreme to be true, undermining straightforward relations between evidence and belief.

Conspiracy theories affect the Mirador debate in two overlapping ways: first, in their epistemic and hermeneutic logics, seen through the content of rumors and stories; and second, through their political action and effect, related to the contexts and ways in which stories circulate. While always linked in practice, analytically teasing these two aspects apart illuminates different effects of conspiratorial thought. First, the contents of rumors provide epistemic frameworks that explain the hidden workings of power, drawing attention to nontransparent political forces, practices, and exclusions (Butt 2005; Nelson 2009; Stewart 1999). Contrary to common assumptions, conspiracy theories provide a more clear explanatory framework, not less, and are able to coherently enfold contradictory statements or evidence through paranoid leaps of logic (Marcus 1999a). Second, the circulation of stories, or context, draws tellers and (receptive) listeners together in the pleasures of mutual trust around a shared secret, forming or reinforcing alliances with clear markers of us/them, right/wrong, and truth/lies (de Vries 2002, 2007; Soares 1999; Wynne 1992). Attending to when and where rumors travel is therefore key to understanding their political effects (Kirsch 2002). Most analyses of conspiracy theories focus on either one or the other of these aspects, but following the thread of knowing a place in order to change it, I read the epistemic and social-political effects of stories about Mirador as the warp and weft of rampant paranoia.

Science and Conspiracy

While unfolding on a vastly different scale, many aspects of the Mirador controversy mirror the role of conspiracy theories in debates over global climate change. In this well-worn debate, Myanna Lahsen (1999) finds two opposing material-political-scientific camps, with accusations of conspiracy and deliberate scientific mishandling flung in both directions at the "other side." She notes that the epistemic coherence of conspiracy theory offers a consistent account that cuts through the often undecipherable reality of scientific and political processes, "characterized by uncertainty, fragmentation, complexity, and competing interests" (Lahsen 1999, 133). Her analysis highlights conspiracy's efficacy as a political tool amid controversy, describing the theories as "one tactic among many" and an evocative "style of argument" (133, echoing Hofstadter's classic essay). In climate change debates, conspiracy theories reinforce networks of trust, shared interests, or worldview, and harden oppositions based on mutual dislike. The parallels with the Mirador controversy are striking, where paranoid rumors move from "one tactic among many" to a dominant form of political action.

To push this analysis further requires taking paranoid epistemologies seriously—not just as an argumentative or political style—by attending to how conspiratorial and scientific thought are entangled in practice. In a political controversy founded on contradictory scientific claims, conspiracy stories are not just tactics but also epistemic frameworks through which data is filtered. Brian Wynne addresses this aspect of conspiracy-science stories in his work with Cumbrian sheep farmers after Chernobyl: "The farmers thus embedded *their reading of the present scientific claim* . . . firmly within the context of the unpersuasive and untrustworthy nuclear institutional body language which had denigrated them for thirty years or more" (1992, 291, emphasis added).

Wynne's emphasis on conspiracy stories as interpretive, not just political, tools is an important addition to Lahsen's analysis.

In the basin controversy, I bring these two aspects of conspiracy theorizing together, showing how conspiracy stories circulating around Mirador establish strong political-scientific networks that divide neatly into two sides, while simultaneously structuring the lenses through which data and scientific arguments are read. In Latour's (1987) classic framing of actor-network theory, both human and nonhuman allies are enrolled in ever-evolving networks, which when large enough stabilize and take on the appearance of fact, nature, or truth. At Mirador, the telling of conspiracy theories—the political style—is a key tactic in recruiting human and institutional allies into such networks. In addition, the prefigured clarity of truth and deliberate falsehood indicated by these stories shapes the reading of nonhuman actants such as maps, satellite imagery, or biodiversity surveys, determining their enrollment or exclusion from pro- or antibasin networks as well. Occupying the same niche in the MBR nooscape, these two networks compete for dominance by securing ever more allies, resources, and material interventions on the Mirador landscape.

The Makings of a Strange Controversy

There is good reason for people to fight over Mirador—it is, without question, an exceptional place. The site is accessible only by five-day guided hike or, for those with money, by helicopter. Making the trek to see it for myself was one of the last things I did after fourteen months of living in the Petén, a capstone to a year of hearing public arguments, secret stories, scientific explanations, and political pleas circling around the ancient city. I finally saw for myself the impressiveness of this last stretch of the MBR jungle not permanently inhabited or harvested by humans, the astounding ubiquity of ancient Maya traces dating back further than 1000 BCE, and the enormous temples and pyramids jutting up above the flat forested landscape. But even from atop La Danta, the Western Hemisphere's largest pyramid, towering above the canopy at over 230 feet tall, I still could not see for myself the "obvious" geological shape of the landscape that I had been promised would be clearly visible by people on both sides of the controversy—I could not see either the presence or absence of a basin.

A geological basin seems a strange thing to fight about. One side of this controversy, led by American archaeologist Richard Hansen and his NGO,

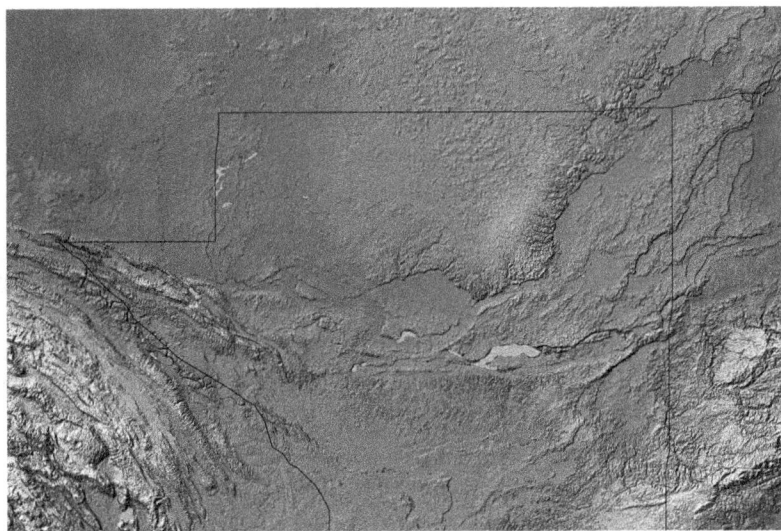

FIGURE 4.1 Topographical map of the Petén and surrounding Yucatán peninsula, from the NASA-SRTM program. The Mirador region shows a gentle slope to the west, rather than a basin (courtesy NASA/JPL-Caltech, cropped by author).

FARES (Foundation for Anthropological Research and Environmental Studies), claims that the area around Mirador is a geological basin, and they use satellite data to prove it. A NASA Landsat image published nearly thirty years ago in *National Geographic* (Stuart 1992) circulates as a key figure on this side of the argument, showing the different infrared signatures of vegetation types based on photosynthetic activity (plate 6). Basinists claim that red areas show relatively high and dry forest, while blue-black areas show low, swampy *bajo* forests. A neatly delineated dark blue area, they argue, shows that water is clearly pooling in this region, indicating a basin. This evidence is met with flat denial by antibasinists, who include the majority of conservation and development NGOs (including WCS) and community organizations working in the MBR. Those on this side of the argument claim that vegetation is not true topographical data, and that the *National Geographic* image shows forest types, not elevation. Instead, they provide elevation maps based on data from NASA's Shuttle Radar Topography Mission (SRTM) program, which show steep rises on the southern and eastern edges of the same region, but then a gentle slope off toward the western wetlands of the reserve, without a western ridge to form a basin (figure 4.1).

The Stakes of a Simple Scientific Divide

Why does the precise shape of what is overall a very flat landscape matter so much to so many people? The proposed basin boundary does not line up with the borders of the parks and concessions that were designated in 1990—and basinists want to redraw the map. They argue that the basin forms an important geophysical barrier, one that shaped unique biodiversity and the cultural formations of Preclassic Maya civilization. Given this natural and cultural significance, territorial limits ought to be revised. Efforts have been made to either change current boundaries inside the reserve or to lay down a new, additional protected area on top of them. While it seems odd to layer protected areas over each other, one law was passed in 2002 to do just this (later struck down as unconstitutional by the Supreme Court), and Manuel Baldizón proposed another to the Guatemalan congress in 2010, making development of the basin part of his presidential platform the following year (figure 4.2) (Escalón 2012).

Redrawing the lines would take away land use and forestry rights from numerous concessions in the reserve's multiple-use zone, notably several community concessions that have deep histories living and working in the forest. Of these, Carmelita is not only the concession that will lose the most territory if basin lines are drawn, but is also the village closest to Mirador, serving as the launch point for most tourist ventures into the ruins. A dusty, end-of-the-road village with fewer than five hundred residents, Carmelita is one of two Petenero resident concessions in the reserve, with the village located inside the concession rather than in the buffer zone (the other is Uaxactún, which would also lose territory under basinist proposals). In a town built up around an old *chiclero* (chicle rubber harvester) camp established in 1925, Carmelita residents formed a management cooperative and were granted a twenty-five-year concession contract by CONAP in 1998. The cooperative, which any resident can join, distributes benefits and income from timber and nontimber products and tourism, and invests in local infrastructure for health and education. Carmelita and its cooperative lie at the heart of the controversy, caught up in the shifting scales of conspiracy theory in which villagers are alternately pawns and key actors.

Hansen and his allies—who include notable people such as Mel Gibson and former Guatemalan president Óscar Berger—have no problem with the redistribution of land rights and access inherent in their model. This side favors a more strict, parklike protection that restricts human use of the forest.

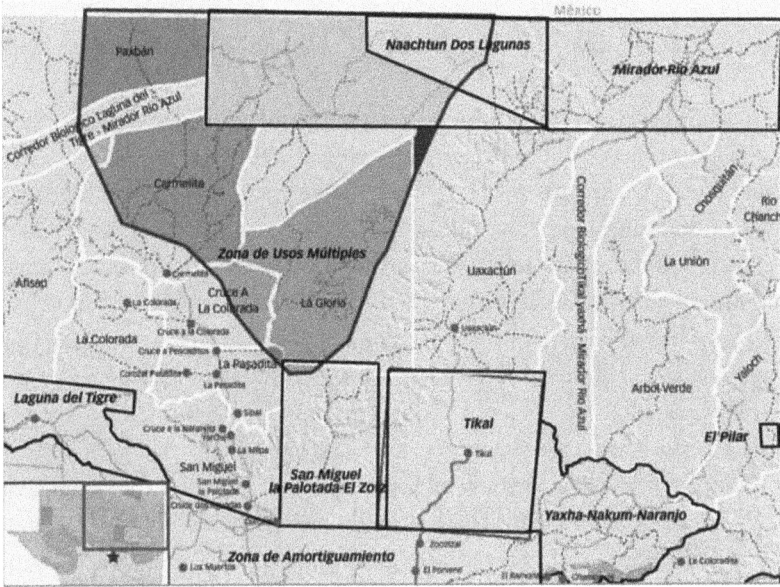

FIGURE 4.2 Overlap between current internal MBR boundaries and the Mirador Basin protected area, proposed to congress by Manuel Baldizón in 2010. Along with several other community and industrial concessions, the village of Carmelita would lose the majority of land currently under its management (marked with shading) (image from proposal for legal initiative #4232, Guatemalan Congress, 2011).

They argue that the tourism brought in by properly developed archaeological sites would provide an economic alternative for local communities. Opposed to this vision, a wide variety of NGO and community actors line up against the basin, supporting the current mixed-use model of the reserve and arguing that local economic benefit through sustainable forestry is the best way to protect the forest in the long term. Both sides produce satellite imagery and GIS maps to demonstrate not only the presence or absence of a basin but also the success or failure of community-based conservation in protecting the forest—a question now inextricably (if illogically) linked to the question of topography. The fact that these contradictory visions of the landscape and conservation philosophy can both be demonstrated with empirical data works against local expectations that technoscientific objectivity might cut through the epistemic murk of postwar politics and lived precarity. These contradictions, then, are read as a clear indicator of political contamination of science, leading to accusations of purposeful mishandling.

From the Village to UNESCO, Mirador Matters

Swirling around the basin controversy are twisted tales of corruption and secret plans, in which scale jumping is the norm.[2] In these stories, discursive links are easily forged between deep history and present politics, between local decisions and global influences, or between events inside a small forest community and a presidential election campaign. Of course, there are actual conspiracies at work—politics in Guatemala do happen behind closed doors, in unofficial, informal, and often illegal channels, and through cliques of allied actors working to further their own interests. Election campaigns are thus a high point for paranoia and conspiratorial thinking, with 2011 and 2015 presidential candidate Manuel Baldizón tying political rumors to Mirador conspiracy.

Baldizón owns huge swaths of San Benito, Flores, and Santa Elena, and his local power was made clear by literally painting much of the urban area red—the color of his political party, Líder (Leader). Called "the Berlusconi of Petén" (Sas 2011), Baldizón was accused during his 2011 campaign of abuse of power through his vast media empire, financial corruption, and links to both old crime families and newer Mexican narco gangs that influence much of the politics, land, and social world of the Petén (InSight Crime 2011). I heard stories about Baldizón's secret plans to change presidential term limits; people familiar with his meteoric rise to power in the Petén were sure that he had dreams of dictatorship. The inclusion of a development proposal for the Mirador basin in Líder's populist right-wing platform heightened these fears of conspiracy, manipulation, and deception among antibasinists.

The 2015 election, which Baldizón was expected to win according to the predictability of postwar presidential cycles, was upended by the Guatemala spring protest movements. Baldizón lost to comedic TV personality Jimmy Morales, and now stands charged with illicit association, bribery, and money laundering in connection with a transnational corruption scandal centered on Brazilian construction company Oderbrecht (Carranza, Robbins, and Dalby 2019). Morales, who emphasized his outsider status to elite power networks, has also been implicated in corruption and money laundering cases. Shortly after taking office in 2016, Morales was given a tour of Mirador by Hansen (by helicopter, skipping over Carmelita). A month later, Hansen co-hosted a press conference with INGUAT (Guatemalan Tourism Institute) to announce progress on a train through the jungle and other tourist infrastructure planned for Mirador (Cuffe 2016). The controversy reignited, but INGUAT quickly retracted its support from the statements after outcry from ACOFOP

(Association of Forest Communities of the Petén, a collective NGO made up of membership from community-run concessions) and other antibasinists that the plans contravened protected area law.

In addition to new laws proposed to the Guatemalan congress or new development policies enacted and retracted, attempts have been made to declare Mirador a UNESCO World Heritage Site. Clear delineation of the site's boundaries (basin or not?) has stood as a major barrier to this goal. The Foundation for Maya Natural and Cultural Patrimony (PACUNAM), an organization composed of elite representatives from Guatemala's wealthiest corporations to "promote sustainable development through the preservation of Guatemala's natural and cultural heritage," long threw its heavyweight support behind the basin model. But in 2011 the group started to shift its alliances toward the NGO coalition who work against the basin, in particular to support the highly controversial capture of Mirador tourism by Carmelita's forest concession.[3]

In 2010, this informal coalition—including WCS, ACOFOP, Asociación Balam, and others—helped Carmelita negotiate a legal agreement with CONAP giving the village a semimonopoly over hike-in tourism to Mirador. CONAP's 2010 Public Use Plan for Mirador-Río Azul National Park established that while any agency can arrange tours to the site, they must hire members of Carmelita's tourism board—managed and licensed by the concession cooperative—to serve as guides, mule drivers, and cooks. This arrangement has been incredibly contentious. Many conservationists and community development workers celebrate this capture of the market as a small victory over Carmelita's geographic and economic marginality, while tourism operators and developers decry the loss of "free-market competition."

As the closest village to the ancient city, the now legally determined center for tourism to the site, and the forest concession with the most to lose from proposed basin-shaped rezoning, Carmelita has become a major player in debates about the future of Mirador. But even inside the village, where it would seem that people should easily align with the antibasin camp that maintains the current concession extension, use rights, and this small pocket of pro-community tourist regulation, there is a small—but extremely vocal—dissenting group. The division between competing visions for the landscape has become entangled with old family conflicts, with a small group of Carmelita residents opposing the community benefit-sharing model of the cooperative. This is especially true now that their ability to run independent tourism ventures to Mirador in competition with the cooperative's tourism council has been declared illegal. One of these villagers, Izabella, railed against the cooperative's influence over community life, which she claimed was bought with intimidation and manipulation: "They tell me that the majority rules, but it's a dirty majority, a dirty process." She kept a list of residents who were not cooperative members, pulling this out to show me evidence of resistance. These families, as opponents rather than members of the cooperative, are more likely to support the anticoncession basin. As a result, both sides of the controversy are able to claim that local people are on their side.

Conspiracy theories include the belief that people are being fooled into participating in something that is against their own interests (Cubitt 1989). This logic is mirrored by the prevalence of duplicity (*engaño*) narratives in postwar Guatemala, the widespread belief "that there is someone behind the scenes, pulling the strings" (Nelson 2009, xvi). Both sides of the Mirador controversy explain the enrollment of local, national, and international allies to the other side through this kind of logic, though rural villagers in Carmelita are particularly subject to this narrative. At the same time, explaining that others have been duped creates a bond between teller and listener, marking both as on the right side of a moral and political divide and indexing unimpeded access to truth (Cubitt 1989).

On the Hunt for Hidden Truths

The tenor of this controversy has grown so intense that the mere mention of Mirador sends people into a frenzy of activity, trying to figure out what hidden connections or interests each new actor brings to the arena, and how to counter the "threat" from the other side without knowing what that threat might consist of, nor whether the other side is even involved. A single word or name can set off cycles of rumor, gossip, and conspiracy theorizing that circulate through casual conversations in the hallways of NGO offices, in the cabs of pickup trucks, in Skype chats between GIS technicians, and between tourists and guides at the tops of temples in the ancient city itself.

Among his opponents, the purported goals of Hansen's secret plans are never quite settled. Rumors I heard ran the gamut from mundane profit motives, to desire for social and territorial control over the area, to dark spiritual motivations. Many think his push for a basin has to do with the money he could make by developing the site for luxury tourism, a theory connected to his proposals for a privately owned train to the site. Others suggest that this imagined payoff is just a way of enrolling powerful allies to support his deeper goals—most often linked to religious motivation based on his Mormon faith.[4]

Although both he and the candidate denied it, it was widely believed among his opponents that Hansen had personal ties to Manuel Baldizón, around whom even darker stories of conspiracy swirl. Through Baldizón, Hansen was linked to rumors of organized crime, drug trafficking, deep corruption, and ruthless power accumulation. Baldizón's arrest in the United States on money-laundering charges only confirms these fears, especially as Hansen has now moved on to the current seat of power, allying himself with Morales.

On the other side, pro-basinists accuse NGOs and their allies of promoting a fundamentally flawed model of conservation—community forest concessions—for their own financial and political interests. Territorial domination is a common theme: "There is a small group in power here . . . that wants absolute control over the [reserve]," Iván, a basin supporter who had previously worked for FARES, told me. He continued that someone from an antibasin NGO had told him that he continued to work in the Petén because this group "allowed it," insinuating total (potentially violent) control over the region. Hansen has publicly accused community concessions of corruption and drug trafficking (Cuffe 2016), while accusations against NGOs include bribing state actors and unlawful accumulation of profit and power. Another of Hansen's supporters counseled me conspiratorially to keep a careful eye on WCS as I carried out my research with them: "Just look at what they do, ignore what they say, and you'll see the truth."

This search for hidden truth is at the heart of conspiracy theorizing. In the Mirador debate, neither side takes the other's scientific or political position as honest truth. Discussing Baldizón's campaign proposal for development of the Mirador area, one NGO worker asked, "What do they get out of supporting this law? Well, part of it is the community development, development of Petén and tourism, conservation stuff, so they look good and get their name in there. . . . But what are the hidden motivations?" Readily apparent explanations of conservation, development, or political prestige are simply not good enough when Mirador is at stake. Instead, differences in scientific data and conservation philosophy are interpreted as hiding the true nature of the other side's nefarious interests.

Doing Paranoid Politics

As stories about Baldizón and his dirty dealings ran wild during the 2011 election season, their occasional intersections with Mirador rumors provided rich fodder for conspiracy theories. While Richard Hansen publicly denied any connection to Baldizón and his Líder party, rumors of their alliance (ranging from financial contributions to secret phone conversations) were only fanned by these denials, with both men seen by their opponents as manipulative, dangerous, and powerfully well-connected would-be destroyers of the MBR. Baldizón's 2010 proposal for a basin protected area was defeated in congress, but members of the antibasin coalition worried about retaliation from the politician. It wouldn't come immediately, they decided, but Baldizón is a "smart, patient man," one who remembers who has crossed him and bides his time before taking retribution.

These rumors were passed back and forth between two antibasin NGO staff in a car ride shared with a tourism development consultant and myself as we headed out to a community event inside the reserve. The consultant, Sebastian, had worked extensively with PACUNAM and FARES, and was skeptical of the connections being posited between Baldizón and Hansen. The others piled on more evidence in response, such as a detailed analysis of language in the candidate's proposal that appeared to be poorly translated, word-by-word, from English descriptions of the ruins. This conflation of poor translation with hidden conspiracy reveals the logic of these rumors: "what distinguishes the paranoid style is not, then, the absence of verifiable facts . . . but rather the curious leap in imagination that is always made at some critical point in the recital of events" (Hofstadter 2008, 37). Beyond these rumors' logics, the telling of stories in the private, convivial space of a shared pickup cab was clearly intended to enroll a new ally in antibasin politics.

Within Carmelita, a similar atmosphere of suspicion and rumor animates village politics. Fights between the concession management cooperative and the village Community Development Council (COCODE) were shrouded in conspiratorial rumors, with regulation of tourism and access to Mirador among the hottest issues. In the run up to a COCODE election in late 2011, the cooperative's board of directors and an antibasin NGO representative strategized in a closed-door meeting about how many days in advance to announce the election assembly in order to prevent "the other side" from having too much time for countercampaigning, organizing, and "manipulating" other community members. This planning meeting was not perceived by those taking part as manipulation or conspiracy, despite being a hidden, coordinated action designed to swing the election toward their own interests. The political alignment of the opposing faction with Hansen and against the cooperative, as well as against community-based conservation and NGO interventions more generally, marked the opposition's actions as based on lies and manipulation for personal gain. In contrast, the meeting was framed as strategizing not for the individual interests in the room, but in defense of the broader community and forest. This kind of preemptive activity simultaneously drives and is driven by the paranoid gossip that builds into full-fledged conspiracy theories, as this meeting designed to cut off the opposition's secret plans would only inspire more rumors from the other side, deepening divisions between them.

How I Came to Conspire against the Basin

I too am entangled in the dynamics of paranoia and rumor at Mirador; these are the conditions for my own knowledge production. Each side of this controversy allowed me access out of the desire to have me see the clear truth of their side, while limiting that access out of fear that I might be hiding my own secret alliances. I was told at one point that there had been careful discussion about whether or not I should be allowed into a particular meeting, a discussion that ended with the conclusion that I was "probably not evil." But rather than uncover a geological truth (though I am more convinced by nonbasin data), I too was enrolled into an antibasin political position by stories and rumors. This was partially due to my preference for community-based conservation, which, while far from perfect, I find more realistic and equitable than strict parklike protectionism. But also, by the time I encountered the basinist position and evidence directly, I had already been turned against them by months of building social ties with WCS and other antibasin NGOs. These ties had been solidified by stories, gossip, and rumor about basinists and their true motivations—stories that I myself later turned to similar political effect.

In 2012, less than a month after returning from Guatemala to write my dissertation at the University of California, Santa Cruz (UCSC), I received an email from an antibasin conservationist: "Hi Micha, Can you please read this email and give us your take on this?" What followed was a forwarded string of messages from a "governance consultant" who was asking about Mirador, and who would be meeting with the UCSC Environmental Studies Department to discuss research funding on behalf of unnamed "friends." My NGO contacts were afraid that Hansen's "hidden hand" was "yet again attempting to plant a seed with a reputable institution to raise their personal profile and line weighty institutions up behind their cause." They asked me to investigate. I managed to get myself invited into a meeting two days later between an academic department I didn't belong to and the consultant, who turned out to be the representative of a sheik from the United Arab Emirates.

The sheik and his daughter had been given a helicopter tour of Mirador by Hansen and had fallen in love with the area, but this consultant had gotten a "bad smell" from Hansen's request for millions of the sheik's dollars. Instead, he had turned to UCSC looking for alternative ways to invest in the region. In the meeting, after tentatively feeling out the consultant's connections, I suggested that he direct research funding through both UCSC and the NGOs and community coalitions that line up against the basin. I was pleased to be able to support the organizations that had supported my research (at least potentially—the funding did not materialize), but at the same time felt uneasy at how I had been drawn into the same preemptive, backroom strategizing that I was writing about. Without the fear of Richard Hansen's secret dealings or my own circulation of gossip in the meeting, this potential alliance between a sheik, a U.S. public university, and the antibasin camp of conservationists would never have been possible. Paranoid politics are thus highly generative—both of political connections and alliances, and of new knowledge: any knowledge about Mirador produced by this funding would be inherently inflected by the paranoia that shaped the possibility of that research.

Paranoid Evidence

Conspiracy stories are powerful tools for creating and solidifying political alliances. Following actor-network theory, the two sides enroll human and institutional actors to their competing networks through paranoia and rumor sharing, though in 2011 neither had yet grown large enough to overshadow the other and stabilize their scientific theory into fact. But what of the nonhuman actors enrolled in these arguments—the GIS maps, satellite images, and biological surveys? What role do the ancient temples play in this struggle, the trees and the understory, the geology, the jaguars? The past, present, and future of the Mirador landscape are all contested, and people struggle to enroll each of these nonhuman players in their visions and versions of truth. How does Mirador declare itself?

An Apocalyptic Landscape

The Mirador controversy is not simply clever humans struggling over passive nature. Landscapes are active, entangled human/nonhuman spaces, which cut human exceptionalism down to size even as human action has serious impacts (Raffles 2002; Tsing 2015; Ogden 2011; Zimmerer 2000; Rose 2004). In one way, Mirador speaks through its refusals to be enrolled fully in one side or the other of regional struggles—the landscape is not so clear in its topography, history, or ecology that it can sit easily with one or another conclusion. It resists easy definition. This resistance is generative; the impossibility of certainty only increases the sense that certainty should be possible, leading to resources and energy poured into the site. Ideas for what could or should be made of the area multiply—new tourism infrastructure such as roads, trains, or hotels, new research projects, new legal designations—even as the site's remoteness and political entanglements shut down most of these possibilities before they begin.

Mirador is a landscape profoundly shaped by human presence, but one that resists human control and domination, physical or political. Its ancient ruins hold an undeniable pull, standing as exceptional monuments to the power of both human and nonhuman forces. The immensity of the Preclassic Maya construction is astounding, beyond compare or easy description, while the ability of the jungle to erase and wind its way into this human past also astounds, making the human contribution seem at once vast and insignificant. The ruins serve as an eerie reminder that while current discourse shrieks that this forest will soon be lost, we too will one day be reduced to traces. One NGO field worker who has visited the city many times often referred to the "dark energy" surrounding the site, and spiritual experiences atop jungle-covered temples are common among Guatemalan and international visitors alike.

Mirador and its Maya history also serve as potent symbols of socioenvironmental ruin and are often used (alongside the controversial "collapse" of Classic Maya civilization several hundred years later) as an allegory for the ravages of hubristic landscape alteration and climate change. In Mirador debates, Hansen in particular is likely to refer to theories of Maya environmental overuse leading to catastrophic population collapse—a popular but contested hypothesis of why Maya civilization abandoned the central lowlands of the Yucatán peninsula centuries before the arrival of Spanish ships. The allure of environmental disaster narratives about the ancient Maya is evident in the popularity of such works as Jared Diamond's (2006) *Collapse* and Mel Gibson's *Apocalypto* (2006, for which Hansen served as a consultant), and shows up in many discussions of the current and future situation of the reserve.

Overlaying historical Maya depopulation with current environmental destruction is a powerful discursive strategy. In a 2004 National Geographic film about Mirador, shots of illegal burning of the reserve's forests frame the film at its opening and conclusion, providing a narrative connection to why the ancient city was depopulated in 150 CE. Featuring Richard Hansen's work prominently, the film explains that ancient Mirador was deforested to provide wood for fires to produce lime, used to build the city's enormous temples. This deforestation, the film argues, drastically altered the ecology of the surrounding landscape and undermined the fragile Maya agricultural system (Townsley 2004). Although today's deforestation is undertaken with different technologies, at different scales, and for different reasons, this ancient tale is framed by shots that warn of current expansion of human presence in the reserve. Humans are presented as once again burning their way through the jungle, heading toward the heart of the Mirador forest to destroy it anew.

These apocalyptic overpopulation/deforestation parables were further bolstered in 2011 by the circulation of Maya "prophesies" of the end of the world in December 2012. This interpretation of the Maya calendar was dismissed by living Maya and Mayanist archaeologists, but fed into broader cultural understandings of the landscape's histories and futures. Research has also indicated that a major drought occurred across the lowlands at the time the Classic Maya civilization disappeared (Gill et al. 2007), a factor easily placed in parallel with predictions of higher temperatures and lower rainfall due to global climate change. These apocalyptic narratives collapse distinctions between pasts, presents, and futures, erasing the differences between cutting wood to burn lime for temples and clearing protected forest for drug-funded cattle ranching, or between a historical drought event and uncertain climate change predictions.

All of these entanglements of human and nonhuman action on the landscape are further generative of conspiratorial epistemologies, as Mirador refuses to cleanly align with one or another powerful vision of what it is, was, or might yet be. When two scientific claims about this landscape conflict, the contradictions between them amplify the mundane paranoia that dominates political life. Each side is convinced that the other is intentionally manipulating or distorting their data. In fact, the more convincing the other side's evidence, the more convinced people become of hidden wrongdoings.

Basin versus Landscape

Richard Hansen and other supporters of the basin make strong claims to scientific evidence, including support from scientists working for the U.S. Geological Survey, the University of Arizona, and Stanford University.[5] But the infrared satellite image that serves as a central pillar in the basinist scientific camp (plate 6) is summarily dismissed by opponents: "A ring of healthy photosynthetically-active vegetation appearing seasonally around the Mirador region does not sufficiently determine the nature of the topography involved in producing such a pattern." In response, one basinist complained about ignorance of bajos, the forests that grow in swampy depressions and appear blue-black in infrared images: "They always say, 'It's not a basin! It's not a basin!' . . . *You* know infrared photographs [addressing me as a researcher interested in satellite imagery]. It's bajo vegetation. Now, water doesn't stand on a hill, it doesn't stand on a plateau, which is what [they're] trying to call it. . . . Let the vegetation tell you what's going on." Nonetheless, when faced with data based on vegetation versus radar topographical satellites, antibasinists stick resolutely to the latter.

Of course, basinists claim not only that a basin exists, but also that it delineates an important natural and cultural barrier—one significant enough to justify the redrawing of political boundaries. Specifically, they argue that many species are endemic to the basin, and that the most important sites of Preclassic Maya civilization lie within its geological boundaries. Iván showed me on a map why current lines ought to be redrawn:

> Scientifically, technically, biologically, there is no reason to have made a park like this. However, here there is a mountain range . . . which is what Richard Hansen calls "the basin." Actually, the majority of Maya construction is inside this. On this side [pointing west of the region] there are some [sites], but not like here. Those same Maya used logic: they saw that there was a natural protection here, the mountains. The water runs generally in this direction [toward the basin's center]. . . . It makes a lot of sense. Biologically, scientifically, the park should have been here.

In contrast, the antibasinists not only claim that there is no special geological feature here, but that the natural and cultural landscapes of interest are much larger and more complex. As a CONAP employee wrote in an email to other antibasinists: "The insistence on differentiating this from the rest [of the reserve] as extraordinary has no foundation. . . . There are two archaeological sites there, more or less out of the ordinary only because of the size of the structures, but there is much more sophisticated and advanced Maya art in other sites, so in reality it's just one of the many important things in the MBR."

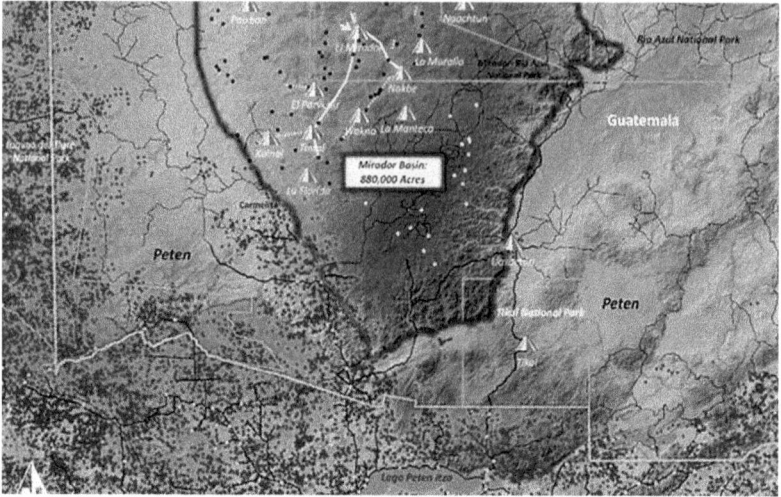

FIGURE 4.3 Map showing NASA MODIS hot spots detected in and around the MBR multiple-use zone from 2001 to 2008. Controlled agricultural fires are permitted in many cases (with restrictions), but here all fires are presented as part of a unified threat. This image circulates as evidence against successful community concession management in a controversy over the Mirador archaeological site, which is contained within the outline of the suggested basin (image: Global Heritage Fund, 2012).

Competing Conservation Philosophies

The two sides of this debate follow different conservation philosophies, with community-led sustainable forestry facing off against tourist-oriented parks. Conflicting technoscientific evidence extends into this realm, with each side presenting data demonstrating the success or failure of the current MBR management regime. The basin side argues that there is no such thing as sustainable timber harvesting, and that community management constitutes a threat to the landscape. To this effect, they present a map with eight accumulated years of MODIS satellite hot spot data showing fires in the MBR, creating a terrifying image of anthropogenic burning sweeping in from the unruly west (figure 4.3). Against this image, antibasinists argue that overlaying many years of fire data creates an exaggerated sense of threat, erases the reduction of fires in recent years (though this argument would be weakened after the catastrophic 2017 fire season), and conflates illegal activities with the permitted, controlled agricultural fires of community concessions.

Antibasinists draw on CEMEC's official knowledges to provide maps and data that back their claim that community concessions are good for conservation. These show that most deforestation in the reserve has occurred in national parks, with concessions protecting forest cover and providing a buffer against further human migration toward Mirador (plate 5). WCS camera trap studies have found higher jaguar densities in well-managed community concessions than in national parks, including Mirador-Río Azul, a charismatic indicator of ecological integrity. Speaking back to this data, basinists point out that tree cover is not a good indicator of ecosystem health, and that the real impacts of selective logging are invisible from the sky. In particular, they point to habitat fragmentation caused by logging roads, ecological depredation due to hunting and harvesting of nontimber forest products, and the trash left on paths and in campsites by unconcerned locals.

Parks, Poverty, People 152

Reading across the Lines

What might in other circumstances be an argument over competing methodologies or types of evidence does not play out in these terms. Instead, both sides attribute differences in scientific argument to deliberate deceit or manipulation. One basinist told me, "Most Peteneros will ignore or *choose to ignore* geographical truths in favor of political or economic expediency" (emphasis added). On the other side, an antibasinist simply stated, "Richard still goes on about his false 'basin,' no matter what the science shows." The lines between truth and falsehood are declared to be obvious and easy, the value of evidence determined by political and social alignment. But there is something more here than just a politically structured system of belief.

Taking seriously the imaginative imputation of nefarious goals and deliberate falsehoods, rumors can undermine the possibility of taking any evidence or source at face value. One day, an antibasin NGO staff member showed me a PowerPoint presentation he had assembled by annotating screenshots of the FARES website. The slides systematically highlighted and contested terminology, numbers, and claims running across all three aspects of the controversy (the existence of a basin, its purported significance, and the degree of ecological threat posed by current management). More than a straightforward refutation of FARES's argument, this PowerPoint slide show was presented to me as evidence of calculated deceit on the part of the opposing NGO, with each additional disputed item adding to the weight of the deception—and therefore to the seriousness of what it might be hiding. Through the twists of paranoid logic, evidence for a basin thus becomes key evidence against a basin (and vice versa), as one's own evidence becomes increasingly solidified in the face of dangerous opposition.

This reading of contradictory data as a sign of powerful conspiracy demonstrates an epistemology that reveals more about the workings of power in Guatemala than it does about the topographical shape of the landscape. Importantly, one's own data and evidence are never held to the same scrutinizing standard as the opposition's; there are no hidden deceptions to reveal, and logical leaps in one's own reasoning are accepted as unproblematic. One basinist cited the discovery of fourteen new species of moth in a three-year period as evidence for the biological uniqueness of the basin. While these discoveries support claims for high biodiversity in the area, they did not demonstrate that the moths are not also found outside the basin, where no surveys were conducted. Similarly, Hansen's Mormon faith was considered a potentially dangerous and important factor in his marshaling of data, while Mormon Guatemalans working in antibasin institutions were left free of suspicion by their peers. Paranoid epistemologies are not only clear about the lines between truth and falsehood, they also impute politics, dirty dealings, and logical fallacy exclusively to the "other."

Reasonable Conspiracies

In the Mirador controversy, conspiracy theories and suspicion are entirely reasonable epistemologies. They are not just contextual to, but deeply entangled with practices of scientific interpretation and argument. There is an insistence on both sides of the debate on a single and knowable truth, something solid and discoverable that is being purposefully manipulated and obscured by the interests of the opposite side. In this controversy, scientific practices designed to present objective images about an external reality cannot be separated from the fearful context in which that science takes place. Dark rumors of dirty secrets like territorial control or plots for Mormon domination create the networks that bolster scientific facts and are embedded within the frameworks through which people read data proving or disproving a basin. Conspiracy theory here is not antiscience; it is coconstituted with scientific understanding itself.

Technoscience, with its promises of access to a clear and knowable reality, works symbiotically with conspiracy theorizing as a way to get a handle on the sheer out-of-controlness of life on an ecologically, historically, and socially complex landscape. Conspiracy theorizing draws together unexpected scales and stories, shapes political strategy, and affects the production and interpretation of evidence, drawing clear lines between fact and falsehood. Conservationists, scientists, villagers, and politicians come together in a world where daily life, hidden powers, and paranoid fantasy bleed into each other, and in which the circulation of conspiratorial stories is political business as usual. Out of the unpredictable shifts of multiple political, scientific, and ecological worlds, paranoid politics and epistemology emerge as a coherent and highly effective way of understanding and acting in the world.

This dynamic of paranoia and scientific controversy is not an exceptional connection found only in this remote corner of Guatemala. All science is political, and conspiracy theorizing is a common way of doing politics around the world (de Vries 2007; Wagner-Pacifici 1999; Briggs 2004; Samuels 2015). These responses to the excesses of reality are exacerbated by violent, unequal, and nontransparent contexts, and exist not only in spectacular displays of irrational calculation but in everyday, mundane conversations and understandings of how the world works. Conspiracy theories are powerful tools for making sense of contradictory information and for providing clear explanations in situations that are anything but. Science, too, aims to provide this kind of satisfying clarity and finality of explanation. As two of the most powerful epistemologies in the MBR nooscape, people draw together science and paranoia as frameworks for hardening certainty, truth, and political power in the face of irreconcilable difference.

PETENEROS AND OTHER
ENDEMIC SPECIES

Endemism, in biology, is the state of belonging to only one place in the world—a native species, in other words, but uniquely so, not found elsewhere. Petenero culture is endemic to the premigration Petén in particular, rooted in particularities of both time and place. It is impossible to grow into the identities of those who arrived later, no matter how many generations may be born there. One can never become Petenero, except perhaps as an honorary title (which I have only seen conferred once, on a white man from the U.S.). As Julio, a Ladino man who moved to the Petén from his family home near the capital, repeatedly told me, "Petén es otro país" (Petén is another country).

Peteneros are known for their stubborn independence, deep connections to the forest, and for living rough and wild. These stereotypes, repeated by both Peteneros and others, naturalize Petenero difference as a kind of endemism to the wild forest. Peteneros were proud of these connotations, people living in Carmelita and Uaxactún especially so. They are the only two Petenero communities living inside their MBR forest concessions, the endemic species in its natural habitat. (Of the remaining ten community concessions in the reserve, six are nonresident concessions granted to communities in the buffer zone, and four are resident concessions made up of more recent migrants to the Petén.) In these two villages, talk of chiclero (chicle harvesting) histories is woven through contemporary forest management practices, collapsing historical time into a naturalized emplacedness.

In the *otro país* of Petén, distinctions between indigenous and Ladino take on a unique cast, as the native Itza' Maya population that forms a key part of Petenero history are now greatly outnumbered by Q'eqchi' migrants. Indigeneity discourses often naturalize connection to place in the way that Petenero discourses do, with similar environmental "noble savage" themes. But Q'eqchi' in the Petén trouble notions of indigenous belonging by virtue of their movements and multiple attachments (Grandia 2012), challenging pan-Maya identity: locally, the word "Maya" typically refers to the Itza', while the Q'eqchi' are always "Q'eqchi'."

If Peteneros are an endemic species, Q'eqchi' migrants must be an invasive one.[1] They are perceived as land invaders by ethnic decree, despite the fact that the vast majority of migrants to the Petén were Ladino. Q'eqchi' are plotted on national ethnolinguistic maps as belonging to other regions of the country: the southern edge of the Petén and neighboring departments of Alta and Baja Verapaz. Q'eqchi' people are often deeply emplaced in the Petén, and their agricultural activities are far from the largest drivers of forest loss. But they, like invasive species, are frequently read as a direct threat to the survival of endemic natures and cultures.

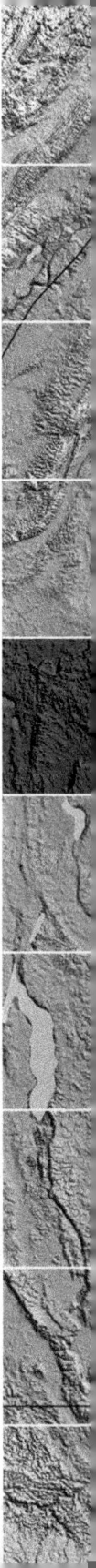

To write a history of ruin, we need to
follow broken bits of many stories and to
move in and out of many patches.
Anna Tsing, *The Mushroom at the End
of the World*

II / PATCHINESS AND

FRAGMENTATION

In landscape ecology, *patchiness* refers to dynamics of uneven
difference over time and space, which produce a shifting mosaic
of ecological relations. Considered a natural part of landscapes,
neither inherently good nor bad, patchiness can enhance biodiversity and help regulate ecosystem functions like nutrient
cycling, and makes landscapes more or less hospitable to particular species. The emergent MBR nooscape is also patchy. Technoscience and paranoia dominate institutional conservation
knowledges, but they are internally complex and differentiated.
They exist alongside many other ways of knowing and changing
the landscape, from local knowledges to nonhuman worldings.
These are distributed unevenly across time and space and come
into different kinds of encounter, with unequal impacts on different places, people, and nonhuman worlds.

Fragmentation is patchiness gone too far. Associated with
human action, ecological fragmentation describes the process
of breaking a landscape into smaller and smaller patches, with

greater and greater difference between them. Relations and exchanges between patches are disrupted. Structural differences between adjacent patches increase, amplifying *edge effects*, the nonlinear processes produced where patches meet. In the MBR, human forces like structural violence, ethnic inequality, and land use change combine to fragment the nooscape. Epistemic edge effects, the patterns and processes that emerge at the meeting of incommensurable enacted worlds, intensify, disrupting possibilities for relation across fields of difference. The fragmentation of the nooscape means that ecological dynamics exceed not only efforts at material control, but also attempts to coordinate a shared definition of what those dynamics are and who is responsible for them. In places where this fragmentation occurs, haunting grows stronger, with too many worlds crowded together into scales that are unable to contain them.

FIVE

A Reserve Full of Rooftops

Population, as a contemporary term describing masses . . . boxes together people living in precarity as a distanced object. It is profoundly entangled with designations of surplus life, of life unworthy, of life contained, of life open to destruction.

Michelle Murphy, *The Economization of Life*

DECEMBER 2011: Pointing to a purple dot marked on an aerial photograph of the small forest village of Uaxactún, my friend Josue exclaimed excitedly, "That house just isn't there anymore. That's where Carlos used to live!" I sat with him and another man, Marvin, in the sweltering midafternoon shade, where my maps, photographs, and questions provided a welcome break from their labor maintaining wcs's local installations. Together we examined the photograph taken and used by CEMEC in its annual estimation of population levels inside the reserve. Poring over the image, with tiny rooftops coded with red, blue, or purple dots depending on how long they had been present, the two men oriented the photograph along the long, abandoned *pista* (landing strip) that ran down the center of the village. They eagerly worked together to fill in the human stories behind the appearance or disappearance of particular rooftops—who had moved in or out, when, and why. They delighted in locating their own houses, and those of their families and friends. Other parts of the image, they told me, were simply wrong, including the location of a small pond, which Marvin insisted was in a different place. As we discussed the use of this photograph to measure the village's population, both men agreed that CEMEC's methodology was deeply flawed, saying, "What CONAP is missing here is to bring this [image/report] here to the community, so that they are using more complete information."

NOVEMBER 2011: Three weeks earlier, far away in the ornate National Palace of Culture in the capital, Guatemala City, I had watched as a PowerPoint slide with a similar aerial photograph, this time of Paso Caballos, flashed on screen (plate 2). The slide was animated to show the increase in rooftops in the village between 2006 and 2009 in the Q'eqchi' migrant community. Part of a formal presentation of the *State of the Maya Biosphere Reserve* report (WCS 2011) to outgoing president Álvaro Colom, the image was followed by a graph projecting population growth across the reserve over the next decade. The presentation named population growth as a key threat to the reserve, alongside climate change, forest fires, and the delicately named "powerful interests."

FEBRUARY 2012: Months later, attempting to replicate my successful image-laden interviews in Uaxactún, I wandered the dusty, trash-littered paths of Paso Caballos with printed aerial photographs and maps in hand. Most villagers were either unwilling or unable to speak to me. Sometimes this was a language barrier—many women and older men speak only Q'eqchi' Mayan, not Spanish—or due to fear that I was a dangerous gringa there to *robar niños* (steal children), making questions about family size particularly unwelcome.[1] Other times, this reluctance was likely an experience-informed distrust of outsiders, especially those asking questions about who lives in the village. Even people who happily discussed other aspects of life and work in the community would not answer questions about the village's population, other than to briefly insist that the rapid proliferation of rooftops in CEMEC's images only reflected the growth of resident families (which often have eight or ten children), and that no newcomers were moving in. Immigration would break the rules of Paso Caballos's agreement with CONAP that allows them to live inside a national park. One or two men admitted that people had moved in that CONAP didn't like. But these people were family, they insisted, and should not really count as outsiders.

~~~~~

These three brief scenes, and the two villages featured and photographed within them, frame my exploration of the patchiness of population enactments in the Maya Biosphere Reserve. What exactly is a population? Does it matter how you count it, and why? Multiple enactments of population arise through different counting practices, such as aerial monitoring or on-the-ground census (Mol 2002; Law and Mol 2008). This is different than saying there are multiple approaches to counting a single real object: there are many different human populations in the MBR nooscape, not one population being measured in different ways. How you decide between them matters. Most often, these decisions are made on an individualized ad hoc basis. Conservationists tend to favor CEMEC's official rooftop counts that reflect state-sanctioned discourses of population growth and environmental protection. But other enactments of population grow in other spaces, tied to alternative practices of counting and ways of inhabiting the landscape. This creates a knowledge-ecological patchiness, a shifting mosaic of population objects that enter into conservation practice (or are excluded from it) at different sites and scales.

A patchy nooscape of enactments shifts away from questions of agency or intentionality (Who made these population estimates, and why?) to think with enacted objects as lively actors (What do different versions of population do?) (Law and Mol 2008). Five enactments of population appear in this chapter: a 2001 census, CEMEC's annual aerial count of rooftops, an imaginary census in Uaxactún, a refusal to discuss population in Paso Caballos, and my own reading of recent village growth in Paso Caballos. The spatiotemporal patchiness of these enactments leads to a proliferation of population-state-environment relationships, relations that are both discursive and material. Here I draw on Sheila Jasanoff's (2004) framing of coproduction, or the simultaneous coenactment of (scientific) knowledge and social order. Population is always coproduced with the state and, in the MBR, with the environment as well. As such, the mobilization or suppression of different versions of population in conservation practice have enormous consequences for the human lives being counted and the nonhuman lives with which they are entangled.

Population and Environment

The creation, measurement, and management of the object known as population are closely tied to debates about modern governance, development, and the environment. Population, as a quantifiable and statistically defined view of humanity, provided the basis for the formation of modern nation-states and governmentality through the nineteenth and twentieth centuries (Foucault 1991). It is closely linked to the rise of the economy as an epistemic infrastructure for neoliberal statecraft, tying together development ideologies, agricultural interventions, notions of global ecological limits, and consumer choice–driven reproductive politics (Murphy 2017). The origins of international development were embedded in nineteenth-century debates over Malthusian population-environment models, in which a predicted resource conflict led to an ideology of directed (as opposed to naturally occurring) progress (Cowen and Shenton 1995).[2] Malthus's models were developed as an explicit ideological defense of capitalism and private property, connections often submerged in more recent versions of population science where social-historically determined terms such as "resources," "technology," "scarcity," or "subsistence" are seen as natural, objectively defined entities (Harvey 1974; Boserup 1976). As such, the idea that growing population poses a threat to natural landscapes has become one of the world's most pervasive "environmental orthodoxies," a powerful standardized narrative that is based more on political ideology than understanding of ecological landscapes (Forsyth 2002).

Population in the MBR also carries the historical weight of the Petén as a frontier region in the late twentieth century. Migration and colonization waxed and waned over the years, but the immense population boom in the lowlands since the 1970s was directly tied to the creation of the reserve (Meyerson 1998). Given this historical trajectory, it is unsurprising that an orthodox population-environment narrative remains powerful among state and NGO agencies working in MBR conservation. Overlaid with new global tipping point discourses and popular theories of Classic Maya collapse due to population growth and environmental mismanagement in the precolonial period, conservationists view growing population in the reserve with apocalyptic alarm, identifying it as a key threat to the forest's future.

Working against this standardized narrative are approaches that aim to differentiate environmental impacts within populations, breaking them down into further categories (e.g., by age, income, or urbanization), or by emphasizing the mitigating effects of technology. It is common, for example, for Anthropocene discourses of a global human population threat (e.g., Crutzen and Stoermer 2000; Steffen et al. 2011) to be countered with the differential impacts of people and practices worldwide, particularly with respect to global capitalism (Moore 2017; Haraway 2015). Another popular reply depends on a form of techno-optimism, in which human technological ingenuity will save the day, providing infinitely increasing efficiency in resource use to offset the impact of growing population.

What's in a Number?

In these popular narratives, the definition of population is left unquestioned: it is a straightforward numerical measure of human individuals. But the populations contained in these narratives might in fact be different objects, even as they describe and debate the same numbers. As Helen Verran (2001) demonstrates elegantly in her study of Yoruba mathematics, numbers can be enacted in fundamentally different ways: they can describe a unity, a (divisible) whole; or a plurality, a sum of parts.[3] The current estimate of the earth's population, 7.7 billion as of this writing, can be read as either a unity, an undifferentiated whole (as in Malthusian population models), or as a plurality, a collection of diverse individuals. Population debates on the global scale are as much about incommensurable enactments of population as they are about technology or politics, locked on the difference between a sum of differentiable individual environmental impacts and a singular collective impact.[4]

In the MBR, both unity and plurality versions of population have been enacted by state agencies at different times through different methods of measurement. Population as a plurality was produced by CEMEC's 2001 census, which gathered extensive information on demographics as well as development and well-being indicators for settlements inside the reserve. This plurality emerged with varied, complex relationships to the landscape, co-producing a bureaucratic state with responsibilities for rational environmental management and for development and service provision to underserved people. In contrast, annual rooftop counts enact the reserve's population as a unity, an undifferentiated mass of humanity. This unity emerges with a sole relationship to the landscape—as a threat—and coproduces a protectionist state, responsible for defending nature against a growing menace.

Aerial rooftop counts enable a reserve-wide view of population, which helps create and maintain a coherent narrative of landscape change and sustainable development needs across the reserve, useful at higher political levels such as the opening scene in the National Palace. It is also significantly cheaper and easier than other counting methods, from a state perspective. Remote monitoring of the MBR's human settlements enacts both a population object and a scale and politics within which that object is particularly meaningful. But for village-level conservation decision making, this information is often inaccurate and can directly conflict with enactments of population emerging out of the villages themselves.

As Diane Nelson (2015) traces in her ethnography of counting and accounting for people lost and killed during the Guatemalan civil war, who counts, and how they count, matters deeply. Differences of identity, ethnicity, method, and memory intersect to produce different numbers, and different meanings associated with those numbers. In the MBR, when official population estimates are at odds with local enactments, it is left up to individual state and NGO practitioners to make sense of the differences, creating a rough patchwork of interpretations and decisions that reflect individual political preferences and social ties. Mostly, aerial estimates are given greater weight than local understandings of population, because of the perceived objectivity and neutrality of CEMEC's photographic methodology—hard adjectives to come by in the MBR nooscape. But this trust in technological truthfulness is a political, not a technical, determination, and one with political consequences.

Enacting Unity and Plurality: State Optics of Population

Census

The first enactment of population is the form most familiar to modern states: a 2001 census of the MBR conducted by CEMEC and allied institutions. Funded by USAID, CARE, and the Austrian Development Cooperation, the census was considered an enormous success. While census methodology was standard in the sense of door-to-door surveying, the particular practices involved differentiated CEMEC's census from other national counts. One CEMEC technician reported, "The work was very good, because . . . the census of the government isn't so good. Here in Guatemala they don't visit all the houses, and the information is really limited. In contrast, here we asked two pages of questions, lots of information. This was [CEMEC's] most important accomplishment up to the present moment." The two weaknesses of national census figures (incomplete and insufficiently detailed data) were overcome with sensitivity to local land politics, careful institutional arrangements in surveying, and a complex two-page questionnaire detailing everything from place of birth to how much land people dedicated to cultivating different crops. Census takers also collected village-level data such as information on infrastructure, local political structures, social services, and institutional support (i.e., NGO presence).

In order to access remote locations and information that many would be unwilling to share, CEMEC contracted the help of two partner institutions. As part of CONAP, CEMEC recognized that tensions over land rights and access inside the MBR would limit many inhabitants from openly sharing information with the reserve's administrators, often perceived as antagonists. The first partner was the National Service for the Eradication of Malaria (SNEM), which had established relationships with most rural villages and was accustomed to difficult journeys to remote places. The second was Asociación Ox'lajú Tsuul Taq'a Maya Q'eqchi', an indigenous rights organization that collected census data in Q'eqchi' villages.[5] Asociación Ox'lajú collected additional information on locally prioritized needs in their surveyed communities (such as road construction, school teachers, composting latrines, etc.), which were listed in an appendix of the published census.

The census report was 850 pages long, including detailed data on 58,781 people in 158 communities. Adding to these door-to-door counts, the document estimated the total population of the reserve at 80,900 people in 175 settlements.[6] The report grouped collected information into six categories: demographics, services, health, education, agricultural and livestock production, and economic activities (Ramos, Solís, and Zetina 2001). Spatially, the census differentiated the reserve into eight subregions, organized by national parks and major transportation routes (along access roads or rivers). Data were presented globally for the reserve, broken down into these subregions, and in detail for each settlement. The census included settlements in the heavily populated buffer zone along the southern edge of the reserve, coproducing an MBR territorial space that corresponds to its official legal boundaries. (Aerial population estimates only count nuclear and multiple-use zones, reflecting the territorial boundaries of conservation practice rather than law.)[7] Yet with the exception of the western national parks, the census subregions do not correspond to legal-managerial zones, lumping together communities in the buffer and multiple-use zones.

Set out in the introduction to the census document was the intended purpose of the data, which was threefold: (1) developing knowledge and analysis of the socioeconomic reality of the MBR, (2) understanding the human factor in protected area management, and (3) development planning in MBR communities (Ramos, Solís, and Zetina 2001). Data were framed with narrative text that directed readers' attention to certain dynamics, for example to the spatial distribution of ethnic groups: "The most numerous ethnic group is Ladinos, with a little more than 80% of the total population, followed by the Q'eqchi' with more than 15% of the total. *Note the difference* in proportions in the Río San Pedro, Sierra del Lacandón National Park, and Laguna Perdida/Río Tamarís subregions, where there is a higher concentration of the Q'eqchi' population" (Ramos, Solís, and Zetina 2001, 10, emphasis added). The report also breaks down population growth into three categories—internal migration (within the Petén), external migration, and local births—then compares nine scenarios of future population growth based on possible trends in these three categories.

Overall, the census enacts a population that is a plurality rather than a unity, a complex set of humans with differentiated histories, identities, and relationships to the landscape and the state. It is individuals, rather than households, settlements, or whole numbers, that count. This population does a variety of things: it threatens the forest, but only sometimes and in some places. It also calls upon the state to provide rights, services, infrastructure, and development. The state that is coproduced with this population is similarly complex and differentiated: it must protect and manage the reserve, but also develop economic opportunities for local communities, provide services such as health and education, and build or maintain infrastructure. It must recognize the difference between indigenous and nonindigenous citizens, address the needs of isolated rural places, and balance conservation and development—a version of state-population-environment relations in tune with global discourses at the turn of the twenty-first century. The census conjured a complex plurality of a population; a modernist, managerial, bureaucratic state; and an environment rendered as territory to be rationally managed, patrimony to be conserved, and natural resources to be sustainably developed. The relations between the three are varied, contextual, and specific, calling forth a wide range of strategies, interventions, and practices distributed unevenly across space and time.

A Reserve Full of Rooftops

CEMEC's strategy of using SNEM and Asociación Ox'lajú worked well to overcome local resistance to the census, but eventually met with trouble. After a few indigenous SNEM extension workers let it slip that the information was destined for CONAP, some villages began to *hacer bulla* (make a commotion). This reluctance to give CONAP information, in addition to the high cost and logistical issues involved in carrying out an on-the-ground census, factored into CEMEC's development of indirect population estimates through aerial photography in subsequent years. As a result, detailed demographic data such as age structure or ethnic identity, or information on livelihoods and various markers of development, are no longer available for yearly comparison and analysis.

MEXICO

Parque Nacional
Biotopo
Monumento Cultural
Reserva Municipal

Concesión Comunitaria
Concesión Industrial
Concesión Comunitaria cancelada

Zona de Uso Múltiple no
concesionada

Zona de Amortiguamiento

MEXICO

Paxbán

Parque Nacional
Mirador-
Rio Azul

Biotopo Naachtún
- Dos Lagunas

Parque Nacional
Mirador - Rio Azul

Carmelita

Chosquitán

Rio
Chanchich

San Andrés

Biotopo Laguna
del Tigre - Rio
Escondido

Parque Nacional Laguna
del Tigre

La Gloria

Uaxactún

La Unión

La Colorada

Cruce a la
Colorada

Las Ventanas

La Pasadita

Yaloch

MEXICO

San
Miguel

Biotopo San
Miguel la
Palotada -
El Zotz

Parque
Nacional Tikal

Parque Nacional
Yaxhá Nakúm
Naranjo

BELICE

Zona de Amortiguamiento

Parque Nacional
Sierra del Lacandón

Reserva
Municipal
Bioltzá

Biotopo
Cerro
Cahui

Parque Nacional

FLORES

N

MEXICO

10   0   10   20   30 km

Área Protegidas
del Sur de Petén

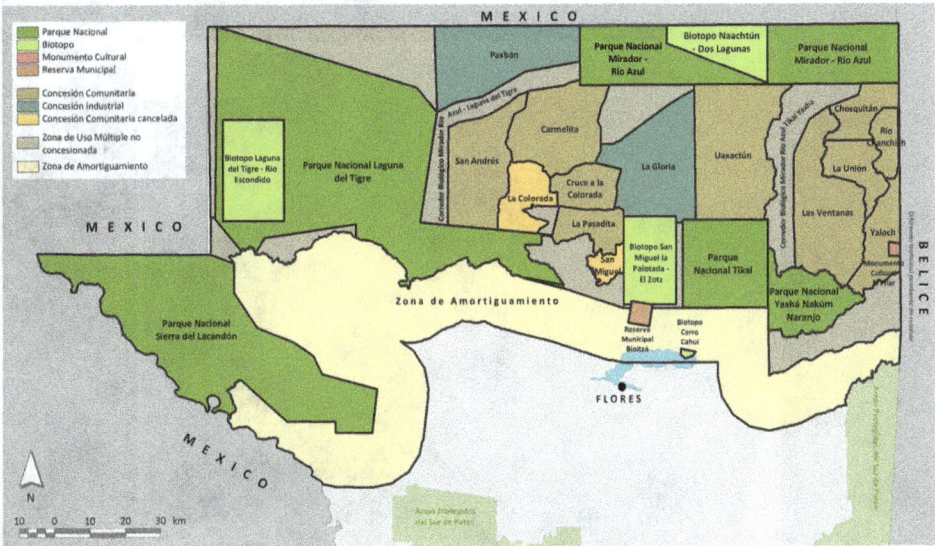

PLATE 1 The Maya Biosphere Reserve. Green and pink areas indicate the nuclear zone
made up of national parks and biotopes; brown and blue areas are the multiple-use zone,
with forest concessions; and the light-yellow strip along the bottom is the buffer zone.
Based on a UNESCO model, these zones are intended to delineate areas for pure nature protection, sustainable resource extraction, and ecologically informed agricultural development, respectively. In practice, however, many nuclear zones are overrun with settlements,
extractive activities, and drug trafficking, and are mired in political controversy. The
multiple-use zone contains lauded community management successes, industrially managed forestry, and sites of violent conflict, militarized evictions, and canceled contracts.
The buffer zone is, in practice, institutionally neglected and unregulated. This map is
ubiquitous in conservation worlds, and its circulation creates possibilities for consensus
about what the landscape is, if not about priorities or strategies in response (image: CONAP
and WCS, 2011).

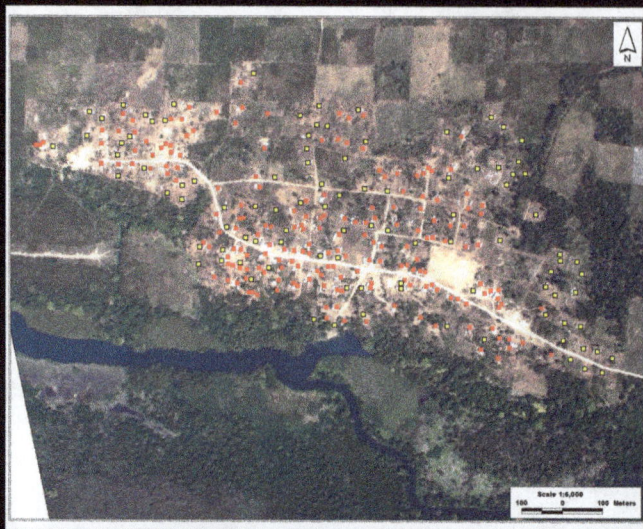

Incremento de la población

Paso Caballos: 2006 (193 casas), 2009 (293 casas)

PLATE 2 PowerPoint slide titled "Population Growth," from the 2011 *State of the Maya Biosphere Reserve* presentation in the National Palace of Culture. The presentation identified population as a key threat to the reserve. The image accompanied an explanation of CEMEC's annual monitoring and estimation of reserve populations using aerial photography, thereby illustrating both the threat of growing populations and the sophisticated surveillance techniques of the state. The featured village, Paso Caballos, grew from 193 houses to 293 between 2006 and 2009 (image: CONAP and WCS).

PLATE 3 PowerPoint slide titled "Institutional Presence," from the 2011 *State of the Maya Biosphere Reserve* presentation in the National Palace of Culture. The map shows the location and staffing institutions for all control posts in the reserve: green represents army, orange CONAP, blue DIPRONA (the environmental branch of the national police), and yellow "other." The "other" category includes NGOs, IDAEH (the national archaeological institution), community representatives, and other institutions. The militarization of the western parks is clearly visible (image: CONAP and WCS).

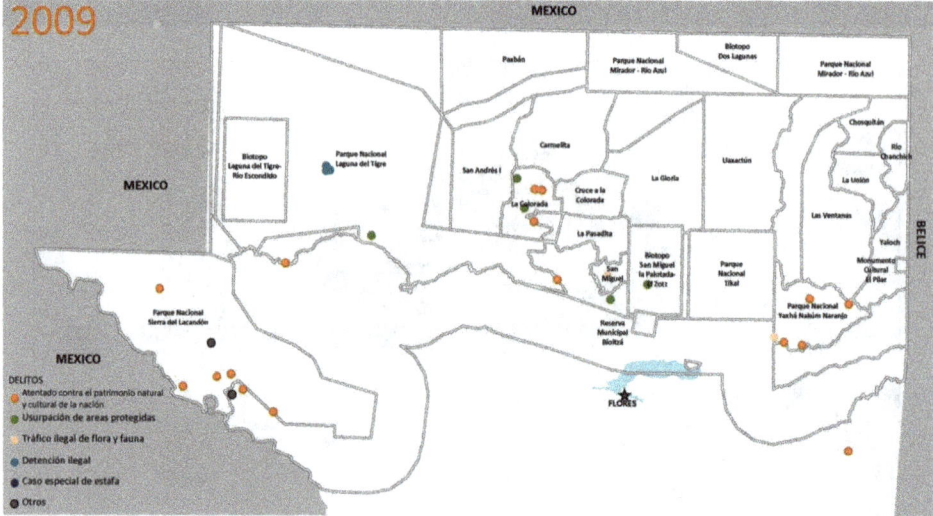

PLATE 4 Map of environmental crimes reported in the MBR in 2009. Orange dots indicate "threat to the natural and cultural patrimony of the nation," green is "usurpation of protected areas," light pink "illegal trafficking of flora and fauna," bright blue "illegal detention" (kidnapping of conservation personnel), dark blue "special case of fraud," and gray "other." The map includes only those cases that were reported to the attorney general's office (Ministerio Público). When viewing this map, NGO and CONAP staff agreed that the data did not represent actual crimes due to underreporting. Specifically, they focused on the lack of dots appearing in Laguna del Tigre National Park, where they collectively perceived the highest rates of crime (image: CONAP and WCS, 2011).

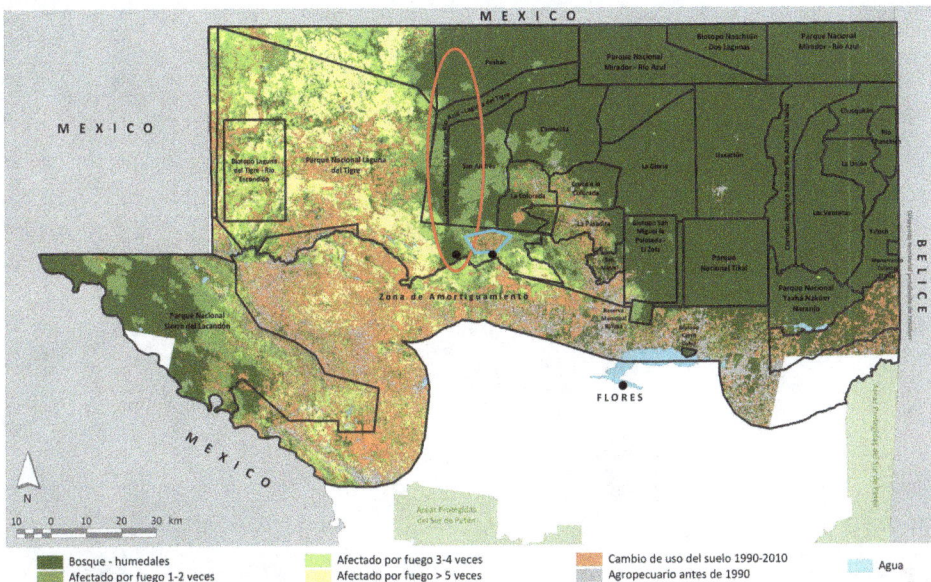

PLATE 5 Map from the *State of the Maya Biosphere Reserve* report showing ecological integrity of the reserve. The legend indicates dark green for forests and wetlands, medium green for areas affected by fire one or two times, light green for areas affected by fire three or four times, yellow for areas affected by fire more than five times, orange for land use change between 1990 and 2010, and gray for agriculture/livestock prior to 1990. Based on this map, the report declares that 79 percent of the reserve's ecosystems are in "relatively good condition." Viewed alongside maps of state presence or illegal activity, conservation actors interpret this map as indicating areas of good governance (green) and of ungovernability (yellow/orange). Approximate locations of "the shield" (red line), Paso Caballos and the Scarlet Macaw Biological Station (black dots, right to left), and the designated agricultural zone of Paso Caballos (outlined in blue) are indicated (image: CONAP and WCS, 2011, modified by author).

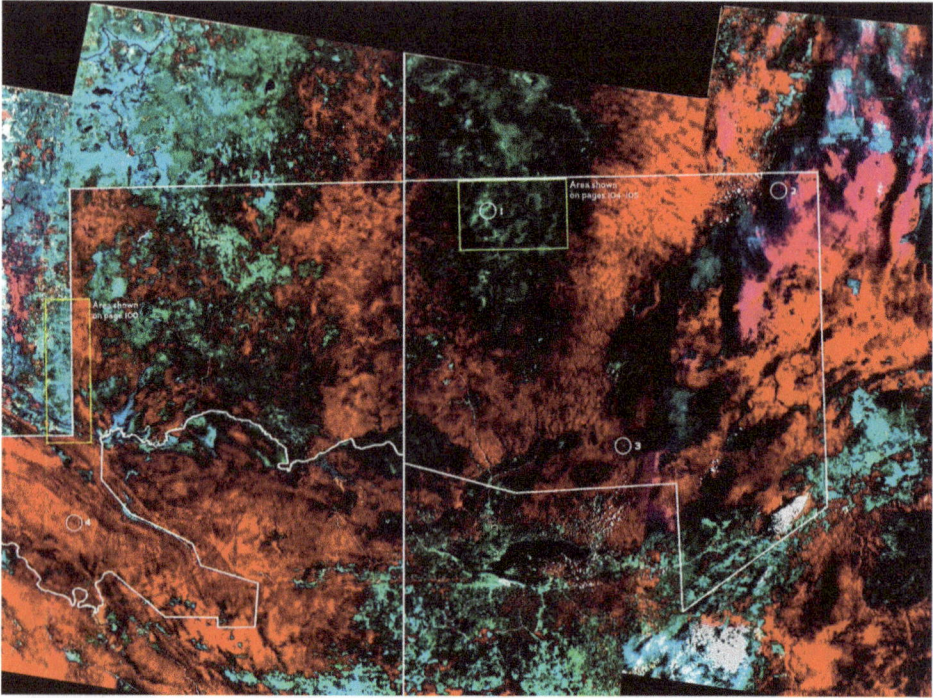

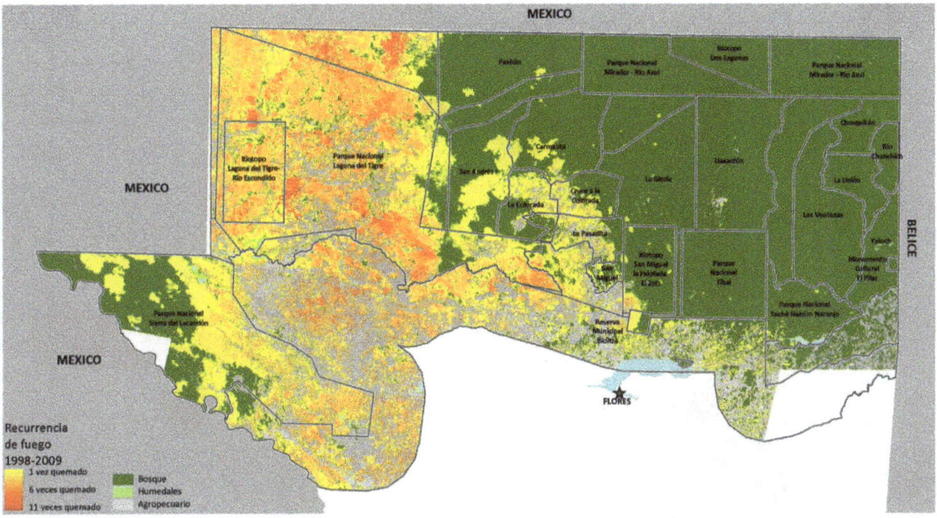

PLATE 7 Map of fire damage from the *State of the Maya Biosphere Reserve* report, based on data from satellite imagery and aerial photography. The yellow-to-red range represents the number of times land was burned between 1998 and 2009, from one to eleven times. Gray areas are those that were converted to agricultural or ranchland before 1998, left uncounted in fire impacts despite being inside protected areas (image: CONAP and WCS, 2011).

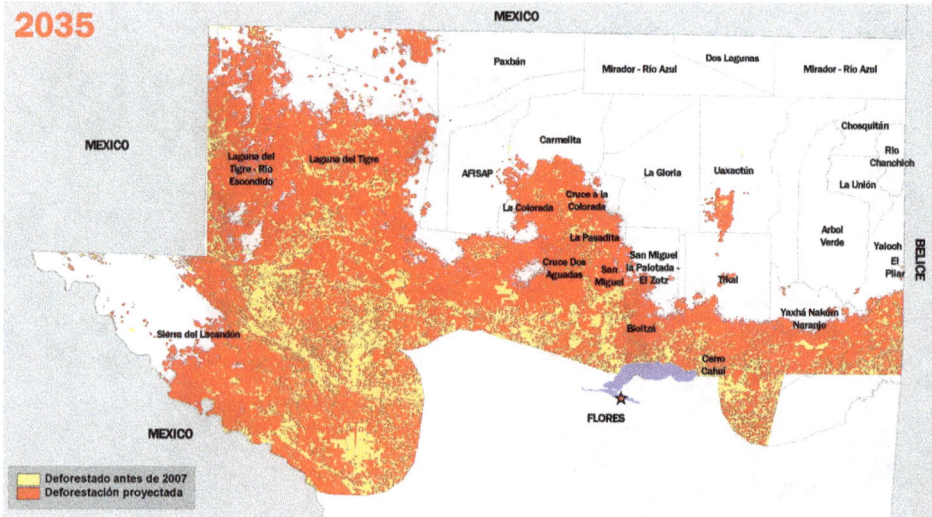

PLATE 8 Map of projected deforestation in the MBR, created for the Guatecarbon REDD+ project in 2011. Yellow areas were deforested before 2007, and red areas are predicted to be deforested by 2035, according to a complex GIS model of social and ecological factors created by CEMEC. The spatialization of future deforestation clearly expands only from measurable past patterns (image: CONAP and WCS).

FIGURE 5.1 CEMEC's digital camera lashed to the side of a small airplane using improvised materials (photograph by author).

CEMEC now conducts remote population monitoring every year. Beginning in 2006, all settlements in the nuclear and multiple-use zones have been annually photographed via airplane, barring budgetary, logistical, or weather problems. Technicians take low-altitude flights to snap photos of the reserve in the dry months from late January through May, rigging a digital camera on the side of the plane. This setup, performed without specialized aerial photography equipment, requires an extraordinary amount of complex know-how developed over the years. A folded tripod, tape, chunks of foam padding, zip ties, and cut-up bicycle tire inner tubes are used to secure the camera apparatus to the plane, ensure proper zoom and angle, and counteract the small aircraft's heavy vibration (figure 5.1). The planes are owned by volunteer pilots, who follow precise flight paths and altitudes plotted by CEMEC, while the camera—wired to a laptop computer and time-matched to a handheld GPS unit—snaps pictures at regular intervals.

Aerial photography is used for several monitoring projects in CEMEC, all of which require a careful location of photographs in space and time in order to compare them with previous years' images. This process, called georeferencing, takes place back in the computer lab by first matching the time stamp of each photograph against the flight's GPS tracker for an approximate location, then matching visually distinct features with previous years' photos until each image is stretched precisely across a grid of latitude and longitude.[8] Precise georeferencing is essential for rooftop counts, as individual houses need to be identified and compared in photographs from multiple years. Once it has been georeferenced, a technician overlays the new photograph with one from the previous year, then manually marks each rooftop with a distinct color to indicate whether it was present in the older photograph or is a new construction, or whether a previously recorded building is now absent. The number of rooftops is then multiplied by 5.5—the average size of MBR families reported in the census—to estimate the population of each settlement and of the reserve as a whole.

Each year's aerial population monitoring results are reported in a three-page document. The report begins with a description of methodology and a sample photograph to illustrate the process; in 2012, the sample image was of Paso Caballos. Two maps represent the total estimated population and percentage population growth for all settlements (figures 5.2 and 5.3, respectively). Finally, the report includes a table providing estimated population and raw rooftop counts for all settlements in all years, along with a few brief comments on noted trends, important communities, and any missing data. This report circulates widely to many state agencies and NGOs working in the reserve. The estimates, maps, and summaries are used in presentations, websites, and other reports, and carried out to the settlements themselves by conservation and development practitioners, including WCS field staff.

Embedded in this estimation method are several assumptions: that each rooftop is a household, that households generally match the 2001 reserve-wide average of 5.5 people per family, and that the number of rooftops in a particular place has a direct linear relationship with population growth. These are simplifications in the service of a quick and easy estimate. The original census measured people per family, not per rooftop seen from above—patterns of household construction, as well as the number of nonresidential buildings in different settlements, vary considerably. The reserve-wide average was the result of differentiated per-family averages across communities: in the census, Paso Caballos's average was slightly over 5.5, while Uaxactún was under 4.8. Finally, new rooftops appear according to complex social, economic, and cultural logics, not just population growth. It makes little sense to imagine a household splitting in two when it reaches a critical mass of eleven people,

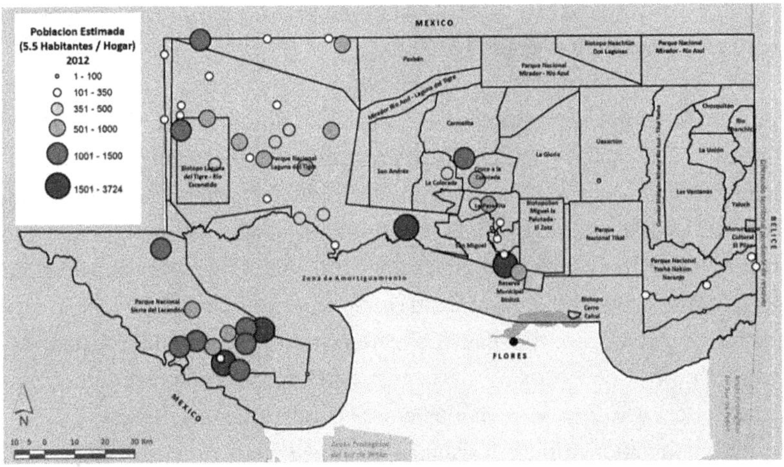

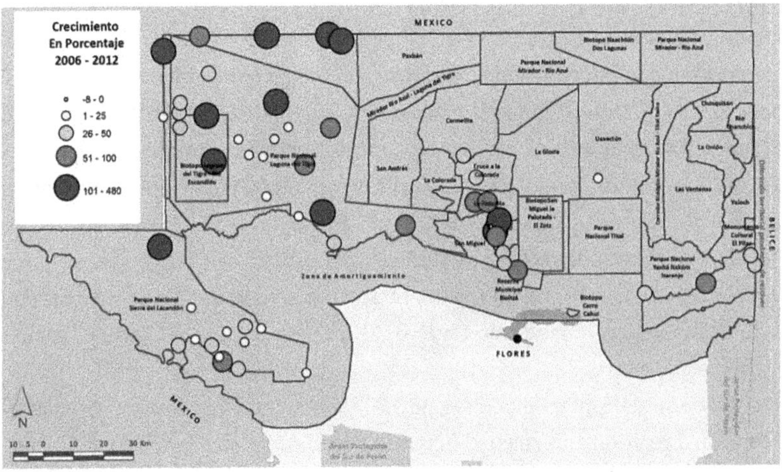

FIGURE 5.2 Estimated 2012 population of settlements in the reserve, calculated based on aerial counts of rooftops multiplied by 5.5 people per household. This image is one of two circulated annually to report CEMEC's annual population monitoring (image: CONAP and WCS).

FIGURE 5.3 Estimated percentage population growth in aerially monitored settlements, 2006–2012. This image is the second of two circulated annually to report CEMEC's annual rooftop counts (image: CONAP and WCS).

but a new house might be constructed by a young couple moving out of their parents' homes to start a family.

The population enacted by this method is vastly different from that of the census. The number produced is a unity, not a plurality—a singular mass of humanity that can do very few things: grow, move, or (occasionally and in particular locations) shrink. This whole is spatially divisible into parts (settlements), but further internal differentiation is absent. Spatially, the multiple-use and nuclear zones are visually and numerically collapsed (differentiated neither on maps nor in the document), while the buffer zone is excluded altogether. This enacts a reserve space that matches conservation practice rather than law—neither CONAP nor NGOs conduct much work in the buffer zone, and most tend to work across park and multiple-use boundaries in flexible ways.[9]

This population, a unity distributed over areas of active conservation intervention in the reserve, also acts as a clear threat to the landscape. The images, maps, and table in the brief reports create a coherent narrative of population growth across time and space, easily digested and moved between contexts, and key to attracting funding from politicians or international donors. The information is useful for requesting support, both for development projects (health and education initiatives for growing villages) and for conservation initiatives that may conflict directly with those projects (more guards, control posts, or evictions). The latter are usually prioritized. When shown in the National Palace to President Colom in 2011, these population data integrated seamlessly with a broader message about the importance of funding defense of protected areas.

This population is appealing in policy contexts because of the vastly simplified relationship enacted between population, environment, and state. Rather than a differentiated plurality of rights-bearing citizens, remote monitoring enacts a unified population limited to the ability to grow and move. This growth and movement, read through environmental orthodoxies, threatens the forest landscape. The state coproduced with this population is more responsible to the landscape than the people; it must protect its territory by funding CONAP, increasing police and military presence in the reserve, and setting policies that defend passive nature against a growing human threat. Emerging from tedious practices of aerial monitoring, the coconstituted objects of the MBR (minus a neglected buffer zone) and its population help create and maintain broad narratives about environmental change, coproducing protectionist intervention at departmental, national, and international political levels.

Meeting the Villages: Population and Pageantry

Fifty-six settlements were aerially counted in 2012, ranging in estimated population from 28 to 3,724 people (CEMEC 2012). Each of these is unique in terms of its mixture of regional origins (migrant, Petenero, or returned refugee); ethnic identities; legal land rights; infrastructure; access to transportation networks and economic opportunities; and health, education, and other services. While many of these structural differences were captured in the census, understanding how birth, migration, and settlement dynamics play out in each village, as well as how population is locally understood, requires a ground's-eye view. Uaxactún and Paso Caballos are not examples of types of village in the reserve, but represent the broader incommensurability of different formations of local village life. As an introduction to these two communities, I use one of the key events through which I myself came to know them—their school pageants.

Who better to serve as symbols of population growth than children? By strange luck of timing, and by virtue of my privileged position as a gringa researcher, I was asked by Uaxactún and Paso Caballos to act as a judge in their annual pageants, in both cases organized by and involving contestants (girls) from the villages' elementary schools. In Uaxactún, the pageant selected a Niña de Independencia and Niña de Guatemala (first and second place) as part of annual Independence Day celebrations. In Paso Caballos, the pageant was an ecologically themed costume contest organized to celebrate Carnaval. In both cases, I accepted the invitation with a cautious curiosity, wary of judging young girls on their appearance. This discomfort never left me, but the contrast that emerged between the two pageants illuminated the differences between each community's social and economic worlds.

Dancing and Disorder: Carnaval in Paso Caballos

My invitation to judge the Paso Caballos pageant came with little formality from a teacher on the day of the event. When I arrived, a chaotic crowd of costumed and beglittered children overwhelmed the handful of adult teachers, parents, and curious onlookers. The kids filled the bare yard in front of the rundown school buildings; the event was to be held on a rickety outdoor wooden stage that doubled as extra classroom space on clear days. I squeezed myself into one of the child-sized desks arranged for the judges, joined by two female teachers and one of their boyfriends. After a ceremonious but unruly opening of flag bearing, anthem singing, and pledge of allegiance, we judges were provided with printed score sheets, listing six contestants' names—one from each grade—and the categories in which we were to score them: costume, dancing, and presentation and speaking. I quickly realized that the names on the sheet were out of order, and missing two contestants who represented the second classrooms of grades so crowded they had been divided in two. Confused, I spent as much time trying to figure out which contestant was which as I did evaluating their performances. To make matters more unclear—but more adorable—an additional tiny girl stood onstage in a beetle costume, dancing, smiling, and waving with the other contestants though she was not officially a part of the competition.

The school had altered Carnaval from its traditional pre-Lent party to reflect ecological themes, and the costumes—some store-bought, some constructed from paper, fabric, and recycled materials—reflected this emphasis. Seven of eight contestants wore costumes representing local wildlife: a blue-headed parrot, a jaguar, a bee, a butterfly, and three scarlet macaws—the last a local icon of conservation due to its endangered status and nesting sites near the village. The eighth girl dressed as *milpa* agriculture, the sole source of income and subsistence for the village. The pageant consisted of a brief introduction, choreographed group dance, and short speeches, but most of the girls seemed unsure what was expected of them throughout. Only one girl (the eventual winner) knew the dance choreography, and during the speeches only she and one other contestant said anything beyond quietly mumbling their name and classroom number into the microphone.

Despite the disorganization—or because of it—the event was extremely fun. Between the three rounds, kids from the audience were invited onto the platform to dance with costumed teachers. After the pageant winner had been chosen, these dances became additional contests, governed by audience applause rather than judges. The dance contests carried the chance to win wrapped prizes, while the pageant winner received only a sash and symbolic victory. No second or third place was awarded; the other girls were simply thanked for their participation and faded back into the crowd. The party that followed, with seemingly endless rounds of dance competition, lasted longer into the night than I did.

Costuming and Controversy in Uaxactún

Uaxactún's Independence Day pageant, in contrast, was a highly formal affair. I was invited to join the judging panel by two women who solemnly approached me to ask a favor. I laughed when their serious demeanor resulted in a request to judge the pageant, but soon learned—through the reaction of my friend Julián, an Asociación Balam field technician—that this pageant was serious business indeed. "Oh no, I'm not doing that again!" Julián cried. "It's different now," insisted Gloria, one of the women: "There's no money involved anymore. It's just for fun [*simpatía*]." They explained to me that in the past, the winner would receive a cash prize as well as the honor of representing the community at ceremonial functions throughout the coming year.

Historically, the community had voted on the winner, but scandals erupted as families made secret alliances and bought votes for their daughters, and the pageants were always followed by bitter fights. Julián had been in charge of vote counting in a previous year, and afterward half of the town turned on him, accusing him of manipulating the result. After some goading from Gloria, he reluctantly agreed to take part in the reformed pageant system: no cash prize, and the judging panel would be composed entirely of outsiders (myself, Julián, and three men from two other NGOs) in an attempt to eliminate bias. The next evening I was seated at a special judge's table at the front of the community meeting hall packed with an audience of all ages, instructed to judge the eight contestants on three criteria: outfit, artistic technique, and charisma and expression.

The pageant opened with the same patriotic ceremonies as in Paso Caballos, but with greater formality and quiet attention from the audience. The contestants were announced as they danced one by one down the center aisle of the hall to the stage, each in an elaborate two-piece outfit with a headdress representing some aspect of local identity and culture. One girl represented the *xate* palm, a local nontimber forest product (NTFP) harvested in Uaxactún's concession; two were dressed as fire and maize, representing agricultural practices; one wore a costume symbolizing conservation; and the rest wore outfits related to the Classic Maya archaeological sites flanking the village, or to local colonial history and legends. The costume presentation was followed by two more rounds: a group dance in which the girls wore their school uniforms, and another in which they emerged in formal gowns and high heels to give speeches about patriotism, local pride, or the future of the community and country—their personal messages as candidates for Independence Day queen. Each of their movements, down to the hand-on-hip pose they took while quietly waiting through competitors' speeches, was tightly choreographed and well practiced.

Between acts, the teacher acting as MC spat surly admonitions at the rambunctious kids pushing up against the stage, and at their parents who let them run free. The time between costume changes for the girls was filled with an alternation of dances from other schoolchildren and the MC's lengthy discourses on order and discipline. He spoke of national and community identity, citizenship, civic responsibility, and the necessity of voting (the pageant was a few days before the 2011 election). He lectured on the centrality of education to Uaxactún's future, particularly a future that would provide alternatives to living off the forest. "Uaxactún," he announced grandly at one point, "is the most important community in the reserve!" He explained that this was due to their "culture of conservation," reminding villagers of the dream of an upwardly and urbanly mobile younger generation closely linked to discourses of forest conservation.

Our determination of winners at the judging table was protracted. We created a new third-place title, the Niña Monja Blanca (named for Guatemala's national flower) to dispel controversy over the second-place winner. And although we judges were from outside the community—a fact repeatedly emphasized by the MC throughout the proceedings—the following day there was still plenty of gossip about who had won, and why. When Julián and I showed up at Gloria's *comedor* (informal restaurant) the next day, it was the sole topic of conversation: "I'm a little disappointed at who did win," Gloria told us, "only because now people are talking. . . . The girl who won is one of my son's students, and since you two and two of the other judges eat here with me, people are talking, you know." It didn't matter that there was no money involved, or that we were unaware of this obscure connection; the stakes were high and rumors were flying. "Still," Gloria reassured us, "it's nothing like it was before."

Ethnicity and Conservation

Two pageants, two vastly different villages. Uaxactún is composed mostly of Peteneros; their families have lived and worked in the region's forests and extractive industries for generations. The village is mostly Ladino (80 percent as of the 2001 census), with a few people claiming Q'eqchi', Itza' Maya, or mixed heritage; Spanish is spoken by all residents. Paso Caballos, on the other hand, is nearly 100 percent Q'eqchi' Maya, composed of late twentieth-century migrants to the Petén. In Paso Caballos, many women and older men do not speak Spanish, isolating them from direct communication with the many state and NGO representatives that pass through their village.

Many people in the Petén echo a common stereotype about Q'eqchi' versus Ladino communities. The indigenous villages are said to be more tightly knit and united, but harder to work with due to being closed off to outsiders. Ladino villages, on the other hand, are said to be more divided and individualistic, with each person out for themselves but happy to use outsiders to their advantage when the opportunity arises. The two pageants can be read along the lines of these stereotypes, with Uaxactún's divisions played against Paso Caballos's communal joyfulness. This difference makes work in Ladino villages easier, according to numerous conservation staff, as Ladinos are adept at understanding the benefits they might accrue through external projects and connections. At the same time, internal divisions in Ladino communities threaten to undermine projects designed for common benefit. These differentiations were repeated to me by Guatemalan and (to a lesser extent) foreign NGO workers, by Guatemalan state actors, and by both Q'eqchi' and Ladino villagers. These discourses of who is and is not capable of participating in conservation reinforce traditional power hierarchies and informally exclude people from the benefits of conservation and development projects in the MBR (Sundberg 2003; Rahder 2008).

Mostly these views were expressed without context, as if they were natural facts about Maya or Ladino social organization. But any truth to the stereotypes has grown from a long historical trajectory. Maya people in Guatemala began to form closed, corporate communities in response to the aggressive agrarian dynamics of first colonial (1600–1870) and then liberal modern (1871–1944) Guatemala, a trend that was solidified in the 1920s when large-scale plantation agriculture overtook rural smallholder land and livelihoods (Handy 1990, 1991; Colchester 1993). A retreat into tightly knit social worlds offered indigenous groups small protection from external forces seeking to take their land and exploit their labor, and this isolation was reinforced by state policies that marginalized Maya populations (Smith 1990a, 1990b). Ethnoracial differentiation between Mayas and Ladinos was simultaneously fractured and fortified by the violence and resettlement programs of the civil war, and by neoliberal social organizing in the postwar period (Tomuschat, de Cotí, and Tojo 1999; Hale 2006; Nelson 2009).

These differences in ethnic identity strongly shape conservationist ideas of who belongs on the landscape, divisions that resonated through the pageants.

In Uaxactún, the girls' costumes represented local identity and history, mixing colonial-era folklore, ancient Maya symbolism, and modern agricultural and forest-based livelihood activities. In Paso Caballos, the costumes were strictly relegated to the ecological world, with the exception of a single costume representing local agriculture. The ease with which identity and belonging were expressed in the former, while no thought was given to Q'eqchi' identity, history, or representation in the latter, is indicative of the differences between those who are seen to belong (or not) on the MBR landscape.

Land Tenure and Livelihoods

The range of costumes in Uaxactún and emphasis on wildlife in Paso Caballos reflect more than racialized imaginaries of belonging; they also indicate the communities' different spatial and administrative locations inside the MBR. Uaxactún has a community-run forest concession in the multiple-use zone, land owned by the state but managed by villagers for sustainable harvest of timber and NTFPs and small-scale milpa agriculture in defined areas. The village's twenty-five-year concession contract and proximity to archaeological and tourist sites provide access to a variety of livelihood activities: salaried work in timber harvesting, milling, or administration; jobs in neighboring Tikal National Park; assisting archaeological studies in the dry season; independent NTFP harvesting; and agriculture (figure 5.4).

Paso Caballos, on the other hand, is inside Laguna del Tigre National Park, part of the human-exclusive nuclear zone of the reserve. The Q'eqchi' who settled at Paso Caballos in 1992 arrived after the official declaration of the park in 1990, making them "invaders," although their presence preceded the park's establishment on the ground by several years. As such, the village signed an agreement with CONAP in 1997 that granted them semilegal status, allotting use rights for highly regulated agricultural parcels and a minimal patch of communal forest reserve from which to gather wood, palm thatch, and other resources for household use. Limited by this strict agreement, the village relies almost entirely on milpa for subsistence and some monetary income. Villagers in Paso Caballos do not describe themselves as poor—based on the criterion that their families are not starving—but they lack financial security, diversity of income sources, good local health or education options, secure access to clean water, and many other markers of well-being.[10]

Both communities have extensive histories of state and NGO intervention into their lives and livelihoods, but they are, in many ways, at opposite ex-

FIGURE 5.4 Image from the 2011 *State of the Maya Biosphere Reserve* report, representing livelihood sources in Uaxactún and Paso Caballos. The relative size of the words indicates amount of income generated by each activity, but it is the range of sources in the two villages that is most striking. Xate is a nontimber forest product sold through Uaxactún's concession management organization, OMYC, which also provides rotating jobs for villagers. Other major income sources in Uaxactún include government positions (*gobierno*), private businesses (*comercio*), and seasonal labor for archaeological projects. In Paso Caballos, both *pepitoria* (squash) and *maíz* (corn) are agricultural products, reflecting the lack of alternative income sources in the village (image: CONAP and WCS).

tremes of conservation and development practice in the MBR. While both have seen many institutions and projects come and go over the years, Paso Caballos has had minimal long-term success with any project, initiative, or institution. It is generally perceived to be a threat held in abeyance—neither destructive enough to forcibly remove from the park nor fully integrated into conservation. On the other hand, Uaxactún has seen slow improvements in village education, employment, services, and infrastructure as a result of their involvement with conservation activities (though not all of these stand the test of postproject time, either). As mentioned by the pageant's MC, the village cultivates a self-conscious culture of conservation that permeates local rhetoric, sense of place, and identity. These outlines gloss over internal differences— there are deeply committed conservationists in Paso Caballos, and would-be forest destroyers in Uaxactún—but reflect their different locations in the reserve and the vastly different opportunities and land use rights afforded to them in those spaces.

These rights and limitations intersect with ethnic differences in community openness to shape local experiences of conservation success and failure. For years, beginning with the negotiation of its 1997 agreement, Paso Caballos worked almost exclusively with ProPetén, the Guatemalan NGO offshoot of Conservation International (CI). ProPetén gained independence from CI in 2002, and soon after changed its priorities from integrated conservation and development inside the reserve to social development in southern Petén. Following these shifts, the NGO ceased working in Paso Caballos and sold its neighboring biological research station to Asociación Balam, and WCS and Balam together moved into the village-level vacuum left behind. ProPetén had worked with the village on many projects: a health outpost, education initiatives, ecotourism development, and environmentally sustainable agricultural improvements. None of these have survived to the present day, the reasons for which include but do not end with ProPetén's retreat from the community. At present, WCS is the most regular institutional presence in the village. The NGO maintains a house there and has a dedicated staff person who splits her time between the village and the WCS office in Flores.

WCS has a similar house and staff person in Uaxactún, although the range of NGOs working in the concessioned village is much greater. While Uaxactún, too, can count an impressive number of failed projects and interventions, slow but steady improvements to village life and infrastructure over the years form a strong contrast to Paso Caballos. Access to education has improved significantly with the institution of a *telesecundaria* (remotely taught secondary school), allowing students to study beyond basic literacy while remaining in the village. Technical support from NGOs for sustainable timber and NTFP harvesting has been constant since the concession was granted in 2000, with more recent support for financial and administrative management as well. Shared community and NGO interest in managing and maintaining forest cover in the concession create a clear set of priorities for which the two can work together.

The villages' locations and relative belonging differentiate their sense of security around long-term land rights. People in both communities expressed concern about losing their land, homes, and livelihoods, as state ownership of all MBR land ultimately trumps all other agreements. Uaxactún's twenty-five-year contract is up for renewal in 2025, and many villagers worry that the state might kick them out if they do not manage the forest well or if outsiders manage to invade the land they are designated to protect. NGO workers dismissed this possibility (at least in the short term) due to the community's strong record of sustainable management; many conservation organizations have invested in Uaxactún as a model for community-led concessions, gaining them an international reputation as forest guardians (e.g., Malkin 2015). Though Paso Caballos's agreement with CONAP has no expiration and has held for over twenty years, it exists in legal limbo, leaving residents and conservationists in delicate positions. By law, nobody is allowed to live in national parks, making access to government approval (let alone funding) for education, health, or other initiatives difficult to secure. Ultimately, while Uaxactún has more legal security and institutional support, both villages are subject to the fundamental uncertainties of the future Guatemalan state.

Village-Level Population Enactments

These two villages provide lenses through which to diffract official state counts of population. Diffractive analysis draws attention not just to differences themselves, but to the effects of those differences (Barad 2007). While many of the structural distinctions described above might have been captured in the plurality of the 2001 census, the ways those differences play out in lived experiences of identity, emplacedness, precarity, and well-being are not. More strikingly, the village scale undermines the usefulness of aerial population counts—a rooftop simply does not mean the same thing in each village. As Michelle Murphy argues in her critical history of transnational population management, "better concepts can be found to describe, study, and politicize the problem of human density as it is entangled in the infrastructural and uneven distribution of waste-making and accumulation" (2017, 141). Such alternative concepts emerge in the MBR from grounded practices of counting or describing local places without reference to state-centric criteria. More than simply providing local perspectives on official population numbers, ways of accounting for human dynamics in Uaxactún and Paso Caballos enact different populations altogether.

An Imaginary Census

In Uaxactún, villagers estimate their own population, estimates that are up to 60 percent smaller than aerial counts. According to CEMEC's 2012 report, Uaxactún had between 1,600 and 1,700 people and had grown by fewer than

100 people since aerial counting began in 2006. Residents and NGO staff who work in the community claim a much smaller population, usually under 1,000. They also contend that the population has been shrinking in recent years, in contrast to the slow but steady growth of rooftops. This understanding reflects new educational programs that have resulted in younger community members leaving for the central urban area around Flores.

In conflict with aerial estimations, many households in Uaxactún have two or three rooftops. Cooking and sleeping are commonly separated into two structures, and legal access to forest materials means that even poorer families are able to construct multiple wood-and-thatch buildings. Uaxactún's concession has slowly increased local incomes and financial security, albeit unevenly. Uaxactún also has a higher proportion of nonhousehold buildings than many MBR settlements: school buildings, churches, a sawmill, a carpentry workshop, small ecotourism hotels, OMYC (Management and Conservation Organization of Uaxactún) offices, and a compound of buildings belonging to NGOs and the national archaeological institute, the Guatemalan Institute of Anthropology and History (IDAEH). Although anyone who knows the village can easily identify these rooftops, CEMEC cannot take the time to get to know each monitored village, so all buildings officially count as 5.5 people.[11]

Uaxactún's population was actively debated among NGO staff and representatives of OMYC, the concession's management nonprofit. External counts have come up with numbers ranging from 724 to 1,700, and per-family averages of between 4.79 and 11 people (Zetina Tún 2011). Part of this variation stems from the complex dynamic of people entering and leaving the village. While the community has prevented new immigration, those who leave the village to seek work (for a season or for years) may return at any time, making exact resident counts difficult. Still, Uaxactuneros and NGO staff familiar with the village agreed that CEMEC's aerial estimate was too high, and its reported trend of slow and steady population growth contradicted the locally perceived shrinking of the village.

Claims that Uaxactún is shrinking are based on the effects of the new telesecundaria, which has enabled young adults to leave for the central urban area for further schooling or to find jobs. Interest in birth control and voluntary sterilization for women have also increased, with a semiregularly staffed health outpost and the periodic arrival of women's health projects in the community. Some prominent women in the community proudly talk about their decision to undergo "the operation" to prevent more children, and of their efforts to convince other women to do the same. During one of my visits,

Gloria explained that reproductive education efforts were clearly working, as 2011 was the first year in recent memory when the school had not lost a female student to pregnancy. Families are getting smaller, and more parents express the possibility and desire for their children to grow up with education and opportunities that will move them away from the village and forest livelihoods. By 2017, this trend was so strong that some local leaders worried whether the village and concession had a long-term future at all.

An alternative local enactment of population emerged in 2011 when WCS's representative in Uaxactún, Juan, sat down with a group of men to conduct an imaginary census. They collectively imagined walking door-to-door through the village, counting the people who lived in each house. This method produced an estimate of around 800 people, reinforcing the claim that the population was getting smaller, not larger. This exercise, unimaginable in larger contexts, closely echoed the way that Josue and Marvin interpreted the aerial village photograph I showed them, using their detailed knowledge of residents' comings and goings to fill an image of rooftops with human names and stories. The population enacted was neither a numerical unity, like aerial counts, nor a plurality of identities like that collected by the census. Instead, it was a collective accounting of social ties—what mattered in this version of population was not ethnicity, age, family size, or household economics, but stories. Who lives where, with whom, for how long, to whom they are related, and how many of their children have completed school and gotten jobs elsewhere.

The imaginary census enacted population as belonging. As a part of its concession contract, Uaxactún must prevent immigration of new people into the village. Partly due to its physical location (you must pass through guarded gates at Tikal National Park to reach the village), Uaxactún has been one of the most successful of all reserve communities at fulfilling this responsibility. The imaginary census was as much about measuring and performing this insider/outsider status as it was about collecting a population number. Echoing the pageant MC's exhortations to celebrate the culture of conservation, this count solidified connections between historic Petenero identity, local social ties, and forest protection. The enacted population has a deep social history in the forest and is shrinking due to conservation-infused dreams of education and urban mobility.

As a result, this population enactment does something that neither censused nor photographed population can: it protects the forest, rather than threatening it. The landscape coproduced matches concession boundaries, providing identity and livelihood to the villagers in exchange for their protection. Finally, the state coproduced with this enactment is also different: instead of protecting or managing the environment, this state should enable and support the population in the latter's protection and management roles. This must be done through further education, health, and reproductive health initiatives, and most importantly, through renewal of OMYC's twenty-five-year concession management contract. From the perspective of Uaxactún's imaginary census, the population is already in harmony with the environment, and it is the state that poses a threat to the forest future.

Refusal to Enact

In Paso Caballos, the aerially estimated 2012 population was just over 2,000 people, a number that has almost doubled since its initial measure in 2006. In contrast to Uaxactún, CEMEC's estimate of 5.5 people per rooftop is more likely to be accurate in Paso Caballos. Families commonly have eight or ten children, and relatively lower cash incomes and less legal access to forest building materials mean that many households fit all their sleeping, cooking, and other activities under one roof. Some households do build multiple buildings, but these can be filled by extended families living together in close residence. Here, there are fewer buildings not used for housing: a scattering of overcrowded schoolhouses, churches, and a single communal meeting hall. As a result, CEMEC's aerial population estimates are more likely to be numerically accurate here than in Uaxactún. But measuring and monitoring an indigenous migrant population inside a national park carries different valences than the same count of a concessioned Petenero forest community.

In Paso Caballos, instead of drawing on local social ties and identity to enact an alternative counting method, questions of population are most often met with elision or refusal. Neither villagers nor NGO staff provide alternative population estimates. Instead, inquiries about the number of residents are either ignored or transformed into a discussion about women's reproductive health or the delicate politics of immigration into the village. While women expressed interest in birth control in the abstract, linguistic barriers, poor project design, lack of education or income-gaining opportunities for women, and male objections have prevented most women from taking advantage of reproductive health initiatives that have passed through.[12] It is common for girls in the village to marry and get pregnant at age fifteen or sixteen. While a few villagers who came to know me over the years were happy to discuss their family size and dissatisfaction with reproductive dynamics, many others were resistant. Attempts to discuss population in indigenous villages like Paso Caballos are often met with distrust and fear, due to long histories of state population control, genocide, forced relocations, illegal adoption schemes, and rumors of child robbery.

Population growth is an especially sensitive topic given the strict prohibition against immigration in the village's agreement with CONAP. Many residents consider their relatives to be exceptions to this rule, while CONAP disagrees. Others expressed an empathetic solidarity with newcomers, based on their own experiences of migration and displacement: who am I to turn another indigenous family away? Above all, villagers would insist that the primary driver of population growth was native births, not immigration. This was repeated like a mantra, an insistence—sometimes directly following stories to the contrary—that Paso Caballos was dutifully fulfilling its responsibilities to CONAP. Beyond historically layered fears of population control, anti-indigenous violence, and manipulation by outsiders, the precarious agreement to stay inside a national park heightens local anxiety over population growth.

Rather than alternative numbers, what emerges in on-the-ground encounters with Paso Caballos is a refusal to enumerate population, either as unity, plurality, or anything else. This refusal emerged not only in my attempts to discuss aerial population counts with villagers but also in my observations of state and NGO representatives meeting with the village. In these encounters with outsiders, the question of number is sidestepped, replaced either by generalized complaints about women's reproductive health or by blunt insistence that any observed growth strictly follows CONAP's rules. This antipopulation is coproduced with a threatening state, one that controls access to land (and therefore livelihood), and which is always on the verge of taking away tenuous land rights.

An Anthropologist Enacts

This refusal was not the only enactment of population to emerge out of my visits to Paso Caballos; another grew from my own observations of human settlement dynamics in the village between my first visit in 2007 and my latest in 2012. As birth rates boom and family members continue to immigrate from outside the reserve, residents still do not cross the strictly delimited village boundaries laid out in their CONAP agreement. Fear of losing land rights leads to a village that has grown noticeably denser in recent years, squeezing more people into the allotted space rather than expanding into nearby forest. This densification has led to increasing pressure on the thin, nutrient-poor soils in the village's agricultural area, less vegetation and more visible trash around houses, and severe pollution of the slow-moving headwaters of the San Pedro River along which the village is built. As reported to me by Rosa, WCS's Ladina technician in Paso Caballos, a 2011 study found one thousand times the safe level of fecal coliform in the river water, which residents use for washing, bathing, and fishing. An oily scum coats the water, and river edges teem with plastic detritus.

This local pollution is exacerbated by lack of health and education infrastructure. The children in the village greatly outnumber the space or teaching staff allotted to the local school—and many children, especially girls, simply do not attend. Sometimes teachers don't show up. Books and supplies are hard to find. In 2011, protesting a decision to institute an agricultural extension school rather than a telesecundaria, large numbers of parents pulled their kids out of school altogether. High rates of serious illness among infants and children were disturbingly visible (adult illness was probably just as prevalent but less visible). On most of my visits to the village, I would by happenstance encounter mothers carrying infants obviously suffering severe malnutrition, illness, or dehydration. Though I did not systematically focus my attention on these issues, their presence was unignorable. Poor sanitation, poor access to clean water, lack of medical care in the village, and a high cost of travel into the central urban area to reach language-inaccessible medical services combine to concentrate serious health issues in the village.[13]

In this enactment, emerging from my encounters with local ways of living with the constraints of a feared state, population is not a number but a dynamic response to historical and present conditions. This population grows, yes, but it grows differently than in standardized MBR narratives: in density rather than by expanding into nearby forest. This growing population does pose environmental problems—those of river health, local sanitation, pollution, soil exhaustion, and environmental health issues. But these are not the problems CONAP or conservationist NGOs are prepared to handle. Prioritization of forest cover as the singular marker of ecological health means that the state is largely unable to recognize these population-environment dynamics. The state coproduced by my enactment is a neglectful and dangerous one—unresponsive to harms inflicted on both human and nonhuman worlds, and threatening to the possibility of ongoing life in the village over the long term.

Decentralized Decisions

The driving question for understanding population-environment dynamics in the MBR has now shifted. The issue is no longer how many people are there, and with what impacts on the forest? But rather, what happens when different population enactments clash? Which versions of population are taken as authoritative, by whom, when, and with what effects? In most contexts, the census is no longer used for understanding human dynamics, as it is over fifteen years out of date (CONAP has been planning another census since early 2012, but this has not yet materialized). Despite CEMEC's pride in the work, the complex plurality enacted by the census does not have the same charismatic pull as annual aerial estimates, which entice with the promise of up-to-date, dynamic information. Aerial population estimates are now used in almost all institutional contexts, from the National Palace to village-level interventions.

In spaces like the National Palace, the aerial enactment of a unified population threat is a persuasive political tool. By coproducing a protectionist territorial state, a coherent reserve scale, and a measurable population object that neatly fits within it, aerial monitoring garners support for protected area funding and conservation initiatives from national governments and international donors. The narrative of population as a threat to the forest is straightforward, digestible, and easily transported, the ultimate in applicable objective information so desired in science-policy contexts. Despite many problems with this framing, it is one of the most familiar and convincing environmental narratives around. In the presidential palace, telling a complex story about ethnic identity, poverty, and failed health projects in a migrant community inside a national park would not lead to greater budgetary allotments for protected areas—and I take funding for environmental protection as generally a good thing. But a problem emerges in the common assumption that this information must be "scalable" (Tsing 2015)—that the knowledge best suited to policy contexts will also work in local practice.[14]

Debates about the science-policy interface often elide this scalar difference with practice, focusing on the former as though it straightforwardly leads to the latter. But as Mosse (2005) and other development scholars have shown, the translation between the two is rarely smooth. Knowledge-making practices designed to respond to policy needs, like aerial population monitoring, can produce "official ignorance" (Mathews 2011) about on-the-ground concerns. But once they reach the villages, workers from state and NGO institutions are confronted with alternative populations. It is left up to these field practitioners—technicians near the bottom of institutional hierarchies—to work out an appropriate response according to their own political beliefs, social ties, and understandings of the evidence. The patchiness of knowledge forms and population enactments across the MBR nooscape is amplified by this patchiness in decision making, leading to wildly uneven effects on different human settlements in the reserve.

In WCS's projects in Uaxactún and Paso Caballos, the responsibility for determining which enactment of population will prevail in local projects falls upon the field staff, Juan and Rosa. In Uaxactún, Juan, a WCS technician and Ladino Petenero man, was explicitly concerned with the question of population, discussing estimates with staff from his and other institutions, village leaders, and me for several months after CEMEC's 2011 report was released. These discussions eventually led to the imaginary census. After this alternate count, Juan struggled over conflicting accounts of population growth or loss, ultimately deciding to accept the local account: a population of around 800 people, either stable or shrinking. Building on his strong social connections to village residents and seven years of working in the community, Juan began including the local estimate in his reports and work plans. He used the imagined number, rather than official state estimates, to decide what kinds of support the community most needed from WCS. This choice met with no resistance; Uaxactún is not generally understood to pose a threat to its concessioned forest, so concerns over local population growth are not especially powerful. What did concern Juan was understanding how and why the village was shrinking, and how that might affect his work and planning. If, for example, young people were leaving for further education, were they likely to return to the village with new skills and expectations? If they were leaving to work, were they sending money back to their families? With what effects? Were they planning on returning? These questions arose directly from local population estimates and understandings, framed by Juan's strong friendships and personal experience in the community.

In Paso Caballos, Rosa was caught between differing enactments of a growing population. Instead of settling into a usable alternative number, questions of population in the Q'eqchi' village have caused conflict and disagreement between community members and state and NGO representatives. When pressed to discuss population, villagers insist that the growth does not include new outsiders in violation of the rules of their agreement with CONAP. They report that any growth is due to high birth rates and to close family members who move to join them—the latter a definition of insider/outsider that differs from state understandings. In meetings with institutions, villagers repeatedly emphasize the need for better schools, economic opportunities, local health services, and access to clean water, while CONAP continues to insist on the priority of intensifying boundary maintenance around the community's territorial limits and on agricultural fire management—priorities determined by an understanding of human population growth as a threat to the surrounding forest.

While Rosa did not explicitly engage questions of accuracy or alternative population counts as Juan did in Uaxactún, she was caught between the priorities framed by official and local enactments. Her job required close coordination with both state and village actors, as well as a commitment to the conservationist mission of WCS. The incommensurability between these enactments of population manifested in a deep sense of uncertainty and anxious changes of plans in her strategies and decision making. Rosa felt a serious responsibility toward villagers and their needs, with whom she had lived and worked for years, but also to the conservationist goals of CONAP and WCS, which pushed back against villager demands. In Paso Caballos, decentralizing responsibility for making sense of competing population enactments led to more conflict and distrust, as Rosa was blamed for changing her story and the ultimate failure of many interventions.

Conflicts over who belonged in the village were particularly problematic for Rosa's work. Both Uaxactún and Paso Caballos have formal, written *acuerdos de conservación* (conservation agreements) with WCS, a CI-led program providing two years of renewable structured funding for local conservation and development activities in exchange for observation of new rules, norms, and participation requirements by villagers.[15] The acuerdo in Paso Caballos included funding for temporary employment of villagers during the fire season, with hires to be selected by the village COCODE and approved by full community assembly and by Rosa. In early 2012, a newly elected COCODE selected two men who were not signatories to the original CONAP agreement. Rosa, as representative of an NGO committed to upholding this original CONAP document as part of its secondary signed agreement with the village, refused to hire the men, causing resentment among the COCODE and delaying work on clearing a fire break. She was forced to publicly contradict the council's choice, even as she argued that her job was to support their decision-making processes. And, as she complained repeatedly, if the delay resulted in a fire passing into surrounding parkland, she would take the blame for failing to work out the problems—not the villagers, not CONAP, not WCS, but her. As field technician, Rosa became responsible for enforcing the question of local belonging, and for the complex consequences of that belonging for the surrounding forest.

The Politics of Patchiness

The decentralization of decision making in village-level conservation and development projects is a double-edged sword. People working in reserve communities come to know the particular local dynamics of the places they work. This can be an incredible boon when they are faced with different enactments, as in Juan's preference for local population estimates in Uaxactún. But it also becomes their individual responsibility to negotiate between conflicting enactments and possibilities, leaving others, like Rosa, in the middle of intense hostility. Overall, this dynamic creates a patchy landscape of decision-making processes that reflect individual practitioners' political preferences, evaluations of evidence, and social ties. The ability to settle upon a single version of population works differently in different places, diffracted by the many structural forms of inequality shaping the encounters through which multiple enactments emerge. In Uaxactún, the relative stability, privileged Petenero identity, and contracted forest concession allow a degree of flexibility within which villagers, NGOs, and state representatives can engage different population enactments with little to no conflict. In Paso Caballos, however, the looming threat of migration into Laguna del Tigre National Park, troubling discourses about indigeneity and population growth, and conflicts over definitions of family and belonging lead to blunt demonstrations of power that overrule local perspectives in favor of state-dominated technical enactments.

The asymmetry between enactments resulting from differently situated practices and epistemologies can deny lived realities, with haunting effects. The triumph of remotely monitored population over local enactments in Paso Caballos may be considered a form of epistemic violence (Spivak 1988)—a cruel suppression of other knowledges and worlds. The image of proliferating rooftops in Paso Caballos is used to illustrate a generic population threat to the reserve's forests, as in the formal presentation to then-president Álvaro Colom. But people in the village, afraid of losing precarious land rights, have densified without infrastructural support rather than expanding into neighboring parkland, resulting in major environmental, health, and social problems that are rendered invisible through this hegemonic lens. The denial of this reality impacts not only villagers, whose lives are dominated by the priorities of protected-area law, but also those who end up caught between competing worlds, like Rosa. Understanding this as a conflict between different populations, rather than different perspectives on a single population, displaces the possibility of turning to rational objectivity as a means of determining action. Seeking a singular understanding of population and growth dynamics in Paso Caballos will not offer a way out of this conflict.

Using marginalized Paso Caballos as the photographic emblem of a population problem in PowerPoint presentations, while Uaxactún is congratulated for its good conservation practices, ignores the incredible social, historical, and economic differences between the two communities, further deepening the gulf between them. The presentation in the National Palace also celebrated and reinforced the militarization of conservation, which is particularly thick in Laguna del Tigre National Park. It is unsurprising that aerial photography has become the standard method inside CONAP to estimate the MBR's population. It is cheaper, quicker, and easier to fly over many villages in a few days than to conduct surveys on the ground, despite the loss of detail that can be gained from a traditional census. Once you factor in notoriously poor national census procedures, reluctance to volunteer information to CONAP, and the charisma of objective photographic methodologies that appear to stand above the fray of the reserve's problems, it becomes difficult to imagine alternatives. Yet other possible populations—with different relations to the environment, and different coproduced states—continue to be enacted in patches of the MBR nooscape. Some are tamed into institutional knowledges, like Juan's enfolding of the imaginary census into official documents and plans. Others, like Paso Caballos's refusal, haunt institutional decisions, policies, and practices, never fully banished by official population counts. These spectral enactments can erupt as unacknowledged determinants of failure in conservation and development projects. The effects and confusions of clashing epistemologies, identities, and power relations in the Q'eqchi' migrant village are the subject of chapter 6, where patchiness disintegrates into fragmentation.

PARKS, POVERTY, PEOPLE

Globalized knowledges about how best to preserve natural areas and ecosystems swing on a pendulum. Strict protectionism and declaration of parks reigned through the mid-twentieth century, inspired and exported from U.S.-based visions of wilderness cleansed of their own genocidal histories (Cronon 1996; Spence 1999; Burnham 2000). Parks were all about human-free Nature left to its own (highly managed) devices. But as decolonized and post-colonial places pushed back against these imaginaries in the late twentieth century, new attempts to integrate poverty reduction strategies grew into the global conservation imaginary (Adams et al. 2004; Adams and Hutton 2007). The UN millennium development goals made sustainable development the new buzzword for poverty reduction, slotting environmentalism in alongside structural adjustments and neoliberal development theories to imagine a brighter future composed of sustainable natural resources and smart managerial resource users. The MBR's community-based forest concessions, including those granted to Petenero communities Uaxactún and Carmelita, reflected this swing. The poor were transformed from population threat to wild areas into communities in need of education leading to better environmental practices.

But these schemes failed to transform the worlds of heterogeneous cultures, ideas, landscapes, livelihoods, and politics into their singular transferrable model of a rationalized *Homo economicus* (Zerner 1994; Sivaramakrishnan 2000; Agrawal 2005; Pacheco et al. 2008). So a movement back toward strict protectionism has begun (Brechin et al. 2002; Bray and Anderson 2005; Brosius and Russell 2003). Now overlaid with post-9/11 security discourses and new metrics of environmental economization, the pendulum is swinging further into a militarized defense of Nature (Duffy 2016; Lunstrum 2015). The poor are now a threat not just to Nature but also to the environmental security of nations. This violent imaginary is spreading its way around the world, including into large patches of the MBR nooscape.

Who are these "poor"? Who counts as worthy of development schemes, of empathy, of assistance? Against whom do forests need to be defended? Asociación Balam and WCS attempted to measure local understandings of poverty through a Basic Necessities methodology (see chapter 7, box 7.1), but even this methodology requires a standardization of local meanings across the highly varied lived worlds of the reserve. Debates over who is really poor circulate among MBR conservationists. Juan Castellanos, who lives part-time in Uaxactún on behalf of WCS, claimed that villagers there were not poor because they had "motorcycles, TVs, resources, and opportunities." Yet he worked hard to support them in garnering even more resources and opportunities. People in Paso Caballos would often claim that they themselves were not poor, because they had land. This of course meant precarious usufruct rights, not ownership, but this access was enough to leave the category of the poor. Still, these claims could then be taken up and twisted by institutional staff, who sometimes used them to argue that Paso Caballos did not need support or resources—they had been given land inside a national park; why should they get anything else?

Others would attempt to untangle poverty from Petenero culture, associated with pride in rough-hewn forest lifestyles. Iván, who worked for FARES, and Julián, who worked for Asociación Balam, repeatedly debated whether people in the reserve village of Carmelita were poor. Iván claimed that people there lived in "terrible, devastating poverty"; this was the root of what he saw as their destructive relationship with the forest, which they were killing by cutting down all the trees. Julián countered by defending community-based forest management, including selective timber harvests, distinguishing Carmelita's activities from clear-cuts. He also said that it wasn't really poverty in the village: "It's cultural. The thing is, even if they had more money, they wouldn't change the way they live. It's because it's part of the culture. They're an old

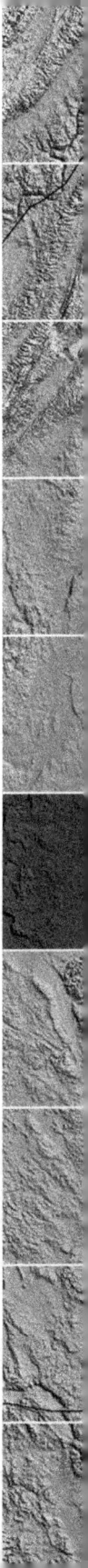

chiclero [chicle harvester] community, so they've always lived off the forest like that, with those conditions of life. And they don't want to change." Jorge, a CEMEC technician, later denied this common narrative about Petenero culture, claiming it was "a myth. . . . I never believe that there are people who voluntarily would have chosen the forest [*monte*] if you had [also offered them] a ton of asphalt and a ton of communication. I don't believe that it was voluntary."

Conservationist understandings of poverty—who is poor, what effects poverty has on people's relationships to landscape or conservation—affect how knowledges move in the nooscape. In WCS, this emerges in debates over the benefits and limits of transparency. Some consider open information sharing with local communities a sign of good faith, important to participatory conservation projects. One project proposed that WCS would share scarlet macaw nest GPS coordinates with local COCODEs as part of community engagement. But a technician, Carlos, expressed doubts: "We have these wishful projects, of open love, transparency . . . and then you get screwed. It takes one bad person in a community of two thousand. That's all it takes! They hear the information, and think, that's five thousand Quetzales! They just told me where I can get five thousand Quetzales! . . . There are limits to transparency." This limit only works in one direction: WCS expects that all local knowledge of macaw nests will be shared openly with their staff. The poor can help conservation; whether or not conservation can help the poor remains an open question.

SIX

Fire at the Edge of the Forest

Fire is many things. Less object or noun than verb, process, or transformation, fire never sits still. In the Petén, it is almost always started by humans, but is never fully under human control. This chapter traces the fragmentation of the nooscape around fire in Paso Caballos, presenting five enactments of fire: (1) a pixelated satellite image of infrared heat, (2) a threat to forests, (3) a tactic of genocidal terror, (4) an expression of discontent of MBR residents, and (5) an agricultural tool. These multiple fires do not separate out neatly from the others; they do not add up to something new, or translate into one another; their distribution across time and space always burns around the edges.[1] The multiple enactments of fire in and around Paso Caballos always coexist in haunted relation, with fragmentation of fire-related knowledges and practices—more and more patches, with greater and greater difference between them—breaking down the ability to create even temporary senses of singularity, closure, or agreement.

This inability is the result of the amplified edge effects of a fragmented nooscape. Paso Caballos sits amid a multiplicity of edges, both epistemic and material. Multiple enactments of fire rub up against each other, resulting in a proliferation of contradictory patterns and processes. At the same time, the forest and wetland ecosystems of surrounding Laguna del Tigre National Park are also increasingly fragmented by settlements, cattle ranches, drug trafficking, oil extraction, and other human activities. This material fragmentation is a process most often led by fire, raising the stakes of knowing and intervening in its unruly effects. As edge effects intensify between patches of knowing and doing, the ability to work together across fields of difference can break down. This breakdown is often identified by conservationists as failure, though meanings of this word too shift and bend through a fragmented lens.

This chapter is fragmented, structured to mirror material and epistemic fragmentation and its effects. I present five enactments of fire interspersed unevenly with six edge effects, all of which share partial connection but do not quite resolve into a whole. Within each fragment there is more patchiness, unevenness of ways of knowing and intervening in fire. The patches work on different spatial and temporal scales, and the relations between them are multiple—some made explicit and others left smoldering, not yet cooled into the ashes of interpretation. The effect should be somewhat disorienting, built to create some lingering uncertainty about how certain patches connect—or don't. You may be left with burning questions. The larger picture, rather than resolving into a singular frame, should create an emergent sense of what no-oscape fragmentation is and does, a haunting sense that your own interpretation of each story, segment, or relation between them might yet be otherwise.

Fire 1: A Pattern of Pixels

FEBRUARY–MAY, 2011: It is the dry season, the Guatemalan summer. Daily temperatures hover around 35°C (95°F), shooting into the 40s (115°F) every week or two. Less than one inch of rain falls across all four months. It is fire season, the hottest time of the year. Yet the CEMEC lab is at its coldest, the aggressive air conditioning explained as technical necessity: with the heat of the machines, the already extreme temperature would become truly unbearable. A temperature gradient traces the office hierarchy. The large air conditioning unit is mounted such that Director Victor Hugo Ramos, along with David and Luis—the technicians who have worked for CEMEC the longest—sit comfortably in diffuse cool air, while at the far end of the room the newest technicians and I stash jackets, blankets, hats, and gloves in our desks to keep out the chill. Like its Skype-mediated silence, this cold marks CEMEC as a space of difference. Moving between the office and the un–air conditioned hallway to the rest of CONAP is a painful shock.

In cold CEMEC, fire is no hotter than any other digital image. Fire is a pattern of pixels, something detected by foreign-owned satellites, downloaded as raw data, electronically decoded, mapped, and distributed via email and website to interested parties. When the computer lab was founded in 1996, they didn't have air conditioning yet and smoked in the office. With a staff of three sharing a single computer, CEMEC's first task was to digitize area and topographical maps of the region, tediously tracing territory into new computerized form. In 1998, the fledgling institution met its first real challenge: an El Niño year, with forest fires raging across the MBR. The lab stepped up and played a major role in the firefights, downloading and analyzing publicly available satellite data from the National Oceanic and Atmospheric Administration (NOAA) website every day. Those old NOAA sensors, David told me, were poorly calibrated. They would show fires in the middle of Lake Petén Itza; each image had to be carefully checked and corrected before they made any sense.

These days, daily reporting of satellite-detected fires is a streamlined process. MODIS satellites, a NASA system for global fire monitoring, pass over the Petén twice a day, in the morning and afternoon. The images produced are available for free at 1 kilometer-pixel resolution; each pixel in which fire is detected is called a "hot spot" (*punto de calor*).[2] The system's second pass captures most daily fires, with data appearing online around 4:30 p.m. This leaves just enough time to download raw hot spot data, create a map of detected fires, and send it out to the fire season email list—hundreds of individuals and institutions—before the end of the office day at 5 p.m. One technician, who was in charge of these daily reports for the entirety of the fire season, described the process to me: "It's not difficult. . . . I have to download the data from the webpage. . . . I download them, export them, put them into the map, and that's it. The map is already made; it's a basic map. You just have to change the date, a few little details, and that's it." Fire as pixel is mundane, easy.

The daily reports include the total number of hot spots detected across the Petén, and a map showing their locations (figure 6.1). On some days, the reports indicate how many hot spots were located inside protected areas, and occasionally include additional maps of specific areas, most often Laguna del Tigre or Sierra del Lacandón National Parks. Sometimes, the reports don't match up with what people find on the ground. Marco Gonzalez, director of the forest fire department of CONAP-Petén, introduced himself to me with the English nickname "Hotman." He noted that fires were sometimes more or less severe than indicated by the reports, happened in places that didn't get picked up by satellites, or were reported in places where his team could later find no evidence of burning. Still, he insisted, the reports were an invaluable tool, making his work of directing CONAP's fire response teams enormously easier.

Once a week, a more detailed fire report is distributed to CEMEC's email list and posted on CONAP's website. These reports fill out the staccato daily alerts with a fuller comparative picture, composed of maps, graphs, photographs,

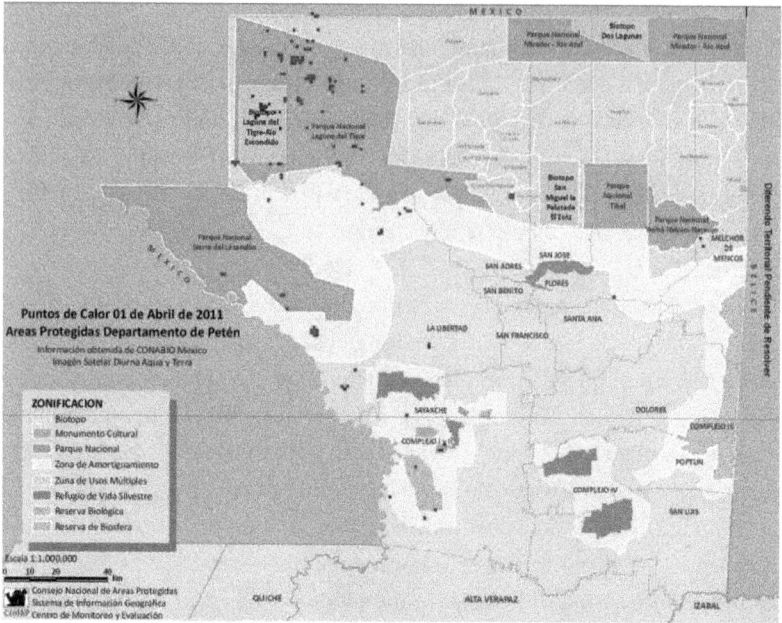

FIGURE 6.1 CEMEC's daily fire monitoring map from April 1, 2011. On this date, seventy hot spots were detected in the Department of Petén. Protected areas in southern Petén are included along with the MBR. A small cluster of spots is visible in the agricultural zone of Paso Caballos, in the easternmost reaches of Laguna del Tigre National Park (image: CONAP and WCS).

interpretive text, and descriptions or images of notable fire events. They cover reported hot spots, cumulative and predicted temperature and precipitation data, drought indices and phenological conditions related to fire risk, and other data, placing all in comparison with the previous ten years of data on similar measures. Good years and bad are called up in the memorializing of the graphs. Occasionally other items are added to these reports: photographs of smoke, detailed reports on particular fires, images from monitoring flights of fires in progress or burned areas, and so on. Each weekly report concludes with a color-coded fire risk alert level for the upcoming week.

CEMEC's staff viscerally live with fire as pixels. They told me that 2011 was a "really good year": more rain than usual, fewer fires, and very few that passed from agricultural parcels into pristine forest. This assessment was made in the computer lab by connecting stories from friends, colleagues, and relatives working field crews with their own daily labor preparing and reading maps and graphs. One day in late April, as a technician was getting ready to send out the daily report, he commented on how few hot spots appeared. Others in the office gathered around his screen as he started opening files, maps, and images from previous years. The technicians began collectively pooling memories of what bad fire years felt like, outside the office:

> We could tell this year wasn't so bad. It wasn't even that hot outside, compared to some years.

> Some years, we would just be dripping with sweat!

> And the smoke. Sometimes the smoke is so thick, even here in the central urban area, that you can barely breathe.

> You can see little pieces of ash floating down like rain from the sky—that's how bad the fires get.

As they reminisced about the worst fire years, they sought out satellite images from those years to illustrate and verify their bodily memories: 2003, 2005, 2006, 2007. David piped up, inviting me into the memories. "I already showed Micha the one where the smoke reached all the way to Miami! But show her 2005," he directed.

David had previously given me a tour of his computer's archives, digging through years of image files that he had saved, including from their very first year of fire monitoring in 1998. This was the NOAA satellite image of smoke clouds blooming up from Central America and crossing the Gulf of Mexico toward Florida. David had saved everything that he had ever worked on. Every map, every satellite image. He showed me the receipt for the first computer CEMEC ever bought. "It's history," he told me. "It's good to save them." He reminisced about the day that he downloaded the 1998 image: "I still remember that day. The dark cloud came up suddenly, and the heat. I went running for the bus. It was 4, 5 p.m., late by then. And the next day I saw the image. They were good images—this one was the best there was. But the hot spots were no good. . . . They showed up here, see? [Opening a map file with a hot spot in the lake.] And why? The lake, was it burning or what? The sensors weren't well calibrated. That problem doesn't happen anymore." He clicked through more images, continuing to reminisce about extremities of fire, wind, and rain: "In '98, after the forest fires from El Niño, there was a hurricane here. Here [in the Petén] it didn't rain much. But I would sit here in the office until 5 every day, looking, watching this [NOAA] site. There was a little wind, but not that much.

But here, I was on this website." The sensors have changed over time, but the experience of fire, climate, and landscape as digital images has not.

Fire 2: An End to Forests

"Wake up and burn nature, that's what I like to do," a conservationist declared bitterly as we flew over a smoldering patch of land. Conservationist fears of an end to the reserve's forests materialize as fire, licking its way, year after year, across the landscape. One of the worst years on record was 2017, especially in Laguna del Tigre, where over 54,750 acres of forest were burned. But this threat is not unified, and the effects of fire are uneven. A patch of forest will be more or less affected by fire depending on whether or not it has burned before, and how long it has had to recover. The swampy bamboo groves in northern Laguna del Tigre might burn ten times, year after year, and still bounce back, barely affected. But just one fire on the steep thin-soiled slopes of the Sierra del Lacandón hills can devastate the land for years to come.

Most MBR fires are set by human hands. There are tiny trash fires in village yards, cooking fires, campfires, and many other small, contained conflagrations. In communities with established relations with CONAP, agricultural fires are strictly regulated and controlled with firebreaks, restrictions on time of day and climatic conditions, and other management practices. Regulated communities are expected to control their own fires, calling on NGOs for resources and technical support, and on state institutions only in the event of a fire getting out of hand and crossing into protected forest. Other fires are set without these measures, sometimes just to avoid the extra labor of control, other times deliberately for maximum damage and spread. When these are detected, by satellite or field crew, they set CONAP's firefighting department in motion.

The fire department only has funding for two regular staff plus Director Hotman Gonzalez. With occasional external funding this number is sometimes raised to ten or fifteen, still paltry in comparison to how many bodies are needed to fight fires in the field. In 2017, hundreds of CONAP and NGO field staff and seasonal firefighters were mobilized with very few resources. President Jimmy Morales declared a state of emergency in the Petén to funnel additional support to the firefighters, including not just the usual SIP-ECIF (National System for Prevention and Control of Forest Fires), but also CONRED (National Coordinator for Disaster Reduction), the Ministry of the

Environment, DIPRONA police forces, and the army. Mexican and Honduran agencies lent helicopters, bodies, and other resources. The firefighters slept in overcrowded camps with little to eat, minimal time to rest and recover between long hard days of labor, and little in the way of firefighting equipment.

Funding for equipment always lags behind need, so old and out-of-date tools are used long past their regulated lifetimes. Even when equipment is available, many on the front lines refuse to wear it, claiming it is too heavy, too hot, or too hard to move in. Getting men to wear helmets was among Gonzalez's biggest frustrations. He explained that unlike visiting gringos, who extolled the virtues of helmets, the men here are too cocky, fearless (*bravo*). Firefighters in the Petén rarely frame their work as a brave defense of nature or noble sacrifice. Machismo and bravado enter the tales, but as a demonstration of personal trial, survival, and ability, not a selfless sacrifice in the name of the forest. Fires are a threat to the forest among conservationists, but a trial of the masculine body among firefighters.

Edge Effect 1: The Threat from the West

When fire as cold pixel meets fire as end to forests, they produce a threat from the west. Hot spot maps begin to look like a single slow-moving fire, spreading steadily over the years outward from settlements and oil or logging roads. Cumulative images collapse many fires into a single destructive force: agricultural field or cattle ranch, lit by drug runner or poor peasant, legal or illegal, practical or vicious—all become part of a unified fire threat, smoldering its way from the western parks toward the heart of forest cover in the reserve (see figure 4.3 and plate 7). Fire data were chosen for CEMEC's 2011 test run of a new Flash-animated mapping program designed for website presentation. MODIS hot spot data from 2001–10 was encoded into a dynamic map of the MBR with a sliding time scale, allowing comparison of fire intensity across the spaces and years of the reserve. This new way of viewing old data opened up discoveries in the computer lab, further solidifying the image of fire as a threat from the west. CEMEC staff had previously assumed that the buffer zone, an essentially unregulated agricultural and ranching landscape along the southern edge of the reserve, would consistently show the highest fire rates. But the yearly slider demonstrated that in 2005, and in every year from 2007 to 2010, fires were in fact more common in Laguna del Tigre.

Laguna del Tigre is the largest national park in Guatemala, its nearly 3,000 square kilometers covering an expanse close to that of Yosemite National Park in the U.S. Created with the MBR in 1990, CONAP had no physical presence within park boundaries until 1996 (Parks Watch 2003). CONAP documents begin their historical review of the park in the year 2000, leaving the first decade of the park's existence unaccounted for (e.g., CONAP 2006). That absent beginning was the beginning of the park's end: deforestation rates in Laguna del Tigre more than doubled between the periods 1986–90 and 1993–95 (Sader et al. 2001). Without institutional presence, waves of migration into the park increased after it was declared rather than slowing down. The park is now widely known as the wild west.[3] This characterization shows up everywhere from casual conversation (inserted in English into Spanish conversations) to refereed publications (e.g., Gould 2006). A North American working on a project with a Guatemalan NGO told me, "It really is the wild, wild west. Land speculation, illegal logging, looting, all this stuff just flowing up into Mexico, people getting shot all the time. And I mean, imagine the kind of people who are drawn to that situation. Pure greed, that's the only thing. I don't know. . . . I don't care if you're some poor campesino, there's no reason to be there except self-enrichment. It's just completely out of control." The poor, often indigenous peasants who formed part of the agricultural frontier mix in Laguna del Tigre with wealthy cattle ranchers (especially drawn to this park due to available water), oil companies, drug traffickers, (rumored) politicians with illegal land holdings, illegal loggers, and archaeological looters.[4]

What to do about this confusion of human action inside Laguna del Tigre? This question was the subject of a 2006 CONAP technical study, which suggested a range of possible interventions for settlements inside the park, from military eviction to assisted relocation to written agreements for remaining in place, similar to those already held by Paso Caballos and a few other communities. Settlements were sorted into action categories based on a combination of geographic, ecological, administrative, and demographic factors, as well as vague qualities like "conflictivity" (*conflictividad*) or "willingness" (*voluntad*) to cooperate with CONAP. In 2011, at a meeting designated for NGO comment on the document and its recommendations, the technical study was inseparable from rumors that traveled with it. The assembled group worked through double visions of each village one by one, combining the document's data with chisme: How many people live there? Are they bordering particularly vulnerable ecosystems? What stories circulate about their political or criminal connections?

One community located near the center of the park, Río Hermoso, was isolated as a special case. The settlement was said to have influence over other villages and to be protected against eviction (through political connections and armed residents), and showed little interest in negotiating with park authorities. One of the study's authors spoke up against the perceived difficulty of evicting the community: "What does it mean if we let them stay, and everybody there is narcos?" An NGO representative replied in support of dangerous compromise: "We know the landscape [el campo], we know the reality of these areas. The case of, for example, Río Hermoso, which is a big community. But in the end, if they stay, they will be able to help get others to leave. And if we can keep them in a polygon where they don't move? Good! I think the proposal should be something like that. I know it's complicated to make it legal. I'm probably forgetting a lot of things, lawyers and all that . . . but that would be the best for the protected areas." As of this writing, no formal action has occurred in this community, although others—like Laguna Larga, also discussed in this meeting as high in conflictividad and connection—have since been evicted by the military.

Some of the paralysis grows from uncertainty over whether land agreements based on compromise would ever work in larger, Ladino settlements. These would equalize landholdings by parceling out standard tracts of land to each household, as in Paso Caballos. How would CONAP deal with the inevitable conflicts and violence that would erupt within each community as a result? "They will kill each other among themselves," one man said. Despite the inability to agree on strategy—let alone begin to implement one—the complexity of human dynamics in Laguna del Tigre was taken seriously. The difference between narcos and poor campesinos was acknowledged, if not fully knowable. A multiplicity of responses emerged in theory, if not yet in practice. But as hour after hour of the meeting wore on, the insurmountability of the challenges grew, and the conversation devolved into cynical jokes about buying up land in the park before the next government undeclared it altogether.

The threat from the west is drawn as an edge in both space and time—how long can any park exist under such conditions? How long until the whole reserve has failed? Reaching its limits along the borders with Mexico, conservationists fear that this frontier dynamic of violent ecological conversion led always by fire will turn toward the east. It will move out of Laguna del Tigre into the multiple-use zone and its better-maintained forest cover. While the multiple-use zone still holds a promise of success for many conservationists, Laguna del Tigre is often considered lost to conservation, a park in name only. Its frontier made of fire is read as failure, one advancing aggressively across the landscape. This threat drives the strategy known as "the shield" (*el escudo*). A line has been drawn, and it is crawled by increased patrols and fire brigades. The shield materializes the edge between areas imagined to be under control and those that have spiraled out of hand. Paso Caballos sits in line with this shield, marking its ambiguity: is the village part of the shield, or part of the threat? (plate 5). One of Asociación Balam's staff, on a boat ride between Paso Caballos and the NGO's neighboring Scarlet Macaw Biological Research Station, insisted that we stop the motor so that I could capture a photo of the clear physical limit between the village and the station's territory. "The agricultural frontier," he named my photograph, despite the fact that this particular frontier had not moved or changed since 1997 (figure 6.2).

Fire 3: Scorched Earth

When the military is mobilized to evict settlements from Laguna del Tigre, as in Laguna Larga in 2017, fire is among their tools. People are less likely to come back if their houses are burned down, so these flames bolster conservationist imaginaries of control rather than reducing them to ashes. These fires also reignite the smoldering historical memory of scorched-earth campaigns during the civil war. Fire was widely used by the state as an anti-insurgency weapon, alongside torture, rape, massacre, kidnappings, disappearances, and other horrific forms of violence. Fire extended the military's genocidal brutality from (primarily indigenous) people to their crops, animals, and homes. By the end of the war, 626 rural massacres had been carried out and over four hundred villages burned to the ground (Tomuschat, de Cotí, and Tojo 1999). Counterinsurgency campaigns operated at the scale of landscapes rather than individuals, indiscriminately destroying entangled human and nonhuman lives: "The state, with its warlike tactics undermined by such a moving target, attacks not the guerrillas but the population and the terrain. Massacres, scorched earth, displacement, defoliants, and resettlement are ways to control, monitor, reorganize, and redeploy insurgent networks and forces. If, as Mao Tse-Tung said, guerrillas move among the population like fish in water, Guatemalan counterinsurgency strategy, especially from 1978 to 1983, was to remove the water from the fish, to transform the milieu" (Nelson 2009, 220). The Guatemalan army used this same metaphor to justify its actions at the

FIGURE 6.2 "The agricultural frontier," as titled by a field staff member of Asociación Balam. The image shows the edge between Paso Caballos's agricultural polygon and forest managed by Balam's Scarlet Macaw Biological Research Station. At this edge, the frontier has not moved in twenty years (photograph by author).

time, aiming to "drain the sea" of civilian support for the guerrilla movement (Jonas 2012).

Villages in the Petén were subject to some of the most extreme violence, including burning, in the country—housing, humans, fields, forests, livestock, all went up in smoke (Tomuschat, de Cotí, and Tojo 1999; Egan 1999; Ybarra 2012). The region was targeted because its thick jungles were welcoming waters for revolutionary fish, providing hiding places for leftist rebels. The unruly agricultural frontier confused categories of people, place, and politics, confusions that the scorched-earth campaign aimed to violently clarify: "the jungle as a guerrilla refuge deepened the military's perceived need for army control of the jungle and a territorial strategy to separate nature from civilization/agriculture" (Ybarra 2012, 489). Rather than settling and securing the landscape, however, this tactic resulted in an intensification of the already temporary and moveable nature of settlements in the Petén. Entire villages would empty of people if the military was known to be approaching, including the former inhabitants of Paso Caballos (Egan 1999).

The current Paso Caballos formed in the ruins of a former Petenero settlement that was abandoned during the war. Vincent, a Ladino Petenero NGO worker, told me of the time he first came to Paso Caballos—over forty years ago, when the world of conservation hadn't yet reached the Petén. Back then, Paso Caballos was a Ladino town, a petroleum and forest resource extraction center with an airstrip used to shuttle people and supplies. The town was "much better then," Vincent told me, with infrastructure for power and water paid for by the oil industry that the village's current incarnation doesn't dream of. It is unclear whether the town was harboring guerrillas, leftist sympathizers, or was simply in the wrong place at the wrong time, but one day in the late 1970s warnings drifted in that the military would be coming to raze the town in three days. By the time they arrived, Vincent recounted, the entire population had disappeared. They never returned.

A few Q'eqchi' migrants found the spot in the early 1990s and brought their families on a long swampy trek to the headwaters of the San Pedro River to found the indigenous community that occupies the location today. Others joined them slowly over the years, coming from the neighboring departments of Alta and Baja Verapaz, Izabal, and southern Petén.[5] The shell of the previous town is still visible in a few places. A large water tank by the airstrip blew down in a storm, the wooden tower supporting it slowly picked apart and hauled off for reuse. The landing strip itself is grown over with thick weeds and grasses, the forest encroaching onto the previously barren stretch, reclaiming the abandoned land of industry. The burned-out husk of half an airplane lies in a stream nearby, a tilted wooden bridge built over it to discourage curious kids from playing in the rusted metal. Paso Caballos was colonized, emptied, ruined, and resettled in fewer than thirty years, leaving scars etched into the land at the source of the Río San Pedro.

Edge Effect 2: War, Peace

Separating war crime from conservation practice when accounting for villages burned by the military requires a clear historical edge between war and peace. The signing of the Peace Accords legally delineated this edge, marking the difference between thirty-six years of civil war and military-dominated dictatorships, on the one hand, and a constitutional democracy, bringing with it land reform and protections for indigenous groups, on the other. But there was more than one endpoint to the war in Guatemala, a multiplicity of edges that fold back over themselves in processes of healing, restitution, and lack thereof (Nelson 2009). One of many transitions, the 1996 accords serve as the major historical monument to the end of war, even as their contradictory effects reverberate through the Petén.

The material and epistemic edge effects produced at the meeting of war and peace are unruly. The accords allowed refugees, including 46,000 who crossed the border into Mexico, to return and legally claim land, a process that began in the early 1990s but was formalized by the new constitution (Egan 1999).[6] Much of this land was in the Petén, overlaying new conservation landscapes with divisions between migrants, internally displaced people, and returning refugees. Human rights discourses and movements flourished along this edge, led by the presence of MINUGUA (United Nations Verification Mission in Guatemala) and other UN officials overseeing the transition. Human rights, including cultural and political rights for indigenous groups, are recognized in the Peace Accords and new constitution. In Guatemala, as around the world, human rights claims can clash with conservationist projects and understandings of land (West, Igoe, and Brockington 2006; Adams et al. 2004; Agrawal and Redford 2009; Ybarra 2012).

International knowledge forms like UN observer reports enter a fragmented nooscape, colliding and combining unevenly with other worlds and knowings. Human rights in the MBR are diffracted through (often unknowable) human difference; those being evicted from parks have access to a new

Silences of Memory
32

set of discourses and allies in Guatemala, whether those evicted are refugees or narcos. Conservationists would tell me that settlers now strategically take up this language to claim rights that they do not legally have, such as rights to buy and sell land inside the reserve, or to raise cattle. In August 2011, an interview with Alberto Brunori, representative of the UN High Commissioner for Human Rights in Guatemala, was published in the newspaper *Prensa Libre* (Valdez 2011). The article argued in defense of human rights for settlements inside Petén protected areas, and set off a rash of email exchanges and conversations in the back rooms of WCS. Reactions ranged from a considered "this will make things a little bit difficult" to a deeply sarcastic "the poor campesinos without rights." One man focused on the citation of a 2004 MINUGUA report in the interview:

> I was there back in 2004. I remember when MINUGUA was preparing that report, and I went down to the capital to talk to them. Because in their report on land conflicts in the Petén, they were talking about all these factors: historical cattle ranching development, the movement of different ethnicities, the impacts of the war. But in all of that, they didn't have anything to say about what I saw as a major factor: organized crime. So I went down there and talked to them, showed them a bunch of evidence of what we knew was happening. And I said to them, okay, so we're not these violators of human rights—they had been seeing things about burning people's houses and that kind of thing—but we do find ourselves clashing with these people, these populations, just based on our work and where they are.

The barely discernable difference between "clashing" and "human rights violation" is drawn here by alluding to the presence of organized crime, which diffracts human rights and environmental discourses into new patterns where militarized eviction becomes acceptable, even laudable, practice. The man continued, "If there is any convergence between an honest human rights agenda and an honest environmental agenda—and let's face it, both of these are easily corrupted by other interests—this is it: the concentration of state lands in the hands of the wealthy few."

Some conservationists read backward from their current fears of forest loss to blame human rights agendas for the failures of conservation in Laguna del Tigre. As one NGO worker, Carlos, recounted, CONAP showed up to implement the park on the ground right when the accords were signed. When they encountered settlements there, they had to decide: either sign agreements allowing them to live inside the parks, or send in the army to kick them out. Carlos explained that they had decided on the former, which he supported: "Right after signing these historic Peace Accords, to send in the army, how would that look?" But he also saw this historical reticence as the origin of current land grab problems in the reserve. Although conservationists (attempt to) distinguish between migrant agriculturalists and powerful land grabbers, they can read agreements like those forged with settlements like Paso Caballos as opening the door to criminal invasion. But contrary to Carlos's historical narrative, CONAP did not simply decide to sign agreements out of respect for human rights. These agreements grew from yet another form of fire.

Fire 4: Burning Down the House

Across the MBR, villagers (Q'eqchi' and Ladino, migrant and Petenero) have burned institutional buildings as an expression of fear and discontent. Like back burning to fight a wildfire, these smaller fires burn in opposition to whole villages lit by those more powerful. Park guard houses, state-run control posts, NGO village residence huts, biological research stations, all of these have burned in the MBR, set alight by the poor, the angry, the dispossessed. Terrifically violent yet potentially subtle, the burning of institutional structures in the reserve has punctuated the slow spread of state (and state-like) territorial control. And in many cases, something new has risen, phoenix-like, from the ashes—new buildings replace the old, transformed in both material and social relations.

Rosa, WCS's field technician in Paso Caballos, used to work in Uaxactún. She left the Petén for two years between these assignments when her house in the Petenero village was burned down. WCS has maintained a part-time residential presence in Uaxactún since 1996, building small houses for their staff to live and work in. Built first in the local style of wood houses with thatch roofs—cheaper, and both cooler in the intense heat and warmer on the rare chilly day—these houses proved too flammable for the institution's inclination toward permanence. One by one, these houses were burned down. The reasons were many: loss of an NGO-paid job, general disapproval of outsiders, project failure, alcohol, personal vendetta. One by one, the buildings were built again, this time with heavy concrete bricks and corrugated tin rooftops that trap the dense midday heat but keep out even hotter flames. The institution rebuilt, replaced, and remained. Rosa left Uaxactún in frustration and fear, but eventually came back to WCS to work in Paso Caballos instead.

The roots of Paso Caballos's agreement inside Laguna del Tigre are awash in this kind of flame. Like shoots of maize in a milpa field growing from the ashes of burned forest, the Q'eqchi' village's agreement with CONAP grew from the ashes of the first Scarlet Macaw Biological Station, constructed less than 6 kilometers downriver from the village in 1996. When the first Q'eqchi' migrants settled the site in the early 1990s, there was no park presence, only the ruins of the former Petenero camp. CONAP arrived a few years later, along with NGOs including CI's Guatemalan offshoot, ProPetén, which undertook construction of the research station. As the NGO built its station, CONAP began the work of evicting communities from the park. Stories from this time report that CONAP was burning people's houses to make them leave, but I do not know for sure whether or not the state revisited this scorched-earth tactic at the time. What is certain is the fear that people felt in Paso Caballos, fear that this land they had found after long histories of dispossession and displacement might again be wrested violently away (Grandia 2012).

So they burned. People from Paso Caballos and other villages combined forces, headed for the station in small boats along the Río San Pedro, kidnapped NGO staff, and burned the brand-new buildings to the ground. The hostages were released two days later, beaten but alive, after ProPetén's leader, Carlos Soza Manzanero, negotiated a settlement between park and people: the villages would be granted conditional usufruct agreements inside the park, and in exchange would help rebuild the station. This tale has now circulated widely with striking variation, reflecting its position along multiple edges in a fractured nooscape. It is used to illustrate the failures of conservation (Parks Watch 2003; Grandia 2012), the duping of Q'eqchi' villagers by other interests who "paid for and orchestrated" the burning (Bray and Anderson 2005), the heroic character of Soza (Nations 2006), or the essential role of community participation in sustainable development (Grandia 2012; Sader et al. 1997). My first trip to the Petén, in 2007, was for master's thesis research on the relationship between Paso Caballos and the Biological Station. During that trip, I collected as many versions of the story as I could: from people who were kidnapped and held hostage, who lived in Paso Caballos at the time, or had since moved into the village and knew the story secondhand.

One of the most striking versions of the story came from my friend Mayron, a ProPetén worker who had been kidnapped. He performed the tale for me as he swept out the station's dormitory rooms, using the broom to gesture wildly and act out dramatic scenes. Like many, Mayron began with a standard opening, one that indicates a clear beginning to a story that might reach back much farther into local and national histories: the trouble began in 1996, he told me, when ProPetén built its new biological station. Bringing the broom down from where he was sweeping cobwebs out of dark ceiling corners, Mayron leaned on the wooden handle and set a scene of confusion: it was November, and after working on construction for nearly a year, they were on the verge of inaugurating the station. From where he was working atop a *bodega* (storehouse) roof, he could see down to the river, where a tangle of motorboats were coming and going—workers from the station off in one boat to get drinking water, others with men fishing, all part of the river traffic that snaked along the San Pedro River between the more than twenty villages that had been established inside the park. "All of a sudden a boat full of men with machetes, with pistols, with guns . . . they started running up toward us with their weapons." Perhaps it was bravado in front of his gringa audience, but Mayron claimed that at this point he turned to the manager of the station and cracked a joke: "It looks like we have some visitors . . . but how odd!"

Mayron continued, "They came because CONAP had been burning their houses, and they were angry. But we weren't burning their houses. They thought that it was us [ProPetén], that we were burning, but we didn't have that authority. We didn't have anything to do with it. So they came running up at us, yelling, 'Hands up!' And what could we do? We didn't have guns, or anything more than machetes to defend ourselves. We couldn't run. They said they would shoot us in the back." The attackers—estimates of their number range from fifteen to 450, the most reliable probably around sixty—came running up from the river, kicking in doors, smashing and breaking everything they could find, and finally using the station's own gasoline stores to set fire to the brand-new buildings. Thirteen workers were forced into motorboats, tied up with rope, and carried downriver close to the Mexican border, where they were held hostage. The fire demolished the station and much of the surrounding forest before it was brought under control.

According to Mayron, ProPetén did not find out that they had been kidnapped for two days. No one was shot, but the hostages were beaten and threatened. The kidnappers used the broad sides of their machetes to—thwack!—slap the hostages across the back. Mayron described how the station's manager, because he was boss, took the worst of it, getting kicked in the stomach. The manager later told me that he was so traumatized that he could not return to work for a year, and his eyes still welled with tears when he told the story a decade later. Pausing his tale, Mayron returned to his sweeping and fell into silence for a few moments, then looked up at me: "You know? We were a little bit nervous."

Enter the hero: "But then ProPetén—back then, the boss was Carlos Soza—he came and sorted everything out." Soza, a Petenero and director of ProPetén until his death from illness in 2002, has acquired a gilded sheen in the memories of ProPetén workers, especially those I met at the biological station in 2007. Bridging a deep passion for conservation, a local feeling for the forest, and an unusual sensitivity for the plight of migrants, Soza deftly coordinated between different groups to start negotiations with the attackers, leading to the formal agreements between CONAP and settler communities that would allow them to stay within the park. His entrance into Mayron's narrative brought it to an abrupt end, much like Prince Charming riding in at just the right moment, followed closely by happily-ever-after. "He made the agreement with the communities, and they all followed it . . . and up to now we're all friends. Everything is fine. There haven't been more problems. *Todo tranquilo* [everything is cool]." After this incident, people "learned the difference" between CONAP and ProPetén. The NGO's work in Paso Caballos dwindled over time, and in 2010 the organization sold the Scarlet Macaw Biological Station to Asociación Balám, the Guatemalan NGO started by WCS.

Other versions of this tale, including that told to me by Norman Schwartz, an anthropologist and social historian of the Petén, emphasize the material transformation of the station. The construction and design of the station were entirely different when rebuilt, a material analogue to the transformation of relations between park and people. The original buildings, according to Schwartz, resembled "pillboxes" or "bunkers." "When you make sudden moves," he explained, "you're likely to confuse and upset people. So the combination of the way the station looked combined with the suddenness of its arrival really freaked people out." The reconstruction effort, led by Soza, redesigned the station's buildings according to local style, with wood from the station's forests, screened but largely open walls, and palm thatch roofs. This transformation is described as a localization of the station's design, implying a power shift from international CI to Guatemalan ProPetén, though the latter was not yet independent. As such, the material reemergence of the station is narrated as a triumph, an allegory for the emergence of locally negotiated agreements standing against national law and international conservationist priorities.

Though published accounts name Paso Caballos as one of two communities that led the attack (Parks Watch 2003), people in the village tend to displace the action onto others. One villager, Don Pablo, focused his version of the story on differences between Q'eqchi' and Ladino migrants to the Petén. When I asked about the burning, his first words were of ethnic differentiation: "It was *castellanos* [Spanish speakers] who burned the station." While Don Pablo never talked about being Q'eqchi' with words like "oppression" or "marginalization," his fear and resentment of Ladino culture were evident. Ladinos, he told me, are *mala gente* (bad people): "When they get mad, they do whatever they want." Today, people from both the village and the station talk about the lawlessness *abajo*, downriver toward the border. The burning of the station was blamed on communities from abajo in almost all stories I collected, a shift in historical attribution that reflects current distributions of threat and fear while quietly covering over the village's conflict-ridden past.

The closest that any in Paso Caballos came to acknowledging responsibility for the burning was by emphasizing their misunderstanding of NGOs versus the state: "We didn't know that CONAP and ProPetén were different things," people repeated. "Now we know better." Still, even if the attackers had confused ProPetén with the state's park authority, Don Pablo pointed out that "CONAP stuck their foot in it. They also wanted to kill the people." When the station burned, Don Pablo told me, they were scared in Paso Caballos, too. Villagers saw the smoke and thought CONAP was coming to burn their houses; people were ready to flee.

One Q'eqchi' woman told me the story as one of fear. It wasn't a tale about who burned the station or why, the agreement with CONAP, or ProPetén. It was simply her memory of the time, filled with the terror and confusion of fire: "When the station burned, we were all scared that our houses would burn next, that there would be a huge forest fire and that all of our houses and clothing would burn. In order to prepare, we put all of our clothing into big *costales* [bags used to store corn]. Everybody got together and put their clothing into these costales so it wouldn't burn. We were scared of the fire, and scared because there were so many boats coming in and out all of a sudden, and helicopters flying over, and we thought the fire was coming." People from Paso Caballos, along with others from other migrant villages, started this fire. But once a fire is lit, it belongs to no one.

Edge Effect 3: Conservation and Development

Growing from the uneven edges between these enactments of fire in Laguna del Tigre—threat to forests, scorched-earth evictions, resistance—are shifting attempts to balance conservation and development. Should conservation NGOS be doing development work? "A philosophical question," as wcs director Roan Balas McNab put it, reworking the boundaries of conservation practice again and again. If people are living illegally inside a national park, do you help them gain access to water, education, and health services, and try to keep them from cutting deeper into the forest in exchange? Or does this signal that invasions are a legitimate and successful path to land access and institutional support, undermining conservation? Roan reflected, "What it comes down to, for me, is that we're here ultimately to work for nature. So which is better for nature, for those beings without voices or votes? That's the ultimate question. And how do you work with those communities to save what you can, while also making sure that the conditions are right so that it isn't easy for others to do that, invade, in other parts of the reserve? These are the kinds of tough questions I grapple with all the time." Roan shifted back and forth on these issues. His questions reflect the entanglements of knowledges and material-ecological worlds in a nooscape, with human presence shaping ideas about human presence, and vice versa. But this is a fragmented part of the nooscape, amplifying epistemic edge effects even within a single institution.

While wcs's director struggles philosophically, his field technician Rosa struggles materially, politically, and personally through projects in Paso Caballos. She notes that while other conservation institutions engage development in terms of economic benefits for communities, wcs does more: working with health or education, for example. Through their 1997 agreement with CONAP and their newer two-year acuerdo de conservación signed with wcs and other institutions, Q'eqchi' villagers trade participation in conservation activities for development assistance: money for the school, seasonal jobs, a village health outpost started and failed and started and failed and started and failed. I ask Rosa why health projects never last here, and she replies, "The people don't want it" (*La gente no quiere*). I ask why the school buildings are so run-down, the construction on a new addition unfinished for years: "The people don't want it." Her statements reflect the fragmented realities of conservation work in the village, contradicting themselves. First, "I'm here to support the community, to do what they want. If they don't want something, that's their choice. I can't do anything about it." And then, "I'm here as the representative of a conservation organization. It doesn't matter what I think is right—I have to prioritize conservation."

Rosa grew up in a middle-class household in Guatemala City, and chose education and career over marriage and family. With degrees in agronomy, anthropology, and protected-area studies, Rosa has dedicated herself for over fifteen years to the difficult work of community-based conservation. This path is uncommon for women in Guatemala, especially to remain unmarried, and Rosa is unusual in other respects as well. Forthright and direct, she frequently alienates people with her disregard for gender norms and open expressions of anxious uncertainty. Yet these qualities serve her well in Paso Caballos: "I don't make any promises that I can't keep. I'm not Santa Claus coming with a bag full of money. If there's a possible project, and people ask me if they can get it, I never promise them yes. I say, 'I don't know, maybe. We'll try. We'll see.' . . . I don't give in to people who try to pressure me or manipulate the situation." In a village where so many projects and interventions have failed over time, refusing to promise success can both frustrate villagers who desire the objects of those promises—such as better schools, infrastructure, or work opportunities—and simultaneously build a slow and steady trust, as people learn that Rosa works harder than most to try to bring projects to fruition.

There are two possible futures for Paso Caballos, Rosa tells me. "Either people will start invading the forests around the village, or . . ." She trails off, failing to provide the alternative. "The soils are already becoming exhausted," she says instead. "With this many people and agriculture this intensive, it can't continue." She has worked on some of the toughest problems in the village with good results: "Fires, cattle, last year some people [classified as invaders] left the community—but I don't count these small gains as 'success,' because the larger goal is always conserving the forest around the community." If Rosa claims any success in Paso Caballos, it is in how villagers engage with institutions. "One thing we've done is to work on reducing conflictividad," she explains to a visiting consultant, "particularly the problems and conflicts they had with CONAP." She describes this work as concienciación, raising awareness, and as building what she calls the "social sustainability" of conservation: cultivating a shared understanding of how to work together within the bounds of legal and institutional constraints.

Rosa feels like she barely understands life in Paso Caballos after nearly a decade working there. Still, it is her favorite place that she has worked. While most conservationists turn to their love of wild species and spaces to keep going, Rosa repeatedly cites her favorite project in Paso Caballos when confronting her frustrations: painting an eco-themed mural on the communal meeting hall with village children. In a community balanced along the edges of so many troubling dynamics—land grabs, drug trafficking, dispossession, racialization, ecological destruction, and remilitarization—a mural can seem unimportant, even a waste of time or resources. But Rosa returns to this moment—to her memories of kids sharing Coca-Cola directly out of large bottles, sticky with candy and paint, creating bright images of macaws, jaguars, and lush vegetation—as a reminder of the possibility of joy and wonder in her work.

Some days are hard, but other days she loves the village, which is quiet and safe. People also put up with things that she couldn't get away with elsewhere—silly things, like yelling out at people while she walks around the village, giving joking answers to questions that aren't addressed to her, loudly inserting herself into conversations where she doesn't belong. "*Pueblo chiquito, infierno grande*" (small village, big hell), she says, explaining that everybody knows everybody's business, is involved in everything. And then, contradicting herself again, Rosa insists that she doesn't stick her nose where it doesn't belong: "I don't get involved in other people's problems."

Sometimes, she simply can't get involved, excluded by the linguistic separation of Q'eqchi' and her native Spanish. In their meetings with state and NGO institutions, Paso Caballos residents frequently slip into Q'eqchi' Mayan to hold private conversations in the shared meeting space, deciding on a course of action or response before switching back into Spanish to address outsiders again. This is a powerful tool, and one which the villagers protect vigilantly: when it was discovered that an NGO staff person was able to understand a good deal of their conversations, they began asking him to leave the room while they continued to hold discussions in front of other visitors. That these villagers take this code switching for granted and do not leave the room themselves is indicative that power relations in these encounters are not straightforward. Outsiders—CONAP, NGOs, and others—have many structural advantages but are repeatedly frustrated by their inability to impose whatever new programs or rules they like on the marginalized migrant community.

Edge Effect 4: The Firebreak

Epistemic edge effects like the shifting line between conservation and development become material effects. Attempts to clarify this philosophical boundary are etched into the Laguna del Tigre landscape as a physical edge: the *brecha*, or firebreak, that cuts a line around the outer limits of Paso Caballos's territorial polygon (*polígono agrícola*). Between 5 and 6 meters wide in most places, the brecha cuts through living vegetation to delimit realms of Nature/forest/conservation from Culture/agriculture/development, ideological limits made manifest by chainsaws, machetes, and leaf blowers. Combined with the smaller firebreaks known as *rondas* around individual agricultural parcels, the land is carved up to resemble the map designating Paso Caballos's use rights.

In February 2012, I attended a fire planning meeting in the WCS house in Paso Caballos where Rosa lives part-time. The meeting involved Rosa and another WCS technician, the director of the Scarlet Macaw Biological Station and two additional Asociación Balam field staff, the director of Laguna del Tigre National Park, a representative from CONRED/SIPECIF (national disaster reduction and forest fire agencies), two representatives from a neighboring community forest concession managed by AFISAP (Integrated Forestry Association of San Andrés, Petén), and Paso Caballos's COCODE. Together, the group worked out responsibilities for clearing the brecha around Paso Caballos before the upcoming fire season. The brecha was divided into three sections: the western border abutting the biological station, the northern border marking the edge between Laguna del Tigre and the AFISAP concession, and the eastern border and internal rondas lumped together in a third category.

The first two sections were given priority. Starting discussion with the western brecha, two men from the COCODE explained that they had finished clearing the line in December. The director of the biological station quickly objected, saying that the break needed to be widened by at least a meter, in order to ensure that even large fires could not pass. Rosa explained that responsibility for clearing that stretch of brecha was shared fifty-fifty between the station and village, but this assertion was met with confusion and disagreement—did this mean equal contributions of funding? Labor? Shared responsibility if a fire should pass? Eventually, the group decided that maintaining this break was not a truly equal collaboration, because any fire that crossed the line would be the community's responsibility first and foremost.

Instead, the station lent its support due to its direct interest in the protection the brecha offered.

In contrast, the second section of brecha shared with AFISAP was considered a true collaboration, with the concession managers coordinating with Paso Caballos over areas remaining to be cleared. One of the men from San Andres reminisced about a fire that passed from Paso Caballos into AFISAP territory in 2009, offering this as explanation for why it was worthwhile to share clearing responsibility with the village. For both of these stretches of brecha, exact responsibilities and contributions of the different institutions and actors present were broken down in detail—how many people each would commit, for how long and on which days, and how much gasoline, equipment, food, funding for equipment repair, and other resources each would contribute. The meeting was tense, with COCODE members frequently slipping into Q'eqchi' side discussions and representatives of each institution pushing back on the others and looking out for their own interests. One institution offered packages of "expired food" (*comida vencida*), an offer met with derisive laughter from another participant: "Do they think we're children? That we want that?"

When the first two brecha sections had been mapped out and negotiated, Rosa noted that the third section would be cleared as resources allowed, downloading this responsibility onto individual agricultural parcel holders. For all three categories, two promoters from the village would be chosen by the COCODE, responsible for brecha-clearing labor, ensuring that other villagers cleared the edges of their own parcels (especially those along the western and northern edges), and coordinating between institutions and community members for all seasonal fire management activities. The promoter positions were seasonal jobs paid from WCS funds via the acuerdo, which meant they had to be chosen from among the families who signed the original 1997 agreement with CONAP. After a few hours of hammering out details, the meeting ended calmly. Despite the tensions and occasional eruptions of conflict during the proceedings, Rosa told me afterward that she was surprised by how smoothly it went.

Fire 5: Agricultural Tool

Firebreaks are necessary because fire is a key agricultural technology in the Petén, as in many parts of the tropical world. This form of agriculture—known as swidden, slash-and-burn, or milpa (the maize-centric version common across Mesoamerica)—has been practiced in the region for millennia. While pyrophobic discourses and inflammatory images of poor people burning down rain forests still dominate many environmental imaginations, other responses are possible. Many argue that swidden agriculture is best practiced with low population densities and large extensions of land, allowing more time and space for the regeneration of forest growth between growing cycles (Dove 1983; Angelsen 1995; Lambin et al. 2001; Fox et al. 2000; Forsyth 2002). From this perspective, it is the overcrowding of swidden-supporting forest landscapes (caused proximately by migration or population growth, and structurally by reconfigurations of land rights and access) that poses a problem, not the agricultural method.

This analysis still distinguishes between the rolling frontier of migrant milpa and Petenero agriculture, long accommodated to a local balance of field, fallow, and forest. Many believe that migrants, especially the Q'eqchi', have brought agricultural practices from other regions, such that they are now ill suited to their new environment (e.g., Nations 2001). Yet there are no substantial differences between Q'eqchi', Ladino migrant, or Petenero milpa practices (Atran et al. 1999). While some environmentalists claim to see differences between local, traditional swidden fields and those of indigenous migrants, these reflect conservationist perceptions of the bodies and histories of those planting the fields, not the fields themselves.

Peteneros and Other Endemic Species 116

Migrants themselves explain how their agricultural practices have shifted in response to the different climate and soils of their new homes. Men in Paso Caballos were quick to tell me about these differences, the most favorable of which was the Petén's hotter, wetter climate. This allows two consecutive maize plantings per year, sometimes three, instead of the single harvest possible in the mountainous regions from which their families came. The varieties of corn you can grow are different, too, and some crops grow only here (rice, spicy chile Petenero) or there (coffee, cardamom).

In the cool month of January, after the rains have slowed but before the heat sweeps in, people in Paso Caballos begin cutting their parcels in preparation for burning. They chop down trees, vines, overgrown agricultural residues, and whatever else may be growing, leaving it rough on the ground for a month or so to dry out. The next step—institutionally mandated and closely watched, though not always carried out to the letter—is to cut a ronda around the parcel. These must be 2–6 meters wide, depending on the height of the *guamil* (fallow, secondary vegetation) you cut, the *botado* (cut material) you now have, and the corresponding potential height of flames. When the extreme heat of the dry season hits, usually in late February, burning begins. Paso Caballos residents must carefully control their fires, accounting for wind direction, slope, and time of day so that they burn only their own patch of land. Fires sometimes accidentally cross from one parcel to another within the village's polygon, but nobody worries too much unless it approaches the outer brecha.

The fires return tangled vegetation to the soil in a quick burst of nutrients. After burning, the land is left to rest. If it rains too soon, there will be trouble—the surface ash carried away in waste. But this is the dry season, so the layers settle, integrate. If the guamil is tall and the botado thick, you can grow on a patch for two or three years; if they are too small, maize won't grow at all. *Pepitoria*, a staple squash plant, is planted first, in March and April. Small mushrooms, called *xiquinché*, sprout from downed logs when the rains arrive, filling corn-dough empanadas for a seasonal local delicacy. The first maize crop is planted late in May, just in time to catch the first rains, and harvested in June or July. This is followed by a second planting, harvested in September or October, and—if conditions are right—a third planting can follow this, harvested in December and January. Two types of corn are planted together, small/Icta and large/Petenero, and they mature and are harvested at slightly different times in this cycle. Rice is planted mid-May and harvested in September. Hot chili peppers are planted in August, with black beans following in September through November, both harvested in January and February.

Some conservationists recognize the necessity of fire in this agricultural system. Their support can be surprising, with conservationists who have worked with reserve communities defending fire to those who fly in from abroad, delivering funding, projects, and authoritative expertise. How could we tell people to give up fire? Petén-trained conservationists ask. When you are living at the absolute end of the rutted, rain-impassable dirt road, with no vehicle, with no supply stores, with no possibility for income beyond the sale of what you have grown in your allotted parcel, how else will you enrich the thin, alkaline soils? Who will buy fertilizers, year after year? Who will deliver them? Who will provide labor to spread them? Fire is the simplest, cheapest, and most accessible source of soil nutrients, these environmentalists explain. Replacing it is unfeasible; better to regulate and control it than to ban it altogether.

Edge Effect 5: Failure

Rosa's optimism about the fire planning meeting's smooth conclusion did not endure for long. The excess of perspectives, possibilities, and lived worlds in play tip even closely coordinated projects over the edge toward failure. Things fall apart. Despite the rule that only villagers included in the 1997 CONAP agreement could be hired as promoters, the COCODE chose two men classified as invaders for the jobs. Two days later, I watched a raucous argument over this choice unfold in a community assembly (though I was linguistically barred from understanding what was happening until it was all over).

The first agenda item of the day was the fire season plan that had been approved in the interinstitutional meeting. The assembly discussion started out involved and attentive, but relatively calm. But people soon grew more and more animated, until they were gesturing wildly, standing to yell their opinions over each other, and finally the whole room erupted in people shouting over and at each other. Eventually things calmed again as agreement was reached, and Geraldo (auxiliary mayor, head of the COCODE) ran through a summary of their final position. People responded with a chorus of "*us*" (pronounced "oos," meaning "good" in Q'eqchi'), then moved on to discussion of a failed satellite internet project. When the meeting was over, I learned that the assembly had decided to reject the entire NGO- and state-proposed seasonal fire plan. When I asked Geraldo why, he responded, "It's because these institutions always offer support, and never follow through." Why should the village uphold their end of signed agreements, if institutions did not?

The fallout was immediate. Rosa, back in Flores, caught wind that something had gone wrong. She started dialing through the cell phone numbers of anybody who might be in the village, trying to get a handle on the damage. The men of the COCODE stood in the communal meeting hall where the assembly had just cleared out, face to face with CONAP and SIPECIF staff who were passing through to check on the proceedings. Unlike the tense but restrained atmosphere of the meeting a few days earlier, this encounter boiled over into open conflict. The state representatives—all Ladinos—spoke loudly and authoritatively, standing taller and broader in their institutional uniforms over the leaner, shorter Q'eqchi' men, who tended to listen quietly or to interject with softer, more cautious voices. Their cell phones rang in turn, unanswered.

The conversation hinged on institutional promises of support (or lack thereof), particularly the question of buying gasoline for brecha-clearing equipment. Each side insinuated that the others' claims of lack of resources were disingenuous. A park representative, Ronaldo, stated that CONAP had no money for fuel: "If I had that money, I'd just come give it to you." One of the COCODE members responded, "What about your salary?," causing a round of nervous laughter. Ronaldo answered evasively that sometimes CONAP staff didn't get paid for months during government transitions, and that his own job was insecure. He then shot back, turning to the Q'eqchi' man standing next to him: "And how many *manzanas* of land do *you* have?"[7]

Edge Effect 6: Fragmented Responsibility

Days earlier, waiting for the fire planning meeting to begin, Rosa and I chatted with Geraldo and Asociación Balam staff. "Which do you think is more difficult," Rosa asked, "being president of the republic [of Guatemala], or president of the COCODE?" One of the Balam technicians clarified: "Which is *más difícil* [technical difficulty], or which *cuesta más* [personal difficulty]? Because being president of the Republic is probably más difícil, but being president of the COCODE definitely cuesta más." Geraldo, holding the latter position, contributed his perspective: "It's definitely *más yuca* [more impossible, intractable] being president of the COCODE." Rosa concurred: "When something goes wrong as the president of the republic, you can send somebody else out to take the blame. But here you've got to face right up to it."

When so many enactments of fire are crowded onto a single contested patch of land, this question of who takes the blame splinters. Who is responsible if a fire crosses Paso Caballos's brechas? Is it the Q'eqchi' agriculturalist in their regulated parcel, who lit the match? The village as a whole, for not maintaining the firebreak and following protocols? WCS, as the primary institution supporting Paso Caballos' fire management? Rosa, as the embodied presence of that institution? Balam, for not maintaining control of the land around the station? CONAP, for not maintaining control of the park as a whole? The anxiety caused by the possibility of an unruly fire, and heated arguments over who will take (potential) blame, spark conflict in the dry tinder of the social, political, ethnic, and economic differences that characterize fire work in and around Paso Caballos.

Rosa often claimed, "If a fire passes the brecha, I'll get blamed. It will be my fault." At the same time, she staked out the boundaries of her responsibilities—to WCS, to the community, and to the forest—very clearly: WCS does not work in firefighting, only in prevention. Once a fire has passed, she may be blamed for failed prevention, but that's where her responsibility ends. It is the state (CONAP, CONRED, and SIPECIF) that is responsible for control if a fire gets out of hand. When planning and coordination in the village seemed to be breaking down after months of hard work, Rosa was overcome by frustration. On a particularly exasperating day, staff from other institutions failed to show up for a meeting in the village, providing flimsy excuses. Exhausted and fed up with interinstitutional bickering, she declared, "I'd rather see it burn than give one cent to fire control."

With greater and greater difference between enactments of fire in Paso Caballos—pixel, threat to forests, scorched earth, resistance, agricultural tool—edge effects amplify. Responsibility for those fires is distributed unevenly, in patches and gaps. Rosa's work on reducing conflictividad in Paso Caballos centered on building local awareness of legal and institutional constraints; clarifying roles and responsibilities was key to this strategy. But the 2012 fire plan fell apart because too many institutions had failed in the past to follow through on their promises. Formally, CONAP is responsible for defining rules and restrictions, the COCODE responsible for enforcing them, and WCS for providing support. But there is a gap between formal responsibility and consequences, an edge effect that pushes the burdens of navigating a fragmented nooscape onto those already most burdened. Individual villagers, the COCODE, and Rosa will all suffer consequences if something goes wrong. Not to mention the forest.

Fragmentation means that knowledges, practices, and enacted worlds are broken into smaller and smaller patches, with greater and greater difference between them. Edge effects between these patches of difference materialize on the landscape as new practices, interventions, patterns, or processes. Fires in Paso Caballos begin as agricultural tool, but are haunted by fire as an end to forests. Fearful of the always-imminent possibility that one will become the other, Rosa calls on pixelated fire in her attempts to compel adherence to rules and regulations. She describes CEMEC's daily emails as though they were high-resolution spy surveillance: "They will see the fire, in CONAP," she tells villagers. "They will see that there is a fire where there is no fire scheduled, and they will call me up on the phone and ask me what happened, who is lighting fires." If too many fires should pass the village's designated lines, a militarized scorched-earth eviction haunts the edges of possibility, calling violent fires of the past into the present. Within each of these ways of knowing and doing fire there are yet more patches of unevenness and difference.

Fragmentation means things fall apart: projects and interventions, but also relations. Fire in Paso Caballos draws together—willingly and unwillingly— villagers, NGO field staff, conservation leaders, remote sensing and GIS technicians, satellites, agricultural and forest ecosystems and their many inhabitants, state representatives, and seasonal weather patterns that are now beginning to shift unpredictably with global climate change. But even as fire draws these actors together, the possibility of relations between them breaks down. Consensus or singularity around fire is impossible. It is simultaneously tedious and terrifying, a tool of oppression and radical expression of discontent by the oppressed, both an ending and a beginning to life on the landscape, and always out of control. Like the fragmented fire sections of this chapter, these enactments haunt each other in ways influenced but never determined by the many edge effects spiraling around conservation knowledges and interventions in Paso Caballos. Lines shift and blur between conservation and development, war and peace, forest and farm, success and failure, individual and institution. Responsibility fragments, but somebody has to take the blame. Fire in Paso Caballos demonstrates the instability of relations between fragmented ecological and social worlds in the MBR nooscape, how these worlds are pieced together and negotiated in practice, and then, too, how they fall apart.

DEATH OF A DOG

In November 2011, I accompanied three WCS veterinarians on a visit to Paso Caballos. As our four-hour journey over bumpy, washed-out dirt roads brought us close to the village, we passed through an enormous ranch, stretching on both sides of the road for miles. "Look at all this land," Luis commented bitterly, "and only, what, a hundred cows? They should call it 'la Lavandería' [the Laundromat]." When we arrived, the vets set up a projector in one of the school buildings, preparing for a presentation to local kids about the proper care of domestic animals. The desks were stamped with the words "Perenco Educación," marking them as a donation from the French petroleum company that drills in Laguna del Tigre National Park. Luis joked again without smiling: "See? Oil is good." The audience was small; it was a Saturday, so most of the children were out working in the milpa fields.

Another vet, Tono, presented detailed information on how to care for horses, chickens, pigs, and dogs to the few kids who had assembled. The presentation was part of the WCS program Conviviendo con Carnívoros (Living with Carnivores), and centered on the message that better animal care and less subsistence hunting would reduce conflicts with the jaguars and pumas inhabiting the forests around the village. But the recommendations, based on abstract standards that assumed access to veterinary care, medicines, and other resources, were a rough fit with village life. Many of the suggestions for animals were better than typical care for humans in this place: twice-annual veterinary checkups, dental care, regular vaccinations, uncrowded housing arrangements to minimize disease. At one point, Tono suggested that horses should be given

ample opportunities for play and recreation, not just labor. The luxury of this proposed equine lifestyle felt absurd as I thought of the absent audience in the fields.

After the presentation, the men encouraged the kids to bring their dogs to the school for free vaccinations and worm testing; two did. The dogs squirmed under the unfamiliar handling of the vets, but received their care. Then the third vet, Vicente, and I were left to wait by the school as the others dropped off supplies across town. A cat ran by, chased by a kid throwing rocks. Watching sadly, Vicente bemoaned the treatment of animals in the community, judging it ignorance and unthinking cruelty: "In some other places, people treat their animals just like their children!"

Later, as we headed back to the truck to leave town, we passed a dog that had been slashed open by a machete blade. I could not believe it was still standing; a ten-inch gash, almost two inches across with raw flesh, streaked across its back. I turned away, unable to face the image. The three vets talked about what they could do, in the end deciding to do nothing. They had no sutures with them, and even if they did sew it up, the dog would have needed antibiotics for thirty days. I was stunned, and the vets filled my silence. "It really would need to be hospitalized to survive," Vicente told me apologetically. It was going to die, they all agreed; the wound was a death sentence. Luis explained: "Even if we had the things here today to put it to sleep, which is what really should happen, you know the owner would just come back at us angry, saying that *we* killed his dog." We drove away, leaving the dog panting with its open wound on the side of the road.

This dog was attacked by a human, but dogs are also preferred prey of jaguars in the MBR. The origins of this veterinary outreach program are rooted in increasing attacks on cattle, dogs, and other domestic animals by jaguars and pumas. This is a kind of multispecies retaliation, violence begat by violence: predator attacks have increased as ranches spread into wild hunting territories. Jaguars displaced by likely narco-connected money-laundering ranches, Q'eqchi' Maya displaced by state violence and land dispossession, national protected-area laws displaced by oil money, institutional care for humans and nonhumans displaced by each other.

Who is responsible for the death of a dog?

Processes of decomposition and renewal
may tell us about the everyday practices
through which not only people but entire
ecologies . . . strive to collectively change
the conditions of their lives. They do so
not by transcending these conditions, but
rather by sinking into them, slowly turning
them over, aerating, and breathing in new
life that also potentiates different possibilities for and relations to death.

Kristina Lyons, *Decomposition as Life Politics*

III / COMPOSING AND
COMPOSTING KNOWLEDGES

All knowing intervenes, composing new worlds through material processes and relations. Knowledges and interventions do
not have to do what they were intended to do to work, that is,
to make a difference. Knowing a place in order to change it is
another way of changing a place, of composing it anew. Many
MBR conservationists have come to recognize this, that learning
through work can be more important than project outcomes.
Making a plan, which requires working with human and nonhuman others, can be more important than having or following
that plan, or expecting a plan to unfold predictably into knowable futures.

Still, these plans and the knowledges they contain compost
into something. In a nooscape, knowledges, documents, stories,
and ideas break down and remix with other worlds to produce
new material patterns, practices, and impacts. This can enrich
MBR worlds, like dead organic matter enriches soil through the
multispecies collaborations of decay. Other knowledges might

compost into toxicity, like agrochemical inputs that increase productivity for a short time but only cause more problems later. Compost politics are about tinkering, growing new modes of attention, knowing-in-practice, and more-than-human relations open to possibilities beyond the pleasant and the positive (Abrahamsson and Bertoni 2014). Turn knowledges into the land, the people, the plants, the waters. See what grows.

SEVEN

A Known Place

Uaxactún is the *pulmón del mundo* (the lungs of the world), Vinicio declared to me proudly. The pronouncement came as we chatted in his kitchen; I had just finished surveying his household's access to basic goods and services for a Basic Necessities study on behalf of Asociación Balam. I had heard the phrase "pulmón del mundo" (often used to refer to the Brazilian Amazon) associated with this village's forest several times. But this time, after Vinicio stated this fact, he asked me to explain it back to him: is it true, he wondered, that forests clean the air, and that the air cleaned by Uaxactún's trees travels far away, like to France? It's true, I answered, doing my best to explain global air circulation and the oxygen/carbon balance of the atmosphere. He was satisfied by my answer, as it explained something else too: why so many foreigners are interested in the fate of this patch of forest and the people who live in it. Our exchange made clear: the forest lungs exhale clean air, then pull international conservation in with their deep inhale.

It is no coincidence that this moment confirming Uaxactún's place in a global conservationist nooscape occurred during a household survey. Surveys and studies conducted by outsiders are a constant, mundane part of village life. There are technical forestry studies, detailed ethnographic examinations of the community's dense social world, and broad ecological and archaeological views of the surrounding landscape. Before I showed up at their doorsteps asking for household characteristics, villagers easily identified me as a researcher (not a tourist) because I had stayed for more than a single day. Children called me by the names of other gringa graduate students who had worked there before, while their parents reminisced pointedly about the gifts those visitors had brought. This is a well-studied place. Knowledge made in and about Uaxactún shapes how the village enters regional, national, and global conversations, but also folds back into the construction of the village and surrounding forest as a local, knowable place.

Uaxactún's forest concession permits villagers to eke out a living from the landscape, harvesting timber and nontimber forest products (NTFPs) for global markets. As villagers extract forest materials, so do NGOs, state agencies, and researchers like myself harvest data points, interviews, names, and numbers, processing them up into global chains of meaning and circulation. A common Spanish verb for conducting a study, *sacar un estudio*, means to extract or take out, perfectly describing this dynamic of removing data from the village in order to turn it into authoritative knowledge. Few study results are reported back to the community. In many cases this knowledge seems to disappear when a researcher leaves the village, but it returns in other ways: in how others enter and interact with the community, in their projects, in their assumptions about ways of life, beliefs, and priorities common to Uaxactuneros (village residents), or even just in the choice to study and work in this village over so many others in the reserve. Just as extraction of forest resources transforms the landscape left behind, constant external study of Uaxactún changes the village.

Knowledge Making and Place Making

A sense of *being known* shapes how Uaxactuneros understand their own and others' place in the forest, shifting ecological relations and livelihood practices. Knowledges produced about Uaxactún by and for institutional outsiders compost back into villagers' daily life, identity, and relations to both human and nonhuman actors—even when those knowledges are largely unavailable to local people. This knowledge making is a form of place making. Seemingly localized places are constructed translocally, amid complex more-than-human relations of power and meaning that are not geographically bounded (Gupta and Ferguson 1992; Massey 1994; Moore 2005; Tsing 2005). In Uaxactún, translocal knots of knowledge, power, place, and identity emerge from evolving relations between villagers, the state, NGOs, other researchers (including myself), and the landscape and its many nonhuman inhabitants.

In contrast to Paso Caballos, where the multiplicity of enacted worlds can lead to fragmentation and failure, Uaxactún serves as a model of community conservation success for institutions. This marks it as an important, if marginal, node in the MBR nooscape.[1] The idea that outsiders, WCS in particular, know more (or know better) about the village and its landscape than villagers themselves is a common sentiment among Uaxactuneros. This view privileges technoscience and formal education over local knowledges, yet has become incorporated into local senses of place and identity. In particular, this perspective is closely tied to Uaxactún's self-aware eco-consciousness (*conciencia*) and forest extraction practices.

This chapter traces two institutional knowledge-making practices in Uaxactún, one that extracts knowledge outward toward funders and donors, and another that is reported back to the community. The first is the Basic Necessities survey described in the opening story; this is designed to assess locally relevant measures of poverty and well-being, creating data for the *State of the Maya Biosphere Reserve* report (WCS 2011). The second is the monitoring of quality (marketability) in harvested *xate* palms, an NTFP that serves as a primary source of income for many in the community. These knowledge practices convert complex social and ecological dynamics into standardized numerical measures in different ways, for different purposes and audiences. In addition, both reveal the complex connections forged between villagers and institutions through knowledge-making practices, relations that can serve and transform both sides in unexpected ways.

Tracing where and how knowledges move is key to understanding their effects in a nooscape. Reports that move outward to serve institutional needs, like the Basic Necessities survey, also provide opportunities for villagers to connect with new actors, access resources, and sometimes to shape future projects and interventions into their lives. Reports that come back into the village, like xate monitoring, not only transform local livelihood and ecological practices, but also provide examples of conservation monitoring practices that are useful to local communities. Just as usefulness is an important institutional product for CEMEC, showing that xate monitoring is useful *to Uaxactún* is key to WCS reports and future funding. Both institutional knowledge projects are enfolded here within my ethnographic knowledge-making practices, themselves moving and growing new connections, including being reported back to Uaxactuneros and MBR institutions in 2015. In one way or another, these knowledges are ultimately turned into *tierra* (earth, land), composted into new projects, practices, land rights, and relations, each of which has material impacts on the more-than-human landscape of Uaxactún.

The Concession Is the People

The name "Uaxactún" refers to several things beyond the ancient Maya site from which it is borrowed: first, it is a village with a deep Petenero identity, established over one hundred years ago and undergoing several transformations and renamings since that time.[2] Second, it is a *unidad de manejo* (management unit), a block of state-owned land that covers 83,558 hectares within the MBR's multiple-use zone. Finally, it is a forest concession, assigning usufruct rights and management responsibilities through a twenty-five-year contract between the Guatemalan state and the village nonprofit OMYC (Management and Conservation Organization of Uaxactún); Uaxactún's is the largest community concession in Central America. The distinctions between these three blur in practice, as one OMYC member's attempt to clarify for me showed: "The unidad de manejo is just the area," he said; "the concession is the people." Echoing this equation of communal identity and contractual obligation, he informed me that a recent survey question (from yet another study) about the concession's benefits to the community didn't make sense: the concession is a "right," he insisted, too fundamental to the community's existence to ask what benefits it brings.

Any village resident is free to join OMYC, membership that offers access to rotating temporary (up to one year) employment and the ability to participate in concession management decisions. Beyond the rotating positions provided by OMYC (timber harvesting, working the sawmill, administration, etc.), jobs are few in the jungle. The village is flanked by two early Classic Maya sites, and the surrounding landscape is rich with many more. This archaeological abundance provides seasonal work for men who are hired to dig and sweep away layers of history in the dry season, or occasionally for women hired as camp cooks. Most men in Uaxactún rely heavily on NTFP harvesting for income, and opportunities for women to earn money are exceedingly few. Only 18 percent of adults had permanent paid employment in 2011, and a third of the community reported that xate, which can be harvested and sold year round, was their primary source of household income (Zetina Tún 2011).

To arrive at the village, you must first drive an hour from Flores to world-famous Tikal National Park, home to manicured lawns, easily viewed wildlife, and stunning temple-top views of forest canopy. The road to Uaxactún runs through Tikal, skirting temple complexes and veering off park roads onto 23 kilometers of bumpy dirt track through the jungle. At the end of the road is a long swath of open grass—a defunct airstrip, now decorated with sports fields and lazily grazing horses and mules—that runs down the center of the village. Houses are arranged in loose clusters snaking off from the landing strip, which until the 1980s provided the only direct access to the village. Entrance through Tikal deeply shapes Uaxactún, providing guard and maintenance jobs for a few Uaxactuneros and fueling villager dreams of developing their own Maya sites for profitable ecotourism. The park's guarded gates also provide protection for the concession against easy invasion from outsiders, illegal logging, and cattle ranching.

Uaxactún and OMYC have been widely praised as an example of successful community forest management due to the concession's well-maintained forest cover (Gretzinger 1998; Nittler and Tschinkel 2005; Radachowsky et al. 2012; Malkin 2015). These accolades generally overlook the fact that the concession generated debt rather than profit for many years, with poor financial management, oversight, and guidance.[3] A fractured, politically diverse membership also challenges OMYC's leadership. By regulation, members elect OMYC's board of directors every two years. In practice, however, each new board quickly takes the blame for any problems that arise in the concession, and has in recent years always been ousted before its term is up. While concession jobs theoretically rotate through all OMYC members, in practice they go to those with friends—or at least, a lack of opponents—on the current board, further hastening the desire for overturn among those left out. Small feuds cost the organization big dollars: in early 2012, a man slashed the tires of a skidder when he was refused an advance on his OMYC salary, doing Q30,000 of damage (almost U.S. $4,000). Factions split along old tender lines again and again, tearing apart the administrative structure from the participatory inside. This tumult is a reflection of how truly democratic OMYC is: social and political divisions run like fault lines through the community, and the concession's institutional structures and ecological landscape are deeply entangled with this social world. After all, "the concession is the people," and Uaxactún's people are infamous among state and NGO staff (who otherwise extol the pleasures of working in Uaxactún's beautiful forest) for their social turmoil.

WCS: An NGO at Home in Uaxactún

The Wildlife Conservation Society has a long history in Uaxactún. The Guatemalan branch of the U.S.-based NGO started with a short-term project in the village in 1996, slowly expanding to its current geographic range and political influence. True to its origins, WCS-Guatemala has maintained a constant, if part-time, residential presence over the years, building up from a single hut to a large compound shared with other institutions. Relations between the NGO and villagers are never conflict-free, especially given divisions within the community itself. Over the years, villagers burned down most of their houses, but WCS rebuilt every time. This demonstration of commitment has built a slow and steady trust between the NGO and many Uaxactuneros that other institutions fail to achieve.

If the concession is the people, WCS's field technician in Uaxactún, Juan Castellanos, is well suited to his position. Born and raised in Flores, Juan is friendly, relaxed, and outgoing. Two of his brothers also work in MBR conservation, a family trait that Juan traces back to his grandfather's agroforestry practices. He grew up on a family farm in San Miguel, across the lake from Flores, where his grandfather grew fruit trees, perennial crops, short-rotation milpa fields of corn, squash, and beans, and raised animals. Juan reminisced about wandering over to Petencito, a small zoo near San Miguel filled with local animals, while his grandfather made lime nearby. After studying forestry in college, Juan quickly found himself drawn into the world of MBR community concessions, first through short-term contracts writing management plans, then slowly settling into his role in Uaxactún with WCS.

Juan now spends between 25 and 50 percent of his time in the village, depending on the season and projects underway. The work in the village is *un rollo social*, he tells me—tricky social business.[4] Echoing the development critiques of Mosse (2005), Juan told me that official measures of success and failure in the village didn't mean much: "Maybe at the end you get something that looks like 'good results,'" he said, "but [projects] won't actually *do* anything without the social aspect." Walking through the village, he greets nearly everybody he passes, calling out friendly hellos to a few and stopping to linger in conversation with most, keeping close tabs on daily happenings, concerns, and small-town gossip. With all this pausing to chat, it takes four times as long to get anywhere. Juan jokes, "It's like we're in Antigua, visiting the stations of the cross." Even when there is nothing much to say, there is a friendly presence to be made felt, an enduring human connection to be maintained with the institution.

Though far from the only institution working in the village, WCS is central to dynamics of knowledge, livelihoods, and identity in Uaxactún. With its mission of scientifically driven conservation, the NGO conducts a variety of studies and monitoring activities in the village. Both the Basic Necessities survey and xate quality monitoring are carried out in part by WCS, as were several other studies conducted during my visits to the village. This knowledge production about Uaxactún goes hand-in-hand with WCS's long-term commitment to its residents and forests and is an important part of the institution's broader work across the reserve. As much as these knowledges primarily serve the institution, they are both composed and composted in Uaxactún. Reported outward to donors or back to villagers, new knowledges of and about the village enliven and entangle villagers, institutional actors, and the more-than-human landscape.

Aggregating and Extracting: The Basic Necessities Survey

The Basic Necessities survey is a prime example of extractive knowledge production about Uaxactún. It displays the many transformations, erasures, and elisions required to translate complex village lives and livelihoods into standardized numerical measures. The 2011 survey was a follow-up to focus groups and surveys carried out by WCS and Asociación Balam in 2009, which established a baseline measure of local poverty for a project funded by the U.K. Department for International Development (DFID; see box 7.1). The survey was reconducted in 2011–12 in four MBR villages in order to assess whether the DFID project was improving the well-being of residents in these target communities. My involvement with Basic Necessities began with my recruitment by WCS as a number cruncher, helping to process and interpret the second iteration of survey data for Carmelita. After struggling to make sense of numerical shifts in perceptions and poverty without local contextual knowledge, I was invited to help conduct the follow-up surveys in Uaxactún.

....

BOX 7.1: BASIC NECESSITIES METHODOLOGY

The Basic Necessities survey is designed to identify and measure locally relevant indicators of poverty and well-being, rather than relying on globally standardized calculations. The methodology begins with focus groups to identify goods and services considered locally necessary, or potentially so. These exercises are used to compile a master list of thirty-five to forty items that might range from clean drinking water to chainsaws to personal computers. This list then forms the basis for the survey: household representatives are asked to indicate first whether they have access to or own the item in question, and then whether or not they consider that item a basic necessity, defined as "things that all families should have and none should live without" (WCS Living Landscapes Program n.d.). Any item that 50 percent or more of surveyed households declare a necessity is included in community-wide calculations of poverty.

Each household's poverty index is calculated, representing the total number of surveyed items that a household has access to weighted according to their communal rating as necessities. For example, if access to medical care is considered a basic necessity by 100 percent of respondents, and cell phones by 85 percent, then a household with access to a doctor but no cell phone would have a better score than vice versa. In WCS's comparison of Uaxactún's survey results between 2009 and 2011, a very slight reduction in overall poverty was seen, with no change in the distribution of poverty within the community.

As it turned out, conducting the surveys in a familiar place only increased my uncertainty rather than diminishing it. Essential to the Basic Necessities methodology was a direct comparison of the same households after two years' time. The 2009 survey was carried out by semicensus, going door-to-door to get a sample representing a broad swath of the community. Each household surveyed was recorded by numbering its rooftop on an aerial photograph, by GPS point, and by recording the family's surnames. In 2011, we were to follow the marked aerial image to find the same families from the first round, in order to directly measure improvements or declines in household well-being.

Unfortunately, the map had been lost. Instead, we only had the list of family names, so it fell to me and my cosurveyor from Balam, Julián, to re-mark the map while trying to find households based on surnames alone. With complex naming conventions and multiply overlapping kinship lines, this was difficult.[5] If the "Alvarez Nuñez" household appeared on the list, was this a family headed by a man surnamed Alvarez Nuñez, or one in which the husband's last name was Alvarez and his wife's Nuñez, giving their children the joined name? I rarely felt certain that I had found the correct household, but wandering packed-dirt paths and calling out to canvass the names of each house I passed provided an exceptional introduction to the geography of kinship in the village. This would soon become a familiar pattern: the things I learned from conducting this survey were rarely those things we set out to measure.

The Basic Necessities methodology translates complex questions of local priorities, preferences, and access to goods and services into a numerical measure, ready for aggregation and comparison across sites. Julián and I acted as instruments of standardization, moving slowly from house to house, matching our observations and inferences with the answers of our interlocutors. We worked to create clear distinctions between "yes" and "no" answers in interaction with respondents who favored evasive gray zones like "*cuando hay . . .*" (We have X item, *when it's available*). Other answers, apparently clear, might be undermined by their accompanying commentary, such as one woman's answer, "Yes, a chainsaw is a necessity, for when I'm fighting with my man!" Our algorithms were inconsistent, evolving, worked out in the interactions within each household—what to mark down when a husband and wife disagree about whether a television is a necessity?—and then again reset between survey days as we conferred about which questions were hardest to get good (yes/no) answers to. We tried to gently rephrase these, without invalidating comparison to previously gathered answers.

More worrying to me than the transformations of some answers was the erasure of others. In one household, the husband returned from working partway through my survey and took over answering while his wife retreated from her previous friendly engagement to a wary, watchful silence. In another, a bare hut of thin poles and thatch built at the farthest edge of town, a Q'eqchi' family answered with hedging "cuando hay" to questions that most households happily joked about: "Access to three meals a day? I sometimes eat five!" This family's survey results proved a blunted reflection of their relative poverty and marginality, but as I walked away from their house, I realized that I had misconducted my surveying: their names did not appear on my list; their data had to be excluded from the overall analysis. By the rules of methodology, this household was erased, its poverty not even sample-able.

Open to Interpretation

Only once villagers' nuanced answers had been coded and quantified did our task turn to making sense of the results. With surveying complete, I set to processing the data in Excel spreadsheets, trying to pull meaning out of the numbers again. This data analysis further obscured the gray zones of survey answers, aggregating yes, no, and necessity answers into household- and community-wide measures of poverty and access. I remembered the stories, jokes, and tentative moments, just how uncertain each data point had felt as

I collected it. But my uncertainty was displaced by an emergent trust in the aggregate results as graphs and statistics surfaced out of my spreadsheet. After all, one family's "cuando hay" had been marked as a "yes" for the question of eating wild game, but another had surely chosen to answer "no" when they ate deer regularly, knowing that the survey was for a conservation NGO that frowned upon hunting. Overall, the measure of well-being in the community seemed fairly accurate, more so than results for individual houses. In the knowledge I helped construct, a charismatic truthfulness emerged from the aggregate of individually untrustworthy data points.

Although the village's poverty indices had not changed much since 2009, patterns emerged that indicated a balance of improvements (more motorcycles) and losses (a broken village water tank), as well as shifts moving faster in people's perceptions of necessity than in their actual access to certain items (like the internet). Factors that did not affect the overall statistics were most important to Julián: he was happy to see more houses where only adults worked, not their children, which he connected to the growing emphasis on education in the village. He was also fascinated by the patchwork of income sources that each household drew on, and the implications for NGO practice. Nearly all families answered with a single income source (usually xate) at first, but upon further digging it turned out that most had three or four minor sources of monetary income in any given year.

Because the poverty index had not changed much, the 2011 survey results failed to reflect what DFID project implementers insisted were widespread benefits and improvements in village life. As such, the survey appeared to have failed as a reflexive measure of institutional practice. Instead, isolated questions ended up being more useful to NGO staff. In response to the question of whether they ate wild game, many people responded, "No hay" (There isn't any). Julián optimistically chose to interpret this not as a reduction in local animal populations due to overhunting, but as fewer people dedicating themselves to hunting as a source of income, resulting in fewer opportunities to buy wild meat in the village. Village-wide results showed that both the consumption of wild meat and its perceived necessity had dropped significantly, while perception of domestic fowl and pigs as necessary had increased without a corresponding increase in animal ownership. Had economic or legal factors, conservationist cultural values, reduced animal populations, or some combination driven the reduction in wild meat consumption? Was the increasing perception of the necessity of domestic animals a response to declining availability of (otherwise preferred) wild meat? The results raised more questions than they answered, and things learned from the Basic Necessities survey were rarely related to its purported purpose.

An Overexamined Life: Surveys and Sense of Place

Concurrent with the Basic Necessities survey, there were at least four other household surveys circulating in the community. Most results never find their way back to the village; the findings are directed outward to international academic and professional audiences, to NGO donors or granting agencies, or into state and NGO project files. Many Uaxactuneros expressed frustration with this dynamic, asking, "What do these studies do for us?" Moving from house to house, I invited respondents to ask questions or to discuss survey items as we went. Responses to this invitation reflected exasperation with the intensely studied nature of life in the village. People asked, "What is this survey for? Who will see the results? Will we? What happens if the results don't look good for the project?"

Some villagers recognized that people conducting studies often brought other benefits along with them, or might return to the community in other capacities. One man pointed out that Roan Balas McNab, director of WCS-Guatemala, first came to Uaxactún for his master's thesis research, and then stayed—the origin of one of the most influential NGOs in the reserve today. At least three others who originally came to conduct studies have returned to work in the village on behalf of NGOs. Foreign researchers like myself often choose Uaxactún as a research site due to its relative accessibility, safety, and the availability of institutional introductions; I crossed paths with two other U.S. graduate students there. While the implications of our academic studies may be even father removed from daily village life than those of NGOs, our presence fuels small-scale local economies and a sense of connection to global ideas, markets, and worlds otherwise inaccessible.

This sense of connection is also a sense of place. Through the experience of being the objects of constant study, Uaxactuneros come to know their place as one defined by its standing forests and the clean air they produce, its lauded example of community-based management, and its cultivated *cultura de conservación* (culture of conservation). This phrase, reminiscent of Agrawal's (2005) environmentality in which local environmental subjectivity is reshaped in the interest of state resource management, is often heard in the local school, community assemblies and meetings, and documents, reports, and presentations about the community. A representative described OMYC's role in the community in similar terms: "We sow ideas and awareness" (Sembramos ideas y conciencia). These understandings of identity and place are constructed in relation with outsider institutions and individuals, and villagers adopt these along with the sense that others know their place better than they themselves. One survey respondent told me (without noticeable irony) that WCS had more information about the community and concession than OMYC, such that now when they want to know something about themselves, they go to the NGO to ask.

Authoritative knowledge about Uaxactún was increasingly recognized as extralocal, while some of the most valuable local knowledge included the ability to access and navigate external discourses, institutions, and resources. This is not to say that there is no traditional local knowledge, ecological or otherwise, but that people recognize *authoritative* statements about Uaxactún as those based on external monitoring data.[6] This is a reflection of institutional and social networks of power in the MBR nooscape. Beyond how these outward-bound studies enter Uaxactuneros' sense of place, others are reported back to community members. These practices, like the monitoring of xate quality, can shape not only senses of identity and place, but also local arrangements of labor, livelihoods, and ecologies.

Caring for Xate, Caring for *Xateros*

Josue paused as we hiked along the forest path and crouched down to untwine a tightly wrapped tendril of climbing vine from a xate palm leaf, twisted and pulled by the vine's pernicious grip. "There are *xateros* [xate harvesters] who don't take these off," he said, "but, oooh! *Pobrecita!* [Poor little thing!]" he declared, delicately smoothing out the crumpled palm. "When it rains it will become more beautiful," he assured me. Implied in this beauty was the leaf's recuperation into being harvestable, marketable, a potential source of income for xateros like himself, to be sold and shipped to the U.S. and Europe where the leaves are used in floral arrangements. Beyond a simple economic relation, however, his actions pointed to the ongoing transformation of xate from a natural, exploited part of the Uaxactún landscape to something to actively *cuidar*, to care for.

Transformations in Uaxactuneros' relationships with xate are at the center of evolving webs of knowledge, identity, institutional alliances, and livelihoods. Xate palms—actually three distinct species with their own ecological and economic idiosyncrasies (box 7.2)—are simultaneously the "daily beans" for most Uaxactún residents, the object of intense study and regulation, a commodity marketable to international floral markets, a marker of local identity, and a ubiquitous part of the forest understory. Between 60 and 80 percent of Uaxactún households rely on xate income at some point during the year, and the palms account for 30 percent of total monetary income in the community (Zetina Tún 2011). Because of this local importance, recent projects designed to increase xate's abundance in the forest understory are a rare example of truly convergent ecological and economic goals in the reserve. NGO-driven practices of study and scientific curiosity are at the heart of these projects, central to ongoing shifts in the relationship between xate and Uaxactuneros.

....

BOX 7.2: XATE

Three species of xate palm (*Chamaedorea* spp.) are harvested in Uaxactún, known by the Spanish common names *jade* (jade, also called *macho* or male), *hembra* (female), and *cola de pescado* (fishtail). Xate are understory plants, preferring dense shade, and grow in rich ecological interaction with several species of beetles and thrips (pollinators), as well as birds and mammals (seed dispersers). Once harvested, xate leaves can stay fresh for four to six weeks, making them an ideal product for international floral markets.

The market for jade (*C. oblongata*) persists year-round, and the palm is found throughout the concession in high abundance. Hembra (*C. elegans*), too, grows abundantly in Uaxactún, but its market is concentrated in the dry season (February–May), with a surge at Easter. Seeds of both species are collected locally by xateros and sold to OMYC for enrichment projects, taking two to four years to mature and produce seed. Jade harvested in Uaxactún is exported to the United States and Europe, while hembra is sold primarily to the Netherlands.

Cola de pescado (*C. ernesti-augustii*) is by far the most valuable of the three species, with a year-round market. Very little of the palm is found in the concession; some people claim that fishtail has never grown in this area, while others report that it used to be abundant but was overharvested to near extinction. It is being (re)introduced into Uaxactún's forests by a municipal project: seeds are bought from dealers outside the community, and the plants will take up to eight years to mature and produce seed.

Ecological Care

I use the term "care" to describe particular relations—affective and practical, material and discursive—both between Uaxactún's xateros and palms, and between WCS (and other institutions) and Uaxactuneros.[7] Care is a logic or ethics that seeks to ameliorate, to make more livable, but without an assumed end of best practice, cure, or solution. Instead, an ethics of care emphasizes that the question of the good is never settled and always unfolds in particular contexts "full of complex ambivalence and shifting tensions" (Mol, Moser, and Pols 2010, 14). Importantly, practices of care are never disembedded from power relations, and care is not an exclusive category—practices can simultaneously be caring and exploitative, instrumental, or oppressive.

Joan Tronto and Berenice Fisher provide a working definition of "care": "On the most general level, we suggest that caring be viewed as a *species activity that includes everything that we do to maintain, continue, and repair our 'world' so that we can live in it as well as possible.* That world includes our bodies, our selves, and our environment, all of which we seek to interweave in a complex, life-sustaining web" (Fisher and Tronto 1990, 40, emphasis in original). This definition is not restricted to care for humans, nor to actions by or on autonomous individuals, but rather recognizes care as fostering complex, distributed, ongoing relations of interdependence. I build on this definition of care to decenter human exceptionalism and to emphasize that xate is an active participant in these relations. What xate likes and needs, how it grows, when it reproduces, all these affect emerging formations of knowledge, labor, and identity in Uaxactún.

I emphasize an ecological notion of care as part of the MBR nooscape, attending to the interplay of knowledge production, power relations, and material practices that shape how care emerges at particular scales and relations, but not others. WCS has led many recent xate projects in Uaxactún, including formal studies, ongoing monitoring of extraction and marketability, understory enrichment, and others. These projects have been instrumental in turning Uaxactuneros' relationships with xate from simple extraction into care. These shifts are partial—not total transformations, but complex, often contradictory processes of change in both material and discursive relationships between villagers, plants, institutions, and the forested landscape. These projects enact multiple scales and types of care—of villagers for understory palms, of an NGO for local people, and of a community-NGO alliance for a forested landscape—revealing how multiple forms of care can simultaneously support and undermine each other, particularly when embedded within broader political ecological contexts.

Caring for Xate . . .

On the day he took me harvesting, Josue showed me how to collect xate according to OMYC's sustainable management plan, leaving at least two full-grown healthy leaves, or one plus a shoot of new growth (called a *candela*, or candlestick), to ensure the survival and flourishing of the plant. But he also cared for plants that he wasn't harvesting as we moved through the underbrush: removing diseased or insect-ridden leaves, or patiently disentangling the palms from aggressive vines. Josue is a xatero, a forest labor identity that builds on histories of harvesting other NTFPs in Uaxactún, particularly chicle, the natural rubber used in chewing gum before the invention of synthetics. Many Uaxactuneros still refer to themselves as chicleros (chicle harvesters), although the market for chicle dropped in the 1960s due to political upheaval and the invention of synthetic gum alternatives.

Xate has since replaced chicle in Uaxactún's forest livelihoods, and now stands as a symbol of regional histories of extraction in which it never really took part. Other NTFPs are harvested in the concession, including chicle (*Manilkara zapota*), allspice (*Pimenta dioica*), ramón nut (*Brosimum alicastrum*, sometimes sold as rain forest nut), and others. But xate has thoroughly permeated the village as a symbol of local identity, even forming the basis for a costume in the village's annual Independence Day pageant. One member of OMYC's board of directors referred to xate harvesting as an *actividad de nuestros abuelos* (activity of our grandfathers), while another told me that xate had always been "everywhere," but until recently was just one more plant on the landscape, without value. The latter is perhaps more historically accurate, but the imaginative memory of xate-cutting abuelos reflects current intersections of identity and livelihood. By entangling xate with old chiclero histories, the palm is tied to deep Petenero traditions of living and working in the forest—a historical claim that also strengthens community demands for ongoing extraction rights inside the reserve.

Learning to Care

The material and discursive underpinnings of xatero identity are shifting, and not just from one NTFP to another. Xateros (those who cut) are becoming conservationists (those who protect).[8] Josue's tender actions as he collected leaves are one example of this shift, an affective connection shaped by his recent six-month job with WCS. Two WCS jobs rotate through OMYC members; these include daily care for xate in nurseries around the NGO's housing compound in the village and in plantations beneath the forest canopy (figures 7.1 and 7.2). At twenty-five, Josue was sweet and optimistic, and often brought his young son along while he worked around the WCS installations. His companion in the rotating positions, Marvin, was far more cynical in discussions of conservation or institutional politics, but when it came time to tend to the xate nurseries he was as delicate and attentive as Josue. Uaxactuneros hired by WCS learn to talk about "what the plants like" and to be mindful in their work with seeds and seedlings. This manifests in many details: xate seeds are neatly arranged in furrowed rows of soil (in contrast with the spatially irregular sowing of crops in traditional milpa agriculture); watering pipes over seed beds are patiently watched and manually rotated so that the water falls evenly; thatched roofs over the nurseries are tended to mimic the shade of the forest; and watering is adjusted to seasonal patterns of heat and humidity—not to replicate natural conditions, but to encourage the palms to survive and mature more quickly.

These micropractices of care grew from projects aiming to increase the abundance of xate in Uaxactún's forests, established through the acuerdo de conservación with WCS. As in Paso Caballos, this agreement outlines material and technical support provided to the community in exchange for participation in conservation activities such as fire management, forest patrols, and administrative reform within OMYC. Through the acuerdo, WCS provides support for village schools, assistance with fire management and monitoring, financial incentives for sustainable xate harvesting, and xate enrichment programs in the forest. Responsibility for xate projects is shared by OMYC and WCS, with OMYC buying seeds or seedlings and WCS paying for the labor (including Josue's six months) involved in germinating and tending seedlings in their outdoor nursery, and in transplanting a minimum of twenty thousand palm seedlings per year into the concession's forest. A few other organizations have xate enrichment projects underway too, but WCS's permanence in the community and acuerdo-structured funding commitment make its efforts particularly influential.

Enrichment projects reflect an institutional shift from focusing on harvesting practices to increasing xate's abundance in the concession's forests. Along with its nurseries, WCS started an experimental xate plantation in an

FIGURE 7.1 A Uaxactunero places xate seeds in furrowed soil in one of WCS's nurseries (photograph by author).

FIGURE 7.2 Xate seedlings receive a drip watering in one of WCS's Uaxactún nurseries. Most of the seedlings are of the feathery *hembra* variety, with a few *jade* seedlings visible in the lower left corner. These seedlings will be transplanted to the concession's forests in areas designated for future NTFP harvest, where they will grow to maturity. The leaves of *cola de pescado* palms (several years old, being grown to produce seed) appear in the photo's lower edges (photograph by author).

abandoned agricultural patch regrown into secondary forest at the edge of the village. In it, schoolkids were given responsibility for 20 × 20 meter plots, taught to transplant, tend, and harvest the palms without permanently damaging them, and allowed to keep the small income from any xate they grew and cut. The plantation was, according to WCS technician Carlos, an experiment in three senses: biological, economic, and social. Biologically, the xate flourished under the guided care of the kids and WCS's rotating staff. Economically, WCS calculated that it would take nine or ten years to see a significant return on investment in such a plantation, but that eventually the plots would produce seed as well as palm leaves, becoming economically as well as ecologically sustainable. But socially, Carlos told me, it was a disaster. Located next to the village instead of a day's walk through the jungle, the experimental plantation was sacked by xateros. The machete slash landed on fresh palm stalks rather than OMYC equipment tires, but reflected the same social conflicts and "law of the jungle" logics as other destructive acts in Uaxactún. Carlos noted that the plantation would need constant patrols to protect against this pillaging, thereby negating any economic benefit. Newer xate enrichment projects from WCS thus depart from this private plantation model. Instead, OMYC selects an area of the concession already designated for NTFP harvest, and palm seedlings are transplanted to enrich the natural abundance of a common resource.

It is in the nurseries associated with this enrichment project that new relations to xate are formed. The ability to reduce germination time for xate was accidentally discovered by a Peace Corps volunteer, who forgot to remove seeds from a diluted peroxide solution meant to wash them. This led to a ten-day soaking practice that causes seeds to germinate about a month before they would with simple watering. This happy accident led to a broader experimental relation to xate growing, requiring hired Uaxactuneros to cultivate curiosity, to learn to recognize the needs of the plants with great sensitivity (signs of sun damage, insect infestation, etc.), and to become familiar with the different growth and reproduction rates of the three different species. The handful of men who rotated through WCS positions during my fieldwork—all of whom usually rely on xate harvesting as their primary source of income—spoke with great pleasure about how much they learned about xate, identifying this new knowledge as their favorite part of the job, and demonstrating tenderness in their interactions with the plants. By engaging in practices of caring for xate, a conservationist love for the plants begins to grow into the bodies of laborers.

Monitoring and Transformation

Interventions on xate abundance and harvesting were triggered by new external monitoring practices that accompanied Uaxactún's concession contract in 2000. In the concession's early years, xate was sold to external contractors by weight, encouraging xateros to cut as much as they could (including damaged or diseased leaves) to earn money.[9] A 2004 WCS study of harvested xate quality (defined as the marketable percentage of harvested leaves) estimated that only 25–30 percent of leaves sold to contractors were being selected for market. Responding to overharvesting and poor economic returns, a xate selection facility was established in Uaxactún, operated by OMYC with NGO accompaniment.[10] OMYC now pays xateros per marketable leaf instead of by weight, doubling the price per leaf earned by harvesters. This allows more oversight and control within the concession and captures a larger proportion of xate's economic benefits within the community by selling directly to exporters in Guatemala City (OMYC 2009). In addition, women from the village are hired for sorting and selection of harvested leaves, adding a frequently touted benefit to local women to the project.

Around the time the selection facility was introduced, WCS conducted another study, on the ecological impacts of xate harvesting. They determined how many leaves could be cut from a plant without killing it, and OMYC developed a management plan based on this information. These days, cutting is not surveyed in the field; instead, continued monitoring of xate quality in the selection facility has become a proxy measure for sustainable harvesting practices—less waste at the market selection point indicates less overharvesting in the forest.[11] All xateros now have individual quality statistics reported back to them as an assessment of their harvesting practices. Similarly, the total percentage of xate selected for market is calculated by WCS and reported back to the concession as a measure of their ecological management. Since quality monitoring began, the percentage of leaves selected for market has remained well above the 70 percent minimum set by OMYC's management plan, and in 2011 stayed consistently above 90 percent.

A poster-sized copy of the xate quality graph hangs in the selection facility, where WCS posted it to communicate monitoring results to xateros and selectors. But reading graphs requires specialized visual and numerical literacy, and this one was not well designed for a nonexpert audience. The graph is hard to interpret even for those familiar with the medium (figure 7.3; look, for example, at the inconsistent time scale on the bottom, the unexplained line

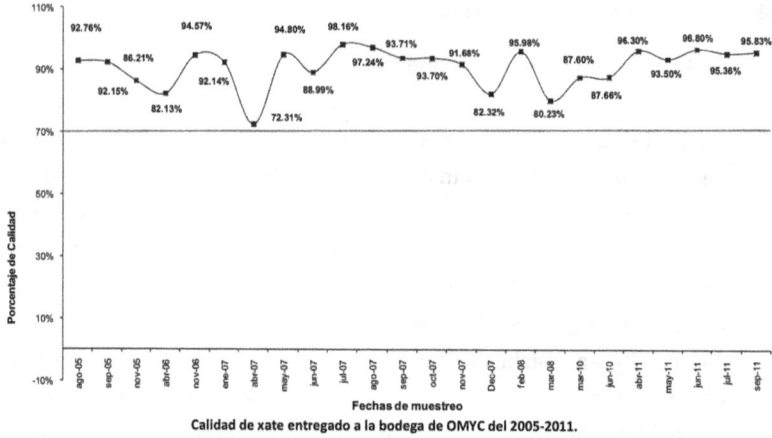

Calidad de xate entregado a la bodega de OMYC del 2005-2011.

FIGURE 7.3 Graph titled "Quality of xate delivered to the OMYC bodega 2005–2011." The x-axis is "sample dates," and the y-axis is "percentage of quality." No further definitions or explanation are included with most presentations of the graph (image: WCS).

at 70 percent, etc.).[12] For people working in the selection facility, the graph is usually interpreted as a reminder that somebody is watching to make sure they're not screwing up. In my visits to the facility, I never once saw anybody glance at the graph without my prompting—until the day a USAID delegation visited and gathered around it to see the impacts of their funding, at which point the graph very successfully communicated responsibility, collaboration, and sustainability to an important donor (figure 7.4).

Reporting Back

Despite its local illegibility, the graph hanging in the selection facility formed a part of WCS's new initiative to report monitoring data back to community-managed concessions throughout the MBR, a strong contrast to most extractive studies. Their ecological evaluations combined broad, remote sensing–based factors from CEMEC (like deforestation or fire damage) with fine-scale indicators particular to each area (like xate quality in Uaxactún or active macaw nests in Carmelita), creating a somewhat general rubric for comparison. After years of collecting these data for institutional use, WCS began in 2011 to present these reports to the leaders of the concessions, including OMYC's board of directors.

FIGURE 7.4 A group of visitors from USAID gathers around the xate quality graph in Uaxactún's selection facility, guided by a member of OMYC (photograph by author).

The first formal presentation to Uaxactún was congratulatory and full of lively discussion, with frequent questions from OMYC board members and commentary provided by Juan Castellanos. Juan acted in a kind of translator capacity, providing local context and explanation for the data projected on-screen. Looking at a map of satellite-detected fires, Juan pointed out that all the fires stayed within the limits of the concession's designated agricultural area, and that although they registered as burned forest according to satellites and technical definition, locals would recognize the burned lands as *guamil* (regrown fallow), not as mature forest.[13] Juan's guiding commentary also reflected his awareness of the gap between NGO lingo and local ways of speaking. Once, he recounted, he had seen a poster in Uaxactún discussing "tools for sustainable development," but people did not seem to understand what it was about. He asked a few men what they understood by the word "tools" (*herramientas*), and they answered: hammers, screwdrivers, saws. Juan made clear that the issue was not with literacy per se, but with the ways that language shifts between formal institutional and rural contexts—a comment that echoed back to me when viewing the xate quality graph in the selection facility.

Still, even basic efforts to report back sets WCS's xate quality and other ecological monitoring apart from most studies of Uaxactún. Even without understanding the xate graph, its presence in the selection facility communicates the presence of external oversight and the supportive message that the concession is sustainably managing a key NTFP. Reporting back also serves the NGO. A WCS biologist explained the interdependency between WCS's monitoring program and OMYC, formalized in the acuerdo de conservación: OMYC gains measures of their ecological success that have high reliability and rigor, as marked by coming from external sources. On the other side, WCS gains the ability to claim that their monitoring programs serve an important purpose for local people, justifying funding for future monitoring of the landscape.

. . . Caring for Xateros?

In the case of xate, external monitoring and reporting back are central to new formations of caring for plants, caring for the landscape, and caring for people. These knowledge-making practices, and the projects attached to them, continue to transform xateros' relationships to the forest landscape and the plants within it, shifting these from pure extraction to more complex interactions characterized by curiosity, nourishing, and care. WCS's xate projects—from germinating, raising, and transplanting seedlings to careful harvesting, selection, and monitoring of marketable leaves—have changed the plant from a natural part of the landscape into something that is actively cultivated and cared for. At the same time, they are changing xateros from ecologically destructive bulk harvesters to careful conservationists. Most xateros have not yet worked in WCS's nurseries, but as people rotate slowly through these jobs and interact with different forms of monitoring and attention, they emerge with transformed perspectives and affective connections to the plant, its place on the landscape, and shared human-xate futures.

As hopeful as these transformations are in many ways, increasing the abundance of xate leaves many problems unaddressed. Most Uaxactuneros rely on xate for subsistence income, and when I expressed my hopefulness about these projects as a way of caring for people by way of caring for the plants and landscape, Juan Castellanos brought me back down to earth. "Maybe . . ." He hesitated. "No, maybe not. In the question of food security, no. It wouldn't cover it. It wouldn't guarantee enough income." Similarly, when Josue spoke to me about working in WCS's nurseries, he emphasized his changed perspective but also pointed to its limits: "Before working here, I didn't know anything about xate—how to grow it, how to . . . nothing. But thanks to God, I learned. I learned. Not just to cut. Not just to destroy. Because to be a xatero is to destroy. But I'm not saying . . . maybe you have a huge need, and if you find a little plant of xate that just has one leaf, you just have to cut it, out of necessity. And then that little plant is going to die." For Josue, who cared for a young son, the need to support one's family outweighed discourses of sustainability and the affective relations he had cultivated with xate plants. On our harvesting trip, he pointed out a palm that had been overharvested, its candela a shriveled grey-brown. "This one is going to die," he reported matter-of-factly, passing no judgment on whoever had cut the plant too deeply. New knowledges and practices of care that appear powerful at one scale can still be undermined by the structural constraints facing individual xateros.

Care Is Not a Panacea

The transformation of local perspectives on xate can be read as a form of environmentality (Agrawal 2005), of making new environmental subjects without transforming broader conditions of life and labor in the reserve. As much as caring for xate may transform perspectives and relations, and will almost certainly help ensure access to the resource in the future, it does not change the basic structures that require men to work as independent laborers, trekking through forest to cut and haul palm in large bundles loaded onto mules, motorcycles, bicycles, and strong backs. The advantage, another Uaxactunero told me, is that whenever you have a free day you can go out and work, and you'll see the money quickly. But, he continued, in the summer it's unbearably hot, and in the rainy season the paths are nearly impassable with mud. It's difficult physical work, dependent on uncertain international markets, and is heavily gendered.[14]

The women hired to work in the selection facility mostly sit around unpaid, waiting for xateros to return from harvesting with bundles of palm, at which point they work in short, ten-minute bursts of sorting. The women separate marketable from damaged, too small, or discolored leaves, count the separated piles, then report the totals to both the xatero and the facility supervisor, who records them in a monitoring log. The selectors, like xateros, are paid by the leaf; on a good day they might earn between 25 and 30 Quetzals ($3–4), compared to the 600 to 800 Quetzals ($75–100) that a xatero can earn in the same day. Packers—also men—trim and roll up bundles of xate after they have been sorted; they are paid more than twice as much per leaf as the selectors they work alongside. The women's work is by no means hard, and there are few other opportunities for paid employment for women. But framing these meager earnings as a great gender-equality benefit is hard to swallow.

A closer look reveals insecurity on the xatero side, too. The potential to earn over $75 for a hard day's work can seem like an extraordinary opportunity in a place otherwise devoid of income sources, but the precarity of this income—especially considering uncertain markets and external subsidies—should not be underestimated. Xate sales operate in a regular way in Uaxactún: OMYC has contracts with midlevel distributors who transport the palms by truck to Guatemala City, at which point they are flown around the world. But this supply chain, and the U.S. and European floral decoration markets upon which it relies, are inherently unstable. There are many points of vulnerability along this chain, any one of which could undermine this vital source of income for Uaxactuneros. For example, there are new attempts to start xate plantations in other regions of Guatemala, where the palm is grown under artificial shade to replicate the forests of the Petén. If these become successful, they may undermine Uaxactún's xate sales through direct competition or via ecological claims to provide the plant without harm to protected forests. The consumer market for the palms could also shift unpredictably in terms of valuation or demand. Chicle, the former economic heart of Uaxactún, is instructive in this regard: chicle extraction shaped the social and ecological landscape of the Petén for centuries, but a sudden drop in market demand in the 1970s collapsed most of these formations (Schwartz 1990). Xate may have replaced this natural rubber in Petenero identity formations, but the regional system of unclaimed territories and unregulated extraction has also disappeared, replaced with an NGO-dominated conservation landscape embedded in globalized neoliberal capitalism.

Conservation priorities are fundamentally at odds with extractive economies, despite many attempts to marry the two. Uaxactún's geographic marginality gives them an advantage in preserving forest cover—protected by poor road access and the buffering effects of Tikal National Park—but at the same time undermines many possibilities for improving access to basic goods and services. The village lacks reliable drinking water, electric, or communication infrastructure, all of which are tightly constrained by protected-area regulations (a single landline serves the community, which receives no cellular service, although a recent NGO project brought satellite internet access to the local school). Uaxactún's twenty-five-year concession contract with the state expires in 2025, with renewal possible but far from certain. Despite praise for its forest management, the threat of losing concession rights or even being evicted from the reserve is strongly feared within the community (Zetina Tún 2011). OMYC documents also point to a lack of political or legal security with changing national governments; lack of political will on the part of state agencies to uphold their end of the concession contract; neoliberal trade agreements that undermine local rights; lack of market regulation for many of the forest products produced; petroleum interests; and other serious threats to the concession (OMYC 2009). At multiple interlocking scales, vulnerability and precarity dominate.

Temporary solutions and improvements, including the xate enrichment and extraction projects detailed here, are deeply subsidized by NGOs, which are themselves constrained by short-term funding cycles and global institutional priorities that may have little to do with local needs. While the Guatemalan branch of WCS enjoys considerable programmatic freedom from the head office in New York City, contradictions between the organization's biodiversity conservation mandate and efforts to integrate local social, political, and economic concerns are many. To maintain its daily operations, WCS must prioritize extensive studies, project writing, assessment and reporting activities, and other work that has little to do with local people. The uneven dynamics of knowledge production, and the recognition that reporting back to local actors is also a generative activity for future NGO funding, are exemplary in this regard. Those working in WCS and other NGOs recognize these contradictions, but recognition is not the same as transformation. Juan Castellano's recognition of the difference between official project success (valuable to the institution and its donors) and positive outcomes on the ground begins to ameliorate this tension, since this shapes his work and decisions in the village. But this itself is precarious, reliant on the social skills and political judgments of an individual who is ultimately unable to change the power relations in which he too is embedded.

The concept of care allows recognition of efforts to ameliorate the situation of marginalized people and environments on multiple scales, while simultaneously recognizing the embedded contradictions and structural limitations to these efforts. If care is a striving toward something better, without assuming that an ultimate goal or solution will be reached, then WCS's xate projects indeed fit the definition, working as they do toward sustainable shared human-nonhuman futures. Overall, these xate projects might best be described by the phrase oft used by Donna Haraway (2008): they are necessary, but not sufficient. While the projects do run in parallel with a strong emphasis on education initiatives (aimed at getting kids out of Uaxactún and forest labor in the future), they are ultimately more concerned with the permanence and well-being of plants than people.

Care describes one way of working through the incommensurabilities produced at this node in the MBR nooscape. By attending to the interplays of knowledge, power, and material practice at multiple scales, it becomes possible to see how care emerges within particular scales and relations, but not others. Care makes it possible to live better in the absence of fundamental changes in the political, geographic, and economic marginality of Uaxactún, but it is this same extension of possibility that means care is never enough. Close attention to the material practices and embedded values of care helps us see that these and other conservation projects are more than just extensions of the structural status quo. Care is a striving, a concerted movement toward something a little bit better, if not an ultimate good. Like Josue's affectionate attention to the health of wild palms and ultimate prioritization of his family's food security, the contradictions of conservation and development are inescapable. And like Josue, finding ways to care even when faced with these contradictions is an essential form of striving, a striving mirrored by WCS in its projects even as these are undermined by other political and economic forces shaping life, livelihoods, and ecologies in Uaxactún.

Turning Knowledge into Tierra

The intensity of external monitoring and knowledge production in Uaxactún has become a mundane—if contested—part of village life, and the practices and outcomes of these studies have effects that range far beyond stated research goals. Xate quality monitoring is based on a strange calculation in which marketability stands in for ecologically sustainable field harvesting practices, but its ongoing practice in the village has been key to transforming local plant-human relations. The Basic Necessities survey is intended to measure NGO-led transformations, not trigger them, but its results end up raising new questions, problems, and sites for further study and intervention. Both contribute to Uaxactuneros' awareness of having little control over the questions and terms of studies being carried out, reinforcing the identity of the village as an externally known place.

Still, these external knowledges about Uaxactún are turned into tierra, which means both earth and land. Earth first: through the lens of knowledge ecology, knowledges are turned into the earth like compost as they are absorbed, digested, transformed, and remade into interventions—new projects, new harvesting practices, new village-institutional relations—each of which has real, material impacts on Uaxactún's more-than-human landscape. Second, tierra as land indexes property rights, or at least rights of access and use, as in Uaxactuneros' reference to their agricultural parcels in the concession as their tierras despite formal state ownership. In this sense, external knowledges can be turned into land rights of the community as a whole: when I presented a draft of this chapter to a group of Uaxactuneros in 2015, discussion revolved primarily around how best to mobilize external knowledge to support OMYC's bid for concession contract renewal in 2025. The more OMYC has direct access to study results, the group decided, the better prepared they will be to autonomously defend their concession rights without having to rely on outside institutions.[15] Far more than the impact of xate monitoring or surveying household well-being, it is in this renewal that WCS's, other researchers', and my own knowledges may prove most useful to Uaxactún.

In the MBR nooscape, institutions are not very good at sharing their information with local communities, but they are getting better. Academics like myself have done a similarly poor job. Constant study and monitoring of all aspects of life is not particular to Uaxactún—it happens everywhere, in different ways. But the visibility and local awareness of this dynamic, combined with the marginality and differences in power and access between extralocal knowledge producers and villagers, strongly affect people's ideas about who they are and where they live. More important than the results of any particular study is how monitoring practices locate Uaxactún in the MBR nooscape, reinforcing the village's place in regional institutional and global environmental orders. Uaxactún is held up as an example of successful community management to other MBR communities and around the world, yet they are marginalized in networks of capital, knowledge, and conservationist decision making, undermining security in the future of the concession itself.

There is much frustration over the amount of study leaving the community and so few direct benefits coming back in. Work is hard to find; local economies are dependent on global markets and extensive certifications; and people are burdened by debt at the household, community, and national levels. Still, most people are relatively content in Uaxactún and happy with where they live. It is, after all, beautiful, and there is always xate to keep one's family afloat. Vinicio, who told me that Uaxactún was the pulmón del mundo, after an extended rant about Uaxactuneros paying for global problems, returned to the same image for comfort, sighing in resignation: "At least we breathe good air, here in the reserve."

CERTAINTY EMERGES

How are facts made in a nooscape? A common saying among modelers and methodologists is "trash in, trash out": if your data collection is poorly designed, if each data point gathered is unreliable, then the analysis built from that data will be similarly tainted. But across the MBR nooscape, aggregations of uncertain moments, answers, or details can cohere into the most useful and clear of knowledges. Into facts. Less trash in, trash out; more uncertainty in, certainty out. How does this certainty emerge?

Emergent phenomena, including life itself, are most often figured in ecology as wholes that cannot be predicted or explained simply by examining their parts. This is like a metaphysical magic trick, the mystery of emergence produced by distracting attention from an epistemic scaffolding of nested hierarchical levels of organization (e.g., from cell to tissue to organism to community, and so on) (Potochnik and McGill 2012). Facts, from this vantage point, are certain wholes arising unpredictably and like magic from many uncertain data parts.

But viewed through a lens of partial connections, phenomena like *certainty* or like *life itself* only emerge in relation with parts outside their wholes, as well as those inside. Facts do not just emerge from data parts and the analytical and political maneuvers that bring them into a whole. Facts can only be facts in relation to rumors, lies, jokes, or other facts. Life only emerges as a distinction to nonlife, a distinction with its own situated entanglements of politics, worlds, and knowings (Povinelli 2016). Parts matter, but only partially. The whole is always constituted, in part, by something outside of itself. Relations of partial connection do not so much make wholes as phenomena that are more than one but less than many (Strathern 2004; Haraway 1991).

To gather up the bits and pieces of uncertain encounter that can build a fact, you must enact a scale at which the fact can emerge, enact an equivalence between data points such that they might be gathered together, enact boundaries of exclusion, and so on—you must build the world you describe. In order to build this world, you must already be situated in another one, always inside and outside of every enactment at once. Certainty, as a property of some knowledges but not others, can grow only in relation with other practices, knowledges, and worlds that remain uncertain. Certainty looks like a whole only when it exorcises the ghosts of uncertainty from its parts, banishing them to other worlds. And banishing, as J.-K. Gibson-Graham remind us, "creates the possibility and the likelihood of a haunting" (1996, 240).

EIGHT

Wild Life

An Adventure . . . and They Pay You!

Luis told me the story of how he came to work as a wildlife veterinarian with WCS. Luis was outgoing, charming, and always cracking jokes; for Halloween, he lent me his WCS-logo scrubs and stethoscope and trained me in the filthiest cursing he could muster to complete my costume as a wildlife veterinarian. After growing up in the western highlands department of Huehuetenango, he enrolled in veterinary coursework at San Carlos University in Guatemala City, focusing on cows and horses—familiar animals from his childhood. He worked while studying to support himself and his family, then sought a professional internship (*ejercicio profesional supervisado*) in order to graduate. He hoped to return to Huehuetenango to work on ranches, but no such internships were available. He looked into opportunities close to the capital, in Santa Rosa or Escuintla, before being drawn unexpectedly up to the Petén.

LUIS: I was supposed to work with goats, but I wasn't very interested. And right then this position here opened up. They told me it was a position for working with jaguars, and it was here in Petén, so I said, "OK, I'll go to Petén." I thought I'd just come to see what happened. When I arrived, we started with surveys and interviews with cattle ranchers. There's a publication that came out of that, about ranchers' perceptions of jaguars. So we were doing that when there was another project here, capturing peccaries. Fernando said I should go and talk to Miguel from ARCAS [Wildlife Rescue and Conservation Association]; he had tried to capture peccaries three times, but he couldn't do it. So Fernando said to me, "You're daring—go try to get some peccaries." And I had never done that! I started reading, and it wasn't that complicated.

MICHA: Really? How do you do it?

L: There was a rifle, and I tried, and I think it was pure fluke. . . . I don't know if it was just luck, but on my first shot, pow! In the exact center [of a target]. And Fernando said to me, "Wooowww. You're going with Miki [Miguel]." So we went with Miki, Jose too [a field tech]—he was with us. We went one time, and sure enough, we couldn't do it. We went another time, and we couldn't do it. And the next time, we went walking, checking out the *aguadas* [water holes] and all that, and when we arrived at an aguada called La Sistal, we heard, "Mmm, mmm, mmm" [making a deep, throaty grunting noise]. Have you heard pheasants?

M: No.

L: Pheasants say "Mmm," and peccaries say "Mmmm, mmmm," a bit longer. So Miki told me, "You stay here." And I heard "Mmm, mmm." [Whispering:] *And here come the peccaries . . .* the peccaries are coming! Miki came up and I said, "*Shut up, man! They're coming!*" "Those are pheasants, you asshole!" he said to me. And the whole time I had been thinking, "Wow!"

After that we went walking to other aguadas, and sure enough there was a herd of peccaries. And Miki said, "We'll wait here. When they're coming near tell me, I'll pass you the rifle and you shoot." And that's how we did it. There were a ton of peccaries, eeeeeee! There were like forty peccaries! Aaaaaand I was scared! Because it was like forty peccaries, and I was crouched down trying to hide, they were so close! At one point I shifted, and a stick on the ground cracked and the noise scared me so much! I couldn't decide whether to stay hidden or run away! And Miki just gave me a hard time: "Why didn't you shoot?!" and I don't know what all. That's how it was.

The aguada was called Cerro Rojo. We were using these 10-centimeter tranquilizer darts. But the one I shot entered wrong, so some of the liquid leaked out and air got in instead, so instead of being knocked out, the peccary was just dizzy. We tried a few things and ended up with darts that are 3 centimeters—they work better. Then we went for the *fifth* time. We got them. Five times. But it was really hard, really hard. . . . That was the first that I had contact, like that, with nature. This was the first time I thought, *ahh, que bonito.* And it was because it was an adventure. An adventure, and they pay you! Even though there is heat, there are ticks, snakes, horseflies, mosquitos—there are tons of things. But it was beautiful.

M: But what did they do with the peccaries?

L: Ah, the peccaries! Once we captured them, we put on GPS collars. Peccaries are indicators of good ecosystems. So where they go, supposedly, the ecosystem is doing really well. So, say this is the MBR [sketching a map]. If they go here, this whole part, they're saying that this area is really good. So we have to prioritize these areas.

M: "Supposedly"?

L: No, it's true. And right in this area [indicating sketch map], on the road out toward Melchor de Mencos, there are a lot of people, growing marijuana, et cetera. So when there are growers in here, we have to focus on that. So that was what happened.

Luis came to Petén conservation by happenstance, but was drawn to stay through the beauty and adventure he found in the wild. This was a common narrative—people take a conservation job because it is a job, then fall in love with the forest. Wild encounters, like Luis's first time tracking peccaries, draw people into the worlds of conservation and keep them working in the face of threats (both human and nonhuman). Conservationist love for the reserve's multispecies worlds has been an understory of this book so far. Here it surfaces, as I focus on conservation work that moves back and forth from office to wild campo (the campo can refer both to rural human spaces and to the relatively nonhuman spaces of forest; here I focus on the latter). In particular, I draw on a few months in fall 2011 that I spent following the biological research and veterinary team at WCS. The biovets, as I refer to them, combine classic biological research with veterinary interventions with both wild and domesticated animals. While the staff includes biologists and veterinarians with different titles, skills, and roles, their work often blends together. The biovets are frequently assisted by WCS's team of field technicians, who also work in patrols, fire prevention, control posts, and other campo labor.

Encounters with the wild campo draw knowledge forms like paranoia, love, and technoscience into new patterns and relations. This chapter follows a trajectory much like that in Luis's story, from wild encounter to technoscientific knowledge to conservation interventions. I begin with the sensorial richness of the wild campo, which is laden with contradictory nuances: threat and thrill, love and fear, intimacy and uncertainty. Across institutions and roles, people in conservation talk about the wild as more *real* than their work in urban offices or policy settings, or than what appears on maps and reports. As Roan Balas McNab explained, "You can read documents and you can look at GIS maps, but you don't get the real, the real accurate picture of what's going on in an area until you see it for yourself." As a result, this sense of immediacy and certainty is enfolded in efforts to bring the campo back into the office as generalizable, useable knowledge.

Technologies ranging from cameras to field reports to GPS wildlife collars are used to tame the unruly sensorial knowledges of the campo, translating them into forms that can integrate with other official knowledge, like CEMEC's remote indicators of forest health. This epistemic taming allows embodied encounters with the wild life of the MBR to become disembodied, creating knowledge of the real that can move across the nooscape, direct conservation intervention, and make a difference. Through these translations, love is excluded from official institutional knowledges, much like paranoia and rumor in other sites of the nooscape. When conservationist desires for useful, applicable knowledge forms take over, love and the real are cut off from each other—as in the sudden change of affect at the end of Luis's narrative, where exciting animals become indicators, adventures get plotted on maps, and the thrill of the chase disappears into rationally directed intervention. But discarded love composts into new embodied practices and relations, subtly shifting the material impacts of conservationist intervention.

Into the Wild

The campo is dense with sensory contradiction. The thickness of vines, the shadows cast by canopy trees, the hot turgid air, the impenetrable hum of insects, birds, and rustling leaves—human senses calibrated to urban life are overwhelmed with too much stillness and too much motion, all at once. The sensorial impact of all this lively nonhuman agency, the nature shock, leads me to describe the campo as "wild." The words "wild" and "wilderness" have a long and fraught history, particularly in the tropics. Colonial projects relied on an imaginative imputation of uncontrolled wild nature (and wild natives) to justify domination and extraction (Stepan 2001; Taussig 1987). Troubling divisions between nature and culture embedded in U.S. American wilderness ideologies have been exported to conservation institutions and policies worldwide, including Guatemala (Cronon 1996). These are potential dangers lurking in my descriptions of wild landscapes, an imputation of tropical Otherness. Yet the wild MBR campo (and other tropical places) *are* exceptional in their sheer density and diversity of life forms, and their resulting sensorial presence; to deny this difference is also to deny nonhuman agency.

While I aim to distinguish my descriptions from colonial wilderness ideologies, I continue to use the word "wild." My use contains a multitude of meanings, building on the work of Sarah Whatmore (2002) and Jamie Lorimer, who defines "wildlife" as an "alternative ontology to Nature to inform future environmentalism. . . . It describes ecologies of becomings, not fixed beings with movements of differing intensity, duration, and rhythm. Wildlife is discordant, with multiple stable states. It is not in any permanent balance. It is shaped by but divergent from the past, multinatural in its potential to become otherwise" (Lorimer 2015, 7). I separate the word "wild" as adjective in order to allow its meanings to apply not just to animal life, but to everything from plants to campo experiences to knowledges.[1] "Wild" does not distinguish between nature and culture, and aims to capture multiplicity and contradiction rather than purity or clarity. The word can describe traditional wilderness spaces (like the deep forest); mean out-of-control or unrestrained violence or fury (as in the wild narcotraffickers of Laguna del Tigre); or point to something that is mind-blowing, full of wonder, as in a hippie's declaration, "That's *wild*, man!" This is the wild of Luis's amazement when he states that campo work is "an adventure . . . and they pay you!": "It's an adventure because you don't know what time you're going to arrive, where you're going to sleep, and the journey is always . . . everything is different. You see animals. It's beautiful. . . . That's it, straight up. And to see jaguars." To see a jaguar in the forest— that's *wild*. Encounters with wild Others fold back the space between certainty and wonder, mind and body, science and affect.

Threat and Thrill

After my first six months of fieldwork, moving from the silence of CEMEC into the boisterous, convivial atmosphere of WCS's Flores office was a pleasant shock. When I soon accompanied WCS staff to the campo, I felt an equally striking shift in social atmosphere. Where the NGO office was friendly with chatter, in the campo talk shifted to action; in the office people took an interest in each other, but in the campo they looked after one another. The wild campo is where deep friendships and connections are made, forged by shared threat and thrill. Food (and often alcohol) is shared, tongues loosen and stories flow, and people band together against snakes, biting flies, wayward scorpions, and dreaded *chinche* bugs, carriers of deadly Chagas' disease. Nothing earned me so much curiosity from WCS field technicians as the time I got a case of leishmaniasis, a skin parasite known locally as "chiclero's ulcer." My small lesion called forth displays of impressive scars and a wave of stories of all the folk remedies they had tried. Though quickly treated away, my encounter with leishmaniasis was a visceral reminder that not all multispecies relations are pleasant or positive (Abrahamsson and Bertoni 2014).

The campo is a place to tell stories of the campo. Many field staff are skilled storytellers, trading their best tales in camaraderie and competition. A common theme is wildlife encounters: tapirs, peccaries, and—most prized—jaguars. Other animals are thrilling to see, but too common to make a good story (foxes, monkeys, paca, deer, anteaters, and others). Birders swap rare sightings. Crocodiles are worthy of stories if particularly large or seen while swimming, and snakes if they posed a threat. Funny stories—like Luis mistaking pheasants for peccaries and fearing for his life—are popular. But the best are the near-death stories. Men recounted these tales with dramatic flair: slowing their words, drawing out narratives with sensual details and dramatic pauses, holding their audiences captive in the buildup to an emotional climax (I always heard these from men, though women would share in other genres like wildlife sightings or recalling humorous pranks on other field staff). Near-death stories included both human and nonhuman threats: a tale of a snake bite while alone in the woods, death narrowly escaped by chewing the bark of the acacia tree and crawling out to safety, would be met with one about an encounter with armed huecheros (archaeological looters).

The distinction between human and nonhuman threat, which can disappear in these performances of survivalist masculinity, returns when it is no longer a question of past encounters, but lived risk. After all, it is not just shared stories that forge bonds in the campo, but also shared bodily dangers and corresponding mutual care. For Roan Balas McNab, these dangers made getting out to the campo a responsibility, one that he didn't see many NGO directors fulfilling. He described this responsibility as an obligation to his field staff:

> We ask a lot of our people. We ask them to take risks. And it's a tough thing, to send those people—men, and some women—into the field, and

say, "Look, you go do this and leave behind your family. You go take these risks." Especially for the pay scale that we have here in Guatemala. "Go take all these risks in the name of conservation and sustainable development of the Petén. Go take those risks, but I'm going to be here sitting at the desk." So, you know, I get out there with them. If they're going to go out on a patrol on the "front line" [air quotes], or going to go exploring out there in dangerous areas, I'll go out there and say, "Look. Hey, let's go. I'm going to be there with you. I'm going to do that." And that's a motivating thing for them, too.

Sharing the threat and thrill of the campo was one way that Roan demonstrated trustworthiness and responsibility to his Guatemalan staff.

Dynamics of risk in the campo amplify the gendered dimensions of conservation work, as women's bodies are differently vulnerable to human violence. Women are more common in biological and veterinary fields compared to their scarcity in other field positions. They were usually part of larger field teams and more likely to be in established camps than exploring remote forest. In shared camps, men took on a caretaking role toward women, looking out for their safety and comfort. "The men of wcs really take care of you," one woman commented. "They feed you to death, and are extremely *cuidadosos* [caring, caretaking]." A visiting American biologist, Lisa, told me the story of her first campo experience years before. How it rained so hard it took them fourteen hours to make the journey from the El Perú campsite to Flores (usually six hours). How the rain, mud, and bugs were overwhelming. How she barely spoke a word of Spanish, but "the guys" took care of her. How the rains formed a *laguna* in the middle of the road, and a wcs biologist found a small crocodile in it. "Like the herpetologist he is," Lisa told me, "Fernando of course grabbed it. So there we were, crocodile wrangling on my first trip out to the campo! I loved every minute of it."

The Dangers of Intimacy

My own visit to the El Perú camp in eastern Laguna del Tigre was less dramatic but similarly convivial. The trip also taught me how the proximity and intimacy of the campo could be tense as well as pleasurable, even bordering on dangerous. Before leaving, a worker from another NGO, Iván, overheard me planning with the biovets and asked wcs if he could tag along. He was free from work obligations that week and wanted to see the forests of Laguna del Tigre, where he had never been. The result was an education in how the social intimacy of the campo could shift dynamics of interinstitutional politics and gossip. People from WCS and Balam later commented to me about distinguishing between Iván as an individual—*muy buena gente* [he's good people]—and his institutional positions, which put them at odds in terms of conservation politics. Iván was an outspoken, even blunt, political critic, making open accusations of corruption or criminal connections among CONAP or NGO staff, politicians, or other powerful people. This made people in WCS and Balam nervous, especially when these stories started to come out in greater detail around the campsite.

Tensions on this trip developed slowly, from coded conversations in the pickup truck in the morning to more frank and candid talk in the evening. On the long, bumpy ride, Iván asked about the area around El Perú, and about WCS's and Balam's projects in Laguna del Tigre. He, Luis, and Fernando began by swapping stories of wildlife sightings, before Iván subtly moved these stories into the realm of spatialized politics, asking, "In your experience, which area in the reserve has the highest biodiversity?" Luis and Fernando hesitated, so Iván clarified: "I'm talking about mammals, when I say biodiversity. Because, you know, some places you might be counting all the insects or something." The men launched into a discussion of definitions of "biodiversity," a safe topic, before Iván brought it back to his original concern: "This topic is very broad. But what is the area with the most mammals?" Fernando answered, "This area, El Perú. I think this is the highest." Iván responded with incredulity: "Really? Compared to Río Azul [National Park], even? Because every time I go to Río Azul, I see lots of animals." "Yes," Fernando insisted, "this area has more. The difference is that here there's water; that's what's missing in Río Azul. There is more forest there, sure, but there's no access to water."

On the surface, this was a straightforward comparison of different areas of the reserve, in which the men (and their NGO employers) happen to work. What remained unspoken was the men's navigation of a potential minefield of differences between institutional priorities, work areas, conservation strategies, and influence. Mirador-Río Azul National Park is home to the controversy that pits Iván's employer, FARES (Foundation for Anthropological Research and Environmental Studies), against a coalition that includes WCS and Balam. The controversy includes arguments over the biological uniqueness of Mirador-Río Azul (implied by Iván's "Really?"), and over community-based versus park-centric approaches to conservation. The pro-park discourse surrounding

Mirador-Río Azul is framed by comparison with the "failures" of Laguna del Tigre, hence tension around claims that the latter had more mammals. All of this stayed behind a polite veneer during the car ride, but after dinner, with whiskey and beer, subtext surfaced into text.

Iván again broached his controversial concerns in a seemingly neutral way, asking the assembled group of men (and me) about the land around El Perú. "How much forest is there around here?" he asked. "*Primary* forest?" "Ohhhh, I don't know . . ." the men hesitated, responding vaguely: "Lots." Iván pushed: "How much, though? Say, twenty square kilometers?" Sure, the others agreed, probably around twenty square kilometers of forest. They started laying out the geography of the surrounding park: there is less forest to the west, where the (illegal) *fincas* (large landholdings) start. But around Balam's Scarlet Macaw Biological Station, east of El Perú, there's tons. "And there are lots of jaguars here?" asked Iván, picking up Fernando's comments from the ride. Again, the group answered that there were many jaguars, only qualifying their statements as Iván pressed for details. Through his insistent questions, Iván cornered the men into talking about places where there were no jaguars: where forest had been lost, where the breaches in conservationist presence and practice were, who was cutting down trees and setting up fincas. Finally, Fernando declared an end to the conversation. Addressing Iván, he said, "You should be careful who you say these things in front of, things like, 'There are no jaguars in Laguna del Tigre.' We're all OK here. We understand. But you have to be careful. People might hear you and interpret it in different ways, that since the park is already cleared it's fine to move in, bring cattle, and cut down more forest."

This concern—that describing Laguna del Tigre as a failed park would lead to more failure—was familiar within wcs. It was not the only tension that surfaced that evening. As the night wore on, Iván told stories about conservation funds misappropriated to buy a gun, about the criminal connections of local politicians, about who had threatened him and his family, when and why. His stories were met with anxious laughter; the field team was captivated by Iván's boasting, fearless persona, but nervous. Who was this character, who would so openly declare the names of his powerful enemies in front of people he had just met? His stories were not matched by the others around the table; unlike storytelling about wildlife encounters or campo adventures, the field crew did not respond with their own tales of confronting organized crime in the reserve. Instead, their responses echoed Fernando's cautionary sentiment:

"We're all OK here. We understand. But you have to be careful." Later, several men checked in with me about his stories and behavior, aware of my ethnographer presence. Buffered again by assurances that Iván was really a good guy, I too was cautioned: "You have to be careful."

The dangers and intimacies of the wild campo are sites for shared caution of all kinds—always check beneath camp mattresses for scorpions before bed; always be aware of who is listening to stories. The double visions of paranoia can become alarmingly concrete (he's buena gente, but be careful), while encounters with the wild begin their translations into evidence. Sharing stories starts the work of taming encounters—a jaguar here, a finca there—into evidence—of biodiversity hotspots, or conservation success or failure. Wild encounters arise in and between sensing and knowing bodies, and remain rooted always in the particular places they occur. Evidence, disembedded and disembodied, can move across the nooscape. Stories start this translation, but they remain too tied to the wild particularities of body, affect, and more-than-human place. So other technologies are brought in to help tame the wild.

Taming the Wild

One thing upon which Iván and the field staff could agree during their trip was on the access to reality provided by the campo. On the truck ride, Iván ranted about how CONAP's directors of Laguna del Tigre National Park had become "too politicized":

> Right now it's all just politics and meetings. You need to actually get out into the reserve to know what's going on. And sure, maybe you need to know how to work with *diputados* [congressional representatives], the governor, the Ministerio Público [attorney general], but you need to get out there too. You can't manage a business without going to it. Imagine you had a large finca. There's no way you could run a finca without actually going to it! All they do now is just sit at a desk, looking at the internet, with a secretary, when what you need is to get out into the park. You need to go to the communities, talk to the people, spend the night there!

Luis chimed in: "To see the reality." "Exactly," replied Iván. "That's exactly right. Right now, you see all this stuff in the Cuatro Balam meetings, the Mesa Multisectorial, and it's the same people saying the same things, over and over again, every time.[2] Everything looks good from there! Things are fine. We've recovered this-and-that number of hectares here. It's all great. But it's *not*—you just can't see it from there."

For Roan Balas McNab, visiting the campo to access this reality was an essential part of his job as director of WCS-Guatemala. In addition to reinforcing trust with his field staff, he noted:

> That field *lectura*, that sort of reading from the field is really important. Also it's an opportunity to sort of do some project "ground truthing," in the sense that sometimes the information that feeds back into our office through the channels of partners . . . Like CONAP field staff in Laguna del Tigre, they'll tell a technician, the technician needs to tell the subdirector, director of the park, [then] it'll get back to us. It's not perfect. And information is provided selectively. You know, there's more of a tendency to get good information back. But not the bad news.[3] Not the other stuff, so . . . so that's one of the things, getting into the field to do that kind of stuff. And the other is just to get in there to refresh myself about the ecological characteristics of areas, all the biological stuff, you know, do my bird lists, just get out there and observe the areas and start thinking about things. A lot of times that's when ideas for projects and next steps of interventions come through.

Roan spoke frequently about exploration and the importance of discovery—of the biological characteristics of unstudied areas, of new damage or threats, and of his own love of the forest. Secondary stories were untrustworthy, changing through a politicized game of telephone. In contrast, inspiration and new interventions grew out of his own encounters with the wild.

Still, even Roan's encounters with the "real" of lively multispecies worlds must be tamed into institutional knowledges if they are to make a difference. Many technologies aid in this epistemic taming: cameras, rifles, bird counts, notebooks, hair traps, GPS collars, wildlife surveys, and many others. These can be distinguished from CEMEC's remote technologies, like satellite imagery, on the basis of material presence in the campo. Like CEMEC's remote sensors, campo technologies do not provide straightforward, objective knowledge without efforts at translation. A variety of wild encounters must be gathered, standardized, codified, and entered into documents, spreadsheets, and other transferable formats, such that they might be able to travel elsewhere and shape interventions across the nooscape.

Here, Kitty . . .

Cameras are a favored tool for bringing wild life into the office. To estimate wild feline populations, especially jaguars, WCS uses camera traps—their shutters triggered by sensors to capture animals in photos. Camera traps seem like a straightforward form of technoscientific monitoring (a cat seen is a cat recorded), but feline counts via camera traps emerge out of shifting, contingent encounters between technologies, cats, and people. First you must design the traps properly, so you get pictures of jaguars. They must have enough battery power and memory to last between technician visits, be water resistant and secure, and have automatic sensors to regulate camera settings (adjusting ISO for day or nighttime photos, for example). Movement-based sensors can result in too many empty images, triggered every time the wind rustles the understory or a heavy rain falls. Temperature sensors are less likely to take pictures without animals, but can suffer from heat blindness when ambient air temperature rises too high (Noss et al. 2013). A continuous series of images is useful for capturing multiple angles or body parts of an animal, but might waste memory (or film, in older cameras) on repeated shots of passing herds of peccaries or tourists. In some locations, traps will be set with an automatic timed delay after each shot to avoid the latter.[4]

These are the equipment requirements; you must also site the cameras properly to maximize animal capture. Traps should be distributed far from human settlements and near known wildlife travel routes, water sources, or other landscape features appealing to felines. The cameras must be distributed across the landscape at scales and densities determined by species—some, like ocelots, have smaller ranges, while jaguars have very large and exclusive territories. Cats can be enticed to linger by the traps through scents; Calvin Klein Obsession is a known feline favorite. Finally, there are humans to consider: the traps should be tamper-proof with antitheft protections, so they are not casually taken or destroyed (although, as a WCS guide notes, "it is virtually impossible to stop a determined camera trap thief"; Noss et al. 2013, 9). In the MBR, placement must take into account which humans live nearby, and WCS sometimes hires men from local villages to check and maintain the traps to minimize conflict.

Once set, memory cards are collected periodically and brought into the office, where a biovet runs through captured images to code them for inclusion in a database. Besides time, date, and special observations (like a mother and cub, or an injured animal), the felines have to be identified as both species and individual. Identifying recaptures (multiple instances of the same individual) is the key to estimating populations. Despite the initial excitement of viewing wild cats, this turns out to be almost as dull as georeferencing in CEMEC—a repetitive, detail-oriented, screen-bound task. Cheny, a young Ladina woman from Guatemala City doing a biology internship with WCS, spent most days sorting through camera trap images. Identification was an iterative process; as Cheny learned to recognize individual felines, she would return to already-processed images to revise her findings. Certain species were difficult to tell apart, like ocelots and margays. At first Cheny had miscoded them all as ocelots: "Before, I didn't have hardly any [margays]. I didn't have as much of an eye. But now I'm getting better at it . . . so now I have three margays, where before there was only one." As her eye developed, cats already in the database changed identities. Some cats remained resistant to categorization due to the contingencies of in-motion photos. Cheny's eventual separation of ocelots from margays was based on the thickness and length of their tails, but she showed me a cat who had its photo snapped several times without ever getting its tail in the frame.

Identifying individual felines is even tougher. Cheny named them after her friends and family, which helped her recognize them. Jaguars could be identified by the unique patterns of their spots, which meant the same side and body part had to be in multiple pictures to identify them as recaptures. Spotless pumas were almost impossible unless they had a special feature, like one with a protuberance of overgrown hair on its belly. If a cat wandered in front of a camera trap showing multiple angles, this would send Cheny digging back through old pictures to figure out if an individual previously identified on the left side might be the same as one identified on the right. In this way, two cats in the database sometimes merged into one. Because of these iterative processes of identification, the WCS feline database is not settled once a picture is coded and included. Instead, it is an ever-evolving set of relations between remote camera technologies, cats, and technicians in the campo and in the office.

Tinkering with Traps

Camera traps work well under the right conditions but are expensive. Cheny's undergraduate thesis examined the potential of using hair traps rather than camera traps to track felines. Hair traps are large wire brushes (like common pet brushes) mounted at the height of a jaguar's shoulders, set over a sponge filled with perfume attractant. The cats are attracted to the smell and induced to rub against the brush, capturing hair samples. These can be identified to the species under a microscope (if the hair is complete and in good condition), and provide a noninvasive way to gather DNA samples, which can allow for identification to the individual and other analyses. Cheny further noted the potential value to WCS, compared to cameras: "Nobody would ever steal a hair trap. And even if they did, it costs, what? Maybe Q35" (around U.S. $4.50).

Cheny's project focused on experimental design, figuring out how to set up hair traps such that jaguars would rub against them and leave usable samples in the forest. Cheny explained previous experiments in captivity that had tested scents for their attraction potential in jaguars, first at the Bronx Zoo in New York City (run by WCS), where CK Obsession and Chanel Number 5 induced the most rubbing behavior. Cheny worked with the biovets and ARCAS, a wildlife rehabilitation center near Flores, to test Obsession-scented hair traps in a local jaguar enclosure. As she showed me video of a jaguar rubbing itself gleefully against a test trap, she explained:

> We set up two hair traps at different heights to see which would work better, and we set up a camera trap as well in front of each one, to see. So that each time the jaguar passed through there, it would be documented in a photograph. From that we could see that the height that worked best was 50 centimeters, and also that the jaguar reacted favorably to this. It loved the perfume. It rubbed all over and left a ton of hairs. So, yes, it works. So then the challenge was to try it in a wild state [*estado silvestre*].

She worked with the biovets to set up ten hair traps and accompanying camera traps in eastern Laguna del Tigre. They dosed the sponges with Obsession, left them for fifteen days, then returned to collect camera memory cards and hair samples for analysis.

Something had changed. While captive jaguars had rubbed all over the Obsession-scented brushes, the wild traps did not elicit the same reaction. A few ocelots reached up to rub against the brushes, as well as one gray fox, but pumas and jaguars were captured by the camera traps just walking by, only one female jaguar briefly stopping to sniff the trap before moving on (without leaving a sample). Cheny had a few hypotheses about why wild jaguars might not interact with the perfume the same way they did in captivity. One possibility was that they don't repeat their scent markings once they've made them in a certain area, no matter what it smells like later. Another explanation was a difference between marking behavior in jaguars' core territory and shared transit routes. The paths along which the test traps were sited were shared by jaguars, pumas, ocelots, and others, while core territorial areas might be distinct, and distinguished by scent. Further experiments were in order.

Cheny's project was an attempt to find a cheap, noninvasive feline population sampling method, a new way to bring wild cats into office databases. Processing hairs for analysis was also a slow, difficult, repetitive process, fraught with uncertainties. But unlike well-developed camera trap protocols, figuring out how to entice and capture the right kinds of animals (and their hair) was still a work in progress. The first field test was a dry-season run; as we spoke Cheny was preparing for a second test during the rainy season. Heavy rains posed new challenges in trap design; Cheny had to ensure that both scent and hairs would stay put. Camera and hair traps offer easy access to animals that are hard to see, but they require complex arrangements of labor, technology, and flexible responsiveness to human and nonhuman agencies—including camera thieves, jaguars, other forest species, rains, and more. While these devices are charismatic ways to tame wild life into the institutional knowledges of the nooscape, direct human experience—the immediate, sensory real—is even more so. But taming human memories of wild life can be even more complicated.

Ojos en el Campo

In November 2011, an American conservation biologist studying scarlet macaws (*Ara macao*) paid a visit to wcs. Lisa had worked with the biovets before, to visit the macaws' habitat and collect blood samples for genetic analysis. This time, Lisa was interested in the birds' behavior and ecological needs, and hosted a daylong workshop for the wcs field team in one of Santa Elena's lakeside luxury hotels. The men, accustomed to working in remote jungle, joked and teased as they gathered in the bright, white-table-clothed meeting room, laughing nervously when asked to speak into one of the wireless microphones provided. Lisa's Spanish was passable but patchy, so wcs biologist Fernando acted as comoderator. He welcomed the men as wcs's "ojos en el campo" (eyes in the field), explaining that the workshop's purpose was to recover and formalize their campo knowledge, which up to that point had been "lost information." Lisa laid out the four key themes she was interested in: monitoring and observation protocols, nest availability and selection, behavior, and predation. The men split into three breakout groups based on their primary field locations, working through Lisa's lists of questions and reporting back to the full group periodically.

The wealth of information that came out of the workshop was extraordinary, although not all of it translated smoothly into official knowledge. Discussions often spun off from Lisa's preset questions into brainstorming sessions for future action, spurred by the field crew's sensitivity to macaw preferences. For example, the observation that macaws did not use artificial falcon-proof nests led to the group collectively determining why not, and how they could change the design in response. For modifications made to existing (nonartificial) nests, the conversation balanced the needs and desires of conservationists and macaws: modifications are designed to increase chick survival rates, but if they are too extreme birds will no longer use the nests. Again, discussion revealed that this equation wasn't straightforward, that the timing and speed of nest alterations also mattered. Had the birds already occupied a nest? Laid eggs? Hatched chicks? Were the modifications sudden or gradual? Each scenario led to different macaw responses, and the gathered men flooded the room with examples and stories from particular birds, places, and years to fill out the details.

Campo stories like these sat in awkward relation to the abstract data Fernando and Lisa were seeking. The biologists' yes-or-no questions were answered with complex narratives of particular experiences rather than generalized responses. Lisa's question, "Do mating pairs return to the same nest year after year?" was met with tales of which birds did or didn't, in which years, in which areas, and what other factors might have affected the birds' selections, like flooded nests or a competing species taking up residence. Each story would draw out stories from other groups, adding complexity and nuance. Lisa was most interested in understanding the birds' preferences in a generalized and abstracted way: identifying preferred tree species, or whether macaws prefer living or dead trees. The men's answers included too much detail, too many qualifications: it depends what season it is, what human activities are happening nearby, whether other species have used the nests.

Throughout the day, Lisa and Fernando guided the men away from narrative and toward generalizable data, trying to tame their wild knowledges. The field crew's answers shifted in response; Lisa noted afterward that the men were "quick learners," able to pick up on the biologists' desired frame. At the same time, she reinforced hierarchies of whose knowledge was valid, expressing later that she learned a lot about macaws despite the fact that the men were not used to talking about science or thinking on a statistical level. For Lisa, the importance of the day was giving the men "a chance to tell their stories. So much is delivered to them: 'Here, we're going to tell you how things are.' But this was really the opposite; *you're* going to tell *us*! It's *your* show!" The exchange of stories was more frustrating to Fernando, who repeated the need for hard data that might help decide where to direct resources to get the greatest value for their conservation buck. When the field techs told stories, he would interrupt: "Yes or no? Yes or no?" As the day went on, he began adding this to Lisa's questions: "Do other parrots compete for nest cavities, yes or no?" The men continued to answer in stories, or responded, "It depends." Finally, when Fernando asked, "Have you observed problems with the quality of nests?" Luis stood, picked up one of the microphones, and mockingly answered with a simple "Yes." Nervous laughter spread through the room. It was exactly what Fernando had been asking for, but clearly insufficient. Annoyed, Fernando added, "An example, please."

That which remained too embedded in narrative, too closely tied to the love of wild encounter, was left aside. At the end of the day, Mario, field staff coordinator, asked gently if others thought the macaws might be able to recognize individual people. A few men chimed in, suggesting that they might be able to learn their voices, hair color, smell, or even how individuals move. Mario continued with a story in which a pair of birds not only learned to recognize him as an individual, but to recognize that he was a harmless (or even helping) presence, rather than a threat. In a soft voice, he recounted how on a visit to check and clean a nest, he accidentally startled the pair, who flew to a sit on a higher branch when he climbed up. They watched his activities carefully, and he wondered if they would return to the nest when he left. When he returned ten days later, he started climbing and realized the birds were still there only when he was very close to the nest, when one again flew out to a nearby branch.[5] When he reached the nest and found two eggs, he expected alarm in the nearby bird, as incubating macaws do not like to leave their eggs unattended (as I learned earlier in the workshop, field techs try to leave incubating females alone until their eggs hatch). But this bird sat calmly, preening its feathers and not calling out—signs that it was relaxed—and waited for him to finish.

Mario's narrative was beautiful, unexpected, and uninteresting to the biologists in charge. Perhaps it sounded too fanciful, like the projection of a romantic wish, although the parrot family is known to be very intelligent, with complex social bonds and communication skills. Maybe it was left aside due to Fernando's desires for useful information, hard data that could be used to increase conservation value (chicks fledged) per resources spent. If correct, however, Mario's finding would not just be a captivating story (useful for media coverage and fund-raising), but could also help direct actions in the campo to reduce birds' stress. Unfortunately, the strength of emotion and wonder—the wild love—in Mario's narrative prevented its translation and uptake into official knowledges. Despite his opening frame of recovering lost information, by passing over this narrative in the workshop, Fernando told Mario's social birds to stay lost.

Stay lost, love. The translations in this workshop, like all translation, incur a loss. While in the campo, love and the real are inseparable parts of personal narrative and embodied experience. As they are translated and tamed into technoscientific frames, love and the real are cut off from one another. Data pertaining to reality or nature are filtered out from the affective and bodily experiences of love, encounter, or adventure. But the haunting remnants of love are benevolent ghosts. They will keep Mario engaged in the fieldwork of conservation, continuing to enter remote forests in the face of kidnappings or death, to collaborate with birds that he knows know him. Macaws that collaborate in their own conservation might never enter institutional knowledges, but they may return to work together with Mario at the same nest for years to come, sharing their own knowledge of what is real. While it is as banished from technoscientific worlds as paranoia, the haunting presences of love are forces for collective ongoingness.

Intervening

The biovet team's knowledge production, like CEMEC's, is always oriented toward usefulness. But the embeddedness of biovet knowledge in the wild campo can wrest usefulness away from straightforward technoscientific frames. Making knowledge about wild species always requires intervention, some active human and/or technological presence on the landscape. Biovet practices take this even further, with wild experiments leading the way to new knowledges, including knowledges about how to intervene or know better. Wild experiments describe conservation practices that aim not for nostalgic stability of landscapes, but future-oriented ecosystem building without ideological assumptions about pure, human-free nature (Lorimer 2015). Wild experiments are risky in the MBR nooscape, where hardline defense of Nature remains a powerful discursive frame. But biovets manage this risk, shifting between enacted worlds of disinterested objectivity and experimental interventions as they work to foster the survival of key species. This shifting is familiar to the discipline of conservation biology, in which moral, ethical, and political claims demote it from the ranks of pure to applied science. In wild experiments, this frame shifting is pushed even further, as the presumed priority of knowing before intervening is reversed or looped—sometimes you have to do before you know.

Unlike most veterinarians and field technicians who came to conservation through job openings, biologists more often arrived through moral commitments that grew out of earlier pure research projects. One of wcs's biologists, Carlotta, told me about her undergraduate and master's research, which focused on seed dispersal by howler and spider monkeys. Her eyes shone with excitement at the memory of setting up controlled experiments, and the *"bien bonito!"* details of what she had learned. Witnessing her love for research, I asked if she had many opportunities to pursue that kind of investigation with wcs. She answered:

> No, no. Look, I started this way, with things that were very [pure research] . . . but it's interesting. In the end you'd always try to put in the implications for conservation. But it was just . . . at a level of . . . not much. So, I was always thinking, how to do something that was really *conservation* conservation, right? Even though the investigations we do here now aren't to *know something, an ecological subject, or because we want to publish* [drawing out her voice in an exaggerated sense of awe]. It's because we need to have it, and it has a practicality for decision making. So that's the beauty of it. Maybe it's not, let's say, pure pure science, to contribute to scientific knowledge in general. But yes, it is science in that they are important questions for conservation, for making important decisions. And for more management things, like all the questions with the scarlet macaws, which are very important, and which give you evident results, Micha. Either twenty-three chicks or three, right? And that can mean either a ton or very little for the population. . . . Maybe we're not doing a lot of primary research, but what we do is useful, and clearly so. You don't have to go searching for the usefulness. . . . I wanted to be a scientist, to continue with pure science. But when you go to the campo, get to know a bit more about the situation of the subjects of your study—for example, the primates that I studied—and you go to conferences to present your work but you listen

to [the experiences of] many others . . . conservation has to come out of it. For me, it's like an obligation [*un deber*].

For Carlotta, conservation work was a moral and practical obligation to the species she had previously studied in (relative) abstraction from their situation in the campo. Motivated by the limitations of traditional scientific research to account for complex human-influenced landscapes, or to contribute usefulness that you don't have to go searching for, she turned away from the pure science that had inspired her and sought ways to make a difference.

Now, Carlotta aims not just to create knowledge about wild life, but also to intervene in it. Biovets from wcs intervene in the lives of jaguars, pumas, peccaries, tortoises, monkeys, trees and other plants, ranchers and their cattle, and, perhaps most intensively, scarlet macaws. These projects walk the line between research and management; they are iterative experimental practices developed over time. And not all experiments can be successful. Carlotta told me about a failed relocation of a troop of nine howler monkeys that had been in conflict with a nearby village—kids had been throwing rocks at them, people tried to poison them, "terrible things." wcs collaborated with Mexican biologists who provided funding, logistical support, and site assessment for the relocation in exchange for blood samples for their research. They found a site on private land with all the right food and ecological resources and without a resident howler troop. But all nine of the howlers died after relocation—killed by a troop of spider monkeys already living at the site, who aggressively defended their territory. After much deliberation, the wcs team decided to publish the results of this attempt. Carlotta explained, "It was interesting, because it was something really awful, right? Disappointing, awful . . . but we learned a ton of things." She noted that in her literature review for the article, not a single published piece she encountered revealed a similar failure. "They were all *qué bonito! Qué alegre! They accepted their new homes, poof!*" The biovet team decided that sharing their failure could help improve future interventions, but this decision was not made without doubt: "I have a bit of fear because a lot of people will just bury you: 'What a bad scientist! You're supposed to protect them, no!?'"

It Takes a Wild Village

Interventions with scarlet macaws are among the most extreme undertaken by wcs on wild life, and have similarly built on past experiments, failures, and reconfigurations. These practices have developed over time from field observations, to climbing to see inside nests, to digital cameras installed in nests, to nest modifications, to artificial nests, and now to intensive veterinary care provided to wild chicks. Scarlet macaws are cavity nesters, preferring holes formed in the trunks of *cantemó* trees. They eat a wide variety of fruits and seeds, and due to their large territories are considered to be an indicator species for ecosystem integrity. Luis explained, "It's a flagship species [*especie bandera*], that is, it flies over a large territory. So to save just one scarlet macaw . . . it's like the jaguar, right? Jaguars and macaws are flagship species, because of their habitat, their very large territories, so to protect those species you protect a lot of other species and flora."[6]

Visiting macaw nests involves trekking out to remote locations, away from cut paths, and using ropes and climbing harnesses to reach the nests. The wcs biovets and field crew monitor known natural cavities and place artificial nests in sites they think will appeal to the birds. Before nesting begins (late January, as the season turns from wet to dry), the staff visit nests to remove debris and water, modify the size of cavity openings, and otherwise prepare the nests. They treat nests with the insecticides permethrin and carbaryl (and are testing other substances) to combat the use of cavities by insects, especially Africanized bees. When macaws are incubating eggs, the field crew refrains from climbing, but when the chicks are born they quickly head up again to check their health and begin interventions. The biovets treat chick injuries and infections with antibiotics, remove parasites, smooth ointment on skin ailments, adjust nest substrates in response to respiratory ailments, and provide supplementary food to the smallest chicks.

Supplementary feeding protocols have changed greatly due to wcs's experimental tinkering. Different foods were tried, with different problems. The chicks didn't like one premade formula; another was too expensive. Luis explained that they tried fresh fruit to simulate the macaws' natural diet: "With fruit we were getting results, but it was so complicated taking fruits out there, and maintaining the fruits, and making them into a smoothie." Eventually biovets found a formula that worked well for budgets, birds, and field crew, but administering the food properly posed another learning curve. The formula had to be warmed, and some field technicians burned chicks with overheated food. In a presentation to other NGOs, Luis showed images of burned chicks, explaining that technicians had been testing formula temperature with their fingers. Field laborers have rough, calloused hands, he continued, so they had to teach them to test on the inside of their forearm instead.

Experiments in supplementary feeding have now evolved into moving some chicks from one nest to another. Previous monitoring showed that in nests with three chicks, the smallest would often die from malnutrition. WCS began removing the smallest chick, feeding and caring for it in a field camp, then returning it not to its original nest but to another with only one chick. Biovets noted that people often wonder if the parents don't have trouble adopting a new chick. But it is the chicks, not the adoptive parents, who can struggle with the transition. Fernando explained, "They've gotten used to being fed by humans, and then all of a sudden there's this strange bright red thing coming at them, trying to feed them, so they get scared." But they adapt, and they survive, better than they would in their original nests. Two sets of macaw parents, veterinarians, field technicians, medicines, and technologies: it takes a wild multispecies village to raise a chick.

The Contradictions of Success

WCS's interventions with scarlet macaws are making a difference in their survival, and in doing so they push conservation beyond its traditional definition of protecting wild species. The interventions have slowly and steadily increased the number of chicks fledged per year; 2011 marked the first year that fledging rates reached over one chick per nest since monitoring began in 2002. Given the awe with which campo workers spoke about *la naturaleza* (Nature), and the anger and despair with which they described human presence on the landscape, the intensity of human action among macaws seems to fit awkwardly in their nature/culture frame. But, as across the nooscape, biovet practices enact a multiplicity of Natures and many versions of the human, and conservationists shift between these as necessary to manage the risks of contradiction.

I asked Luis what he thought about humans actively maintaining wild macaws versus simply protecting natural processes:

LUIS: The macaw isn't disappearing for natural reasons. Rather, it's pure intervention of man [*intervención del hombre*]. So I think that the intervention of man should recover them as well. Because it's nothing natural, what's happening, that the macaw [population] is going down. It's something influenced by the hand of man [*la mano del hombre*].

MICHA: So the "hand of man" isn't natural.

L: In this ecosystem, no. But what we're trying to do with the macaws is the most natural possible.

M: . . . In what sense is what you're doing the most natural possible?

L: We're not . . . Just in terms of food, for example, at first it was really stressful [for the chicks], but now, we just give them a bit of food and boom, done. We're not standing around holding onto the birds, "Oooooo!" [mimicking cooing at a chick in his hand], no. And about twenty days before they fly, we put them back in the nests. So that there is, what do they call it, "imprinting" they say in English, with the parents and everything. Because the parents have their vocalizations—they have to teach them that, and it's a bond with the parents. Because another kind of . . . a thing called "soft release" [in English], *una liberación suave*. In that, they take down macaws, and they raise them. Up to one, two, or three years old, in big cages. And it's just them, all like orphans, then comes a moment when *whoom*, they free them all. But they're released, and they don't know which fruits to eat, when to eat them, where they are—they don't know anything! So that isn't so "natural."

For Luis, human intervention justifies human intervention, and nature is more like a sliding scale than one side of a dichotomy. There is subtle shifting between enactments here, as Luis (and others) use the term "natural" to describe both the absence of humans and the presence of well-intentioned humans. This kind of multiplicity allows WCS staff to work with the contradictions of conservationist action. In this case, "natural" shifts to accommodate new forms of measurable success—a key good in state and NGO institutions.

This shifting becomes clearer still when considering the use of pesticides in macaw nests and WCS involvement in Paso Caballos, which sits in macaw nesting territory. In the village, Rosa and others provide macaw-centric environmental education, using the birds to teach children about the importance of the forest. She also helps implement the village's settlement agreement with CONAP, ensuring they do not use chemical pesticides or fertilizers on their agricultural plots.[7] Yet in forests nearby, WCS applies pesticides to macaw nests. There is a clear difference of scale here, of course: agricultural plots are large, and nests small. Fernando explained that the chemicals they use in nests have very specific and localized action, so insects have to touch them directly to be affected, and larger animals (including macaws) would need to "grab the bottle and start chugging" before they would feel any effects. Beyond the question of scale, to use any pesticides inside a national park requires clear and compelling reasons. The justification given is that the primary insect threats inside scarlet macaw nests are nonnative Africanized bees. As in Luis's narrative, human intervention (bringing new bee species to the Americas) justifies human intervention and displaces questions of Nature. There is a second rift that becomes visible here: foreign versus native. Q'eqchi' migrants, indigenous to another region, fall on the wrong side of this divide.

A final frame-shifting contradiction emerges in the contrasts between the macaws' importance as an indicator species for the ecosystem, and WCS interventions at the level of individual birds and nests. As biovet interventions focus intensively on the survival of individual chicks, their use as an ecosystem indicator makes less sense. Rather than landscape integrity, the macaw population now indicates the success of WCS nest alteration and veterinary practices. As a scientist reader commented on an early draft of this chapter, the biovets seem to be systematically undermining their own data on ecosystem function. Her reading was grounded in the worlds of pure biological science, prioritizing the enactment of the macaw as indicator species, or sentinel. Sentinels are "living beings . . . that provide the first signs of an impending catastrophe" (Keck and Lakoff 2013). Sentinel species provide warnings enacted through technoscientific practices of counting and population surveys: "[Species] inventories are defined as devices to measure acceptable variables in relation to a previously determined desired state of nature. These inventories . . . act as whistleblowers in case of a threat to a site or to a species" (Manceron 2013). In the MBR, the sentinel macaw is enacted through knowledge practices that foreground the birds' territorial size and feeding practices, and link population size to ecosystem health. In this enactment, macaws exist as a normative, natural species, with stable, scientifically describable habits and habitat needs set apart from human presence or intervention.

WCS's biovet interventions into macaw chick survival enact a very different bird, in which the sentinel role is set aside in the name of species survival. The macaws are the thing to be saved, not the landscape by way of birds. This version is enacted by practices like nest monitoring, veterinary interventions, and numerical measures of fledging rates. In this survival enactment, both naturalness and the birds' ecological relationships across the landscape disappear, except when elements of that landscape (like predatory species or distribution of nesting trees) directly affect the rates in question. This enactment thus strays from pure biosciences into the contaminated realms of wild experiments. Like Carlotta's care for monkeys, the goal for biovet researcher-practitioners is not to maintain the purity of macaw data for measuring ecosystem integrity, but to make a difference.

WCS reports collapse the differences between species survival and sentinel enactments. In documents and presentations summarizing ecological integrity, the biovets' graph of fledging rates is included to demonstrate increasing scarlet macaw populations. Narrative text surrounding the graph flips back and forth between the two enactments. The reports explain that veterinary and other interventions into nests have caused the increase, drawing attention to species survival via wild experiments. But the data are also described as a fine-scale indicator of ecological integrity, set alongside CEMEC's landscape-scale indicators like forest cover and fire damage.

These two enactments suggest different conservationist interventions. In the sentinel enactment, landscape-scale protection of whole ecosystems is the strategic priority. In the survival-rate enactment, biovet interventions are the most useful means to increase desired fledging success rates. Biovet practices work against the sentinel enactment by undermining the usefulness of the species as ecosystem indicator. That these two are contradictory is of little or no concern to WCS conservationists; the NGO engages both strategies, which helps their contradictions disappear. Moving through the partial connections between enactments is smoothed by conservationist priorities oriented toward charismatic species and relatively easier-to-achieve measures of success. It takes fewer resources, and is less risky, to increase macaw survival by deparasitizing and feeding chicks than by removing *narcoganaderos* from landscapes adjacent to their territories. As well as nest-level intervention, WCS does engage in habitat protection; the shield strategy for eastern Laguna del Tigre sets patrols crawling through macaw nesting territory. Bridging the two further, the presence of biovet staff in the campo to intervene on nests is also counted as a deterrent to illegal activity in the area.

Risky Experiments

Admitting to wild experimentation is risky. Jamie Lorimer's (2015) description of wild experiments grew from conservation practices on the landscapes of northern Europe, with their politics, cultures, and histories of human habitation very different from those of Guatemala. In Guatemala, conservationists may be less open to describing their strategies as wild experiments, turning—in rhetoric, if not always in practice—to nostalgic protectionism, which tries to hold an idealized state of Nature steady. Capital-N Nature is beguiling, and remains dominant across global conservation knowledges that move power-fully through the MBR nooscape. It offers a clear solution to the problem of disappearing species and turns the question of human lives and livelihoods into a technical issue rather than a political one. Official institutional priori-ties, reports that emphasize ecosystem integrity, and romanticized encounters with wild animals and places all tend toward nostalgic idealizations of a pure, natural landscape. But intensive veterinary care, animal relocations, or the xate enrichment programs in Uaxactún are wild experiments; these sidestep or rewrite Nature in order to make a place for caring, conservationist humans. These two are jumbled in practice; wild experimental actions are often justi-fied by nostalgic discourses.

Good human presence is haunted by the strict purity of a nature/culture divide. Fernando's warning about describing human presence in Laguna del Tigre resonates here, as does Carlotta's anxiety about publicizing experimen-tal failures. According to Fernando's fears, stepping away from a strict nature/culture dichotomy makes it harder to justify keeping destructive humans out. For conservationist presence to make sense on this natural landscape, it must be a defensive stopgap, not an enduring part of MBR ecosystems. Following Carlotta, conservationist presence should only protect and strengthen wild species, not kill them (even accidentally) by intervening. Otherwise, the line between good and bad human presence is similarly threatened. So while wild experimentation might be a more realistic and successful long-term strategy for maintaining desired MBR species and ecosystems, fears are too great that acknowledging the depth of human intervention might somehow open the door to rampant forest loss. That knowledge of experimentation might com-post into toxic futures. Nostalgic conservation is thus likely to remain the larger strategic discourse for WCS, within which wild experiments can be tol-erated as necessary but somewhat unsettling reactions to human destruction.

Death of a Dog 185

Experiment/Experience

The Spanish verb *experimentar* translates as both "to experiment" and "to experience, feel, or undergo." This doubling captures something of the wild experiments of the WCS biovets, whose interventions are suffused with feeling and embodied experience. Bodies, knowledges, and life are wild in the MBR, in part because they are uncontainable by attempts at description, including my own. There is an affective immediacy of encountering an animal in the wild that is unrivaled by camera trap images, population estimates, or biodiversity surveys. There is a wild openness in veterinary care for scarlet macaws that unravels closed discourses of Nature. The sensorial impact of the wild campo produces love, builds social bonds, motivates conservationist action, and reinforces desires for certainty and clarity promised by the moments in which one touches the "real." These encounters also motivate attempts to tame the wild, to bring the campo back into the official, portable knowledges of the nooscape, such that they might be used to direct future interventions and make a difference.

The relations between love and technoscience in conservation are almost parasitic—the latter relies heavily on the former, but can evacuate much of its power. This is particularly true when embodied affect threatens to overwhelm objectivity, as in Mario's collaborative birds, or when love becomes care in the form of wild experiments, threatening to undermine Nature as a thing worth protecting. Love is thus as excluded from the official, institutional knowledges of the nooscape as paranoia, cut off from the useful data of the real. Yet unlike the violent and reactive effects of paranoia, the hauntings of love in the MBR nooscape compost into rich interrelations and ongoingness, holding multiple contradictory worlds together in the embodied present.

Love changes institutional interventions and their temporal orders. Despite overwhelming conservationist desires to know the MBR in order to change it, wild encounters, experiments, and love reject the framework that knowledge has to come first. To know the wild, one must be present in it—and human presence is already an intervention, as the shifting lines of biovet nature/culture descriptions make clear. To change the wild, to do conservation biology or conservation veterinary care, one must leave desires for "pure, pure" science behind and stay attuned and open to the unexpected: to competition between monkey troops across species, or how jaguar scent preferences shift in and out of captivity. Admitting to this kind of tinkering is frightening for its possibility to be read as evidence of failure—failure to know before acting, to properly calculate risks, to defend Nature against "the hand of man." The usefulness of technoscience suggests a one-way movement between knowing and intervening. Love means intervening before you know for sure.

APOCALYPSE SOON!

It is 2000, and the Anthropocene is upon us! The Holocene is over—time itself has ruptured!

It is 2006, and Mel Gibson's *Apocalypto* is a box office hit! Contemporary landscapes and languages of the Yucatán peninsula, masquerading as ancient worlds, spread around the world carrying a message of violent corruption and ecological degradation leading to massive societal collapse!

It is spring 2011, and followers of American Christian Radio host Harold Camping buy dozens of billboards lining the roads of Santa Elena and San Benito to advertise the approaching end of the world: May 21! The Rapture is coming!

It is fall 2011, and two NGO staff discuss climate change: "In twenty years, what's this area even going to look like?" Juan wonders, "It could be a *bosque seco*!" (dry forest, which grows in southeastern Guatemala). "Or a desert!" Julián responds, joking, "You'll be walking along and see peyote growing in the middle of the forest!" He laughs about ecotourism projects for gringos coming to the Petén to get high. Because the forest could be all gone!

It is 2012, the Maya End of the World! (Well, not for Maya people themselves, who know how to read their own calendar.) But for tourists visiting ancient temples, and for those who want the tourists' money—ancient prophecies spell apocalypse! Why save for later when the world is coming to an end? Buy! Buy! Buy!

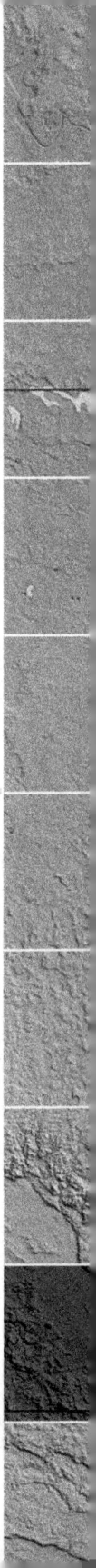

It is 2017, and the sky is falling! Look how low it hangs, heavy with the weight of smoke! Thousands of fires lit! Tens of thousands of hectares of forest burned!

Urgency! Urgency! The land is burning—act now or all will be lost! Buy time for forests, even if the costs are more each year! Even if the costs are human rights! Livelihoods! Lives! Urgency, urgency, urgency!

NINE

REDD+ Queen Futures

Aquí estamos, trabajando siempre

Conservation work is never done. While fundamentally a future-oriented project, conservation has no ends, no ultimate success after which its practitioners can hang their hats, clap each other on the backs, and declare their work complete. In the Petén, the success most hope for is maintaining enough forest cover to keep conservation as a viable and worthwhile activity. This is a fundamentally defensive position, one that keeps conservationists in a constant state of emergency and reaction. Rather than planning and strategizing for a long-term future, people watch for emerging threats to the forest, shifting and changing their strategies and alliances in response to an ever-shifting landscape. As such, conservation in the MBR comes to look much like the dynamic expressed by Lewis Carroll's Red Queen, who stated, "Now, *here*, you see, it takes all the running you can do, just to keep in the same place" (1872, 43).

In fact, MBR conservationists might argue, staying in the same place would be an exceptional achievement. "Aquí estamos, trabajando siempre," people say (here we are, always working). This phrase and another, *siempre en la lucha* (always in the struggle), circulate among people in the MBR (conservationist staff and village residents alike), signaling resignation to a dynamic of always reacting, always working, working hard, struggle never ending. These phrases serve as a common way to end conversations with no end, to close meetings over contentious projects that find no resolution, to acknowledge together the always ongoingness of conservation work.

At the same time, futures must be planned: projects proposed, park management plans written, climate change impacts projected. When people talk about these imagined futures, it is with skepticism. For any five-year plan, the first year might be a real plan, the second a sketch of possibility if the first year brings no major surprises, and the years beyond that a fiction directed at funders and bureaucratic regulations. Instead of solid predictions, people work to build flexibility and emergency funds into their budgets and projects. But this need for flexibility and ability to react to unforeseen futures clashes with the technocratic rationality underlying institutional structures.

This final chapter turns to the unimaginable future of the MBR and its embeddedness in the unimaginable global futures of the Anthropocene. I draw on a carbon credit project, known as Guatecarbon, that requires precise technoscientific modeling of future deforestation in the reserve. Guatecarbon, developed through the UN Collaborative Programme for Reduced Emissions from Deforestation and Forest Degradation in Developing Countries (REDD+), has been under planning and development since 2007. The project's first generated carbon credits were verified in 2017, though as of this writing no legal mechanism for their sale exists. The extended length of financial negotiations for this project is due to the tensions involved in determining legal rights to carbon stored in the trees of the MBR and elsewhere in Guatemala. As framed by REDD+ project leaders, these political battles are entirely distinct from the GIS model of future deforestation, prepared by CEMEC, which sits at the heart of the project. This model is widely praised as a major technological achievement and a source of pride for project leaders, CEMEC technicians, and others. Yet few if any of these actors place faith in the model's predictions. Still, as I argue, this model works—if not as a source of accurate predictions, then as the source of new technical expertise, new alliances, new funding and investment, and new scales of imagination and response. Despite the haunting relations between the temporal orders of the model and lived experience, the REDD+ project composts into material ecological worlds of the MBR, though never in the ways that were planned.

Rejected Projections

UN-REDD+ is a speculative carbon market program designed to reduce deforestation in developing countries. Its projects follow a three-step process of prediction, prevention, and sale of resulting carbon credits. First, the projects must produce a statistically reliable prediction of future deforestation, like the GIS model developed by CEMEC for the MBR. Second, actions must be undertaken to prevent some portion of this predicted deforestation from taking place. After a few years, the difference between the original prediction and successfully saved forest can (theoretically) be sold as carbon credits on international markets, where prevented forest loss is translated into prevented release of those forests' carbon stocks into the atmosphere. These credits would then be bought to offset emissions elsewhere. The conservation actions that reduce deforestation must be directly linked to an official REDD+ project, in addition to other forest protection activities; in other words, if deforestation turns out to be less than predicted but is due to business-as-usual conservation practice, this success is not salable as carbon credits.

REDD+ is extremely problematic, with an ever-growing number of critiques of the program (and similar payment for environmental services models) in theory and practice around the world. The program relies on market logics to compensate developing countries (usually inadequately) for maintaining their forests, while allowing richer countries or corporations to buy these carbon rights rather than reduce their own emissions (Redclift and Sage 1998; McAfee 2012). The valuation of forests is based on translating complex ecosystems with multiple functional and symbolic relations to human and nonhuman well-being into a new commodity, carbon, extending neoliberal capitalist logics into new ecological realms (Milne 2012; Mahanty et al. 2012; Sullivan 2009, 2013; Corbera 2012). Finally, the question of property rights over the carbon content of forests (including below-ground biomass) is incredibly complex, especially in forests that are inhabited or managed by indigenous or other groups (Filer and Wood 2012; Dressler et al. 2012). These challenges have led to extended conflicts in many places, with the implementation of REDD+ projects often exacerbating existing inequalities while doing little to protect forests over the long term (Fletcher 2012; McElwee 2012; Milne and Adams 2012; McAfee and Shapiro 2010). There have been efforts within the UN-REDD+ program to respond to some of these critiques, including the addition of the "+" to the program's name to acknowledge the complex worlds of tropical forests that extend far beyond carbon content; as one Guatemalan NGO worker commented, "the 'plus' stands for 'everything else.'"

Guatecarbon, situated in the MBR's multiple-use zone, is the largest of several "pro-poor" REDD+ projects under development across Guatemala, and one of the most contentious (another inside the reserve is in Sierra del Lacandón National Park, headed by the NGO Defensores de la Naturaleza). The project's development has dragged on for years due to complex negotiations over who will obtain eventual rights to carbon credits and potential payouts.

In the multiple-use zone, these rights must be negotiated between the state, which owns the land, and the industrial and community forest concessions that manage and work its forests, and in some cases live in them. Concession contracts, dating to the pre-REDD+ era of the late 1990s and early 2000s, do not include language about carbon rights or payment for environmental services. Instead of adding to the many analyses and critiques of these political aspects of REDD+ projects, however, I focus here on the ways that new technoscientific predictions created for the Guatecarbon project are composed into the MBR nooscape, shaping its ecological futures in nonlinear and unexpected ways.

Boundary Work and the Performance of Rigor

People promoting the Guatecarbon REDD+ project clearly and repeatedly differentiate between the technical and political (legal-economic) aspects of the program. This is a familiar performance of "boundary work," or drawing a strict contrast between science and politics in order to make the former available as a neutral decision-making tool for the latter (Gieryn 1983; Guston 2001). One example of this boundary work occurred during a formal presentation in late 2011 to the Mirador region multisector roundtable meeting featuring representatives of environmental state agencies, elected representatives, the police and military, Guatemalan and international NGOs, local community members, academics, and the private sector. In this meeting, the line between the technical and political aspects of the REDD+ project was so explicit that they were separated into two different PowerPoint presentations, prepared and given by different people from different institutions.

The political side of the project, widely acknowledged to be much more difficult and slow moving than the technical side, was presented by representatives from the U.S.-based Rainforest Alliance (RA, involved in REDD+ projects across Guatemala) and ACOFOP, who together lead the Guatecarbon project. Their presentation reviewed the process for determining the distribution of rights to carbon credits, as well as the legal and economic structures through which potential earnings from the sale of those credits might be filtered—both hotly contested questions. The number of interests and stakeholders to be balanced in these negotiations was overwhelming: the NGOs involved in the project (RA, ACOFOP, Asociación Balam, WCS, IUCN, PACUNAM, Defensores de la Naturaleza, and others at various points in the project's history), multiple state agencies and politicians (CONAP, INAB, MARN, municipal leaders, the governor of the Petén, and congressional representatives), and the many community and industrial management organizations for forest concessions inside the project area. That these negotiations have dragged on for years is unsurprising, especially when many of these groups and institutions experience conflict and divisions among their own members. The presentation to the roundtable attempted to present an optimistic picture of making progress, but the legal and financial structures of the project remained hazy.

These issues were presented at the meeting as entirely independent of the project's deforestation model, which was praised by RA and ACOFOP as the most complex and well-designed model of its kind yet completed in Central America—praise that I heard repeated many times, in many contexts. Following these NGO speakers, Victor Hugo Ramos stood up to begin his presentation on the technical side of the project: a baseline measurement of forest carbon stocks and a GIS model of predicted future deforestation. The former pooled data from multiple sources and studies to estimate the carbon content of different forest types within the reserve. Victor Hugo commented, "We probably have one of the richest databases for carbon stocks in the whole country." But the deforestation model was the real star of the show. Sixteen PowerPoint slides were dedicated to explaining the data sources and analysis put into the model, which was nearly complete.

The presentation of these data to the roundtable meeting was styled toward the technical. Most slides showed images of GIS layers, presented quickly and with little context or explanation other than a list of data types and sources (figure 9.1). These slides, displaying complex information and imagery, flashed one after another in front of a room filled with nonspecialists. Victor Hugo's guiding commentaries were brief, dry, and generally emphasized the robustness of the various data, analytical tools, and finally, the resulting model predictions (plate 8). Overall, Victor Hugo's role at the roundtable meeting was to play out a Star Trek–like model of science, where an expert, armed with incomprehensible imagery and language, provides a charismatic image of technical mastery rather than actually communicating any technical content or ideas.

This dry technicality was deliberate. When I asked Victor Hugo about his presentation, pointing out the strangeness of the technical details given the nonexpert audience, he told me that this was explicitly requested by Guatecarbon project leaders: "I could have talked more about the process, the challenges, but they asked for this specifically." His role was to simply present the

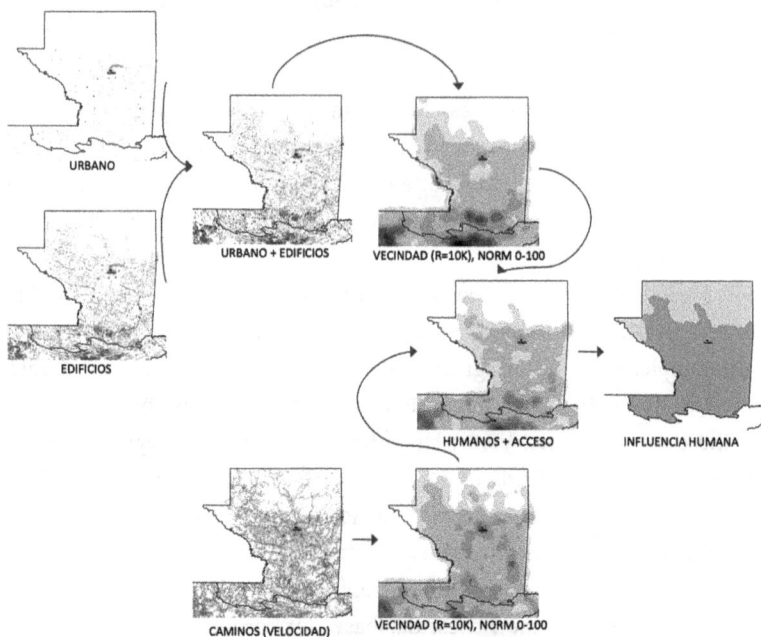

FIGURE 9.1 Image from a PowerPoint slide presented in 2011 to a multisector roundtable meeting by Victor Hugo Ramos, on behalf of the Guatecarbon REDD+ project. The image was one of several demonstrating the layering of data sources and analyses used to build a GIS model of future deforestation. The GIS layers here represent urban areas, buildings, and road access, combined via proximity analysis to create an overall measure of "human influence" (image: CONAP and WCS).

model and its data, to provide a solid symbol of technoscientific expertise, and to assure the gathered people that, despite its many political troubles, the technical half of the REDD+ project was running smoothly, and something to be proud of.

Boundary Crossing

Despite these efforts at boundary work, the model's deforestation projections are still read in entirely political ways. A tourism development consultant, Sebastian, reacted to this model by wondering if the data had been intentionally manipulated. "It struck me as surprising, as biased, and as really sad. . . . If that's really the road we're on, all this effort to preserve the MBR that has been operating for twenty-two years has been in vain, will be in vain." This consultant read bias and manipulation into the model's map both because of the extent of deforestation predicted and because of the spatial distribution of that deforestation—more in parks and less in community forest concessions. While the extent was explainable by the strange logics of REDD+ projects (where the worse the future looks the more money you stand to make by preventing it, encouraging the development of the worst-case scenario allowable within technical specifications), the distribution was directly opposed to Sebastian's pro-park, anticoncession stance. He refused to accept a future in which the concessions were predicted to do so well against deforestation, holding deeply to his belief that local communities were fundamentally ecologically destructive.

Corrupted
Data
57

The spatialization of predicted forest loss was also the source of dispute between representatives of different community concessions. Unlike Sebastian, these men did not challenge the REDD+ data or the model's validity, just its implications for predictability. At a Guatecarbon budget planning meeting between WCS, RA, ACOFOP, and concession representatives, the men struggled to reconcile their organizations' interests with the logic of distributing funding based on CEMEC's spatialized projections. According to the projections, certain areas would receive a greater proportion of (potential) funds from carbon credit sales for monitoring and control of their territory, in particular those concessions with borders along the buffer zone to the south, close to Laguna del Tigre National Park, or along the road to Carmelita that cuts through the center of the multiple-use zone. Representatives from the areas considered safe from deforestation, those in the northeast portion of the reserve near the Belize border, saw this as unfair.

The ACOFOP facilitator running the meeting urged the gathered men to focus on "harmony" and "building a united front." Viewing a map, he asked them to mentally erase all of the lines between their concessions, and to focus on the larger project outline (a red line marking the edges of the multiple-use zone). One of the men responded by asking Victor Hugo, who was present, to show and explain the projections to the group, to "turn up" the red line so the men could see it better; this was, of course, impossible on a static map image. Another suggested that such collaboration was doomed to failure: "We've learned how to fly, how to swim, but we haven't learned how to live as brothers." The conflict between concession and REDD+ project scales was clear, as the community forest managers repeatedly rejected proposals for budget allocation based on the projection model in favor of their own knowledge and experience. From their perspective, the threat of deforestation was inseparable from the financial interests of their own concessions, not a shared problem. A representative of one of the "safe" northeastern concessions commented, in reaction to the model's varied levels of projected risk: "Wherever there is a tree, there is danger of deforestation."

The Unimaginable Future

This quote, while simple, is very telling. It expresses a fundamental disbelief in the predictability of the landscape's future, by technical or other means. This disbelief is shared not only by those who object to the political implications of REDD+ deforestation projections, but by nearly everybody—including the lead developers of the Guatecarbon project. When I asked Jorge, one of the CEMEC technicians who built the model (which he was very proud of) if the output matched what he imagined the future of the landscape might look like, he replied quickly and resolutely: "No." He continued,

> I think it's going to be much worse than the worst scenario that we're considering. If things continue the way they are, and if in thirty years we're where the model says, we'll be doing *well*. There are too many things that can't be modeled. For example, construction of new roads—to use this inside the model, we need to have a document, or a plan, or something official that says they're going to build a road here. . . . We can't predict new settlements either. But if somebody builds a road that cuts the MBR in two . . .

This technician, with over fifteen years of experience in the reserve, rejected the idea that the landscape's future was predictable based on past patterns or current plans.

Throughout my interviews—with GIS technicians, NGO workers, state park service representatives, community members, and others—when I asked about the future of the reserve, the question was met with frustration, lengthy pauses, vague statements, and frequent exclamations of "Saber!" (Who knows!):

- The future of the reserve in the long term is that without . . . if there . . . there aren't . . . state policies . . . well-defined state policies . . . although . . . in the long term . . . the way we're going . . . we could be losing it, if there are no state policies. Now, if there

were state policies, we could talk about, about . . . gobernabilidad, conservation, we could talk about . . . we could keep this
biggest piece [of the forest], right?

- Well . . . what do I think of the future? Well, I don't know.
No . . . the way things look with . . . with . . . with the advance
of the agricultural frontier, the, the, the people, the political
will . . . lots of times that's what, what . . . in the end, those who
are making the decisions don't do anything, because it doesn't
suit them, you know?
- Ohhh [*grimacing*]. Well, there are a lot of areas being recuper-
ated, but narcotrafficking is increasing a lot as well. . . . I don't
know. But if you trust that they're going to recuperate a lot of
area, and maintain it, maintain what they've got . . . who knows.
- Oh man! Every day . . . you always fight, but . . . I don't think,
I don't think . . . I don't know if I'm thinking badly, if I'm a
pessimist, but . . . every year a little is conserved, but something
is lost in another area, and that's how it goes.
- It depends on which people are in the government, so . . . you
can't predict.

Across the MBR's many worlds, there is a widely shared sentiment that reliable
prediction—of any kind—is simply impossible.

At the Guatecarbon meeting with community concessions, the group
struggled with setting future project budgets based on too many unreliable
predictions. The uncertainty in the meeting was extreme, as the men tried
to plan what to do with future earnings that were based on a series of wildly
contingent possibilities: if Guatecarbon can determine a legal structure for
sale of carbon credits, and if that structure is recognized by the UN program
and credits are released to markets, and if future deforestation in the reserve
is at least 50 percent less than CEMEC's modeled predictions, and if carbon
markets are selling at a price that will make those differences profitable, then
how and where will we spend those earnings? The gathered men were asked
to determine the answers to this *how* and *where* on the basis of yet another unreliable prediction, the GIS model. The group made multiple attempts to build
flexibility or emergency response funds into the budget plans, widely agreed
among those assembled (including NGO representatives) to be the most
important thing they could do with future payouts. But the rigid structures of
the UN-REDD+ program did not allow for this kind of flexibility, leaving the

men struggling with not just how to predict the future, but how to budget for the widely expected unexpected.

What Does a Good Model Do?

The rejection of the REDD+ model's predictive accuracy by project opponents, participants, and leaders alike seems like it would lead to rejection of the model itself—but in fact, quite the opposite was true. Despite informal rejection of the project's claim to a foreseeable future, the model itself continued to be upheld as a singular technical achievement in Guatemala and across Central America. The statistical standards for a UN-REDD+ deforestation model's predictive power must be at or above 80 percent (measured as the model's ability to predict current patterns based on past inputs). In late 2011, CEMEC estimated the statistical validity of their model at 88–93 percent, well above the baseline—a sign, along with the numerous data types and sources used as inputs for the model, of technical expertise exceptional for both the country and region. Despite the fact that nobody believes in the model's highly sophisticated predictions, nearly all agree that it is an excellent model (the singular exception of Sebastian's accusation of bias was even tempered by disclaiming his own lack of technical expertise).

Even if it doesn't predict the future, CEMEC's REDD+ model works. It works in two particularly strong ways, neither of which have anything to do with the model's predictive output. First, the model has generated new forms of technoscientific knowledge about the present state of the reserve, resulting from project seed funding and international data standards linked with the UN-REDD+ program. Second, the model serves as a shared enactment of the landscape which draws institutions, individuals, and areas of the landscape into novel connections and scales, as well as drawing new funding and investment into the reserve. The model's new ways of knowing the MBR intervene on it, even if neither the knowledge nor the intervention are quite what they were imagined to be by UN policy makers.

Creating the model has enabled CEMEC to achieve new levels of data acquisition, analysis, and standardization, all of which have had secondary effects on CEMEC's other projects throughout the reserve. REDD+ criteria required CEMEC to standardize its definition of forest (minimum 5 meters in height and 30 percent crown cover), which had previously been evaluated by eye in aerial photography and satellite imagery. In order to properly assess forest cover by this definition, the Guatecarbon project included funds for the purchase of high-resolution satellite imagery and orthophotos (geometrically corrected aerial photographs) to verify their data, including images from previous years. These high-resolution data, usually unavailable on CEMEC's precarious budget, have led to much more detailed spatial and numerical measures of the reserve's historical deforestation than had previously existed. They have also allowed for calculations of statistical error based on comparison of multiple data sources (an alternative to ground truthing). Reading backward through this book, these Guatecarbon-funded data are everywhere: CEMEC has incorporated them into a wide variety of other contexts, including the *State of the Maya Biosphere Reserve* report and WCS's ecological monitoring presentations to community forest concessions.

Beyond these improvements in data access and analysis, the REDD+ program also requires inclusion of metadata for all deforestation measurements and projections. Metadata is "data about data," including both methodological and contextualizing information and technical details about data structure and design—for example, metadata for CEMEC's aerial photographs might include flight altitude, camera equipment, time and date, map projection used for georeferencing, or other factors secondary to the data contained within the photographic images. The inclusion of metadata is essential for sharing raw data (rather than complete analyses), but CEMEC has historically been limited in its ability to document metadata because of the emphasis on rapid turnaround for their analyses. Victor Hugo reported, "A problem with metadata is that usually we have to work under so much pressure, and so quickly, that sometimes there really isn't very much time for putting metadata into things. But we want to change that. Really, we want to change everything—that all the information should have metadata, that all the information is described very scientifically, with the limitations it has, or if it's possible to include a numerical measure of probabilities or error values. We want to do it—we'll see if it's possible for us to do it." CEMEC's work on the REDD+ model was a first step toward this goal: "We're forced to do [metadata] for the REDD+ project, so we're starting to change perspective to try to document things more rigorously." Technically, the development of the REDD+ model has resulted in access to new, high-resolution data, novel analyses of factors that led to current deforestation patterns in the reserve, new advanced skills and technical capacity in CEMEC's technicians, and the lab's ability to participate in internationally recognized standards of data management as signaled by the inclusion of metadata.

The REDD+ model also does a lot of political work in the reserve. It provides a new boundary object around which a wide variety of people and institutions can gather, allowing coordination without consensus (Star and Griesemer 1989). Although little faith is placed in the content of the model's predictions, its status as a rigorous technoscientific object allows the Guate-carbon project to continue despite years of social and political conflict. While these conflicts may never settle, and the project may never result in carbon market earnings, the long process of trying to determine a legal and eco-nomic structure for REDD+ credits has created novel alliances, perspectives, and scales and has drawn new funding into the reserve. The above meeting with NGOs and community representatives was exactly one such new alliance, drawing concessions together into a united front despite ongoing tensions. Similarly, WCS joined the project after it had been under development for sev-eral years, creating new shared interests between this institution and others like the Rainforest Alliance.

The model also succeeds in providing access to new forms of conserva-tion funding that rely on monetary valuation of environmental services. Of course, the promise of future financial return from REDD+ is met with disbe-lief similar to that for deforestation projections, a market-based future even less reliable than that of the landscape. Instead, a tense calculation between potential future payouts and current funding needs determines participation and investment in the project's planning stages. Seed grants and other devel-opment funding for the Guatecarbon project draw in actors that otherwise would choose different conservation strategies. Those developing the proj-ect are well aware of REDD+'s many problems and likely failures—one WCS consultant referred to the program as a *porquería* (junk, useless)—but that's where conservation funding is coming from now. As one project developer said to me, "REDD+ is a total mess, but that's the game now, so we have to play. Otherwise the MBR is going to lose out in the short term. Now, if I were in charge of the world, I'd change the whole way things were run. I'd try to make things more fair. But we're on the bottom step, you know. We can't make these decisions. So we just have to play the game."

The Unpredictable Present

Conservationists are reluctant to believe in technical or financial predic-tion or to offer alternative predictions in interviews. This reluctance reflects the rapid social and environmental changes that have drastically altered the Petén landscape over the past fifty years, themselves the product of ongoing and entangled histories of violence, social and ethnic inequality, corruption, and political instability. The rapidity and unpredictability of these historical changes, combined with continued impunity, nontransparent power structures, and too many competing enactments of and interests in the landscape, lead to understandings of more-than-human ecological dynamics that reject the separation of the technical and political inherent in the REDD+ project. These lived understandings express an anxious refusal of linear prediction that far exceeds typical scientific definitions of uncertainty like those built into the deforestation model, which can be measured and reported in neat statistical packages. Instead of predicting and planning for anticipated futures, conservationists are locked into patterns of reaction, anxiously awaiting new emergencies.

A temporal dynamic of interruptive emergency permeates every aspect of conservation in the reserve. Work plans on all time scales are rearranged to deal with sudden, unexpected occurrences: a fire set out of place, armed assault in an isolated community, or the proposal of a new law or regulation by a politician with rumored connections to organized crime. Rhythms of emergency are amplified by the rippling effects of lack of coordinated planning across actors and institutions, such that meetings might be abruptly canceled when key individuals are found to be out of town, or simply decide they have something better to do. When, instead of canceling plans, people suddenly show up in CONAP or NGO offices without them, schedules are rearranged such that unplanned meetings now interrupt other (planned) work, and so on. People may not like these interruptions, but they learn how to take advantage of them. These are the unpredictable rhythms of daily life, met with sighs of resigned acceptance: *ni modo* (nothing to be done).

The regular work rhythms of CEMEC are also subject to this constant interruption and unexpected urgency. The office's work is temporally structured by the orbital movements of satellites, office hours from 8 to 5, CONAP bureaucratic requirements, WCS's grant funding cycles that affect staffing and equipment, and the four-year political cycles of Guatemala. The computer lab's annual work rhythm also closely follows the cycling of the seasons. February through June are the most intense months of work, packed with daily, weekly, and monthly fire reports, the best satellite images all year (due to less cloud cover), and the carrying out of monitoring flights. The rest of the year is then spent processing the enormous number of images that flowed in during the dry season and preparing annual reports. All of these regular schedules are interrupted daily by sudden emergencies in the field that require maps or data, last-minute requests from other agencies, or other unexpected and unscheduled work. Victor Hugo told me,

> There are things that are clearly urgent. For example, somebody comes in saying, "Look, we have reports of a fire in the heart of Tikal [National Park]." Clearly that has to be priority number one over anything else we're doing. But usually, too, people have their own priorities, and also expect that we act really quickly. They're probably not very used to that. Here, we act almost instantly. People expect their things to come out in one hour, twenty minutes, and sometimes we have whole things to do with a half-hour notice, right? And we're doing other things, which are also priorities, so sometimes it's a little bit frustrating. But that's the way CONAP functions. Here, almost everything is unforeseen. There are emergencies all the time. You just have to get used to it. There's no alternative.

This dynamic repeatedly pushed back the completion of several major CEMEC projects, including the *State of the Maya Biosphere Reserve* report and the REDD+ deforestation model, which, even when presented to the multisector roundtable meeting as a major technological achievement, was not yet fully realized.

Alternative Presents, Multiple Futures

The rejection of the REDD+ GIS model's predictions are based in these lived experiences of emergency, which rework temporal orders from presumed linearity. The model, following international standards, can only predict deforestation based on extrapolation of observed patterns. This reflects a temporal logic in which the past is the basis for predicting the future, filtered through an ostensibly depoliticized rational calculus that directs activities in the present. Besides its incommensurability with daily emergency, this temporal frame also excludes conservationists' deepest fears: that the government of Guatemala will simply give up and undeclare the reserve (or large pieces of it) altogether. Instead of representing this as a potential future, CEMEC can only map the landscape of the northern Petén without the MBR as a nightmarish alternative present: What would have happened without the declaration of the MBR in 1990 (figure 9.2)? In this image, the forest is lost not in the unpredictable future, but in a haunting alternative present where ungovernability, lack of political will, nontransparency, and reckless profiteering have won out over

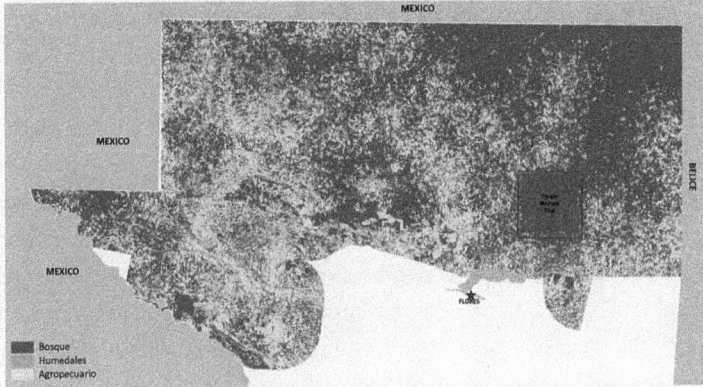

FIGURE 9.2 PowerPoint slide from a 2011 *State of the Maya Biosphere Reserve* presentation, titled "What would have happened without the Maya Biosphere Reserve?" The slide was the first in the final section of the presentation, which focused on the future of the MBR. As a result, the image is framed by a temporal double vision, in which the reserve's pasts, presents, and futures collapse into patterns of widespread deforestation (image: CONAP and WCS).

ecological concerns, erasing the reserve from history altogether (though the image still maps its ghostly outline).

This map is a product of pure imagination, an exercise in modeling a fearful future without remaining beholden to standards of rational predictability. Victor Hugo explained the process of creating the image: "We assumed the construction of two or three roads that we had heard talked about. One of those was from Carmelita to Mirador, another was the road to Uaxactún, and the other from here in Flores to the border with Belize. And we applied the same deforestation rates from the buffer zone, inside. But it was not a scientific exercise, but rather a visual one." The map emerged as a workaround attempt to include the fears and rumors of reactive conservation practice into objective technical realms. Its title frames the image as a counterfactual present, but it was given another layer of temporal effects when embedded within the "future of the MBR" section of *State of the Maya Biosphere Reserve* presentations and reports.

This alternative-present/future was the final slide of the presentation delivered in November 2011 to President Álvaro Colom, just before he left office. Carefully crafted to correlate CEMEC's monitoring data with state funding history, the presentation was a pitch for funds. The temporal juxtaposition of the slide produced a politically savvy double vision of the landscape: First, it was a laudatory celebration of past and present conservation efforts, positioned in contrast to the current ecological state of the reserve that had been shown minutes before (plate 5). The accompanying text, read by executive secretary of CONAP Mariela López Díaz, played up this positive message, emphasizing the collective effort it had taken to achieve the reserve's current protections. Second, overlaying these congratulations, the image was a subtle warning against potential anticonservation impulses in the executive branch, including for the incoming government, with its power to make this nightmare yet come to pass.

This temporal layering helped secure a conservationist future by reinforcing state control over the reserve and shoring up future budgets. At the same time, the map doubled as an imaginative exercise in feared futures, bringing lived anxieties about the MBR's cancellation by the state into the GIS maps from which they are usually excluded by the rules of rational predictability. To name this fear outright or explicitly warn against cancellation would be irrational (why argue against that which has never been proposed?) or even dangerous (signaling access to hidden agendas), but by enfolding it within a counterfactual present the map was able to be presented as a congratulatory, rather than cautionary, message. CEMEC's creative manipulation of temporal imaginaries brought feared apocalyptic futures into the realm of predictability, thereby guarding against their potential unfolding.

The map visualizes local imaginations of an entropically inevitable future, held at bay for as long as possible by conservationists and their allies. Another of CEMEC's technicians told me, "[The current situation] is critical ... lots of people, working in protected areas for twenty years. The reserve has been here for over twenty years now, and it still exists. It's still here. Seventy-five percent of what was here before, 75 percent. So, I think that the destruction process is slow. . . . What we do here—among all of us, the whole work team—is make the process of destruction of the Maya Biosphere Reserve slower." That the continued existence of the reserve after two decades should be so notable— "it's still here"—points to the haunting presence of a reserve-less reality, always just out of sight. Like a REDD+ Queen, it takes all the running you can do, not just to keep in the same place, but to move backward just a little more slowly.

Hopeless Conservation

If there is no knowable future, there is no hope. Hope remains tied to the future, and thus to predictive knowledges which suggest that careful intervention might lead in some way to desired outcomes. The futures of the reserve will never unfold as predictably as REDD+ projects would have it. The Guate-carbon model—like the rest of CEMEC's maps, reports, statistics, and official data—never accomplishes the stabilization of a single, coherent enactment of the landscape. It may not lead to a knowable future, but, like all of CEMEC's enactments, the model is composted into new relations and material impacts on the more-than-human landscape—though these are never the ones officially planned. Technoscientific knowledges, though they are powerful in the nooscape and always intervening, never lead in expected directions.

Despite strong desires for this kind of linear, singular reality, when faced with direct questions about the future, conservationists must confront the haunting sense that their practices exist in a very different, multiple world. That the MBR is more than one thing, but less than many. The pasts, presents, and futures of the northern Petén are too many to hold together, and meet in ways that are sometimes violent, sometimes profitable, sometimes hopeful, and always unequal. From the ruined structures and ecological traces of the ancient Maya to powerful claims of Petenero forest identity to social memory of scorched-earth genocide, the histories of the region refuse to stay neatly relegated to the past. From territorial battles between drug cartels to overlapping protected area declarations to the fragmented knowledge worlds of fire, multiple enactments of the reserve jostle and interrupt each other in constant emergencies in the present.

The futures of the reserve are as multiple as its pasts and presents. In early 2014, CONAP-Guatemala finally approved the publication and distribution of the DOI project report on gobernabilidad, which was under construction in 2011—a sign that the government of Guatemala may be moving toward accountability and acknowledgment of its own weaknesses. At the same moment, Claudia Paz y Paz, the attorney general who had done so much to bring accountability to the country's legal system, as well as Judge Yassmin Barrios Aguilar, who oversaw the conviction of former dictator Efraín Ríos Montt for genocide, were being forced out of their positions under questionable legality in clear retaliation for their effectiveness in standing up to historical and current impunity. Redesigns of the Mirador region continue to be pushed at the highest political levels (FARES 2014), while community forest concessions continue to garner international praise for their conservation success (Chow et al. 2013; Malkin 2015). Fears of governmental undeclaration of the MBR continue to haunt every hope for the forest's future.

But it turns out that conservationists don't need hope to keep working—they have love. The love that grows from the bodily sensations of wild encounters can exist only in the immediacy of being present, and through memories of past encounters that can be called into the present body and mind. Who needs the future, when the continued presence of the reserve—*it's still here*—is a wild encounter in itself. Love makes this place worth fighting for, here and now, no matter the outcome. To reverse the previous formulation: wherever there is a tree, there is the possibility of conservation. Accountability and impunity, parks and people, conflict and collaboration, all are still here, along with their many clashes and contradictions. Love and fear mix in anxious double visions, where the more things change, the more they stay the same (or move backward, just a little more slowly).

MODEST INTERVENTIONS

Late one night in Flores, I met up with a group of CEMEC technicians, already well into the drinking portion of their evening by the time I arrived. Freed from the quiet (and sober) confines of the office, they hounded me with questions: "We see you typing all the time in the office—what are you writing?!" My explanation of field notes—that most of what I was writing was quite boring, just what I observed—was not enough to quell their curiosity: "But how are we doing? What do you *really* think of us?" A couple years later, when I sent drafts of the chapters examining her work in Paso Caballos to Rosa, she commented that she was accustomed to applied anthropology (in which she has a master's degree), and that my writing was more descriptive than she expected. She offered concrete revisions, but also wanted to know that my book would do something for people. In a 2015 workshop presenting this research back to those who had supported it, the NGO directors in attendance requested more applied, concrete suggestions.

These desires for me to provide evaluation, recommendations, or other actionable knowledges—usefulness—were pressed on me repeatedly. Knowing is intervening, and my ethnographer presence in a room already makes a difference to what happens there. I offered minor interventions during fieldwork: technical things like recommendations on survey language, or, more commonly, comments or questions that pushed against troubling discourses of machismo, anti-indigeneity, and the like. People often sought me out for advice about data presentation, or reporting or sharing conservation data with communities in the reserve, and most recently for potentially revising CEMEC's procedures for handling data requests from foreign researchers. Other minor interventions into the nooscape come in the form of taking my own knowledges back into the worlds of institutional practice. Some knowledges lost or excluded from official documents and studies may reenter institutional realms via copies of this book, which will be sent back. Indeed, sending copies of earlier drafts and publications on this research already caused modest shifts in some reporting practices, including gobernabilidad reports.

Still, many conservationists yearn for more—for my own study to offer the kind of clarity and usefulness that is impossible among too many partially connected worlds. My own knowledges about the MBR are inseparable from the dynamics I describe throughout this book. This also means that my own attempts to transform something of this knowledge into usefulness is a patchwork of successes and failures, shifts and gaps. This was most evident in the series of workshops I ran in 2015, designed to report back and generate discussion on my analysis of conservationist knowledge and practice in the reserve.

I tailored different versions of these workshops for NGO staff (from WCS and Balam), CEMEC, and for the villages of Uaxactún and Paso Caballos. The first workshop, with the two NGOs, resulted in the most discussion and the most tension. Familiar with anthropological critiques of conservation, some entered the room ready to defend themselves, then expressed surprise at the analytical focus on the challenges and questions they confront in their daily work. Many attendees were glad of the opportunity to step outside their frantic daily rhythms to reflect on broader dynamics affecting their decision making, while others repeated their desires for immediately applicable recommendations, unable to resist the lure of the useful. The CEMEC technicians, in contrast, were more interested in discussing ideas about objectivity, the politics of knowledge, trust, and communication. Those in attendance at Uaxactún were most excited that I had simply come back to report results—even before delving into the details. They were also curious about how to best harness my understanding of knowledge dynamics for their own uses—particularly gaining access to research and reports on the village and OMYC that might help them in the renewal of their concession contract in 2025.

The planned fourth workshop, for Paso Caballos, fell apart due to a confluence of poor timing, miscommunication, and troubling dynamics. I ultimately learned that some organizations—especially political parties, as it was an election year—had been paying community members to attend meetings. I did not realize until too late that the COCODE members with whom I had been communicating were attempting to squeeze similar payments from me. In the end, this failure was beyond my control. But it haunted me, replicating the same dynamics of exclusion that often lead to conservationist failure in the village rather than providing a space to reflect on those dynamics as the workshop was intended to do.

When I expressed my disillusionment to Rosa, through whom I sent short written summaries of the presentation instead, she replied, "I'm sorry. I really am sorry. But what can you do?" I sighed. "If the people don't want it, they don't want it." (Si la gente no quiere, no quiere.) Rosa's eyes widened in recognition: "You know, there's a part in your study where I say exactly that?"

AFTERWORD

> The ideas which seemed to be me can also
> become immanent in you. May they
> survive—if true.
>
> Gregory Bateson, *Steps to an Ecology of Mind*

So, what on earth is a nooscape?

It is the way that knowledges are like seeds, which flourish, perish, or lie dormant, depending on their relations with all that is around them. It is the way that seeds are like knowledges, growing from containment and immanent possibility into material worldly presence. It is the way that knowledges grow out of ecological relations and into human bodies and minds. It is the way that immaterial human ideas compost into material worlds. It is the partial connections between too many ways of knowing, and intervening, and intervening-to-know, and knowing-to-intervene. It is the emergent more-than-human mind of partially connected, situated worlds. Confused, paranoid, contradictory, uncertain, fragmented, and imaginative, lively and deadly all at once. It is more than one but less than many.

In the Anthropocene, the global has increasing influence over environmental thought and action even at the smallest scales. We are encouraged to "think globally, act locally." The Anthropocene has revived the idea of the noo*sphere*—the emergent global mind of life on earth (Wyndham 2000; Wyly 2015). As originally framed, the noosphere was both material and ideational, a global sphere of human thought that would manage the biosphere primarily in human interest (Turner 2005). This resonates with more technocratic takes on the Anthropocene—the idea that just the right geoengineering intervention, or just the right arrangement of global governance institutions, will set us, and the whole earth, back on the right path. Like new synaptic connections between neurons in an infant brain, this noosphere incorporates the growing web of communications and monitoring technology as it develops, and then acts on the biosphere from which it emerges in the interests of self-protection. The UNESCO Man and the Biosphere Program, from which the Maya Biosphere Reserve was born (along with over 670 other reserves), is exactly one such intervention.

Appealing as it may be, there are gaps in this account. Critics point to exclusions and injustices perpetuated by Anthropocene discourses (Gibson-Graham 2011; Moore 2016; Haraway 2016). These repeat what was said of the noosphere six decades before. In 1959, "American ecologist Eugene Odum categorized the [noosphere] as dangerous on the basis that it implied that humanity was ready to take over management of the biosphere" (Turner 2005, 506). Attempts have been made to broaden both concepts, especially to take nonhuman agency (Lorimer 2015; Latour 2014) and nonhuman knowledges (Kohn 2013, 2014; Margulis and Sagan 1995) more seriously. But the global holism of both concepts remains, even if it is a confused or contradictory or more-than-human whole; and the whole remains a problem for understanding how to respond if you are figured as a part (Haraway 2016; Morton 2016; Tsing 2015).

Instead of working ourselves through strange loops of being both part and whole, of thinking globally and acting locally, I suggest instead that we think and act nooscapically—attending to the nonhierarchical relation between scales (including the global and the local) as they emerge from multiple situated encounters and relations. In a nooscape, there is no meaningful separation between environmental knowing and intervening, as doing either automatically transforms the other. There is no meaningful separation of human cultural ideas from material more-than-human natures, as each compose and compost into the other. This is why I have used ecological terms and theories to understand knowledge projects throughout the book, as more than metaphor—because knowledges are embedded in ecological worlds, and vice versa. There is no neat relation of parts and wholes, only situated, partially connected enactments of ecological change. This text itself enacts the existence of a particular, situated, conservationist nooscape. This also means that the book is rooted—materially, like a plant in soil—in the more-than-human landscape of the MBR. Nooscapes are always in motion, always becoming. They resist singularity and completion at every turn, offering instead a multiplicity of scales, paths, and possibilities, none of which will solve all problems.

MBR conservationist desires to know a place in order to change it lead to a proliferation of knowledges and enacted worlds, each an attempt to create change—whether this is the policy-oriented usefulness of CEMEC's data, the violent anticipatory logics of paranoia, or the growing of care into relations between Uaxactuneros and plants. Throughout this book, I have described haunting relations between these multiple enactments. Haunting is not the only relation possible between worlds; it is produced by attempts to render the world singular, to act as if other enactments were not already present and clamoring for attention: as if maps told a whole story, as if fires were containable by regulation, as if scientific objectivity did not need wild love to survive. As if just the right way of knowing could enact a better, singular world to finally erase those of inequality, corruption, violence, and loss. Attempts to banish these worlds produce a haunting that disturbs linear time, twisting histories, presences, and predictions together in strange formations. What is yet to be disturbs ancient pasts, what might once have been erupts into the present.

Anna Tsing suggests, "Freedom is the negotiation of ghosts on a haunted landscape; it does not exorcise the haunting but works to survive and negotiate it with flair" (2015, 76). What might this "freedom" look like in Guatemala? What alternatives might there be to haunted conservation in the MBR? I can no more offer a solution to conservationist entanglements with dynamics of violence, inequality, corruption, or exclusion than can any other situated, partial perspective. But I can hope that my own attempt to know the MBR in order to change it might push other knowledges and interventions in more equitable directions. For one thing, while the risks of recognizing copresent worlds are real, denying them does not prevent them from erupting as threat, loss, or failure.

I argue that opening to this recognition, of not just different perspectives on a single world but differently situated worlds coming together in partial connection, is necessary in order to work more justly through the effects of difference. This recognition is necessary in order to diminish the power of the enacted world that causes so much haunting—that of a singular nature, passively set aside from active human knowing and action. It is necessary in order to face the nonlinear scale-jumping effects of knowing and intervening, to understand that there will never be a better science that will solve controversies or end conflict. It is necessary to slow the rush to solutions that only cause new and different problems.

Through recognition of multiple copresent worlds, conservationists might learn to recognize new forms of responsibility. Although they are not responsible for the brutality of the war, they are responsible for calling its ghosts into the present through alignments with the military. Although they are not responsible for racist anti-indigeneity in Guatemala, they are responsible for reenacting ethnic inequalities on the microscales of mundane daily practices. Although they are not responsible for globally circulating neoliberal ideologies and priorities, they are responsible for reenacting these in the worlds of the MBR through projects and documents, and therefore responsible for what they do to entangled human and nonhuman lives.

Being responsible does not mean being in control, nor being in charge of finding a solution—it means being called to respond to the effects, intended and unintended, of conservationist knowledges and worlds. Reparations may be in order. Love should be nourished, cultivated, and allowed more space and time to grow, including in the sometimes-infertile soils of institutional structures. That love should extend to humans, some of whom are as essential to the ongoingness of this landscape as others are to its destruction.

Siempre en la lucha.

Introduction

1 Other versions of knowledge ecology have been framed, many of which overlap significantly with my approach. These tend to focus more on relations between knowledge forms and their institutional and disciplinary contexts, with less emphasis on embeddedness in more-than-human ecological worlds (Bowen 1985; Rosenberg 1998; Star 1995). Boaventura de Sousa Santos (2007), a theorist of Latin American social movements, proposes "ecology of knowledges" as a framework for emancipatory global politics. His is a vision for new relations between existing epistemologies (indigenous, subaltern, modernist science, etc.), while mine is an analytical framework for describing how epistemic multiplicity and contradiction emerge from complex situated relations. The multiplicity of knowledges in the MBR is not always linked to emancipatory politics, but can be as easily linked to violent, destructive, profit-seeking, or oppressive ends.

2 Vernadsky's noosphere emphasizes human dominion of the biosphere through science and technology, while Teilhard de Chardin's is deeply theological and imagines a progressive evolution toward divine unification of humanity through Christ. Both describe the noosphere as a new stage of the evolutionary history of life on earth.

3 For example, one attempt by Felice Wyndham (2000) to resurrect the noosphere in ecological anthropology describes a series of nested levels of mind, from individual to social group to noosystem to noosphere. I do not follow the cybernetic "ecology of mind" proposed by Gregory Bateson (1972) for similar reasons, though my approach to an ecology of knowledges owes much to his work.

4 Ecological theorizations of emergent phenomena are locked into debates about reductionist versus holistic approaches; even attempts to reconcile these two by

moving away from hierarchical levels, as in the work of Ponge (2005), end up re-producing a fundamental dualism of parts and wholes. Philosophers of science Potochnik and McGill (2012) offer a helpful critique of hierarchical thought in ecology, arguing that flexible and context-dependent analyses of scale are more empirically useful than conceptualizations of static, discrete, nested levels. The no-oscape builds on the scalar ecology of their approach, sidestepping questions of part-whole relationships in favor of situated process and interaction.

5 In this way, my work aligns with what Anna Tsing calls "world making," which "focuses us on practical activities rather than cosmologies. . . . While most scholars use ontology to segregate perspectives, one at a time, thinking through world mak-ing allows layering and historically consequential friction" (2015, 292n7).

6 Swapping in the nooscape for the figure of the cyborg, Strathern's description of multiplicity in a field of partial connections is apt: "The cyborg observes no scale: it is neither singular nor plural, neither one nor many, a circuit of connections that joins parts that cannot be compared insofar as they are not isomorphic with one another. It cannot be approached holistically or atomistically, as an entity or as a multiplication of entities" (2004, 54).

7 This definition of haunting aligns with that of Barad, who argues against subjective or purely epistemic interpretations of the term segregated from ontological reality. She writes, "Hauntings . . . are not mere rememberings of a past (assumed to be) left behind (in actuality) but rather the dynamism of ontological indeterminacy of time-being/being-time in its materiality" (Barad 2017, G113).

Chapter 1. The Many Worlds of the Maya Biosphere Reserve

1 While the number of massacres in the Petén was lower compared to other regions, relative to population density the region was heavily targeted. This was due in large part to the use of the region's forests as bases for guerrilla groups, as well as to long-standing military interest in establishing territorial control over the region (a major factor in the establishment of FYDEP). One key difference from other regions was that many of the massacres and much of the scorched-earth village destruction in the Petén were carried out on Ladino, not Maya, villages.

2 For a more complete history and analysis of this early NGO landscape, see Sundberg (1998).

3 For example, CI started a local NGO branch called ProPetén, which built the Scarlet Macaw Biological Station in Laguna del Tigre National Park and worked extensively with the neighboring village of Paso Caballos. I visited ProPetén's projects in these locations in 2007 during my master's thesis research at Yale University, at which point the local organization was already fully independent from CI. By the time I returned in 2009, ProPetén had sold the biological sta-tion to WCS's local offshoot, Asociación Balam (also by this time independent),

and had shifted its work and priorities to issues in southern Petén, outside MBR boundaries. The Paso Caballos and biological stations I visited in 2011–12 were sedimented with material and discursive traces of these shifting institutional encounters.

4 What is meant by "neoliberalism" in these critiques can be slippery: it can refer to a global economic model, a specific set of policies implemented by multilateral institutions beginning in the early 1980s, or a range of political philosophies with particular ideologies of personhood, property, and agency (Bebbington and Thiele 1993; West 2006; West, Igoe, and Brockington 2006). It is the presumed foe of many social and political movements across Latin America, as well as dominating the work of many scholars working there. While David Harvey's (2007) fundamental work on neoliberal globalization acknowledges uneven distribution of effects across the world, it (and many other works) still assumes a largely unitary global neoliberalism. But Noel Castree's (2008) review of critical geographic work on the neoliberalization of nature reveals that the term is used to refer to vastly different and often fundamentally incomparable situations.

5 For ethnographic examples, see Das (2007), Hetherington (2011), Hoag (2011), Mathews (2011), and Mitchell (2002).

6 Guatemalans would frequently ask me comparative questions about my life in the U.S. versus the Petén, and their omnipresent awareness of my otherness brought an inflection of comparison to many of the encounters that appear throughout this book. That said, I do not want to unintentionally reinforce a hierarchy of U.S./Global North versus Guatemala/Global South, even when this frame is coming from interlocutors themselves. Instead, I use terms like "gringa" or include such moments of comparison for what they indicate about the transnational power relations that shape knowledge and action in the reserve.

7 While I have updated aspects of argument and narrative beyond my primary fieldwork in 2011–12, I have not updated most versions of these artifacts, particularly maps. I retain the versions encountered in 2011–12 for two reasons: first, as these objects are also actors, their actions exist in thick relation with those of humans I followed, watched, listened, and spoke to at that time. To update just the images but not the humanistic portions of fieldwork would leave my analysis lopsided. Second, because I have remained in contact with CEMEC, WCS, and others in the MBR, sharing different versions of this research in writing and oral presentations, some of the representation and monitoring choices that I write about have changed in response to my feedback, analysis, and critiques. I note these shifts where I am aware of them, as ways that my own research practices enter the nooscape as both knowing and intervening.

8 In 2018, Guatemala was the one of the most dangerous countries in the world for environmental defenders, with the highest rate of murder of environmental activists per capita (Global Witness 2019). The vast majority of those targeted in these attacks are indigenous community defenders, not institutional actors.

9 This does not mean that neoliberal ideologies of transparency do not maintain a strong presence in the conservationist nooscape. As Kregg Hetherington notes, transparency is not so much about pure and open information as about the politics of representation amid uncertainty: "In a climate of suspicion of all things representational, transparency is the ability to claim, however briefly, that unlike anyone else's, one's own representations of past attempts at representing provide a glimpse of the *really real*" (2011, 159).

10 If the word "meaning" feels like a stretch in this nonhuman context, consider the work of Eduardo Kohn (2013). Kohn articulates a semiotic theory of life itself, in which tropical forests are particularly dense with meaning. For Kohn, the forest is "an emergent and expanding multilayered cacophonous web of mutually constitutive, living, and growing thoughts" (2013, 79). The living MBR forest is very much a contributor to the nooscape. Following the metaphor of culture shock, a newcomer to the forest is unable to recognize or decipher the local signs embedded in forest life.

11 The parallel here to the ethnographic fieldwork of anthropologists does not escape my notice. More than once, in conversations about the campo, it came up that Flores and conservation institution offices were my campo, that I too was in the field, accessing the real.

Chapter 2. Eye of the Storm

1 The term "keystone actor" plays off the definition of keystone species in conservation biology. In ecological terms, a keystone species is one that plays a central role in the structure and function of a larger ecosystem. The influence of sea otters on kelp forest ecosystems is a commonly used example: if the otter population drops, the sea urchins they eat will consume too much kelp, undermining a larger multispecies system that relies on the seaweed forests. Similarly, if you imagine removing CEMEC from the MBR, major systemic shifts in conservationist policy and practice would occur across multiple scales.

2 For a few years, CEMEC researched the possibility of using small drones to replace monitoring flights, another unprompted step into new technologies. Ultimately, these plans were set aside due to complex aeronautical regulations and insurance requirements.

3 Traditionally, "ground truthing" refers to sending people out on the ground to verify interpretation of aerial or satellite imagery. Due to budgetary and logistical constraints, however, most of the ground truthing performed by CEMEC is actually triangulation and verification of data sources with other imagery of higher resolution—either aerial photography to verify satellite data, or sometimes purchased high-resolution satellite imagery to verify freely available lower-resolution Landsat images.

4 The interruption of this pattern in 2015 was the result of widespread protests in response to a major corruption scandal in the office of the president, Otto Pérez Molina, which resulted in his resignation and arrest. The unfolding of the scandal coincided with election season, creating powerful political momentum that overturned expectations and common electoral complacency. Instead of electing the 2011 runner-up, Manuel Baldizón (anticipated as the next president by most people in 2011–12), Guatemalans voted in a right-wing comedian running as a political outsider, Jimmy Morales.

5 See, for example, Brechin et al. (2002), Brosius (1999), Fairhead and Leach (2003), Ferguson (1990), Forsyth (2002), and Li (2007), among many others. For related critiques of conservation in the MBR, see Sundberg (1998, 2003) and Ybarra (2012).

Chapter 3. Mapping Gobernabilidad

1 The nonhuman worlds of the reserve's landscape are also ungovernable in many ways: the ranging of endangered jaguars out of the forest onto nearby ranches where they are shot to defend cattle; the unpredictable vagaries of global climate change or regular climatic fluctuations like El Niño; the violent incursions of hurricanes. These elements contribute to institutional senses of powerlessness and lack of control, though I do not attend to the governability of nonhuman worlds in this chapter.

2 This definition is different from typical academic discussions of (environmental) governance and represents my analytical separation of emic uses of the term "gobernabilidad" in the Petén rather than any formal definition. There is a distinct Spanish term for governance, *gobernanza*, but it was rarely used by MBR conservationists.

3 Much scholarship has covered this ground at the national scale of Guatemala (Brands 2010; Grandin 2005; Howard, Hume, and Oslender 2007; Musalo, Pellegrin, and Roberts 2010; Nelson 2009; Sanford 2003; Sieder 2011).

4 These include a USAID grant devoted to improving gobernabilidad in the MBR, administered through cooperation with the U.S. DOI; and the *State of the Maya Biosphere Reserve* report, funded by DFID, which included gobernabilidad as a key theme. Both DOI and DFID projects involved multiple state and nonstate institutions, including CONAP, WCS, Asociación Balam, and the Association of Forest Communities of the Petén (ACOFOP). The DOI and DFID projects were so similar in theme and practice that the institutions carrying them out had to be careful not to double charge the two funders for a single activity.

5 This website, State of the Maya Biosphere Reserve (formerly at estadodelarbm.org), is no longer maintained as of 2019.

6 López was promoted from regional director of CONAP-Petén to national executive secretary of CONAP in fall 2011, so she appears in both roles throughout the text.

7 "Biotopes" (*biotopos*) refers to special protected areas indicated for education, research, and preservation, managed by the public University of San Carlos. These preceded the MBR in the Petén, and when overlaid with national parks, created not a shared, but technically a doubled, administrative structure.

8 Baldizón carried the election in the Petén by a wide margin, but I did not encounter a single Petenero working in CONAP, conservation NGOs, or elsewhere who claimed to vote for him. Instead, people explained his local victory either as a product of duping the local population with his charismatic promises and exorbitant media campaign (see Nelson [2009] on narratives of duplicity in Guatemala) or as a result of vote buying, such as providing tin roofs to rural villages.

9 Mano Dura politics have become popular across Central America, a conservative backlash against the high rates of violent crime generally attributed to gang activity. For an excellent comparative case, see Moodie's (2009) analysis of Mano Dura in El Salvador.

10 It is important to note, however, that despite the dismantling of particular programs, the presidential office has been dominated by right-wing candidates with strong neoliberal platforms, with only a partial exception in the more centrist party of Álvaro Colom (2008–12).

11 "Environmental justice" carries a different meaning in the Petén than in typical U.S. usage. It refers to the pursuit and prosecution of environmental crimes, defined as those that break protected area laws. The category is often extended to include violence or threats of violence against conservation actors, including in retribution for reporting other environmental crimes.

12 NGOs do not cooperate directly with the army, but communicate areas of need and priority to CONAP, which then directs associated armed forces. In this way, NGOs are able to keep military alliances at arm's length while encouraging militarized conservation—yet another enactment of state/nonstate boundaries.

Chapter 4. But Is It a Basin?

1 Two industrial forest concessions would also lose territory under a basinist rezoning, but these losses were not usually raised in debates over the area, as both sides were more focused on representing themselves as providing benefits to local communities.

2 Scale jumping emerges as a key characteristic of political scandal in anthropological analyses; see Mathews (2014) and Tsing (2000).

3 It was unclear whether PACUNAM's support would be permanently withdrawn from Hansen's archaeological work and the basin model, or why this shift was taking place. One FARES worker suggested these elites might be "suspicious" or "envious" of Hansen because they were not being given the adoration or godlike treatment they desired. Antibasinists were happy to attribute the change to the elites begin-

ning to "see through Hansen's lies"; they were also meeting directly with PACUNAM in Guatemala City to persuade them of the importance of the MBR beyond Mirador. In 2016, Hansen was quoted in a news article as saying, "Pacunam's one of my sponsors. I formed Pacunam. I actually gave them their name. I gave them their logo. But I've created a monster" (Cuffe 2016). I was not able to secure an interview with a PACUNAM representative who might directly answer these questions.

4 There is a long and controversial history of Mormon archaeology in Mesoamerica, although Hansen has never connected his own research to this explicitly religious legacy. For more information, see Sides (1999).

5 Evidence from actors in these institutions remained in the realm of claims made in interviews and other conversations; I never saw firsthand testimony or evidence from these connections.

Peteneros and Other Endemic Species

1 Many have debated the influence of anti–human immigrant sentiments on anti–invasive species rhetoric (see Coates 2007; Simberloff 2003). I do not mean to engage these debates here, but rather to play with these metaphorical overtones by reversing their usual direction.

Chapter 5. A Reserve Full of Rooftops

1 Rumors of Americans stealing children (and their organs) from indigenous groups in Guatemala are widespread, sometimes resulting in violent retaliation.

2 Michelle Murphy's transnational historical analysis of population as an object of twentieth-century state management hinges on a shift from Malthus's framing to that of Raymond Pearl. She shows how Pearl's technoscientific formulation of population—one universally describable (even across species) by an experimentally and mathematically defined S-curve growth pattern—was coproduced with twentieth-century states organized around management of something called "economy." Pearl pushed discussions away from early twentieth-century eugenic discussions that focused on the evolutionary quality of individuals toward the management of quantity by state policies and technologies in the interest of national economy. While Malthus's models of finite environmental resources inevitably end in crisis, Pearl emphasized the possibility of rational state management of population to avoid such crises. Murphy argues that the "natural environment" in Malthusian models was overtaken by the "economy" in Pearl's as the fundamental external condition that shapes population dynamics. Her argument is persuasive, but I do not think either Malthusian models or the environment-as-population-limit have disappeared so much as they have been carried along as patchy enactments with

variously coproduced protectionist or conservationist states. Indeed, these may now be reemerging into broader spheres with the rise of Anthropocene discourses and globalized environmental anxiety.

3 In Verran's study, these different numbers are enacted through the different counting and calculating practices of Western and Yoruba mathematics—the epistemologies of different mathematical systems enact different number-objects.

4 According to Timothy Morton (2016), these two versions of global population form a "strange loop" known as the human species. Strange loops are like Mobius strips, where two incommensurable truths are coconstitutive of each other yet exist with an uncanny valley between them.

5 The association only surveyed those Q'eqchi' villages that were members of the organization, so some Q'eqchi' settlements, including Paso Caballos, were surveyed by SNEM instead.

6 The uncensused estimates included 16,620 people in the urbanized buffer zone, 3,835 in unsurveyed rural villages, 240 in institutional or temporary settlements, and 1,500 on ranches or agricultural lands. These estimates were based on existing SNEM records, a survey conducted in 1998, and CEMEC's aerial monitoring.

7 According to CEMEC, it is too expensive and laborious to annually survey the densely populated buffer zone, even aerially.

8 Georeferencing is widely recognized among CEMEC technicians as their most time-consuming and tedious task, with the staff almost entirely consumed by the activity for months during and after the flight season. During these months, even the office receptionist is recruited to the dull work of photo matching.

9 There are a few exceptions to the buffer zone rule, for example, the WCS program Living with Carnivores (Conviviendo con Carnívoros), which targets ranchers near core zones of the reserve in efforts to reduce the killing of wildlife that strays across reserve boundaries.

10 It is not my intention here to reproduce typical development indicators as the best measure of human well-being. As Anna Tsing kindly pointed out to me, this list implies that state-like development interventions would increase local well-being, when in fact it is often rural places with the least state intervention that are better off on their own terms. It is important to remember, however, that the state is not absent in Paso Caballos—it is exceedingly present, though not as a system of support for human life. Villagers are not isolated from state projects, but rather caught in the awkward position of occupying a heavily contested protected area due to historical displacement.

11 I was able to identify twenty-five nonhousing rooftops in the most recent photograph, accounting for nearly 10 percent of the current population estimate, and I am unfamiliar with the locations of small stores and churches.

12 One family told me about a project that brought Depo-Provera birth control shots to the village, considered a good fit by NGOs due to low cost and long-term ef-

fectiveness. The wife had taken advantage with her husband's support, but then suffered major side effects for months, long after the mobile clinic had left. No information about these effects or follow-up care was provided, and she and her husband ended up discouraging others from using this birth control method, spreading a story about how the shots made women sick. As in this story, even well-meaning projects and real interest from villagers can go awry due to lack of permanent, accessible health infrastructure.

13 In 2015, round-trip bus fare from Paso Caballos to Santa Elena was Q100, or almost $13 U.S.—exorbitant when compared to local incomes. This journey also relies on a single privately owned bus, which would unpredictably cancel journeys due to impassable roads, bus repairs, or other issues.

14 Technicians at CEMEC are aware of the scalar limitations of their estimates and agree that aerial population counts may be inaccurate at the village level. But these limitations were discussed only in response to my questions and are not included in the published annual reports. In the latter, the word "estimate" is left to do all the work of describing limits to official knowledge.

15 These acuerdos de conservación are part of an international CI-led initiative that is slowly spreading, via partnership with WCS, across the reserve. Uaxactún was the first village to sign an acuerdo in 2009, with Paso Caballos following in 2010, along with several other villages. In both cases, the village's COCODE, WCS, CI, and CONAP are signatories, along with OMYC in Uaxactún, and all acuerdos are approved by majority vote in an open community assembly.

Chapter 6. Fire at the Edge of the Forest

1 These terms—"addition," "translation," "distribution"—come from Annemarie Mol (2002), who presents them as mechanisms through which multiple enacted ontologies coexist while appearing to be singular.

2 NASA MODIS satellites capture data at three resolutions and multiple levels of sensitivity. The 1 km2 resolution images of hot spot data used by CEMEC are available online quickly as part of the MODIS Rapid Response program. The sensitivity of the instruments can be much greater than 1 km2; the satellites can detect fires as small as 30 × 30 meters (900 m2), but will mark the whole 1 km2 pixel within which the fire was detected as a hot spot.

3 Sierra del Lacandón National Park can also be included in this wild west and has similar but distinct dynamics at play. In early 2018, two conservationists in different institutions forwarded me a petition in support of eviction of a recent land invasion in Sierra del Lacandón, arguing that the invasion marked the park's turn toward becoming "another Laguna del Tigre." Sierra del Lacandón does not share any borders with intact regions of the reserve as Laguna del Tigre does, so while it

is the subject of major concern for its own forests' sake, it is not seen as constituting the same level of threat toward the rest of the reserve.

4 The French-owned oil company Perenco operates wells in the park under questionably legal terms. The renewal of their expired contract in 2010 was the subject of heated debates over protected-area laws. Rumors indicate that the executive secretary of CONAP was replaced by President Álvaro Colom specifically to support the fifteen-year extension of the oil company's concession. In exchange, Perenco contributed funding to the army's Green Battalion for the park, directly bolstering military protection of their own extraction sites.

5 See Grandia's (2012) *Enclosed* for an ethnographic history of Q'eqchi' migration into the Petén lowlands, including into Laguna del Tigre National Park.

6 An estimated 150,000 people fled into Mexico during the war, but only around a third of these gained formal refugee status from the United Nations High Commissioner for Refugees (Tomuschat, de Cotí, and Tojo 1999).

7 A manzana is a Spanish colonial land measurement, equivalent to 6,987 m² or about 1.7 acres.

Chapter 7. A Known Place

1 I do not mean to imply that a similar dynamic of being known does not exist in Paso Caballos. The Q'eqchi' village is less constantly studied than Uaxactún, though it is also deeply shaped by the knowledge making and interventions of external actors.

2 The name was chosen by U.S. archaeologist Sylvanus Morley in 1916 to refer to the ancient Maya city next to which the current village sits. The words *waxac* and *tun* mean "eight stones" in Mayan and were also chosen because they sound like "Washington."

3 Early NGO inputs and accompaniment focused on sustainable timber harvesting practices and infrastructural development, with financial management left up to inexperienced local administrators. By 2009, OMYC owed 2.29 million Quetzales (approximately U.S. $310,000) to suppliers and lenders, which meant that any income from the sale of timber or NTFPs immediately left the community. With OMYC nearing bankruptcy, external institutions and OMYC began collaborating to implement administrative and financial training and assistance. This shift was reinforced by neoliberal transparency and accountability measures that were increasingly important to international donors. WCS included the assignment of an external financial manager for OMYC in its acuerdos de conservación, the first of which was signed in 2009. By 2013, OMYC no longer held any high-interest loans, and the concession operated with more stable finances. Now, income from forest harvesting activities is directed toward community conservation and development projects like forest fire prevention or education.

4 The term "rollo" carries rich connotations that are difficult to translate—in this context, it most directly means "business" or "matter," but also calls up something complicated, messy, or difficult to navigate.

5 Naming conventions in (Ladino) Guatemala use the paternal surnames of a person's father and mother, in that order. In some cases, married women take on their husband's paternal surname in place of their own maternal surname.

6 In practice, much of what becomes official, external knowledge has actually been passed to institutions through informal interaction with villagers, like Juan's use of imaginary census numbers in chapter 5. This knowledge gains new authority and is considered external when it is entered into documents.

7 The term "care" has been used with different definitions and theoretical orientations, most often in feminist analyses of feminine-gendered labor, especially childcare, health care, and education (Held 2006; Hochschild 1995; Mol 2008). Care has also appeared in environmental contexts, particularly in ecofeminist work critiquing associations between caring women and nature (MacGregor 2004, 2011; Salleh 1993). In Uaxactún, it is men who are involved in the discursive and labor formations that I describe as "caring," requiring a broadening of the term from these female-gendered contexts.

8 Not all previous harvesting practices were purely destructive. Historic chiclero practices of leaving chicle-producing trees to recover for several years between rubber extractions is often cited as proof of a long-standing sustainability or conservationist ethic among Uaxactuneros (and Peteneros more broadly), though these practices were not understood in these terms at the time.

9 Local, independent NTFP extraction sold to extralocal contractors was the dominant form of labor organization in the Petén throughout most of the nineteenth and twentieth centuries (Schwartz 1990).

10 The term "NGO accompaniment" refers to a model of NGO-community relations that centers community responsibility and decision making for projects. The language and associated practices are a response to critiques of authoritarian, nonparticipatory interventions but can also leave communities with more responsibility for failures, debts, or other problems that arise from shared projects.

11 Field monitoring of xate extraction is CONAP's responsibility, although this has recently been part of a strained relation that has focused more on penalizing nonharvesting activities of xateros, such as hunting or leaving trash in campsites.

12 Due to a lack of funding for ecological monitoring in WCS that year, 2009 is absent from the graph. Previous years were funded through the WCS Living Landscapes program, and beginning in 2010, xate monitoring was funded by the acuerdo de conservación.

13 Forests are defined by CEMEC as 30 percent or more canopy cover and a minimum 5 meters in height, based on the international standard for UN-REDD+ (Reduced Emissions from Deforestation and Forest Degradation) projects like the one described in chapter 9.

14 People say that there used to be *xateras*, female harvesters, but nobody could tell me exactly when or why women stopped harvesting xate, nor think of any woman currently living in the community who ever cut xate.

15 One of the concrete ideas that emerged from this conversation was to start a collection or database, housed in OMYC, for all the academic studies, media accolades, institutional reports, and other external knowledge about Uaxactún and its forest management. As one woman pointed out, it is easy enough to ask for copies of things from WCS when they are needed, but many institutions implement short-term projects or leave Guatemala altogether, making it virtually impossible for the village to get copies of reports later on. I suggested that OMYC and the COCODE not only could request copies of project reports and documents after the fact, but also could make sure that the request was formally included in project agreements during the planning process.

Chapter 8. Wild Life

1 In a similar move, Kristina Lyons mobilizes the word *selva* (jungle) in her work on Amazonian soil science. Following the conceptualizations of her farmer guides in the Colombian Amazon, she writes, "*Selva* becomes vital entanglement, co-adaptive construction, complexity, and laboriousness. It speaks of intimate, on-going, and mutually obliging relations among organisms and elements—of which farmers are a part" (Lyons 2014, 223). *Selva* contains linguistic echoes of the Spanish word for wild, *silvestre*, and Lyons's description of farmers' attentiveness and entanglements with complex forest life mirrors the ways that WCS biovets interact with wild MBR life.

2 Cuatro Balam was a program initiated by the Colom government in 2008 to increase tourism to the MBR, focused on development of the Mirador archaeological site. The project instituted a series of multisector roundtable meetings (the Mesa Multisectorial) to foster dialogue about the Mirador area between government agencies, NGOs, communities, academics, and the private sector.

3 In contrast to Roan and Iván's comments here about things looking better in the office than in the campo, field reality can push the other way as well. In a climate change roundtable meeting, a local NGO representative presented on the challenges of setting strategy for Laguna del Tigre National Park. He described a technical study regarding human settlements in the park as "stuck," mired in bureaucratic and political uncertainties. He then told a story about a recent encounter between one of his field staff and a tapir inside the park. The encounter was used as motivation and proof, in contrast to the intractability of human presence, that there was still ecological value in Laguna del Tigre, and that it was "worth it" to continue work.

4 There is far more detail than I can include here on properly siting and setting up camera traps, including recommendations like crawling in front of the camera like

a cat to make sure it takes your photo. The WCS guide to camera trapping for jaguars includes a delightful photograph of a Bolivian field technician on all fours mimicking a jaguar (Noss et al. 2013).

5 That two birds are encountered on the first visit and one on the second is due to the different stages of the nesting season. Scarlet macaws usually pair bond for life. Before laying, both males and females will inhabit and prepare the nest. After laying, the female stays in the nest to incubate the eggs, while the male forages during the day. After hatching, both males and females tend the chicks and protect the nest, while males continue to provide food for the young.

6 Indicator and flagship species have different definitions in conservation biology; the former is usually an environmentally sensitive species that indicates ecological damage or integrity, while the latter refers to charismatic megafauna that symbolize conservation, like pandas or elephants. Luis collapses these two in terms of macaws, peccaries, and jaguars, as they are both symbolically important and indicators of large swaths of intact forest.

7 It is CONAP's responsibility to oversee and enforce the rules of this agreement, including with respect to agricultural practices. But NGOs like WCS play a large part in making sure it is feasible for villagers to do so—for example, by facilitating the use of organic compost or pest control methods.

Abom, B. 2004. "Social Capital, NGOs, and Development: A Guatemalan Case Study." *Development in Practice* 14 (3): 342–53.

Abrahamsson, Sebastian, and Filippo Bertoni. 2014. "Compost Politics: Experimenting with Togetherness in Vermicomposting." *Environmental Humanities* 4 (1): 125–48.

Adams, William M., Ros Aveling, Dan Brockington, Barney Dickson, Jo Elliott, Jon Hutton, Dilys Roe, Bhaskar Vira, and William Wolmer. 2004. "Biodiversity Conservation and the Eradication of Poverty." *Science* 306 (November): 1146–49.

Adams, William M., and Jon Hutton. 2007. "People, Parks and Poverty: Political Ecology and Biodiversity Conservation." *Conservation and Society* 5 (2): 147–83.

Agrawal, Arun. 2005. *Environmentality: Technologies of Government and the Making of Subjects.* Durham, NC: Duke University Press.

Agrawal, Arun, and Kent Redford. 2009. "Conservation and Displacement: An Overview." *Conservation and Society* 7 (1): 1.

Angelsen, Arild. 1995. "Shifting Cultivation and 'Deforestation': A Study from Indonesia." *World Development* 23 (10): 1713–29.

Appadurai, Arjun. 1990. "Disjuncture and Difference in the Global Cultural Economy." *Theory, Culture and Society* 7 (2–3): 295–310.

Aretxaga, Begoña. 2003. "Maddening States." *Annual Review of Anthropology* 32: 393–410.

Atran, Scott, Douglas Medin, Norbert Ross, Elizabeth Lynch, John Coley, Edilberto Ucan Ek, and Valentina Vapnarsky. 1999. "Folkecology and Commons Management in the Maya Lowlands." *Proceedings of the National Academy of Sciences of the United States of America* 96 (13): 7598–603.

Bailliet, Cecilia. 2000. "Preventing Internal Displacement: Conciliating Land Conflicts in Guatemala." *Refugee Survey Quarterly* 19 (3): 187–208.

Barad, Karen. 2007. *Meeting the Universe Halfway: Quantum Physics and the Entanglement of Matter and Meaning.* Durham, NC: Duke University Press.

Barad, Karen. 2017. "No Small Matter: Mushroom Clouds, Ecologies of Nothingness, and Strange Topologies of Spacetimemattering." In *Arts of Living on a Damaged Planet: Ghosts and Monsters of the Anthropocene*, edited by Anna Lowenhaupt Tsing, Heather Anne Swanson, Elaine Gan, and Nils Bubandt, G103–20. Minneapolis: University of Minnesota Press.

Bateson, Gregory. 1972. *Steps to an Ecology of Mind: Collected Essays in Anthropology, Psychiatry, Evolution, and Epistemology.* Chicago: University of Chicago Press.

Bebbington, Anthony, and Graham Thiele. 1993. *Non-governmental Organizations and the State in Latin America: Rethinking Roles in Sustainable Agricultural Development.* New York: Routledge.

Berger, Susan A. 1992. *Political and Agrarian Development in Guatemala.* Westview Special Studies on Latin America and the Caribbean. Boulder, CO: Westview.

Blum, Leonor. 2001. "International NGOs and the Guatemalan Peace Accords." *Voluntas: International Journal of Voluntary and Nonprofit Organizations* 12 (4): 327–53.

Bocarejo, Diana, and Diana Ojeda. 2016. "Violence and Conservation: Beyond Unintended Consequences and Unfortunate Coincidences." *Geoforum* 69 (February): 176–83.

Boserup, Ester. 1976. "Environment, Population, and Technology in Primitive Societies." *Population and Development Review* 2 (1): 21–36.

Bowen, Margarita. 1985. "The Ecology of Knowledge: Linking the Natural and Social Sciences." *Geoforum* 16 (2): 213–25.

Brands, Hal. 2010. *Crime, Violence, and the Crisis in Guatemala: A Case Study in the Erosion of the State.* Carlisle, PA: Strategic Studies Institute.

Bray, David Barton, and Anthony B. Anderson. 2005. "Global Conservation Nongovernmental Organizations and Local Communities." Conservation and Development Series, Working Paper 1. Miami: Institute for Sustainability Science in Latin America and the Caribbean, Florida International University.

Brechin, Steven R., Peter R. Wilshusen, Crystal L. Fortwangler, and Patrick C. West. 2002. "Beyond the Square Wheel: Toward a More Comprehensive Understanding of Biodiversity Conservation as Social and Political Process." *Society and Natural Resources* 15 (1): 41–64.

Briggs, Charles L. 2004. "Theorizing Modernity Conspiratorially: Science, Scale, and the Political Economy of Public Discourse in Explanations of a Cholera Epidemic." *American Ethnologist* 31 (2): 164–87.

Brosius, J. Peter. 1999. "Green Dots, Pink Hearts: Displacing Politics from the Malaysian Rain Forest." *American Anthropologist* 101 (1): 36–57.

Brosius, J. Peter, and Diane Russell. 2003. "Conservation from Above: An Anthropological Perspective on Transboundary Protected Areas and Ecoregional Planning." *Journal of Sustainable Forestry* 17 (1/2): 39–65.

Bryant, Raymond. 2002. "Non-governmental Organizations and Governmentality: 'Consuming' Biodiversity and Indigenous People in the Philippines." *Political Studies* 50: 268–92.

Burnham, Philip. 2000. *Indian Country, God's Country: Native Americans and the National Parks*. Washington, DC: Island Press.

Butt, Leslie. 2005. "'Lipstick Girls' and 'Fallen Women': AIDS and Conspiratorial Thinking in Papua, Indonesia." *Cultural Anthropology* 20 (3): 412–42.

Carr, David. 2006. "A Tale of Two Roads: Land Tenure, Poverty, and Politics on the Guatemalan Frontier." *Geoforum* 37 (1): 94–103.

Carranza, Camilo, Seth Robbins, and Chris Dalby. 2019. "Major Odebrecht Corruption Cases and Investigations in 2019." *InSight Crime*, February 20, 2010. https://www.insightcrime.org/news/analysis/major-latam-odebrecht-corruption-cases-investigations-2019/.

Carroll, Lewis. 1872. *Through the Looking-glass: And what Alice Found There*. London: Macmillan.

Castree, Noel. 2008. "Neoliberalising Nature: The Logics of Deregulation and Reregulation." *Environment and Planning A* 40: 132–52.

CEMEC (Centro de Monitoreo y Evaluación de CONAP). 2012. "Población y tasa de crecimiento de asentamientos humanos determinada por el incremento en el número de viviendas en zonas núcleo" [Population and growth rate of human settlements determined by the increase in number of houses in nuclear zones]. San Benito, Petén, Guatemala: Consejo Nacional de Areas Protegidas (CONAP).

Chapin, Mac. 2004. "A Challenge to Conservationists." *World Watch* 17 (6): 17–32.

Chow, Jeffrey, Gabriela Doria, Rachel Kramer, Tina Schneider, and Jeff Stoike. 2013. "Tropical Forests under a Changing Climate and Innovations in Tropical Forest Management." *Tropical Conservation Science* 6 (3): 315–24.

CICIG. 2015. "El financimento de la política en Guatemala" [Political financing in Guatemala]. Guatemala City: International Committee against Impunity in Guatemala. http://www.cicig.org/uploads/documents/2015/informe_financiamiento_politicagt.pdf.

Coates, Peter. 2007. *American Perceptions of Immigrant and Invasive Species: Strangers on the Land*. Berkeley: University of California Press.

Colchester, Marcus. 1993. "Guatemala: The Clamor for Land and the Fate of the Forests." In *The Struggle for Land and the Fate of the Forests*, edited by Marcus Colchester and Larry Lohmann. London: Zed.

CONAP. 2006. "Estudio tecnico integral asentamientos humanos: Parque Nacional Laguna del Tigre-Biotopo protegido Laguna del Tigre-Río Escondido" [Integrated technical study of human settlements: Laguna del Tigre National Park and Laguna del Tigre–Río Escondido protected biotope]. Guatemala City: Consejo Nacional de Areas Protegidas de Guatemala.

CONAP and WCS. 2015. "Monitoreo de la gobernabilidad en la Reserva de la Biosfera Maya" [Monitoring governability in the Maya Biosphere Reserve]. San Benito, Petén, Guatemala: Consejo Nacional de Areas Protegidas de Guatemala and Wildlife Conservation Society.

Corbera, Esteve. 2012. "Problematizing REDD+ as an Experiment in Payments for Ecosystem Services." *Current Opinion in Environmental Sustainability* 4 (6): 612–19.

Cowen, Michael, and Robert Shenton. 1995. "The Invention of Development." In *The Power of Development*, edited by Jonathan Crush, 27–43. London: Routledge.

Cronon, William. 1996. "The Trouble with Wilderness: Or, Getting Back to the Wrong Nature." *Environmental History*, 7–28.

Crutzen, P. J., and E. F. Stoermer. 2000. "The 'Anthropocene.'" *IGBP Newsletter* 41: 17–18.

Cubitt, G. T. 1989. "Conspiracy Myths and Conspiracy Theories." *Journal of the Anthropological Society of Oxford* 20 (1): 12–25.

Cuffe, Sandra. 2016. "Controversial Park Plans in Guatemala's Maya Biosphere Reserve." *Mongabay*, June 17, 2016. https://news.mongabay.com/2016/06/controversial-park-plans-in-guatemalas-maya-biosphere-reserve/.

Das, Veena. 2007. *Life and Words: Violence and the Descent into the Ordinary.* Berkeley: University of California Press.

de Chardin, Pierre Teilhard. 1956. "The Antiquity and World Expansion of Human Culture." In *Man's Role in Changing the Face of the Earth*, edited by W. L. Thomas, 103–12. Chicago: University of Chicago Press.

Devine, Jennifer. 2014. "Counterinsurgency Ecotourism in Guatemala's Maya Biosphere Reserve." *Environment and Planning D: Society and Space* 32: 984–1001.

Devine, Jennifer. 2017. "Colonizing Space and Commodifying Place: Tourism's Violent Geographies." *Journal of Sustainable Tourism* 25 (5): 634–50.

de Vries, Pieter. 2002. "Vanishing Mediators: Enjoyment as a Political Factor in Western Mexico." *American Ethnologist* 29 (4): 901–27.

de Vries, Pieter. 2007. "The Orchestration of Corruption and Excess Enjoyment in Western Mexico." In *Corruption and the Secret of Law: A Legal Anthropological Perspective*, edited by Monique Nuijten and Gerhard Anders, 143–63. Farnham, UK: Ashgate.

Diamond, Jared. 2006. *Collapse: How Societies Choose to Fail or Succeed.* New York: Penguin.

Doane, Molly. 2012. *Stealing Shining Rivers: Agrarian Conflict, Market Logic, and Conservation in a Mexican Forest.* Tucson: University of Arizona Press.

Dove, Michael R. 1983. "Theories of Swidden Agriculture, and the Political Economy of Ignorance." *Agroforestry Systems* 1: 85–99.

Dressler, Wolfram, Melanie McDermott, Will Smith, and Juan Pulhin. 2012. "REDD Policy Impacts on Indigenous Property Rights Regimes on Palawan Island, the Philippines." *Human Ecology* 40 (5): 679–91.

Duffy, Rosaleen. 2014. "Waging a War to Save Biodiversity: The Rise of Militarized Conservation." *International Affairs* 90 (4): 819–34.

Duffy, Rosaleen. 2016. "War, by Conservation." *Geoforum* 69: 238–48.

Egan, Brian. 1999. "'Somos de La Tierra': Land and the Guatemalan Refugee Return." In *Journeys of Fear: Refugee Return and National Transformation in Guatemala*, edited by Liisa L. North and Alan B. Simmons, 95–111. Montreal: McGill-Queen's University Press.

Escalón, Sebastián. 2012. "El Mirador: El incierto futuro de unas ruinas." *Plaza Pública*, September 17, 2012. http://www.plazapublica.com.gt/content/el-mirador -el-incierto-futuro-de-unas-ruinas.

Escalón, Sebastián. 2017. "El Peruíto: Fuego y lucha en una antigua fortaleza Maya." *Plaza Pública*, June 5, 2017. https://www.plazapublica.com.gt/content/el-peruito -fuego-y-lucha-en-una-antigua-fortaleza-maya.

Fairhead, James, and Melissa Leach. 2003. *Science, Society and Power: Environmental Knowledge and Policy in West Africa and the Caribbean*. Cambridge: Cambridge University Press.

FARES. 2014. "Investigation, Conservation, and Development in the Mirador Basin, Guatemala: A Summary of the Annual Activity of the Mirador Basin Project, 2013." Rupert, ID: Foundation for Anthropological Research and Environmental Studies.

Ferguson, James. 1990. *The Anti-politics Machine: "Development," Depoliticization, and Bureaucratic Power in Lesotho*. New York: Cambridge University Press.

Filer, Colin, and Michael Wood. 2012. "The Creation and Dissolution of Private Property in Forest Carbon: A Case Study from Papua New Guinea." *Human Ecology* 40 (5): 665–77.

Fisher, Berenice, and Joan Tronto. 1990. "Toward a Feminist Theory of Caring." In *Circles of Care: Work and Identity in Women's Lives*, edited by Emily K. Abel and Margaret K. Nelson, 35–62. Albany: State University of New York Press.

Fletcher, Robert. 2012. "Using the Master's Tools? Neoliberal Conservation and the Evasion of Inequality." *Development and Change* 43 (1): 295–317.

Forsyth, Tim. 2002. *Critical Political Ecology: The Politics of Environmental Science*. New York: Routledge.

Foucault, Michel. 1991. "Governmentality." In *The Foucault Effect: Studies in Governmentality*, edited by G. Burchell, C. Gordon, and P. Miller, 87–104. Chicago: University of Chicago Press.

Fox, Jefferson, Dao Minh Truong, A. Terry Rambo, Nghiem Phuong Tuyen, and Stephen Leisz. 2000. "Shifting Cultivation: A New Old Paradigm for Managing Tropical Forests." *BioScience* 50 (6): 521–28.

Freedom House. 2012. "Freedom in the World 2012: Guatemala." http://www .freedomhouse.org/report/freedom-world/2012/guatemala.

García, María Cristina Fernández. 2004. *Lynching in Guatemala: Legacy of War and Impunity*. Weatherhead Center for International Affairs, Harvard University.

http://programs.wcfia.harvard.edu/sites/projects.iq.harvard.edu/files/fellows
/files/fernandez.pdf.

Gibson, Mel, dir. 2006. *Apocalypto.* Touchstone Pictures. DVD.

Gibson-Graham, J. K. 1996. *The End of Capitalism (as We Knew It).* Minneapolis: University of Minnesota Press.

Gibson-Graham, Julie Katherine. 2011. "A Feminist Project of Belonging for the Anthropocene." *Gender, Place and Culture* 18 (1): 1–21.

Gieryn, Thomas F. 1983. "Boundary-Work and the Demarcation of Science from Non-science: Strains and Interests in Professional Ideologies of Scientists." *American Sociological Review* 48 (6): 781–95.

Gill, Richardson B., Paul A. Mayewski, Johan Nyberg, Gerald H. Haug, and Larry C. Peterson. 2007. "Drought and the Maya Collapse." *Ancient Mesoamerica* 18 (2): 283–302.

Global Witness. 2019. "Enemies of the State: How Governments and Business Silence Land and Environmental Defenders." https://www.globalwitness.org/documents/19766/Enemies_of_the_State.pdf.

Godoy, Angelina Snodgrass. 2002. "Lynchings and the Democratization of Terror in Postwar Guatemala: Implications for Human Rights." *Human Rights Quarterly* 24 (3): 640–61.

Gould, Kevin A. 2006. "Land Regularization on Agricultural Frontiers: The Case of Northwestern Petén, Guatemala." *Land Use Policy* 23: 395–407.

Grandia, Liza. 2012. *Enclosed: Conservation, Cattle, and Commerce among the Q'eqchi' Maya Lowlanders.* Seattle: University of Washington Press.

Grandin, Greg. 2005. "The Instruction of Great Catastrophe: Truth Commissions, National History, and State Formation in Argentina, Chile, and Guatemala." *American Historical Review* 110 (1): 46–67.

Grandin, Greg. 2017. "A Brutal Expulsion in Guatemala Shows How Neoliberalism Gets Greenwashed." *The Nation,* June 8, 2017. https://www.thenation.com/article/a-brutal-expulsion-in-guatemala-shows-how-neoliberalism-gets-greenwashed/.

Gretzinger, Steven. 1998. "Community Forest Concessions: An Economic Alternative for the Maya Biosphere Reserve in the Peten, Guatemala." In *Timber, Tourists, and Temples: Conservation and Development in the Maya Forest of Belize, Guatemala, and Mexico,* edited by Richard B. Primack, David Bray, Hugo A. Galletti, and Ismael Ponciano, 111–24. Washington, DC: Island Press.

Gupta, Akhil, and James Ferguson. 1992. "Beyond 'Culture': Space, Identity, and the Politics of Difference." *Cultural Anthropology* 7 (1): 6–23.

Gupta, Akhil, and Aradhana Sharma. 2006. "Globalization and Postcolonial States." *Current Anthropology* 47 (2): 277–307.

Guston, David H. 2001. "Boundary Organizations in Environmental Policy and Science: An Introduction." *Science, Technology, and Human Values* 26 (4): 399–408.

Hale, Charles R. 2006. *Mas que un Indio: Racial Ambivalence and the Paradox of Neoliberal Multiculturalism in Guatemala*. Santa Fe, NM: School of American Research Press.

Handy, Jim. 1990. "The Corporate Community, Campesino Organizations, and Agrarian Reform: 1950–1954." In *Guatemalan Indians and the State*, edited by Carol A. Smith, 163–82. Austin: University of Texas Press.

Handy, Jim. 1991. "Anxiety and Dread: State and Community in Modern Guatemala." *Canadian Journal of History* 26 (1): 43–65.

Handy, Jim. 2004. "Chicken Thieves, Witches, and Judges: Vigilante Justice and Customary Law in Guatemala." *Journal of Latin American Studies* 36 (3): 533–61.

Haraway, Donna. 1991. *Simians, Cyborgs, and Women: The Reinvention of Nature*. New York: Routledge.

Haraway, Donna. 1997. *Modest-Witness@Second-Millennium.FemaleMan-Meets-OncoMouse: Feminism and Technoscience*. New York: Routledge.

Haraway, Donna. 2008. *When Species Meet*. Minneapolis: University of Minnesota Press.

Haraway, Donna. 2015. "Anthropocene, Capitalocene, Plantationocene, Chthulucene: Making Kin." *Environmental Humanities* 6: 159–65.

Haraway, Donna. 2016. *Staying with the Trouble: Making Kin in the Chthulucene*. Durham, NC: Duke University Press.

Harvey, David. 1974. "Population, Resources and the Ideology of Science." *Economic Geography* 50 (3): 256–77.

Harvey, David. 2007. *A Brief History of Neoliberalism*. New York: Oxford University Press.

Held, Virginia. 2006. *The Ethics of Care: Personal, Political, and Global*. New York: Oxford University Press.

Hetherington, Kregg. 2011. *Guerrilla Auditors: The Politics of Transparency in Neoliberal Paraguay*. Durham, NC: Duke University Press.

Hoag, Colin. 2011. "Assembling Partial Perspectives: Thoughts on the Anthropology of Bureaucracy." *PoLAR: Political and Legal Anthropology Review* 34 (1): 81–94.

Hochschild, Arlie Russell. 1995. "The Culture of Politics: Traditional, Postmodern, Cold-Modern, and Warm-Modern Ideals of Care." *Social Politics: International Studies in Gender, State and Society* 2 (3): 331–46.

Hofstadter, Richard. 2008. *The Paranoid Style in American Politics*. New York: Vintage.

Howard, David, Mo Hume, and Ulrich Oslender. 2007. "Violence, Fear, and Development in Latin America: A Critical Overview." *Development in Practice* 17 (6): 713–24.

Howe, Cymene, Jessica Lockrem, Hannah Appel, Edward Hackett, Dominic Boyer, Randal Hall, Matthew Schneider-Mayerson, et al. 2016. "Paradoxical Infrastructures: Ruins, Retrofit, and Risk." *Science, Technology and Human Values* 41 (3): 547–65.

InSight Crime. 2011. "Grupos de poder en Petén: Territorio, política y negocios." http://plazapublica.com.gt/sites/all/themes/custom/plazapublica/images /informefinalgpd.pdf.

Inter-American Commission on Human Rights. 2017. "Situation of Human Rights in Guatemala." Country Report OEA/Ser.L/V/II. Guatemala. http://www.oas.org/en /iachr/reports/pdfs/Guatemala2017-en.pdf.

Jasanoff, Sheila. 2004. "Ordering Knowledge, Ordering Society." In *States of Knowledge: The Co-production of Science and Social Order*, edited by Sheila Jasanoff, 13–45. New York: Routledge.

Jonas, Susanne. 2012. "Guatemala: Acts of Genocide and Scorched-Earth Counterinsurgency War." In *Centuries of Genocide: Essays and Eyewitness Accounts*, edited by Samuel Totten and William S. Parsons, 355. London: Taylor and Francis.

Keck, Frédéric, and Andrew Lakoff. 2013. "Preface: Sentinel Devices." *Limn*, no. 3 (June). http://limn.it/preface-sentinel-devices-2/.

Kirsch, Stuart. 2002. "Rumour and Other Narratives of Political Violence in West Papua." *Critique of Anthropology* 22 (1): 53–79.

Kohn, Eduardo. 2013. *How Forests Think: Toward an Anthropology beyond the Human*. Berkeley: University of California Press.

Kohn, Eduardo. 2014. "Toward an Ethical Practice in the Anthropocene." HAU: *Journal of Ethnographic Theory* 4 (1): 459–64.

Kull, Christian A. 2000. "Deforestation, Erosion, and Fire: Degradation Myths in the Environmental History of Madagascar." *Environment and History* 6 (4): 423–50.

Lahsen, Myanna. 1999. "The Detection and Attribution of Conspiracies: The Controversy over Chapter 8." In Marcus, *Paranoia within Reason*, 111–36.

Lambin, Eric F., B. L. Turner, Helmut J. Geist, Samuel B. Agbola, Arild Angelsen, John W. Bruce, Oliver T. Coomes, Rodolfo Dirzo, Günther Fischer, and Carl Folke. 2001. "The Causes of Land-Use and Land-Cover Change: Moving beyond the Myths." *Global Environmental Change* 11 (4): 261–69.

Latour, Bruno. 1987. *Science in Action: How to Follow Scientists and Engineers through Society*. Cambridge, MA: Harvard University Press.

Latour, Bruno. 2014. "Anthropology at the Time of the Anthropocene—a Personal View of What Is to Be Studied." Lecture, American Anthropological Association Annual Meeting, Washington, DC, December. http://sector2337.com/wp-content /uploads/2015/06/Latour_Anthropocene.pdf.

Latour, Bruno, and Steve Woolgar. 1986. *Laboratory Life: The Construction of Scientific Facts*. Princeton, NJ: Princeton University Press.

Law, John, and Annemarie Mol. 2008. "The Actor-Enacted: Cumbrian Sheep in 2001." In *Material Agency*, edited by Carl Knappett and Lambros Malafouris, 57–77. New York: Springer.

Lewandowsky, Stephan, Klaus Oberauer, and Gilles E. Gignac. 2013. "NASA Faked the Moon Landing—Therefore (Climate) Science Is a Hoax: An Anatomy of the Motivated Rejection of Science." *Psychological Science* 24 (5): 622–33.

Li, Tania Murray. 2007. *The Will to Improve: Governmentality, Development, and the Practice of Politics*. Durham, NC: Duke University Press.

Lorimer, Jamie. 2015. *Wildlife in the Anthropocene: Conservation after Nature*. Minneapolis: University of Minnesota Press.

Lowe, Celia. 2006. *Wild Profusion: Biodiversity Conservation in an Indonesian Archipelago*. Princeton, NJ: Princeton University Press.

Lunstrum, Elizabeth. 2014. "Green Militarization: Anti-poaching Efforts and the Spatial Contours of Kruger National Park." *Annals of the Association of American Geographers* 104 (4): 816–32.

Lunstrum, Elizabeth. 2015. "Conservation Meets Militarisation in Kruger National Park: Historical Encounters and Complex Legacies." *Conservation and Society* 13 (4): 356.

Lyons, Kristina Marie. 2014. "Soil Science, Development, and the 'Elusive Nature' of Colombia's Amazonian Plains." *Journal of Latin American and Caribbean Anthropology* 19 (2): 212–36.

MacGregor, Sherilyn. 2004. "From Care to Citizenship: Calling Ecofeminism Back to Politics." *Ethics and the Environment* 9 (1): 56–84.

MacGregor, Sherilyn. 2011. *Beyond Mothering Earth: Ecological Citizenship and the Politics of Care*. Vancouver: UBC Press.

Mahanty, Sango, Sarah Milne, Wolfram Dressler, and Colin Filer. 2012. "The Social Life of Forest Carbon: Property and Politics in the Production of a New Commodity." *Human Ecology* 40 (5): 661–64.

Malkin, Elisabeth. 2015. "In Guatemala, People Living Off Forests Are Tasked with Protecting Them." *New York Times*, November 25, 2015. http://www.nytimes.com/2015/11/26/world/americas/in-guatemala-people-living-off-forests-are-tasked-with-protecting-them.html?_r=0.

Manceron, Vanessa. 2013. "Recording and Monitoring: Between Two Forms of Surveillance." *Limn*, no. 3 (June). http://limn.it/recording-and-monitoring-between-two-forms-of-surveillance/.

Manz, Beatriz. 2004. *Paradise in Ashes: A Guatemalan Journey of Courage, Terror, and Hope*. Berkeley: University of California Press.

Marcus, George E. 1999a. "Introduction: The Paranoid Style Now." In Marcus, *Paranoia within Reason*, 1–11.

Marcus, George E., ed. 1999b. *Paranoia within Reason: A Casebook on Conspiracy as Explanation*. Chicago: University of Chicago Press.

Margulis, Lynn, and Dorion Sagan. 1995. *What Is Life?* Berkeley: University of California Press.

Massey, Doreen. 1994. *Space, Place and Gender*. Cambridge: Polity.

Mathews, Andrew S. 2011. *Instituting Nature: Authority, Expertise, and Power in Mexican Forests*. Cambridge, MA: MIT Press.

Mathews, Andrew S. 2014. "Scandals, Audits, and Fictions: Linking Climate Change to Mexican Forests." *Social Studies of Science* 44 (1): 82–108.

McAfee, Kathleen. 2012. "Nature in the Market-World: Ecosystem Services and In-equality." *Development* 55 (1): 25–33.

McAfee, Kathleen, and Elizabeth N. Shapiro. 2010. "Payments for Ecosystem Services in Mexico: Nature, Neoliberalism, Social Movements, and the State." *Annals of the Association of American Geographers* 100 (3): 579–99.

McElwee, Pamela D. 2012. "Payments for Environmental Services as Neoliberal Market-Based Forest Conservation in Vietnam: Panacea or Problem?" *Geoforum* 43 (3): 412–26.

Meierotto, Lisa. 2014. "A Disciplined Space: The Co-evolution of Conservation and Militarization on the US-Mexico Border." *Anthropological Quarterly* 87 (3): 637–64.

Meyerson, Fred. 1998. "Guatemala Burning." *Amicus Journal* 20 (1): 28–31.

Milne, Sarah. 2012. "Grounding Forest Carbon: Property Relations and Avoided Deforestation in Cambodia." *Human Ecology* 40 (5): 693–706.

Milne, Sarah, and Bill Adams. 2012. "Market Masquerades: Uncovering the Politics of Community-Level Payments for Environmental Services in Cambodia." *Development and Change* 43 (1): 133–58.

Mitchell, Timothy. 1991. "The Limits of the State: Beyond Statist Approaches and Their Critics." *American Political Science Review* 85 (1): 77–96.

Mitchell, Timothy. 2002. *Rule of Experts: Egypt, Techno-politics, Modernity*. Berkeley: University of California Press.

Mol, Annemarie. 2002. *The Body Multiple: Ontology in Medical Practice*. Durham, NC: Duke University Press.

Mol, Annemarie. 2008. *The Logic of Care: Health and the Problem of Patient Choice*. New York: Routledge.

Mol, Annemarie, Ingunn Moser, and J. Pols. 2010. *Care in Practice: On Tinkering in Clinics, Homes and Farms*. Piscataway, NJ: Transaction.

Moodie, Ellen. 2009. "Seventeen Years, Seventeen Murders: Biospectacularity and the Production of Post–Cold War Knowledge in El Salvador." *Social Text 99* 27 (2): 77–103.

Moore, Donald S. 2005. *Suffering for Territory: Race, Place, and Power in Zimbabwe*. Durham, NC: Duke University Press.

Moore, Jason W. 2016. *Anthropocene or Capitalocene? Nature, History, and the Crisis of Capitalism*. Oakland: PM Press.

Moore, Jason W. 2017. "The Capitalocene, Part I: On the Nature and Origins of Our Ecological Crisis." *Journal of Peasant Studies* 44 (3): 594–630.

Morton, Timothy. 2016. *Dark Ecology: For a Logic of Future Coexistence*. New York: Columbia University Press.

Mosse, David. 2005. *Cultivating Development: An Ethnography of Aid Policy and Practice*. Ann Arbor, MI: Pluto.

Murphy, Michelle. 2017. *The Economization of Life*. Durham, NC: Duke University Press.

Musalo, Karen, Elisabeth Pellegrin, and S. Shawn Roberts. 2010. "Crimes without Punishment: Violence against Women in Guatemala." *Hastings Women's Law Journal* 21: 161.

National Democratic Institute. 2017. "Turning Point: Challenges to the Political and Electoral System" [Un modelo en transición: Desafíos al régimen político electoral]. Guatemala: National Democratic Institute. https://www.ndi.org /publications/turning-point-challenges-political-and-electoral-system.

Nations, James D. 2001. "Indigenous Peoples and Conservation: Misguided Myths in the Maya Tropical Forest." In *On Biocultural Diversity: Linking Language, Knowledge, and the Environment*, edited by Luisa Maffi, 462–71. Washington, DC: Smithsonian Institution Press.

Nations, James D. 2006. *The Maya Tropical Forest: People, Parks, and Ancient Cities.* Austin: University of Texas Press.

Nelson, Diane M. 2009. *Reckoning: The Ends of War in Guatemala.* Durham, NC: Duke University Press.

Nelson, Diane M. 2015. *Who Counts: The Mathematics of Death and Life after Genocide.* Durham, NC: Duke University Press.

Nittler, John, and Henry Tschinkel. 2005. "Community Forest Management in the Maya Biosphere Reserve of Guatemala: Protection through Profits." U.S. Agency for International Development (USAID) and Sustainable Agriculture and Natural Resource Management (SANREM), University of Georgia.

Noss, A., J. Polisar, L. Maffei, R. Garcia, and S. Silver. 2013. "Evaluating Jaguar Densities with Camera Traps." New York: Wildlife Conservation Society. http://guatemala.wcs.org/DesktopModules/Bring2mind/DMX/Download.aspx ?EntryId=14156&PortalId=115&DownloadMethod=attachment.

Ogden, Laura. 2011. *Swamplife: People, Gators, and Mangroves Entangled in the Everglades.* Minneapolis: University of Minnesota Press.

OMYC. 2009. "Reseña historica" [Historical overview]. Uaxactún, Guatemala: Organización Manejo y Conservación.

Pacheco, Pablo, Deborah Barry, Peter Cronkleton, Anne Larson, and Iliana Monterroso. 2008. "From Agrarian to Forest Tenure Reforms in Latin America: Assessing Their Impacts for Local People and Forests." Presented at the conference of the International Association for the Study of the Commons, July 14–18, Cheltenham, UK.

Parks Watch. 2003. "Park Profile—Guatemala: Laguna del Tigre National Park." http://www.parkswatch.org/parkprofiles/slide-shows/ltre/ltnp01_eng.pdf.

Pearce, Jenny, and Jude Howell. 2002. "Civil Society Discourses and the Guatemalan Peace Process." In *Civil Society and Development: A Critical Exploration.* Boulder, CO: Lynne Rienner.

Ponge, Jean-François. 2005. "Emergent Properties from Organisms to Ecosystems: Towards a Realistic Approach." *Biological Reviews of the Cambridge Philosophical Society* 80 (3): 403–11.

Potochnik, Angela, and Brian McGill. 2012. "The Limitations of Hierarchical Organization." *Philosophy of Science* 79 (1): 120–40.

Povinelli, Elizabeth A. 2016. *Geontologies: A Requiem to Late Liberalism.* Durham, NC: Duke University Press.

Primack, Richard, David Bray, Hugo A. Galletti, and Ismael Ponciano, eds. 1998. *Timber, Tourists, and Temples: Conservation and Development in the Maya Forest of Belize, Guatemala, and Mexico.* Washington, DC: Island Press.

Radachowsky, Jeremy, Victor H. Ramos, Roan McNab, Erick H. Baur, and Nikolay Kazakov. 2012. "Forest Concessions in the Maya Biosphere Reserve, Guatemala: A Decade Later." *Forest Ecology and Management* 268 (March): 18–28.

Raffles, Hugh. 2002. *In Amazonia: A Natural History.* Princeton, NJ: Princeton University Press.

Rahder, Micha. 2008. "Forest Knowledge and Power in the Maya Biosphere Reserve, Petén, Guatemala." Master's thesis, Yale School of Forestry and Environmental Studies, New Haven, CT.

Ramos, Victor Hugo, José Nery Solís, and Julian Enrique Zetina. 2001. "Censo de población en seguimiento a la base de datos sobre población, tierras y medio ambiente en la Reserva de Biosfera Maya." San Benito, Petén, Guatemala: Centro de Monitoreo y Evaluación de CONAP (CEMEC).

Rayner, Alan. 1997. *Degrees of Freedom: Living in Dynamic Boundaries.* London: Imperial College Press.

Redclift, Michael, and Colin Sage. 1998. "Global Environmental Change and Global Inequality North/South Perspectives." *International Sociology* 13 (4): 499–516.

Ribot, Jesse C., and Anne M. Larson. 2005. *Democratic Decentralization through a Natural Resource Lens.* New York: Routledge.

Robinson, William I. 2003. *Transnational Conflicts: Central America, Social Change, and Globalization.* New York: Verso.

Rose, Deborah Bird. 2004. *Reports from a Wild Country: Ethics for Decolonisation.* Sydney: University of New South Wales Press.

Rosenberg, Charles. 1998. "Toward an Ecology of Knowledge: On Discipline, Context, and History." In *Rise of the Knowledge Worker,* edited by James Cortada, 221–32. New York: Elsevier.

Sader, S. A., D. J. Hayes, J. A. Hepinstall, and C. Soza. 2001. "Forest Change Monitoring of a Remote Biosphere Reserve." *International Journal of Remote Sensing* 22 (10): 1937–50.

Sader, Steven A., Conrad Reining, Thomas Sever, and Carlos Soza. 1997. "Human Migration and Agricultural Expansion." *Journal of Forestry* 95 (December): 27–32.

Salleh, Ariel. 1993. "Class, Race, and Gender Discourse in the Ecofeminism/Deep Ecology Debate." *Environmental Ethics* 15 (3): 225–44.

Samuels, Annemarie. 2015. "Narratives of Uncertainty: The Affective Force of Child-Trafficking Rumors in Postdisaster Aceh, Indonesia." *American Anthropologist* 117 (2): 229–41.

Sanford, Victoria. 2003. "The 'Grey Zone' of Justice: NGOs and Rule of Law in Postwar Guatemala." *Journal of Human Rights* 2 (3): 393–405.

Santos, Boaventura de Sousa. 2007. *Another Knowledge Is Possible: Beyond Northern Epistemologies*. New York: Verso.

Sas, Luis Angel. 2011. "Baldizón, el Berlusconi de Petén." *Plaza Pública*, September 7, 2011. http://plazapublica.com.gt/content/baldizon-el-berlusconi-de-peten.

Schwartz, Norman B. 1990. *Forest Society: A Social History of Peten, Guatemala*. Philadelphia: University of Pennsylvania Press.

Scott, James C. 1998. *Seeing Like a State: How Certain Schemes to Improve the Human Condition Have Failed*. New Haven, CT: Yale University Press.

Sides, Hampton. 1999. "This Is Not the Place." *Doubletake Magazine*, spring.

Sieder, Rachel. 2011. "Contested Sovereignties: Indigenous Law, Violence and State Effects in Postwar Guatemala." *Critique of Anthropology* 31 (3): 161–84.

Silva Ávalos, Hector, and Felipe Puerta. 2018. "Iván Velásquez: Guatemala's Elites Are Vying for Total State Control." *InSight Crime*, February 1, 2018. https://www.insightcrime.org/news/analysis/ivan-velasquez-guatemala-elites-vying-total-state-control/.

Simberloff, Daniel. 2003. "Confronting Introduced Species: A Form of Xenophobia?" *Biological Invasions* 5 (3): 179–92.

Sivaramakrishnan, Kalyanakrishnan. 2000. "Crafting the Public Sphere in the Forests of West Bengal: Democracy, Development, and Political Action." *American Ethnologist* 27 (2): 431–61.

Smith, Carol A. 1990a. "Origins of the National Question in Guatemala: A Hypothesis." In *Guatemalan Indians and the State*, edited by Carol A. Smith, 72–95. Austin: University of Texas Press.

Smith, Carol A. 1990b. "Social Relations in Guatemala over Space and Time." In *Guatemalan Indians and the State*, edited by Carol A. Smith, 1–30. Austin: University of Texas Press.

Soares, Luiz E. 1999. "A Toast to Fear: Ethnographic Flashes." In Marcus, *Paranoia within Reason*, 225–39.

Spence, Mark David. 1999. *Dispossessing the Wilderness: Indian Removal and the Making of the National Parks*. New York: Oxford University Press.

Spivak, Gayatri Chakravorty. 1988. "Can the Subaltern Speak?" In *Marxism and the Interpretation of Culture*, edited by Cary Nelson and Larry Grossberg, 271–313. Chicago: University of Illinois Press.

Star, Susan Leigh. 1995. *Ecologies of Knowledge: Work and Politics in Science and Technology*. SUNY Series in Science, Technology, and Society. Albany: State University of New York Press.

Star, Susan Leigh, and James R. Griesemer. 1989. "Institutional Ecology, Translations, and Boundary Objects: Amateurs and Professionals in Berkeley's Museum of Vertebrate Zoology, 1907–39." *Social Studies of Science* 19 (3): 387–420.

Steffen, Will, Jacques Grinevald, Paul Crutzen, and John McNeill. 2011. "The Anthropocene: Conceptual and Historical Perspectives." *Philosophical Transactions of the Royal Society A: Mathematical, Physical and Engineering Sciences* 369 (1938): 842–67.

Stepan, Nancy. 2001. *Picturing Tropical Nature*. Ithaca, NY: Cornell University Press.

Stewart, Kathleen. 1999. "Conspiracy Theory's Worlds." In Marcus, *Paranoia within Reason*, 13–20.

Stewart, Kathleen, and Susan Harding. 1999. "Bad Endings: American Apocalypsis." *Annual Review of Anthropology* 28 (January): 285–310.

Strathern, Marilyn. 2004. *Partial Connections*. Lanham, MD: Rowman Altamira.

Stuart, George E. 1992. "Maya Heartland under Siege." *National Geographic* 182 (5): 94–107.

Sullivan, Sian. 2009. "Green Capitalism, and the Cultural Poverty of Constructing Nature as Service-Provider." *Radical Anthropology* 3: 18–27.

Sullivan, Sian. 2013. "Banking Nature? The Spectacular Financialisation of Environmental Conservation." *Antipode* 45 (1): 198–217.

Sundberg, Juanita. 1998. "NGO Landscapes in the Maya Biosphere Reserve, Guatemala." *Geographical Review* 88 (3): 388–412.

Sundberg, Juanita. 2003. "Conservation and Democratization: Constituting Citizenship in the Maya Biosphere Reserve, Guatemala." *Political Geography* 22 (7): 715–40.

Taussig, Michael. 1987. *Shamanism, Colonialism, and the Wild Man: A Study in Terror and Healing*. Chicago: University of Chicago Press.

Tomuschat, Christian, Otilia Lux de Cotí, and Alfredo Balsells Tojo. 1999. *Guatemala: Memory of Silence, Tz'inil Na'tab'al*. Report of the Commission for Historical Clarification. Guatemala.

Townsley, Graham, dir. 2004. *Dawn of the Maya*. National Geographic Television.

Tsing, Anna Lowenhaupt. 2000. "Inside the Economy of Appearances." *Public Culture* 12 (1): 115–44.

Tsing, Anna Lowenhaupt. 2003. "Natural Resources and Capitalist Frontiers." *Economic and Political Weekly* 29 (November): 5100–106.

Tsing, Anna Lowenhaupt. 2005. *Friction: An Ethnography of Global Connection*. Princeton, NJ: Princeton University Press.

Tsing, Anna Lowenhaupt. 2012. "Unruly Edges: Mushrooms as Companion Species." *Environmental Humanities* 1: 141–54.

Tsing, Anna Lowenhaupt. 2015. *The Mushroom at the End of the World: On the Possibility of Life in Capitalist Ruins*. Princeton, NJ: Princeton University Press.

Turner, David P. 2005. "Thinking at the Global Scale." *Global Ecology and Biogeography* 14 (6): 505–8.

Valdez, Sandra. 2011. "'Petén refleja al país.'" *Prensa Libre*, August 8, 2011.

Vernadsky, W. I. 1945. "The Biosphere and the Noösphere." *American Scientist* 33 (1): xxii–12.

Verran, Helen. 2001. *Science and an African Logic.* Chicago: University of Chicago Press.

Votes without Violence. 2018. Votes without Violence: Guatemala. http://www.voteswithoutviolence.org/guatemala.

Wagner-Pacifici, Robin. 1999. "The Judas Kiss of Giulio Andreotti: Italy in Purgatorio." In Marcus, *Paranoia within Reason*, 299–318.

WCS. 2011. *State of the Maya Biosphere Reserve.* Flores, Petén, Guatemala: Wildlife Conservation Society.

WCS Living Landscapes Program. n.d. "Assessing the Impact of Conservation and Development on Rural Livelihoods: Using a Modified Basic Necessities Survey (BNS) in Experimental and Control Communities." New York: Wildlife Conservation Society.

West, Paige. 2006. *Conservation Is Our Government Now: The Politics of Ecology in Papua New Guinea.* Durham, NC: Duke University Press.

West, Paige, James Igoe, and Dan Brockington. 2006. "Parks and Peoples: The Social Impact of Protected Areas." *Annual Review of Anthropology* 35: 251–77.

Whatmore, Sarah. 2002. *Hybrid Geographies: Natures, Cultures, Spaces.* London: Sage.

Wittman, Hannah, and Laura Salvidar Tanaka. 2006. "The Agrarian Question in Guatemala." In *Promised Land*, edited by Peter Rosset, 23–39. Oakland, CA: Food First.

Wyly, Elvin. 2015. "Gentrification on the Planetary Urban Frontier: The Evolution of Turner's Noösphere." *Urban Studies* 52 (14): 2515–50.

Wyndham, Felice S. 2000. "The Sphere of the Mind: Reviving the Noosphere Concept for Ecological Anthropology." *Journal of Ecological Anthropology* 4 (1): 87–91.

Wynne, Brian. 1992. "Misunderstood Misunderstanding: Social Identities and Public Uptake of Science." *Public Understanding of Science* 1 (3): 281–304.

Ybarra, Megan. 2012. "Taming the Jungle, Saving the Maya Forest: Sedimented Counterinsurgency Practices in Contemporary Guatemalan Conservation." *Journal of Peasant Studies* 39 (2): 479–502.

Ybarra, Megan. 2016. "'Blind Passes' and the Production of Green Security through Violence on the Guatemalan Border." *Geoforum* 69 (February): 194–206.

Zerner, Charles. 1994. "Through a Green Lens: The Construction of Customary Environmental Law and Community in Indonesia's Maluku Islands." *Law and Society Review* 28 (5): 1079–122.

Zetina Tún, Julio Francisco. 2011. "Línea base para el monitoreo socio-económico: Unidad de manejo 'Uaxactún'" [Baseline for social-ecological monitoring: Management unit "Uaxactún"]. Acuerdo de Conservación Para la Concesión de Uaxactún. Uaxactún, Guatemala: WCS/OMYC-Uaxactún.

Zimmerer, Karl S. 2000. "The Reworking of Conservation Geographies: Nonequilibrium Landscapes and Nature-Society Hybrids." *Annals of the Association of American Geographers* 90 (2): 356–69.

INDEX

Note: Page numbers followed by *f* denote figures; P indicates a color plate.

Association of Forest Communities of the Petén. *See* ACOFOP

attorney general (office), 10, 81, 86–87, 227, P4

awareness, environmental, 87–88, 90, 152, 175, 200

Baja Verapaz, 117, 166

Balam. *See* Asociación Balam

Balas McNab, Roan, 199, 221, 228, 284n3; and CEMEC, 39, 42, 53; conservation philosophy, 174; the state, perspective on, 74–75, 77; and WCS field technicians, 27–28, 30, 223–24

Baldetti Elías, Roxana, 62, 75

Baldizón, Manuel, 76; and Mirador controversy, 100–102, 105–6, 277n4, 278n8

Barad, Karen, 5–6, 24, 274n7

Basic Necessities, 153, 189, 191, 194–99, 214

Bateson, Gregory, 269, 273n3

Berger, Óscar, 100

biologists, 232–34, 236–37. *See also* biovets

biotopes, 74, 278n7, P1

biovets, 220, 224, 229, 231–32, 243–44, 284n1; interventions by, 235–42. *See also* biologists; veterinarians, wildlife

brechas. *See* firebreaks

buffer zone, 116, 261, P1; exclusion of, 132, 280nn7–8; fire in, 161; population in, 127, 280n6

burning, of institutional buildings, 169–73, 194

CALAS (Center for Legal Action in Environment and Social Issues), 77, 80

camera traps, 31, 244; and jaguars, 113, 229–32, 284–85n4

campesinos, confusion with drug traffickers, 1–2, 15, 17, 83–84, 162–63, 168

campo, 23, 276n11; conservationist presence in, 57, 238–39, 242 (*see also* institutional presence, in MBR); gender and, 92, 224; intimacy of, 222–27; in

MBR nooscape, 29–31, 220–22, 243–44 (*see also* love; real, the)

CARE (Cooperative for Assistance and Relief Everywhere), 19, 126

care, 243–44, 283n7; ecological, 202; and xate projects, 200–206, 210–14, 271

Carlos (NGO technician), 15, 154, 206; views on military, 82, 84, 89, 168–69

Carlotta (WCS biologist), 236–37, 241, 243

Carmelita, 13, 23, 195; and Mirador controversy, 94–95, 100–104, 106–7; Petenero history, 14, 116, 152–54

Casasola, Oliverio, 16

Castellanos, Juan, 10–11, 86, 143, 153, 209–10, 245; Uaxactún, relationship with, 148–51, 194, 213, 283n6

cattle, 15, 237; deforestation and, 1, 15–18, 22, 62, 64, 70f, 168; drug trafficking and, 110, 185–86 (*see also* narco-ranchers); jaguars and, 2, 186, 277n1; in Laguna del Tigre National Park, 155, 161–62, 226; monitoring of, 41–42, 65; removal from MBR, 72f, 175

CEMEC (Center for Monitoring and Evaluation of CONAP), 22–25, 37–38, 60, 222; author interventions in, 265–66, 275n7; as keystone actor, 25–26, 38–40, 52–54, 263, 276n1; knowledge production in, 41–48, 65–71, 156–61, 259–62, 276nn2–3, 280n8, 281n14; Mirador controversy and, 113; neutrality of, 39, 48–51, 54–56, 58, 74; stability of, 51–52; technical capacity of, 44, 256–57, 281n2, 283n13; WCS coadministration of, 39–41, 47–48, 52–54, 75, 78. *See also* maps; monitoring data, interpretation of; monitoring data, use of; *individual monitoring projects*

census, imaginary, 123, 143–44, 151, 283n6

census, MBR, 43, 123–30, 141, 147–48, 280n6

certainty, 6, 221–22; desire for, 3, 25, 35, 244; impossibility of, 22, 95, 109; production of, 95, 109, 115, 198, 216–17. *See also* uncertainty

Cheny (WCS intern), 20, 230–32
chicle, 203, 212, 283n8
chicleros, 100, 116, 154, 203, 283n8
chisme. *See* rumor
CI. *See* Conservation International
CICIG (International Commission against
    Impunity in Guatemala), 58, 61, 75–76,
    79–80
Civil Patrols, 17, 62. *See also* civil war
civil war, 26, 32–33, 62, 92–93, 126, 137,
    164–67, 271; genocide, impunity for,
    18, 83; in the Petén, 14–17, 59, 274n1;
    presidents and, 76, 80–81. *See also* peace
    accords; refugees, returned; scorched-
    earth campaigns
climate change, 109–10, 122, 184, 245,
    277n1; and conspiracy theory, 96–97;
    projections of, 43, 247
COCODES (Community Development
    Councils), 154; in Carmelita, 106; in
    Paso Caballos, 149, 177–78, 181–83, 267,
    281n15; in Uaxactún, 281n15, 284n15
Colom, Álvaro, 33, 59, 278n10; and the MBR,
    18, 69, 122, 132, 150, 262, 282n4, 284n2
Commission for Historical Clarification
    (CEH), 32
community-based conservation, 31, 86,
    152; debates over, 95, 101, 105–7, 112–13,
    153, 174, 253; success of, 190–91, 193, P1
Community Development Councils.
    See COCODES
community forest concessions, 74, 116,
    141, 152, 264; critiques of, 39–40, 95,
    105, 112f; and Mirador controversy,
    101, 112–13; monitoring of, 43, 208; and
    REDD+, 250–55, 258. *See also individual
    concessions*
composting (knowledge), 9, 187–88, 243,
    269–70; of love, 221, 244; of REDD+
    project, 248, 250, 263; in Uaxactún,
    190–91, 195, 214–15. *See also* materiality
CONAP (National Protected Area Council),
    14, 23, 38, 47, 53, 283n4; bureaucracy, 48,

57, 259–60; communities in MBR, rela-
    tions with, 127–28, 151, 162–63, 168–69,
    281n15; corruption in, 225, 282n4; elec-
    toral transitions and, 51–52, 78, 92; field
    technicians, 50, 228; forest fire depart-
    ment, 157, 160–61; gobernabilidad and,
    63, 87, 90, 277n4; military, alliance with,
    15, 81–82, 89, 278n12; Mirador contro-
    versy and, 103, 111; NGOs and, 40–41, 74;
    Paso Caballos, agreement with, 138, 141,
    170–76; Paso Caballos, relations with, 122,
    145–46, 148–50, 181–83, 285n7; presence
    in MBR, 18–20, 66–68, 69, 132, P3; REDD+
    and, 250. *See also* CEMEC; state, the
conflictivity, 162–63, 175, 183
congress, Guatemalan, 19, 46; and Mirador
    controversy, 95, 100, 101f, 103, 227, 251
CONRED (National Coordinator for Disas-
    ter Reduction), 160, 177, 183
conservation agreements. *See* acuerdos de
    conservación
conservation biology, 20, 232–37, 244,
    276n1, 285n6
Conservation International (CI), 19, 140,
    149, 170, 172, 274n3, 281n15
conspiracy theory, 94–96; about Mirador,
    100, 102, 104–7, 110; technoscience and,
    97–98, 108, 114–15
contradiction, in conservation strategy, 19,
    25, 174–76, 239–42, 264; and haunting,
    7–8, 31, 155; and the state, 21, 89–91
Conviviendo con Carnívoros, 185–86, 280
coproduction, 26, 123; of population and
    state, 125, 128, 132, 143–47, 151, 279n2
corruption, 17, 57–58, 88, 245, 271; CEMEC,
    lack of accusations of, 39–40, 51, 58; of
    justice system, 80–81; Mirador con-
    troversy and, 102, 105; monitoring of,
    65–66, 70, 82; rumor and, 28–29, 255; of
    the state, 21, 41, 61–64, 70, 75–76, 277n4;
    technoscience and, 54
Cuatro Balam, 227, 284n2. *See also* Mesa
    Multisectorial

Das, Veena, 27

David (CEMEC technician), 45, 49, 60, 65, 156–59

death threats: against conservationists, 28; and justice system, 61, 81

Defensores de la Naturaleza, 47–48, 74–75, 80, 249–50

deforestation, 25, 110, 113, 208, 261, P5; gobernabilidad and, 62–63, 85, 88; locals, blamed for, 14, 17, 179, 253; monitoring of, 26, 37, 42, 45, 55–56, 257; in Petén, 14; visibility of, 22. *See also* deforestation model, GIS; land cover change; land use change; *under names of individual protected areas*

deforestation model, GIS, 39, 43, 248, 256–59, P8; interpretations of, 252–54; praise for, 251–52. *See also* Guatecarbon; REDD+

Department of the Interior, U.S. (DOI), 74, 78, 263, 277n4

depoliticization, 53–55, 71, 243, 260, 277n5

DFID (United Kingdom Department for International Development), 64, 78, 195, 198, 277n4

diffractive analysis, 7, 24, 141, 150, 167–68. *See also* agential realism

DIPRONA (Nature Protection Division of the National Civil Police), 82, 161, P3

diputados. See congress, Guatemalan

discovery. *See* real, the

district attorney (office), 66

DOI (U.S. Department of the Interior), 74, 78, 263, 277n4

Don Pablo (Paso Caballos resident), 173

Dos Erres, 32–33, 59

double vision, 227, 261, 262, 264; of communities in MBR, 84, 162–63; conspiracy theory and, 95; of the state, 61–65, 74, 79, 81, 83, 88–90; technoscience and paranoia as, 27, 35–36. *See also* haunting

drug traffickers: identity, uncertainty of, 1–2, 6, 17, 83–85, 90, 162–63, 168; MBR, presence in, 1–2, 10, 17–18, 20, 155, 255, P1; narco-ranchers, 17, 110, 185–86, 242; violence and, 15, 54, 63. *See also* Zetas (cartel)

drug trafficking: land grabs and, 17; maps of, 60, 65–66; militarization and, 62, 83–84; politicians and, 75–76, 102, 105; prosecution of, 80; references to, coded, 29, 55, 65, 70, 72, 82, 89–90. *See also* organized crime

ecology, 3–4, 11, 23, 269–70; conservation biology and, 236, 285n6; hierarchical thought in, 216, 273n7; terms from, 119–20, 276n1

ecology of knowledges, 3–6, 214, 273n1, 273n3; CEMEC, as keystone actor in, 40, 47; ethnographic method and, 21–23. *See also* nooscape

edge effects, epistemic, 120, 155–56, 167, 174, 177, 183–84

education, environmental. *See* awareness, environmental

elections, presidential, 13, 51, 102, 105, 277n4, 278n8; and instability, 64, 75–78, 81, 267

El Niño, 47, 157, 159, 277n1

El Perú, 224–26

emergence, 4–5, 24, 119–20, 269–70, 273n4; of certainty, 198, 216–17; of usefulness, 46

emergency, rhythm of, 247–48, 259–60. *See also* urgency

enactment, 3–6, 270–72, 280n3, 281n1; of fire, 155–56, 174, 182–84; of the MBR, 25–26, 30, 55–56, 88, 256, 263, P1; multiplicity of, 7, 24, 91, 120, 190, 217, 259; of Nature, 236, 239–42; of population, 122–26, 128, 132, 141, 143–51, 279n2; of the state, 21, 62–64, 66, 73–77, 79, 278n12

environmental crime, 10, 66, 73, 79–81, 86–88, 278n11, P4

environmentality, 199, 211

Environmental Justice Forum, 80–81, 89

environmental orthodoxy, 124, 132

environmental services, payment for, 20, 249, 258. *See also* Guatecarbon; REDD+

epistemic taming, 31, 221, 227–35. *See also* real, the; wild life

epistemic violence, 150

epistemology: and agential realism, 5; of conspiracy theory, 96–98, 110, 114–15; multiplicity of, 25, 31, 35–36, 40, 95, 150, 155–56, 273n1, 280n3. *See also* love; paranoia; technoscience

Estación Biológica Las Guacamayas. *See* Scarlet Macaw Biological Station

ethnic inequality, in Guatemala, 76; and the civil war, 16, 32, 137, 274n1; in MBR, 120, 127–28, 136–38, 163, 173; and the Petén, 16, 117, 179

ethnicity, and conservation, 8, 117–18, 136–38, 140, 271–72

evictions, of MBR communities, 14, 18, 31, 132, 162–64, 183, 281n3, P1; backlash against, 63, 83–85, 88; justification for, 168. *See also* militarization, of conservation; settlements, illegal

facts, 7; construction of, 5, 50, 98, 108, 216–17; and rumors, 106, 114–15. *See also* objectivity

failure, 29–30, 244, 267, 271, 283n10; community conservation and, 101, 140, 151, 155, 169–70, 174–75, 181–82; of experiments, 237, 243; Laguna del Tigre as, 163–64, 168, 226–27; MBR as, 14, 19, 112; success and, 35–36, 85, 88

FARES (Foundation for Anthropological Research and Environmental Studies), 99, 105–6, 113, 153, 225, 278n3. *See also* Hansen, Richard

Fernando (WCS biologist), 218–19, 224–26, 232–35, 239–40, 243

fire, 47, P5, P7; as agricultural tool, 178–80 (*see also* milpa); gobernabilidad and, 70; management of, 177–78, 204; MBR, as threat to, 70f, 109–10, 112, 161–64; monitoring of, 42, 156–60, 209, 281n2; multiplicity of, 155–56, 174, 182–84; responsibility for, 182–84; urgency of, 86, 246, 259–60. *See also under protected area names*

firebreaks, 160, 177–82

firefighting, 160–61, 183. *See also* SIPECIF

Flores, 20, 39, 60, 93, 194, 265, 276n11; institutional offices in, 22, 37, 47, 140, 222; Manuel Baldizón and, 102; MBR sites, travel to, 142, 181–82, 224; tourism and, 59. *See also* San Benito; Santa Elena

fragmentation, 97, 119–20, 155–56, 167, 170, 174, 263, 269; failure and, 182–84; habitat, 113

frontiers, 17, 162–66. *See also* Petén: as frontier

future, of MBR: communities, 136, 141, 143, 175, 213–15; and the past, 109–10; plans for, 187; predictions of, 83–85, 128 (*see also* deforestation model, GIS; REDD+); responsibility for, 79, 243; unknowability of, 247–48, 254–56, 259–64

FYDEP (National Enterprise for the Promotion and Economic Development of Petén), 15–16, 274n1

gender: in campo, 161, 223–24; care and, 283n7; violence and, 23, 92–93; xate projects and, 207, 211, 284n15

Geographic Information Systems/Science. *See* GIS

georeferencing, 42, 129–30, 230, 257, 280n8

Geraldo (Paso Caballos mayor), 181–82

Gibson, Mel, 95, 100, 109, 245

Gibson-Graham, J. K., 13, 217

nooscape (continued)

22, 191, 227–28, 269–70; epistemologies, relations between, in, 35–36, 115, 221, 244 (*see also* double vision); fragmentation of, 97, 155–56, 167, 170, 174, 182–84; heterogeneity of, 119–20, 239; love in, 29–31; nonhumans in, 24, 30, 187, 232, 276n10; objectivity in, 39, 216–17; paranoia in, 26–29, 89, 95; patchiness of, 123, 148; power in, 79, 200, 215; technoscience in, 25–26, 126, 263. *See also* ecology of knowledges

noosphere, 4–5, 269–70, 273nn2–3

NTFPS (nontimber forest products), 43, 100, 113, 138, 140, 190–92, 203. *See also* chicle; xate

nuclear zone, 127, 129, 132, 138, P1. *See also individual national parks*

objectivity: and the campo, 228, 236, 244 (*see also* real, the); of CEMEC, 39–41, 48–50, 53–55, 78, 126, 266; desires for, 35, 147, 151; haunting and, 24–25, 36, 56, 71, 217, 260–62, 271; paranoia and, 27, 64, 101, 114. *See also* facts; technoscience

oil extraction: in MBR, 17, 20, 84–85, 155, 185–86; militarization and, 18, 62, 82, 282n4; in Petén, 15, 166

OMYC (Conservation and Management Organization of Uaxactún), 87, 142, 192–93, 281n15, 282n3, 284n15; concession contract, 144, 215, 266; livelihoods and, 139f; xate projects and, 201–13

ontology, 5–6, 40, 222, 274n5, 274n7, 281n1

organized crime, 10, 17, 168; confronting, 226; references to, coded, 70, 72; rumors about, 105, 259; and the state, 21, 61–62, 66. *See also* corruption; drug trafficking

PACUNAM (Foundation for Maya Natural and Cultural Patrimony), 103, 106, 250, 278n3

pageants, village, 133–36

paranoia, 4, 269; conspiracy theories and, 94–97, 114–15; corruption and, 58, 61–62, 75, 79, 102; drug trafficking and, 17; as epistemology, 25–29, 114, 271; love and, 220–21, 235, 244; militarization and, 83, 85, 88; as politics, 48, 105–8; technoscience and, 35–36, 54–56, 64–66, 71, 73, 108, 110 (*see also* double vision)

partial connection, 4–5, 8, 63, 156, 242, 266, 269–71, 274n6; and certainty, 216–17

Paso Caballos, 13, 23, 133–34, 281n13, P5; acuerdo de conservación in, 149, 281n15; ethnicity in, 136–38; fire management in, 158f, 177–80, 182–83; history, 20, 166–67, 274–5n3; institutions and, 139–40, 180–82; knowledge, external, access to, 266–67, 282n1; legal status, 14, 138, 141, 162–63, 280n10; in MBR nooscape, 150–51, 155, 164–65, 184; population in, 122–23, 130, 144–46, 280n5, P2; poverty in, 138, 153; and Scarlet Macaw Biological Station, 170–73, 274n3; violence in, 26–27; WCS projects in, 148–50, 174–76, 185–86, 240

patchiness, 122–23, 148, 150–51, 226, 279n2; and fragmentation, 119–20, 155–56, 183

patrols: community participation in, 204; danger of, 1, 28, 224; efficacy of, 10, 90; funding for, 69; institutions involved in, 18, 81, 220; spatial distribution of, 11, 67f, 164, 242; reporting of, 66–68, 70, 72–73. *See also* institutional presence, in MBR; territorial control, of MBR

Paz y Paz, Claudia, 80–81, 263

peace accords, 18, 167–69; and state reform, 20–21, 58. *See also* civil war; refugees, returned

peccaries, 218–20, 223, 229, 285n6

Perenco, 82, 185, 282n4. *See also* oil extraction

pesticides, 238, 240–41

rumor, 39, 54, 82, 136, 145, 261, 279n1; drug
trafficking and, 17, 65–66; Mirador controversy and, 94–97, 104–8, 113–14; in
nooscape, 19, 24–25, 40, 216; paranoia
and, 26–29, 48, 64, 73, 83; politicians
and, 102, 162, 259, 282n4

Salguero, David, 80
San Benito, 22, 37, 40, 47, 69, 79, 102, 245.
    See also Flores; Santa Elena
San Pedro River, 127, 146, 166–67, 170–71
Santa Elena, 22, 32, 102, 232, 245, 281n3.
    See also Flores; San Benito
satellite images, 42, 228, 259; of fire, 155–60,
    209, 281n2, P7; Mirador controversy
    and, 98–101, 108, 111–12, P6; processing
    of, 45, 256–57, 276n3. See also monitoring
    data, interpretation of; remote sensing
scale: conspiracy theory and, 100, 102, 115,
    278n2; contradictions between, 31, 141,
    211, 213–14, 240–42, 253; in ecology, 35,
    229, 273–74n4, 276n1; enactments of, 68,
    125, 147, 202, 217, 248, 256, 258; knowl-
    edge, as limitation of, 281n14; nooscape
    and, 4–5, 7, 22, 24, 120, 123, 156, 270–72,
    274n6; policy and, 147
Scarlet Macaw Biological Station, 140,
    164–65, 274n3, P5; burning of, 169–73
scarlet macaws, 30, 154, 208, 285n5; as
    symbol of conservation, 134, 176, 285n6;
    wcs interventions in, 232–42
Schwartz, Norman, 172
scorched-earth campaigns, 16, 59, 76,
    164–66, 263, 274n1. See also civil war
Sebastian (tourism consultant), 106,
    252–53, 256
sentinel species, 241–42
settlements, illegal, 14; conap, agreements
    with, 168–69, 172; human rights and, 84,
    168–69; strategies for, conservationist,
    162–64; support for, international, 18.
    See also evictions, of mbr communities;
    under individual park names

shield, the, 11, 164, 242, P5
Sierra del Lacandón National Park, 60,
    249; coadministration of, 47–48, 74–75
    (see also Defensores de la Naturaleza);
    fire in, 157, 160; settlements, illegal, in,
    19, 127, 281n3
silence, 72, 80; in cemec, 37–38, 44, 48–50,
    156, 222; civil war and, 32–33; paranoia
    and, 25, 28–29, 36, 55–56, 65, 88–89
    (see also drug trafficking: references to,
    coded)
Sinaloa cartel, 83
sipecif (National System for Prevention
    and Control of Forest Fires), 73, 160,
    177, 181, 183
Skype, 24, 44, 49–50, 60, 104, 156
slash-and-burn. See milpa
snem (National Service for the Eradica-
    tion of Malaria), 127–28, 280nn5–6
Soza Manzanero, Carlos, 170–72
state, the, 40–41, 280n10; boundaries of, 64,
    73–75, 80, 278n12; cancellation of mbr (or
    parts), fears of, 141, 163, 212–13, 254–55,
    260–63; coproduction of, with popula-
    tion, 123–25, 128, 132, 144–47, 151, 279n2;
    instability of, 51–52, 75–77, 92; maps of,
    31; multiplicity of, 21, 63–64, 90–91; ngos
    and, 47, 77–79, 173, 183. See also corrup-
    tion; elections, presidential; gobernabi-
    lidad; territorial control, of mbr
state of siege (2011), 59–60, 62, 83
State of the Maya Biosphere Reserve, 37,
    139f, 257, 260, P5, P7; alliance building
    and, 40; construction of, 45, 67–68, 191;
    gobernabilidad and, 64–65, 77, 277n4;
    National Palace presentation of, 69–72,
    122, 261f, 262, PP2–3
strange loops, 270, 280n4
success: community conservation and,
    101, 140, 143, 163, 190–94, 210, 215, 264;
    failure and, 29, 35–36, 85, 88; measures
    of, 69, 88, 112, 213, 239–43; partiality of,
    31, 63, 175, 247

Velásquez Gómez, Iván, 61, 76. *See also* CICIG

Vernadsky, Vladimir, 4, 273n2

Verran, Helen, 125, 280n3

veterinarians, wildlife, 185–86, 218–20, 236. *See also* biovets

Vinicio (Uaxactún resident), 189, 215

violence: conservationists, against, 35, 169, 278n11; conservationists, by, 9, 83–85, 88–91, 153 (*see also* evictions, of MBR communities); drug trafficking and, 5, 15, 54, 63; elections and, 75–76, 278n9; gender and, 23, 92–93, 224; gobernabilidad and, 61–65, 72f, 80–81, 85–86; history of, 15–18, 32–33, 137, 145, 164–66 (*see also* civil war); multiple worlds and, 6–8, 24–25, 263, 271, 273n1; nonhumans and, 17, 163, 186, 277n1; paranoia and, 27–29, 54–56, 95–96, 115; structural, 120. *See also* gobernabilidad

WCS (Wildlife Conservation Society), 22–23; in campo, 222–24, 228; CEMEC, coadministration of, 40–41; community conservation and, 140, 148–50, 153–54, 169–70, 281n15, 285n7; conservation strategies in, 168, 174, 243, 280n9; funding, 277n4, 283n12; the military and, 15; Mirador controversy and, 95, 99, 103, 105, 107; and other NGOs, 80, 225–26; in Paso Caballos, 26–27, 146, 174–78,

182–83, 185–86; REDD+, involvement in, 250, 253, 258; the state and, 74–75, 77; in Uaxactún, 10, 143, 191, 193–96, 199–210, 213–14, 282n3, 284n15; wildlife interventions, 30, 220, 229–42, 284n1 (*see also* biovets)

wilderness, 152, 221–22. *See also* Nature

wild experiments, 235–39, 241–44

wild life, 25, 220–22, 284n1; intervening in, 235–43; love and, 30, 244; the real and, 31. *See also* campo: in MBR nooscape; epistemic taming

Wildlife Conservation Society. *See* WCS

world making, 5–7, 9, 187–88, 217, 269–72, 274n5; nonhuman, 25, 30, 119. *See also* enactment

Wynne, Brian, 97–98

xate, 200–203, 284n14; identity, as symbol of, 135, 203; as income source, 139, 192, 198, 211–12; monitoring, of quality, 191, 195, 207–10, 214, 283nn11–12; projects, in Uaxactún, 204–6, 210, 213

xateras, 284n14

xateros, 200–203, 206–8, 210–12, 283n11

Ybarra, Megan, 82

Zetas (cartel), 59–60, 83. *See also* drug traffickers; drug trafficking

www.ingramcontent.com/pod-product-compliance
Lightning Source LLC
Chambersburg PA
CBHW050333270326
41926CB00016B/3439